Aarif Abraham

A Constitution of the People and How to Achieve It

What Bosnia and Britain Can Learn From Each Other

Balkan Politics and Society

Edited by Jelena Dzankic and Soeren Keil

1   Valery Perry (ed.)
    Extremism and Violent Extremism in Serbia
    21st Century Manifestations of an Historical Challenge
    ISBN 978-3-8382-1260-9

2   James Riding
    The Geopolitics of Memory
    A Journey to Bosnia
    ISBN 978-3-8382-1311-8

3   Ian Bancroft
    Dragon's Teeth
    Tales from North Kosovo
    ISBN 978-3-8382-1364-4

4   Viktoria Potapkina
    Nation Building in Contested States
    Comparative Insights from Kosovo, Transnistria, and Northern Cyprus
    ISBN 978-3-8382-1381-1

5   Soeren Keil, Bernhard Stahl (eds.)
    A New Eastern Question? Great Powers and the Post-Yugoslav States
    ISBN 978-3-8382-1375-0

6   Senada Zatagic
    A Neglected Right
    Prospects for the Protection of the Right to Be Elected in Bosnia and Herzegovina
    ISBN 978-3-8382-1521-1

7   Aarif Abraham
    A Constitution of the People and How to Achieve It
    What Bosnia and Britain Can Learn From Each Other
    ISBN 978-3-8382-1516-7

Aarif Abraham

A CONSTITUTION OF THE PEOPLE AND HOW TO ACHIEVE IT

What Bosnia and Britain Can Learn From Each Other

Bibliografische Information der Deutschen Nationalbibliothek
Die Deutsche Nationalbibliothek verzeichnet diese Publikation in der Deutschen Nationalbibliografie; detaillierte bibliografische Daten sind im Internet über http://dnb.d-nb.de abrufbar.

Bibliographic information published by the Deutsche Nationalbibliothek
Die Deutsche Nationalbibliothek lists this publication in the Deutsche Nationalbibliografie; detailed bibliographic data are available in the Internet at http://dnb.d-nb.de.

Cover image: Pikist. Public Domain.

ISBN-13: 978-3-8382-1516-7
© *ibidem*-Verlag, Stuttgart 2021
Alle Rechte vorbehalten

Das Werk einschließlich aller seiner Teile ist urheberrechtlich geschützt. Jede Verwertung außerhalb der engen Grenzen des Urheberrechtsgesetzes ist ohne Zustimmung des Verlages unzulässig und strafbar. Dies gilt insbesondere für Vervielfältigungen, Übersetzungen, Mikroverfilmungen und elektronische Speicherformen sowie die Einspeicherung und Verarbeitung in elektronischen Systemen.

All rights reserved. No part of this publication may be reproduced, stored in or introduced into a retrieval system, or transmitted, in any form, or by any means (electronical, mechanical, photocopying, recording or otherwise) without the prior written permission of the publisher. Any person who does any unauthorized act in relation to this publication may be liable to criminal prosecution and civil claims for damages.

Printed in the EU

Contents

ACKNOWLEDGMENTS 9

FOREWORD 11

INTRODUCTION 15

1. "A text about a text": constitutions of Britain and Bosnia .. 37
   1.1 Searching for the soul of a state 37
   1.2 Overview of the British constitution 44
   1.3 Overview of the Bosnian constitution 53
   1.4 Comparative constitutional histories 59

2. "Look a shoot is sprouting": measuring culture 93
   2.1 Political culture in theory 96
   2.2 Political culture in practice 103
   2.3 Political culture applied to Bosnia and Britain 107
   2.4 Problem of political apathy 117

3. "Going back to whence I sprang": assessing apathy 127
   3.1 A-systemic orientations 128
   3.2 Anti-systemic orientations 131
   3.3 Absence of interpersonal trust 135
   3.4 Institutions as an explanation 140

4. "We've still not found a cure": constitutional rules 153
   4.1 Constitutional choice and change 153
   4.2 Recurrent crisis and rarefied reform in Bosnia 158
   4.3 Rising strain amidst weak reform in Britain 175
   4.4 Reform dilemmas and deadlock 194

5. "We need to uncover lost paths": modelling change 213
   5.1 Modelling intransigence 213
   5.2 Modelling the failure of reform 230
   5.3 Modelling successful evolution in the short run 235
   5.4 Modelling future co-operation and participation 239

6. "A text about hope": lessons from Bosnia and Britain 257
   6.1 Debate, deliberation and participation 257
   6.2 Lessons for Bosnia and post-conflict societies 260
   6.3 Lessons for Britain and pre-conflict societies 270
   6.4 Pathways out of constitutional quagmires 293

BEYOND LAW, PRESCRIPTIONS AND CONCLUSIONS 319

AFTERWORD 333

APPENDICES 339

GLOSSARY 351

REFERENCES 353

In tribute to my teachers
— past, present and future —
with particular gratitude
for my mother, aunty, and uncles

ACKNOWLEDGMENTS

This book would not have been possible without the conversation, counsel and guidance of a great many friends and colleagues who have added immeasurably to my understanding of politics, law and international relations over the course of my academic and professional callings. Our interactions have made writing this book enjoyable and highly rewarding.

I am very grateful to Professor Philippe Sands QC, Sir Geoffrey Nice QC, Baroness Helena Kennedy QC, Hon. Dr Brett Mason, Dr Valery Perry, and Margaret Owen OBE for their contributions to this book, as well as their critical thoughts and reviews. A much better book is the result.

I am indebted, in particular, to my friends and mentors: Helena Kennedy, Geoffrey Nice, Valery Perry, Kyrie James and Salim Ibrahim. They have often given up their valuable time, without asking for anything in return, to help resolve dilemmas and difficulties. In this case, they have extended their kindness to tackle seemingly intractable ones in Bosnia and Britain.

I would like to give thanks to a number of colleagues who contributed directly to the preparation of this book. Valery Perry is a leading scholar on Bosnian constitutional reform. Without her constructive, challenging and critical comments whatever nuance and distinction there is in this book would have been lost.

I was very privileged to have been taught, and encouraged in my thinking about Bosnian constitutional reform, by the late Zdravko Grebo. He never once suggested that *conventional* thinking might be the answer to elusive endeavours in pursuit of peace and justice. As one of the young leaders of the first mass protests in Yugoslavia, he inspired many a mind to stand upright, and without fear, in the face of powerful and insurmountable behemoths. I hope I am a worthy student.

I had insightful discussions about constitutions with Dr Kurt Bassuener, Professor Daniel Sewer, and Ewelina Ochab. Kurt Bassuener provided much food for thought drawing upon his many decades of experience and scholarship on the Bosnian constitution.

Dr Rachel Kurian and Alina Trkulja provided useful comments and direction as to the structure of my original thesis and Dr Mansoob Murshed, a specialist in game theory, helped develop the models adopted in this book through his feedback.

I received very helpful critical suggestions on either the proposal or parts of the draft manuscript from: Dr Miles Jackson, Mark George QC, Andrew MacDowall, Dalila Sadinlija, Kate Young, George Mitchell, Kerim Suruliz, and Natasha Jackson. This book, in style and substance, is much improved as a result. Among the kind readers of the manuscript was Patrick Page. As a master of the written word, he led me on a testing, but extremely rewarding, journey in questioning all my defaults as to style. I am grateful to him.

Lily Lewis, through a fortuitous turn of events, assisted me with some further research on political culture in Bosnia and Britain and contributed to those chapters. I had remarked to Lily, knowing she had no prior connection with Bosnia, that it was no coincidence that the Golden Lily happened to be the symbol of Bosnia. I hope this book, and Lily's contribution, will help add to the corpus of knowledge on good political culture and its cultivation, growth and bloom in both Bosnia and Britain.

Last but not least, I would like to thank my colleagues at Ibidem Press who have been unfailingly kind, supportive and helpful from proposal to publication: Jakob Horstmann, Valerie Lange, Dr Soeren Keil, and Dr Jelena Džankić.

Although the suggestions and comments of these readers greatly improved the final manuscript, I alone am responsible for the interpretations appearing in this book and for any flaws, errors or omissions that remain.

Aarif Abraham
Garden Court North Chambers

Manchester, February 2021

FOREWORD

Fifteen years of involvement in international cases that followed the collapse of the Socialist Federal Republic of Yugoslavia, or SFRY, made me acutely aware of the particularities of the constitutional situation that faced Bosnia and Herzegovina, the sovereign State which emerged from that collapse. It also left me cognisant of the apparent differences with the situation faced by the United Kingdom of Great Britain and Northern Ireland.

I recognised that matters of history and politics, of culture and identity, will combine to weave distinguishable constitutional arrangements. Yet I also knew, not least from the research that went into my book East West Street, that a situation which exists at one moment in time can, within just a few years, change very radically. That was the case for the city of Lemberg, which had, in the late 1920s, a diverse and multinational population, but within two decades found itself with a totally different population.

As a part of the Austro-Hungarian empire, and then the SFRY, Bosnia was largely made up three majority communities — Bosnian Muslims, Catholics and Orthodox Christians. There were other minority groups too. As the SFRY dissolved, a violent conflict in Bosnia exposed all populations to such unimaginable horrors that — eventually and belatedly — the international community was catalysed into action. A 'peace' was negotiated, then concluded in 1995 at a military base in Dayton, Ohio. Out of this process a new constitution emerged.

Britain's unwritten constitution, by contrast, is said to be ancient, one that establishes a parliamentary democracy that threads together the four 'nations' of Scotland, England, Wales and Northern Ireland. The composite constitution goes back many centuries, through and beyond empire. It is said to be unwritten and characterised by a particular flexibility.

The differences between Bosnia and Britain appear stark. What might be learned from an exercise in comparison?

Bosnia's constitution was imposed. It is codified, rigid, difficult to amend. The people had no direct say in its creation, on the basis that they harboured "ancient ethnic hatreds." The constitution is seen by some to institutionalise divisions that many believe to be debilitating. It seeks to ensure a formal equality of the three main ethnic groups, with strict rules on elite power-sharing, which some consider to undermine the freedoms and rights of individuals. Aarif Abraham poses some important and searching questions about a constitutionally-imposed system of group segregation, one that arose in the context of international crimes. If the people of Bosnia do not harbour supposed ancient hatreds but have a political culture that is democratic, tolerant and accommodating, he asks, might another constitutional future be envisaged? What circumstances might cause the different groups and their elites to abandon this structure for a different one? Can the people of Bosnia truly control their own democratic destiny within the current constitutional straightjacket within which they now exist?

With its different model, Britain claims, by contrast, a high degree of constitutional longevity and slow evolution. Yet it has faced its own challenges, all the more so today, following its departure from the European Union and the real possibility that Northern Ireland and Scotland may, within the foreseeable future, leave the Union. Such a fundamental change to the system has not happened for 350 or so years, but new divisions and polarisations appear to be eating away at some constitutional fundamentals. There is contestation over devolution and independence of the four nations, as well as the various regions, over distributions of wealth and socio-economic entitlements, and in respect of human rights (and, it might be asked, who would have imagined, just a few years ago, that Scotland would be able to shut its border to visitors from England, in the face of a health pandemic?) Such developments cause Mr Abraham to raise other questions, equally significant. Has a practise of moderate constitutional tinkering put the entire structure at risk? Has there been a fracture in the delicate balance between executive, legislative and judicial power and authority? Can the British constitution resist the challenges of extreme nationalisms and populisms?

This important and original book seeks to unwrap these and more challenging questions. Mr Abraham embarks on a comparative exercise, one that contrasts what some view as a pre-conflict society (Britain), on the one hand, and a society viewed as having frozen and embedded a conflict (Bosnia), on the other. As readers, we are invited to reflect on a most fundamental issue of our times: the relationship between a country's political culture and its constitution.

Mr Abraham sees the cultures of both countries as increasingly moderate and inclined to a broad and democratic political participation. He is maybe optimistic, or right. If he is right, the discrepancy between elite preferences and people's preferences becomes acute, a space in which the constitutional rules will play themselves out, and the forces for change will be overwhelming.

Could Bosnia adopt some of the flexibilities of the British system? Mr Abraham imagines a *revolving constitution*, one that would subject existing constitutional arrangements to fixed and regular public debate, to the deliberation and approval of succeeding generations. Properly institutionalised, and with procedural safeguards, he argues, no one should be worse off. At best, everyone might have an opportunity for an enhanced constitution than is currently the case. He seeks a coincidence between the people's and elite's preferences.

In a certain sense, Britain already has a revolving constitution, one in which elites are regularly confronted with constitutional issues in the hurly burly of generational day-to-day of politics. Yet, Mr Abraham argues forcefully that some of the conventions, rules and practises that allowed fair and measured constitutional changes are no longer functional. On his view, Britain need not make its constitution as fixed and rigid as Bosnia's in order to represent all of its communities. It can, however, imagine a more inclusive national debate and process of deliberation, and a four-nation settlement around a new constitutional statute, one that all of Britain's people might have contributed to.

The book argues that a constitutional settlement owned by all the people will have a greater authority and stability. Mr Abraham offers no prescription on the content of a constitutional settlement but a road map as to how it may be achieved. As such, he succeeds in inviting us to think about our individual and collective roles in constitution-making. He encourages us to be more creative and careful. He asks us to reflect seriously about a people's political culture, and to cultivate, maintain and enrich that culture so people can contribute to change the way in which they are governed. Such transformation, he argues, requires practice and action, and not just words.

Professor Philippe Sands QC
University College London & Matrix Chambers

London, January 2021

> "Words abound in everything
> So words are everything but everything is bound by words
>
> For just one word we wait and pray
> An ancient word from far away
>
> But we have heard a new word
>
> Verily we have heard a word so new
> That be it but whispered the heavens ring"
>
> - Mak Dizdar, *The Stone Sleeper* [1]

INTRODUCTION

Britain has an almost unique constitutional position among States. It is a long-established democracy, comprising four diverse nations, with an uncodified, non-federal constitutional arrangement. The constitution itself is a miscellaneous collection of flexible conventions, norms and rules governing political behaviour. It cannot be found written down in a single place and some aspects of it are not written down anywhere at all. To the 'outsider', as well as the most intimate of 'insiders', it can be difficult or even impossible to comprehend. The current monarch of the United Kingdom, Queen Elizabeth II, is reported to have remarked that "the British constitution has always been puzzling and always will be."[2] While that may be the case, the constitution has endured for almost three and a half centuries without armed conflict threatening its core structure. The foundation on which the constitution is built goes back further still to the Kingdom of Athelstan, over a thousand

---

[1] An extract of a poem called "BBBB" by Mak Dizdar [1917-1971] (2009, 50).
[2] These, possibly apocryphal, remarks were widely reported to have been made by the Queen at a lecture being delivered by Prof. Peter Hennessy at Queen Mary College, London. See further, Hennessy's (1995) own account of the event. Bogdanor (2009) gives an account of another incident. The Queen attended an event at University College London where she came upon a book called *The Changing Constitution*, edited by Prof. Jeffrey Jowell. She reportedly said to Jowell, who was standing nearby, "Changing, Professor Jowell, what changes? I haven't noticed any changes!" Jowell replied, "Well, evolving, Ma'am, evolving." She responded, "Yes, but in what direction?"

years ago. That thousand-year period was punctuated by armed conflict and bloodshed. Even Britain's recent history saw armed conflict at its periphery and within its imperial dominions. Its constitutional structure, however, has had an undeniable longevity and continuity.

Bosnia and Herzegovina, by contrast, is a relatively recent democracy with an ethnically diverse population (though perhaps less diverse than Britain's).[3] Bosnia emerged in 1995 from three and a half years of devastating inter-ethnic armed conflict. The Bosnian constitution is not in any sense conventional, drawn up, as it was, as Annex IV to the Dayton Peace Agreement.[4] With the signatures of the war's main protagonists, the Dayton Peace Agreement successfully ended the war that ravaged Bosnia following its declaration of independence from the former Yugoslavia.

Neither the Dayton Peace Agreement nor the Bosnian constitution within it, however, created the successful democratic and functioning State envisaged by its chief proponents.[5] Instead, it set out complex procedures for governance that have institutionalised ethnic division and led to governmental paralysis. Bosnia, for instance, is composed of two devolved entities, three 'constituent peoples', and five layers of governance which, together, count among them a tripartite State presidency, two entity presidents, and fourteen prime ministers and governments.[6] In a country of no more than 3.53 million inhabitants (AfS 2013), Bosnia has the highest number of presidents, prime ministers, and ministers *per capita* in the world. Such a proliferation has made streamlined and efficient government difficult (Belloni 2010, 99).

---

[3] Bosnia and Herzegovina is referred to throughout as "Bosnia".
[4] The State constitution was agreed as Annex IV of the *General Framework Agreement for Peace in Bosnia and Herzegovina*, initialled at Dayton on 21 November 1995 and signed in Paris on 14 December 1995. It is referred to throughout as the "Bosnian constitution".
[5] Richard Holbrooke, the principal negotiator of the Agreement, maintains that "on paper, Dayton was a good agreement; it ended the war and established a single, multi-ethnic country." His caveat is that "the results of the international effort to implement Dayton would determine its true place in history."
[6] There is also the self-governing district of Brčko in the North of Bosnia which is under international supervision.

The Bosnian constitution has no popular mandate and lacks any features that may allow future democratic legitimacy. It has been imposed on the people and like other constitutions created in—or mostly *for*—seemingly 'divided societies', it has proved immune from change.

Most written constitutions are a product of war or revolution and are imposed by political elites who do not formally consider the views of 'their' people, even if they occasionally invite them to ratify the new arrangements. The absence of popular participation is not *always* fatal to the working of a constitution, but it *can* be if the political culture of the people differs from these rules-that-create-all-rules which the people are then required to respect.

This book seeks to contrast the two very different models of constitutional design in Britain and Bosnia. They sit at very different ends of a spectrum. The comparison goes to the heart of what a constitution is understood to be. Is it imbued with meaning, culture and history and, as such, is the soul of a State and its people? Or is it merely a functional, abstract and prescriptive set of rules which create the practical environment in which the people go about their everyday business?

In Bosnia, abstract and prescriptive constitutional rules have real world consequences. The Bosnian constitution has maintained and reinforced ethnic division and led to governmental deadlock. There are critical aspects of the constitution that require reform and there has been no shortage of proposals for reform.[7] All reform proposals since 2005 to amend the Bosnian constitution, however, have been driven by political elites and have failed. These failures are to the immense detriment of individual human rights,[8] and

---

[7] There have been three substantial reform processes since 2005 all of which have failed as a result of intransigent, ethno-nationalist positions taken by the elected representatives. There have also been two missives for reform that are very significant. These are all addressed in Chapter 4.

[8] The constitution contravenes international law in a number of ways. For instance, only members of the three main ethnic groups are allowed to run for the office of president; members of the country's many minorities, such as Roma and Jews, are excluded as candidates. Also, individual rights are subservient to ethno-national group rights which permit vetoes, quotas, and exclusive ethno-national representation to the elected representatives of the groups.

amount to at a colossal economic cost to the electorate. Up to 55 per cent of the entire State budget,[9] some 3 per cent of the country's GDP, is spent on government administration, largely as a result of Bosnia's highly complex system of government (PIC 2020). By comparison, the cost of the Britain's central government administration is approximately 1.36 per cent of the State budget, some 0.5 per cent of the country's GDP.[10]

Why has reform not succeeded? As this book will seek to show, efforts have been impeded by intransigent, narrow, and nationalist positions adopted by the political representatives of Bosnia's three official 'constituent peoples': Bosniaks (Muslims), Bosnian Croats (Catholic Christians) and Bosnian Serbs (Orthodox Christians). These representatives sit in a number of constitutionally created institutions: the Parliamentary Assembly, the State Presidency and the two federal entities of Bosnia (Republika Srpska and the Federation). Intransigence is made possible due to vetoes, strict ethnic quotas and decentralised powers accorded exclusively to the three constituent peoples, all at the expense of such individuals or groups as are not specifically recognised by the Bosnian constitution. The constitution collectively and dismissively describes, although does not define, those not falling withing the three constituent groups as "Others" or "Citizens". Others loosely comprise those identifying as "Bosnians and Herzegovinians" or those refusing to politically affiliate with any of the three constituent groups and the corresponding ethno-national political parties.

The Bosnian constitution was premised on the notion that the people, harbouring 'ancient hatreds', are divided, meaning that it is preferrable to leave decision-making in the hands of political

---

[9] Approximately 613.22 million USD in 2019 (PIC 2020).
[10] The comparison between Bosnia and Britain is not straightforward as the accounting for the cost of government administration is different in the two countries. The figure for Britain is a composite of the following: costs of government administration for the state at 10.1 billion USD, 2019 (HM Treasury 2019); cost of running both Houses of Parliament at 766.25 million USD, 2019 (IfG 2020); cost of the running the central government estate at 3.56 billion USD, 2018 (Cabinet Office 2018); total budgetary receipts 1,054.21 billion USD (OBR 2020). The UK GDP for 2019 was 2,829.10 billion USD (World Bank 2020).

elites.[11] Meanwhile, experts warn about the latent desire of political elites for renewed armed conflict. In the international arena, powerful countries like Russia, China and Turkey are pursuing their own narrow self-interests in the Balkans and this has exacerbated local ethno-national competition. The economic and political manoeuvring of these powers demonstrates their intention to rescind the international communities' guarantee to maintain the peace in Bosnia. In the domestic arena, ethno-nationalist elites in Bosnia are vying with each other for support in their secessionist ambitions by appealing to predatory neighbours, namely Croatia and Serbia. These international and domestic pressures are compounded by US dis-engagement from the region over the past decade. This has created a power vacuum in the region for other international actors to fill.

In Britain, the constitutional arrangements seem to have worked relatively well historically in maintaining stability and adapting to needed political as well as socio-economic change.[12] The British constitution does not have a formal mechanism to give priority or permanence to one piece of legislation above another.[13] This is generally true of statutes that have constitutional significance and means that, where political practice is accommodating and respectful of traditions, adapting the constitution in accordance with changes in society is evidently much easier. A number of recent crises, however, have put the constitution to the test. These crises include: the process leading to the UK withdrawal from the European Union ("Brexit"); constant appeals for secession from Scotland and Northern Ireland; the breakdown of centuries-old conventions as seen with the unlawful prorogation of Parliament by the Prime Minister in 2019; the

---

[11] This issue is touched upon in Chapter 1 and further elaborated upon in Chapters 3 and 4.
[12] This claim in no way relates to policy issues and the very severe crises that emanated over the past 350 years. It also does not discount the violations of rights by the British state, whether domestic or international.
[13] The common law, however, does provide that certain statutes that are deemed, by the courts, to have constitutional significance may only be repealed, amended or abrogated if done so expressly by Parliament. This is further discussed in Chapters 4 and 6.

placing of limits on Parliamentary scrutiny by the government; and a lack of adherence to important international norms and rules as seen by a sustained government campaign to dilute people's human rights protections.[14]

On one view, these crises have all been resolved precisely *because* Britain has a flexible constitution and a sovereign, representative Parliament. The current government maintains that there are checks and balances between the branches of government, that human rights protections for the individual under common law go back centuries, and that arrangements for devolved and local decision making has ensured continued responsiveness to local needs. Ironically, the same government had planned radical changes to the British constitution because they believed changes were needed to address "trust" and a "destabilising and potentially extremely damaging rift between politicians and the people" (Conservative Party Manifesto 2019).

On another view, however, these recent crises have emanated precisely from a lack of formalised rules which could provide some clarity. The political opposition, for instance, characterise as ambiguous the arrangements for power distribution between institutions (horizontal power), power sharing between the central government and regional administrations (vertical power), and the human rights protections accorded to individuals under domestic legislation. Human rights legislation can be repealed by an express majority vote, as in the case of European Union rights post-Brexit and as the government has threatened with the European Convention on Human Rights.[15] There have been calls for a far deeper entrenchment of constitutional rules in respect of some of the existing arrangements seen to be under threat. In respect of horizontal power distribution, there is said to be a strong case for

---

[14] This is notwithstanding the fact that it was Conservative politicians who helped pioneer and draft the international instruments that protect fundamental rights including the European Convention on Human Rights ("ECHR").

[15] In leaving the European Union, British citizens lost a host of rights that have not been directly transposed into domestic law, the most significant of which were rights enshrined in the Charter on Fundamental Rights. In respect of the ECHR, it has been a Conservative Party Manifesto commitment, since 2010, to leave the ECHR.

institutional checks and balances on the executive through greater legislative and judicial scrutiny. In respect of vertical power distribution, this might mean securing a firmer statutory footing for the devolution settlements of three of the four nations of the United Kingdom. In respect of human rights, this would mean a permanent statute guaranteeing certain socio-economic, civic and political rights that cannot be repealed by a simple parliamentary majority. The debate has centred on whether it is finally time for Britain to codify and entrench its constitutional foundations as almost all other modern democracies have done.

What might Britain and Bosnia learn from each other, and what might other countries learn about the process of creating or amending constitutions by considering these two contrasting cases?

This book challenges the acceptance and proliferation of overly legalistic and/or entrenched constitutional models. Those models are largely characterised by abstract, prescriptive, and mechanical rules created in a single constitutional moment.[16] They have gained almost universal acceptance in both developed countries and countries transitioning to democracy. But these models have sometimes created and reinforced the very divisions and polarisations that they were intended to resolve. If, however, the culture of the people is conducive to accommodation, trusting of difference, and democratically oriented, then introducing the capacity to change the constitution need not be feared.

In Bosnia, informed public participation and deliberation in a constitutional design process, on a fixed and repeated basis, with some procedural safeguards, could introduce a flexibility in political life in Bosnia that was, perhaps still is, present in long-evolved democratic polities like Britain. The capacity to change the constitution every new generation (a 'revolving constitution') could allow, with careful calibration, the possibility of catalysing evolutionary outcomes in the short run. Britain itself may be reminded of its own tradition.

---

[16] See further Ackerman (1991, 1992). Constitution moments are understood to "emerge from an exceptional moment of higher-order law-making under the liberal constitutional paradigm" (Bali and Lerner 2016).

Unlike Britain, Bosnia cannot afford to wait to evolve towards a new constitutional settlement. One unfortunate and very real pathway out of the current deadlock in Bosnia is collapse and the other is a return to violent conflict. If the people in Bosnia are much more accommodating than the ethno-nationalist political elites representing them, then the presumption upon which the current constitutional arrangements were built were incorrect. Furthermore, that presumption has helped to perpetuate a collective socio-economic and political malaise from which there is, seemingly, no escape.[17]

This book's suggestions for reform are predicated on the fact, as demonstrated, that the people are accommodating, human rights oriented and tolerant. The political culture of the people in Bosnia is conducive to democratic reform. It is, contrary to popular opinion, open to popular participation and retains the capacity for inter-ethnic cooperation and engagement. One of the tests for this claim is whether or not there is evidence proving that political culture in Bosnia is as democratic as its close EU neighbours' culture. If so, the second test is whether both Bosnia and Britain respectively have political cultures conducive to greater democratic participation. If they do not, then surely this needs immediate and critical attention. If they do, then the objective is to introduce context and an ear for justice into fixed and rigid legalistic constitutional documents by involving the people in key constitutional decisions.[18] The aim, ultimately, is to reorient political life towards an inherently democratic political culture.

The current debate in Bosnia is on reforming the *content* of the constitution by tweaking or changing specific constitutional provisions. The paradox is that reform continues to be unlikely given the special constitutional guarantees accorded to the three constituent peoples. There are few incentives for political elites to compromise their intransigent positions. If anything, the reality is the opposite. Any attempt at reform by one group of elites is seen

---

[17] This is based on the case study of elite behaviour in the State institutions (Chapters 4 and 5) together with the quantitative analysis (Chapters 2 and 3) demonstrating the scope for accommodation amongst the population at large.

[18] See the very cogently argued piece by Bonnie (2001, 801).

as an attempt to undermine one group at the expense of the other (at least that is how ethno-nationalist leaders present proposals for reform to their respective ethnic constituencies). It is a classical "beggar thy neighbour" problem. Political elites explain that this conflict, and their own intransigence, is because of the political culture. They claim to behave as they do in the name of 'their people' in their respective Bosniak, Bosnian Croat and Bosnian Serb electoral silos. The irony is that the electoral silos correspond closely to ethno-territorial silos created by ethnic cleansing during the war. The same people indicted for international crimes, as a result of responsibility for the ethnic cleansing, were the principal negotiators of the Bosnian constitution.[19]

It has been taken for granted, by political commentators and academics alike, that conflict between elites in the constitutional structures of Bosnia is a mirror reflection of the latent desire for conflict within the population-at-large. The people of Bosnia are characterised as anti-democratic and pro-ethno-nationalist. Political apathy and deadlock within State institutions, therefore, are held to be a consequence of a lack of citizen initiative and will. A lack of will that emanates from an apparently intrinsic, non-participant political culture.

But this narrative is not supported by Bosnia's variegated, multi-ethnic and thousand-year history. For much of their history, the Bosnian people have come under the strong influence of foreign powers depriving them of agency. Despite that, Bosnian history is, in fact, predicated on participation, accommodation and tolerance. This book will seek to show that the contrary view is not supported by the evidence including data relating to people's political preferences since at least 1992. If the people are momentarily apathetic, intransigent, or intolerant, this is because that orientation is a consequence of the war rather than being endemic to the political culture. Later that orientation has been strengthened directly by the constitutional structure agreed—or rather imposed—by the Dayton Peace Agreement. Either way, this

---

[19] The incentive structures built into the peace agreement is, unsurprisingly, to the advantage of those negotiators (Bassuener 2020, 225).

Dayton-driven emanation of poor political participation has no reason to remain fixed or unchanging. There is always a possibility for change where there is the capacity, as there is in Bosnia. Such change is imperative before it is too late.

The example of Bosnia is of immediate significance to the British constitution. The constitution of the former provides a cautionary lesson that written codification, federalisation and entrenchment of some rules above others cannot be, in and of itself, a panacea. This book considers whether the lesson from Bosnia is that misunderstanding political culture, ignoring the preferences of people in all their manifestations, and *imposing* rather than *agreeing* constitutional arrangements will simply lead to failed institutions and instability.

There is no doubt that dissatisfaction exists in Britain. Dissatisfaction is prevalent among the devolved powers, among the regions, among the haves and have-nots, in the quality of political elites, and in the manner in which political elites carry out their duties and how they are elected (or not, as in the case of the House of Lords—Parliament's upper chamber). There is a clear need for *something* other than the status quo to address constitutional issues in Britain outside the day-to-day of parliamentary politics. The classic British fudge, muddling through with partisan, ad hoc, changes to its constitution are not sustainable. The underlying constitutional issues have precipitated many crises and have resulted in attacks on judges by the media and the executive. The executive has failed to understand the significance of fundamental unwritten rules and practices and the consequences of attacking them for short-term political gain. With a rise of nationalism, different political parties, have precipitated centrifugal and centripetal forces which wrestle with secession from the Union, or, on the contrary, further centralisation. Meanwhile, there are calls for a reassertion of nativism, originalist or 'orthodox' (depending on your view) interpretations of people's fundamental rights. These calls compete against international norms that Britain is bound faithfully to interpret, apply and fulfil either by treaty or custom.

This book demonstrates that, when it comes to constitutional issues, there is a significant discrepancy between the preferences of the elites and those of the people in both Britain and Bosnia.

In Bosnia, constitutional structures, when combined with the legacy of the war, have tended to favour the election of ethno-nationalist elites. The Bosnian constitution, and by extension its institutions, is the most significant impediment to the bridging of societal divides. Its reform, therefore, must be the priority. But such reform must have a popular mandate. Elites, isolated from the people,[20] are unable and/or unwilling to undertake reform that is conciliatory, moderate and accommodating. These elites are seemingly locked in revolving doors without an exit. Using adaptations from game theory (mechanism design and implementation theory) and behavioural economics (prospect theory) a 'revolving constitution' is proposed to break the impasse. A revolving constitution would subject parts of the constitution—as opposed to ordinary legislation—to greater civic participation and input (through, referendums, civic initiatives and deliberative assemblies) on a fixed basis every new generation.[21] Fixed and repeated interaction between elites and the people would introduce a flexibility and democratic legitimacy into political life that is currently lacking these characteristics. A widely agreed constitutional covenant would ensure such a process would be transparent, properly institutionalised, and contain procedural safeguards. These safeguards would ensure no one is cut out of the process or that current arrangements are not simply torn-up by one group. This can be achieved with: rules requiring joint and concurrent referendums in all significant entities, municipalities and cantons; civic initiatives that cut across ethnic lines; and inclusive constitutional conventions for deliberation. With these

---

[20] On the issue of constitutional reform, at least, and arguably on almost all policy issues given the way the electoral laws and districts operate.

[21] The term 'deliberative' has helpfully been defined by Ghai and Galli (2006) to mean "a process of negotiation which is based on clear goals (of the national interest and social justice) and sufficient information and knowledge, aimed at exchanges of ideas, clarification of differences, persuasion and agreement. This requires a degree of facilitation, and a critical question is who does this and under what procedures."

safeguards, it is clear that the people and elites would be no worse off than under the status quo; even if the people might be as intransigent as elites. A revolving constitution would guarantee that the outcomes of reform would accord with the median or average voter. Elites in the constitutional reform space, currently interacting only with each other in the parliamentary or presidential arena, would be incentivised or 'nudged' towards considering the preferences of the people in the electoral arena.[22] If the people are just as intransigent as the elites then current constitutional arrangements will remain in place. If it is true, however, as the evidence suggests, that the people are more accommodating than political elites then regular interaction between elites and the people can lead to far greater constitutional change than is currently possible and a far greater likelihood of accommodating behaviour amongst elites. The revolving constitution can help publicly manifest the underlying political culture of the people: democratic, tolerant and accepting.

The revolving constitution is far from being a revolutionary construct. It does not, like revolutions in general, impose a winner takes all solution by immediately empowering or disempowering one group over another in the political game. Repeated interaction and engagement by the people and elites in the constitutional reform arena would tend to speed-up constitutional evolution, recreating a *process* that allows flexibility to be established in polities like Britain. If it is right that the people are more conciliatory and accepting than political elites (as this book demonstrates they are) then this evolution will stand in bold defiance of exclusive ethno-nationalism. The possibility of regularly (though not too frequently) amending the constitution, with civic involvement, would set in motion a process rather than determine an outcome. A process whereby political elites are incentivised to pursue moderate and accommodating reform could, incrementally, alter the shape of everyday politics in Bosnia. A standard may even be set for other

---

[22] The idea that political elite's decision-making is in the name of 'the people' would no longer ring hollow and the people would find it more difficult to blame political elites alone for intransigence given that all the people will now have an opportunity to participate.

plural, multi-ethnic polities to follow—both to help regulate existing conflict and avert conflict in the future.

In Britain, it is evident that piecemeal and partisan constitutional changes and the use of modes of decision making that are outside the accepted rules and norms has had a corrosive effect on the institutions of parliamentary democracy. Parliamentary democracy is predicated on representative institutions rather than institutions of direct democracy. It is evident that there is a need for inclusive, participatory and deliberative processes to reform aspects of the British constitution so that a fairer settlement can be achieved to address disparities in: wealth and regional equality; the equality of the four nations; the application of human rights and the international norms thereof; and the representation of the people in Parliament. There is a strong case for a constitutional covenant to begin a process: to inform the electorate and elites, to understand the significance of reform and where it might be really needed through consultation; and, ultimately to open an informed national debate and deliberation—among political elites and the people—in order to form a cross-party consensus as to which aspects of Britain's unwritten constitution are fundamental. This might include the production of an impartial code or guide to the current arrangements to facilitate understanding and debate (HoC 2014). The process towards a covenant is not utopian in nature but rather a practical mechanism: the people can be nudged into this process given the preferences they have expressed in favour of more involvement, participation and a need for a change from the status quo.

The Bosnian experience shows that there are some principles which must be at the forefront of any constitutional reform endeavour in Britain. The process of any reform proposal is all critical. Measuring political culture is as important as carrying out polls on the day-to-day issues that concern the electorate. This enables a better understanding of where the electorate stands on the fundamentals of democracy, participation and the idea of living together. Public participation in the process must be provided for and ought to be genuine and meaningful to help nurture, consolidate, and develop good political culture. And, finally, pragmatic buy-in of political elites is necessary to avoid spoilers and to avoid scenarios where it is perceived that at the end of the process the winner will take all. With some of these principles it may well be possible to consider whether the British people, across all four nations and in all their diversity, may come to new political understanding, perhaps towards a kind of Magna Carta of the People, around which political elites, stakeholders and the people may coalesce.[23] There will be no shortage of questions requiring answers, for example:

- How do you accommodate different national interests in a union of nations without descending into a nationalist "race to the bottom"?
- How should constitutions deal with veto rights on decisions by national or minority communities?
- What are the risks of entrenching some rights above others, in particular, the rights of whole groups or nations?
- What are the pitfalls of using referenda in a blunt manner (as was done in the referendum to leave the EU) and what might be more 'sensible' ways of ascertaining people's preferences?
- Why is constitutional change without considering the preferences of the people doomed to fail?
- Should political culture (both civic and political values) be given equal, if not more, attention as proposals for reform of constitutional rules?

This book aims to provide those answers and an opportunity to re-evaluate Britain's current uncodified constitution. In doing so, it provides some insight as to a possible transparent, inclusive, participatory pathway around current impediments. It posits a recurring but controversial question: is Britain's historical unwritten arrangement really worth defending? Any such defence, if it is to occur, would be made through a re-development of core political and civic virtues through greater political interaction

---

[23] Another title may be the *Millennium Magna Carta* or the *Charter of the People*.

between political elites and the people. Reliance simply on written rules, duties and responsibilities is not enough. Some form of social entrenchment of human rights (if not legal and political) is clearly necessary to allow the unrestricted cultivation of good political culture. Game theory and behavioural economics suggest that, where the conditions are right, the British model, with certain adaptations, could be favourable to better constitution-making. The British model may make less confrontational a process by avoiding any 'constitutional moment'. It allows, not unlike a 'revolving constitution', inter-temporal bargains to lessen the 'winner-takes-all' effects of a new or amended constitution. It also encourages an active constitutional culture to develop across generations so that new generations may *feel* that they have something at stake and a genuine solidarity and fraternity with others who decide the new rules.

Britain though may need a way to reset the terms of its political arrangement. A one-off constitutional covenant leading to a constitutional convention to deliberate on key constitutional problems may provide a truly participatory and deliberative constitutional statute to renew, reinvigorate and revitalise political relationships. Such a constitutional statute could ensure that Parliament, the Government as well as the devolved administrations benefit from greater popular legitimacy rather than suffer collective malaise, disdain and apathy.

The book is organised as follows. Chapter 1 provides an overview of what a constitution is and the debate that surrounds its nature. An outline is provided of the British unwritten or uncodified constitution: its operation, its historical origins, and the recent trends challenging its unwritten status. The Chapter also provides an outline of the Bosnian constitution: its creation, the hopes of its drafters, its imposition, and the practical reality of its operation. It explains why comparing these two particular States is important and what we might hope to gain by questioning their design and amendment processes. It emphasises that no *particular* constitution is paradigmatic. An unwritten one is not necessarily superior to a written one. The *process* of creation or change, however, necessarily entails a consideration of political culture and history.

Chapter 2 introduces theoretical ideas about political culture, what it is and how it can be measured. It explains falls in political participation in Bosnia and Britain and the variables that can help explain why people are (or can become) apathetic in a given constitutional structure. In particular, the Chapter looks at how people form views that are not conducive to democratic engagement, as well as views that are hostile to a democratic form of government. The sub-chapters define concepts such as 'political culture', 'political apathy', 'political participation', and proposes a working model for analysis. The Chapter presents the findings of quantitative research (see Appendix A) in respect of political apathy in Britain and Bosnia, with Croatia as a reference point.

Chapter 3 presents the detailed findings of quantitative research in respect of political culture in Bosnia. The Chapter, in particular, considers whether a 'poor' political culture (defined in Chapter 2) is the main variable explaining Bosnia's political problems or whether there are more persuasive explanations such as institutional failure stemming from foundational constitutional structures. The Chapter roots the questions of constitutional design and amendment in the context of the real political culture of the Bosnian people and sets out why the failure to consider this culture may be helping to perpetuate conflict and simply freeze violent conflict. If Britain and Bosnia have pro-democratic political cultures, the question is posed as to what they may learn from one another in terms of their design and amendment processes.

Chapter 4 sets out the literature and theoretical principles of institutional design and amendment. It explains why changing formal rules when the underlying beliefs or values of societies remain rigidly opposed will result in failed institutions; and why a failure to change the formal institutions when belief systems are conducive to change imperils those institutions. The sub-chapters set out the three major proposals that have been made to date to reform the Bosnian constitution and the reasons for their failure.

The sub-chapters will contrast that experience with the outlier case of the unwritten constitution in Britain and various reforms made to it (with a focus on those made since 1997). The sub-chapters focus on Brexit, Scottish and Northern Irish secessionism, and the unlawful constitutional practices of recent British governments. They interrogate whether it is the existing unwritten constitution (which creates a system of representative parliamentary democracy) that is the source of these crises or, rather, the by-passing of existing constitutional conventions, rules, and institutions. In the one (Britain) it poses the question of whether abandonment of its traditional unwritten constitution is the problem and in the other (Bosnia) it asks whether the foundational moment of the imposed constitution is the source of all the problems. In essence, what can one State learn from the other as calls for reform ring loud?

Chapter 5 draws on the literature in the fields of game theory and behavioural economics to model the impasse in Bosnia in light of the practical operation of Britain's flexible constitutional arrangements. It uses game theory to present how ethno-nationalist political elites play a 'zero-sum' game in the current Bosnian institutions. Suggestions are made as to how they may be incentivised to give-up their strong ethno-nationalistic decision-making in the current system by introducing a third and critical actor: the people. The Chapter then suggests a solution to the impasse in Bosnia: a *revolving constitution*.

Chapter 6 develops the practical lessons for two disparate constitutional reform debates—that in Britain where codification is being increasingly talked about, and that in Bosnia where any hope of reform is marred by the actions of ethno-nationalist elite spoilers who benefit greatly from the current constitutional status quo. The Chapter sets out the mechanics of how a revolving constitution for Bosnia might operate and the careful calibration that is required to ensure safeguards for minority groups, human rights and stability. The Chapter also looks at how Britain may address current and future constitutional crises that clearly require redress. A model for greater deliberation and participation of the public is proposed which is in true keeping with British political culture and tradition.

The <u>concluding remarks</u> suggest how best to characterise a constitution and draws together the wide scholarship consulted in writing this book. The remarks identify the main lessons learned in comparing Bosnian and British constitution-making and design; some practical policy suggestions are provided on possible reform of the British and Bosnian constitutions. General lessons are drawn from the comparison made between Bosnia and Britain for both post-conflict and pre-conflict States.

Technical Methodology

This book makes use of two research methods to answer the primary research questions: (a) quantitative research to understand political culture, political apathy and political division in Bosnia and Britain; and (b) the use of rational choice models (game theory and veto player theory) and behavioural economics (prospect theory) to analyse the behaviour of political elites and the people (together 'players') in the current constitutional framework.

The quantitative analysis uses value-based surveys produced by the *World Values Survey (WVS)* and *European Values Study (EVS)* to make operational the terms 'political culture', 'political participation' and 'political apathy'. Croatia is used as a comparative case study.[24] The dataset produced by WVS and EVS conducted seven waves of studies with four each of Bosnia, Croatia and Britain in the period from 1990−2020 (Bosnia *1998 (N=800), 2001 (N=1200), 2008 (N=1512), 2019 (N=1735)*, Croatia *(1996 (N=1196), 1999 (N=1003), 2008 (N=1525), 2017 (N=1493) and Britain (1990 (N=1484), 1999 (N= 994), 2008 (N=1561), 2018 (N=1794)*.[25]

---

[24] Given the different paths Croatia and Bosnia have taken following the war and the relative political 'success' of Croatia the comparison is immensely useful in analysing variations, if any, in 'culture' and levels of apathy.

[25] The *World Values Survey* is a global database for social scientists studying changing values and their impact on social and political life. The WVS has been carried out in close collaboration with the *European Values Study* and encompasses data of representative national surveys from ninety-seven societies around the globe, containing almost 90 percent of the world's

WVS and EVS are used as they are the only dataset that collated time-series data cross-nationally on issues concerning political participation over a significant period of time. Given the lack of any other serious time-series data, and gaps in the datasets which exist, the analysis is supplemented by data obtained from other local studies where available and relevant.

The quantitative analysis forms the basis for the rest of the study. The quantitative data together with the case study on Bosnia's institutional failure (Chapter 4) is necessary to form some of the assumptions about players' substantive preferences and institutional structures in the rational choice analysis that follows (Chapter 5). These assumptions give empirical content to the theory and hence make it testable (Ganghof 2009). Rational choice models have explanatory power and predictive potential: in Bosnia they serve to elucidate why substantive proposals for constitutional reform are failing and suggest possible ways to break the reform impasse. The Bosnian case study allows a clearer comparison with constitutional reforms suggested for Britain. The game theory approach helps to explain complex political behaviour in a systematic way; why the behaviour of political actors is an optimal response to conditions of their political environment and the behaviour of others. Changing the context or institutions (the 'rules of the game') leads to changes in preferences and, therefore, outcomes. The models, therefore, provide theoretical clarity and strong explanatory power by eliminating chance or ad hoc explanations whilst acknowledging that the model is only an approximation of reality although a relatively good approximation (Tsebelis 1990, 40-47). They also explain why certain conditions and behaviour prevail, as equilibria, in a State such as Bosnia. The veto player approach, in particular, can integrate a number of approaches to institutional analyses by focusing on actors within institutions that actually matter—those that can set, alter and veto legislation (Tsebelis 1999; 2002; Ganghof 2009; Hallerberg 2010, 21).

---

population. These surveys show pervasive changes in what people want out of life and in what they believe. In order to monitor these changes, the EVS/WVS has executed seven waves of surveys, from 1981 to 2019. Data set sources: World Values Survey 1981-2019.

The game theory and veto player approaches are used to model the game played by the elites in the parliamentary arena in Bosnia. The preferences of elites, however, are influenced in another important space: the electoral arena where interaction with the people (or the electorate) can alter preferences and, therefore, outcomes. The objective of the study is not to discuss the shortcomings and benefits of various institutional structures generally for Bosnia but to compare all of these structures consistently with respect to one particular objective (Tsebelis 1995): the capacity for meaningful constitutional change.

Given that the use of such models has been neglected in the study of Bosnia's political paralysis, this book aims to add to existing work by identifying the precise causes of failure in the institutional structures in Bosnia inhibiting meaningful constitutional reform and civic participation in politics. That would go some way to creating a Bosnia based on individual rights and equality rather than the presumed collective equality of ethnic groups. For Britain, this book seeks to draw together disparate thinking on suggestions for constitutional reform and attempts to reconcile competing models. The analytical models deployed allow a pathway out of constitutional paralysis, contestation and crises. Practical proposals are provided as to how States can enjoy higher civic participation in politics, fairer bargains between groups and increased democratic legitimacy. Britain and Bosnia may benefit, but so might others.

A Constitution of the People and How to Achieve It

"And when we saw this script we'd
never seen before
In front of our very eyes from far-off
times of yore
A long silence
Fell between
Us

This stillness was broken by a voice
that was calm but
outspoken –
No scribe wrote this text for sure
It looks like someone
Was trying to
Draw

And then a second says racking his
brains —
Look at the right that might be
where it begins
And it's merrily flowing leftwards
Widdershins
Who was such writing
Written for

Those who insist on reading from
right to left
Are wrong all along —
A third one says half crazed

And half
Amazed

Look it's a secret text from the
darkest days of old
Rising it seems from the depths of
our murkiest
Dreams
Its signs are like writing
Seen in a mirror —
Mutters
A mouth
Calm and
Cold

The fifth with clenched fists and
trembling fingers tries to hold
This mirror of clear redeeming grace
But it slips
To the
Floor

For in it that instant he recognises
His own
Ancient
Forgotten
Face."

— Mak Dizdar, *The Stone Sleeper* [26]

---

[26] A poem called "A Text About A Text" by Mak Dizdar [1917-1971] (2009, 71).

1. "A text about a text": constitutions of Britain and Bosnia

1.1 Searching for the soul of a state

Constitutions have existed for time immemorial. Whenever groups of people have come together for political, social, or economic association, some form of rules, practices or principles have inevitably followed: a constitution of the people for some particular purpose. Rules, practices or principles would have helped people ascertain the terms of their association particularly where differential power dynamics existed among the group. The historical record shows differential power dynamics existed in much of Britain's and Bosnia's royal histories.[27] There would have been a single monarch, his and sometimes her court, and then the mass of the people. In much of Bosnia's and Britain's early histories, differential power dynamics would have also existed between outside influences (such as invading rulers) and the indigenous peoples.

In Bosnia's case, the major outside influences were Illyrian, Celt, Roman, Slav, Hungarian, Ottoman, Austro-Hungarian, Yugoslav[28] and, today, American. The outside influences were interposed by relatively long periods of independence. One such period, in particular, saw the rise of the Bosnian Kingdom (Banate or *Banovina*) and its associated Bosnian Church in the 12th and 13th centuries. In Britain's case, the conquering or outside influences were Roman, Norwegian Viking, Danish Viking, Anglo-Saxon, and finally Norman. The Normans were the last of the major conquering forces who won control and, ultimately, assimilated into the English population.

As people's associations, both internal and external, started to become more akin to communities, with repeated engagement and

---

[27] As noted in the Introduction, Bosnia and Herzegovina is referred to throughout as "Bosnia".
[28] In so far it came to be dominated by Serbia and Croatia and silenced the agency of Bosnians.

interaction, the relevant rules, practices or principles may have been written down. Very early in human history those written rules would have been on scraps of bone or skin or stone.[29] The earliest known written rules in England are said to be that of Ethelbert of Kent believed to date from c.602-603 which was very early in the formation of kingdoms *in* England and long before we can talk of a Kingdom *of* England. In Wales, a type of Celtic law, the Cyfraith Hywel, was codified by Hywel Dda in c.942–950. In Scotland, the earliest preserved code of Scots law appears to be the *Leges inter Brettos et Scottos*, promulgated under David I (c.1124–1153). Equally, however, a great deal would have remained unwritten. The unwritten rules would have been in the thoughts and, more importantly, practices of men and women. Irish law, for instance, in origin, consisted of the accumulated decisions of the *Brehons*, or judges, who were guided entirely by an oral tradition developed from custom.

Constitutions of formal political communities were (and remain) not altogether different in nature to the rules, practices or principles formed whenever groups of people have come together for some economic, social or political purpose. Today, we might categorise these formal political communities in a hierarchical pyramid at the top of which sit 'States' as the predominant and pre-eminent form of political organisation. A State may be considered, loosely speaking, to be a formal political community bound by some geographical limits. A State in modern political parlance is often synonymous with the idea of a nation or a national community. It is sometimes thought, albeit not without controversy, that a nation can only truly manifest itself when it

---

[29] The Cyrus Cylinder, from the 6th century, on which is written a declaration in the name of Persia's Achaemenid king, Cyrus the Great, is one such example. Some scholars such as MacGregor (2012) have considered it as "the first attempt we know about running a society, a state with different nationalities and faiths—a new kind of statecraft." Even today the Acts of the British Parliament and those of the Irish Oireachtas are printed on vellum for archival purposes (Oireachtas 2012). Controversially in Britain, since 23 January 2017 only the front and back covers of Acts of Parliament are retained on vellum in an effort to save money (House of Commons 2018). In Bosnia, the link between the political and traditional heritage has disappeared altogether.

controls all the machinery of the State. This conception culminated in the post-1648, Westphalian idea of 'nation-states'. By nation-states we mean that there is, or ought to be, some congruence between the perceived idea of the nation and the boundaries of the State. In practical terms, this means that group characteristics (such as race, ethnicity, language, or religion) which together constitute the nation come, or are brought, together as a formal political community.[30] There may be one or more nations within a State and sometimes there may be none.

Within that context, we can locate the idea or concept of citizenship that may or may not coincide with other identities such as nationality or ethnicity (Džankić 2015, 7). Citizenship concerns the legal relationship people have with the State, giving rise to their rights and duties, as well as their emotional attachment to the State and their willingness to take part in the day-to-day functioning of the polity (Ibid, 5). This book concerns itself with States as the formal and formative form of political community.

Formal definitions of what exactly a modern constitution is differ greatly. Generally, we might understand a constitution of a State to serve three principal purposes. The first is to delineate the authority given to the State institutions or organs. A constitution thereby acts as a constraint on the power—as opposed to formal authority—of its principal institutions and, in particular, on the executive which functions as the government. The principal institutions are often the executive, the legislature and the judiciary. The second purpose is to set-out the basis for interaction between the State institutions and its constituents, the people. It is useful for

---

[30] Beneath that pre-eminent form of political community as a nation-state, there are other conceptions of 'nation' which may be subsumed within an existing State. Nations themselves are complicated. They are often, as scholars have explained, "imagined communities" as non-self-conscious abstractions (Anderson 1991). Alternatively, nations can "will themselves" into persistence sometimes as a fiction (Gellner 1983). Nations can have a collective shared identity which is manifest or sometimes that identity manifests over time. Nations can be solely civic in nature if they are successful in removing perceived problematic differences if those can be considered 'problems' at all. They may also be civic in nature if there is another common bond rooted in custom or tradition around which groups can coalesce.

a constitution to resolve the issue of the participation, or the representation, of the people within those institutions and whether that participation is to be formal or informal and direct or indirect.[31] The third purpose is to outline the rights and obligations of the people *vis-à-vis* the State and in some cases their responsibilities. Responsibility can mean two things. Responsibility of the people to State institutions and people's responsibility to each other via the machinery of the State itself such as its justice system. This threefold typology for defining a constitution is relatively modern. The typology does, however, loosely model constitutions that were premodern.[32]

It is difficult to ignore that the terminology used to describe constitutions and their function are distinctly anthropomorphic. It is, however, not by chance that we have inherited such terminology. A constitution, for instance, we say, is 'created'. Creation necessarily entails a maker and even, perhaps, a higher power. A power which somehow 'births' the foundational moment of the State, particularly a nation-state, into being. A State we say is 'born' and popularly, in the context of male-dominated power structures, it is perceived often as female on conception. Just as gender is socially constructed, the nation-state too is socially constructed. It incorporates ideas about 'manhood' and 'womanhood' (Yuval-Davis 1997). As such, a nation-state, in societies with patriarchal norms, is characterised as 'feminine' in nature. She is expected, as the ideal mother, to reproduce the nation with her children. In that process, the nation-state, sometimes, also impermissibly lays physical claim to women's bodies which by inference are an extension of the nation-state.

A State which coalesces with the idea of the nation is seen to have boundaries around 'her' as well as her body politic (her sons and daughters). Both of these require protection from alien

---

[31] For instance, even medieval European monarchs had to have in mind the support of the great landed gentry who may have been empowered (informally, of course) to speak on behalf of smaller landholders and sometimes even the 'tenants' within the monarch's realm.

[32] The pre-modern era would be considered to be before the 18th century enlightenment in Western Europe or the United States of America ("US").

intruders which may infect, harm or penetrate the body (Duhaček 1997) and, therefore, the 'organs' of the State are mobilised for State-sanctioned violence. This violence in the cause of protection emanates, usually, from the 'sons of the nation' imbued with the rhetoric of loyalty, betrayal and sacrifice. They are, in turn, often led by a founding father who stands, all powerful, as the Godhead (Iveković 1993, 115-116, 120-122). In some instances, States have notably taken on board this almost religious iconography and conceived the birth of their State as immaculate in conception. The father figure, of course, co-opts, or becomes synonymous with, that higher power alluded to earlier. Sometimes the nexus between the dear father figure transforms the motherland into the fatherland. And then the power and control of the leader becomes tantamount with the power and control of the State itself over others.[33]

The ascribing of human characteristics to a clearly non-human thing goes to the heart of how a constitution is understood and perceived. The further one goes with the metaphor, the further one moves away from the idea of a constitution as an abstract or functional document simply concerned with rules and institutions. People ascribe such human characteristics to a constitution for myriad reasons, which are relevant to the issue of constitutional creation, design or change.

- Is a constitution, to carry the metaphor yet further still, the *soul* of the body politic and, therefore, its real, pure and metaphysical core?
- Is a constitution rather the *skeleton* providing some foundational structure to the body politic that allows the

---

[33] There is discomfort in some quarters on this gendered characterisation of constitutions and the suggestion that this has an impact on real world outcomes is often dismissed as being 'non-demonstrable'. The reality, however, is that constitution-making has been an almost universally man-led exercise (in most of modern recorded history). It is not possible to verify gendered bias in constitutional design when there is nothing to compare it against: the claim is not possible to falsify. The fact is that man-led constitution making necessarily results in man-oriented norms, practices and rules. Men (still predominantly) make war and exercise state-sanctioned violence and then recreate the State after conflict. Only when a different (more equal or women-led) construction of the State is realised can a meaningful comparison be made.

body to function but is, in and of itself, of no further dynamic utility?
- Is a constitution perhaps the skin or the outward *cosmetic form* of the body providing a surface presentation, in a manner of speaking, of this more complicated and esoteric inner core? Or,
- Is a constitution something disconnected from the body such as the *environment* within which the body may find function and meaning in order to truly manifest itself?

The metaphor, one might think, can be stretched to breaking point but scholars have alluded, or expressly considered, the constitution, over the centuries, to be each of these humanly things.

Aristotle was considering the nature of political association as early as the fourth century BC. For him, the formal cause of the city-state was its constitution (*politeia*). Aristotle defined the constitution as "a certain ordering of the inhabitants of the city-state" and the political community as "the form of the compound" (Politics, III.1.1274b32-41). He argued that whether the community is the same over time depends on whether it has the same constitution of the people which bring with them certain ideals, values and objectives (III.3.1276b1-11). The constitution, according to this formulation, is not a written document, but an immanent organizing principle, analogous to the soul of an organism. The constitution, therefore, is "the way of life" of the citizens (IV.11.1295a40-b1, VII.8.1328b1-2).

But the citizens in the Aristotelian city-state were those of the (minority) resident population who were privileged enough to possess full political rights (III.1.1275b17-20). Women, slaves, working-class men and non-residents were excluded. It was much like Britain until the movements for universal suffrage or the Britain of the colonies. It was only until the passing of the voting rights acts in the 19th and 20th centuries that most men and then women were granted suffrage. It was long after then that Britain granted to its imperial possessions in the British Empire independence and self-determination. A constitution, therefore, can include as well as exclude even when it is conceived of as the soul of a State.

An intermediary view has seen the constitution as much less esoteric and more akin to a skeleton around which the body politic is formed. Whilst the skeleton is intimately connected and indeed is critical for the functioning of the body, in day-to-day life it is not particularly relevant until things go wrong. On this view, political turmoil "can operate like an X-ray, lighting up the bones around which the body politic is formed. And we suddenly realise that we can no more live without a constitution as we can without a skeleton to support our flesh" (Stourton, BBC 2017). This view sees the constitution as far removed from the people but paradoxically inescapably close.

A somewhat different use of the metaphor is to consider the constitution as not human at all. Rather it is more analogous to the environment in which the critical human component of a State, the body politic, must operate. This strand of thinking is most prevalent in the modern age. The constitution *in extremis* is merely an abstract construction. An important abstraction but without very much relevance to the way people really live their lives. It is simply concerned with the form and function of government: the right to, and frequency of, elections; the provision of some basic human rights protections; and ultimately little else more. Constitutions are just the 'rules of the game' so to speak. Rules that only concern a handful of people at the top.

Discussions and indeed disagreements about constitutional creation, design or amendment go back to the very beginning of political action and thought.[34] Broadly, discussions on constitutional design relate to two major aspects. The first aspect is whether the foundational moment of a constitution is an imposed legal settlement or a freely negotiated social contract upon which all members of society agree to govern their affairs. The second aspect is about content. Should a constitution include a link to important social or moral values, delineate the authority and powers of institutions, and provide for individual or group rights

---

[34] In the Western tradition, at least, we may think of, a great many thinkers: Plato (375 BC); Aristotle (335-323 BC); Locke (1690); Hobbes (1651); Burke (1770); Paine (1792), de Tocqueville (1835-1840), Hamilton, Jay and Madison (1787); Mill (1859); Rawls (1971); Habermas (1998, 2001); and Derrida (2002).

including representation in institutions? Some of these issues are resolved expressly at the outset and others are determined through time as a constitution becomes a 'living instrument'. In taking either of those routes to a constitutional settlement, what is deemed *essential* to a constitution must necessarily come before what is the *desirable* content of a constitution. That is why the *process* of constitution-making becomes highly important. It is the sole concern of this book.

In terms of form and substance, therefore, constitutions can be as close to the soul of a State as one might want them to be. A constitution may reflect the social, cultural and moral virtues or norms of the people who expressly or tacitly accept the State, and the way it functions, as legitimate. And accept it they must if the State, bound by constitutional rules and norms, is to function properly. A constitution, however, may be devoid of any sociological or metaphysical basis if all it is considered to be is an abstract, prescriptive and instrumental document setting-up an environment in which *any* State or people may operate. Over time, an empty vessel may indeed be filled with something worthwhile should it remain intact. The question, however, of whether it remains intact and what exactly is worthwhile cannot be answered simply by gauging the political opinion of the majority at a particular snapshot in time through national elections. Longer term social, moral and cultural norms, collectively known as 'political culture', must be ascertained in a far more rigorous way if the process of constitution making is to be truly reflective, participatory and inclusive. This is where considering the British and Bosnian constitutions as well as the histories of their development is relevant.

1.2 Overview of the British constitution

The British constitution, famously, is not written or codified in any single document. Some elements are not written anywhere at all. Those unwritten elements are rather a product of experience, whether that was the experience of the monarch, the monarch's government in Parliament, or the monarch's counsel (as a precursor to the judiciary). Over time, experience became custom and even later still hallowed convention until, of course, such time that the convention is dis-applied. Even the British constitution's most important written elements—legal rules created by Parliament or by the courts under common law—may be unwritten just as easily as they were made. Parliament may repeal any previous Act of Parliament by simple majority vote. Important constitutional principles, however, may only be repealed if the intention to do so is made express by Parliament.[35]

It is a great strength of the British constitution that many important constitutional documents, particularly in relation to fundamental rights, have stood the test of time. They have remained on the statute books and have been faithfully applied by the courts. But that such fundamental rules or practices may not succumb to popular whims, prejudice or 'transient passion', as Turpin and Tomkins (2012) call it, is not guaranteed at all.

Certain rules or practices that most people might consider fundamental have been diluted by Parliament despite vociferous and principled opposition. These include the defendant's right of peremptory challenge of jurors, or their right to silence when charged with a crime or the right to trial by jury. In each of these cases the right has either been expressly removed, diluted or abrogated by Parliament (Turpin and Tomkins 2012, 7).

In some instances, the courts, where they have had sufficient legal basis and authority, have declared such attacks on fundamental rights as incompatible with the British constitution. Famously, in the case of *A v SSHD*,[36] the House of Lords held that indefinite detention without trial of non-British nationals, who were suspected of being terrorists, was contrary to right to liberty and security of the person because it discriminated against foreign nationals (contrary to Art. 14 of the European Convention on Human Rights ("ECHR") although it was not unlawful *per se*. Following a tradition of judicial conservatism and considering the

---

[35] *Thoburn v Sunderland City Council* [2002] EWHC 195 (Admin) at [63-64]; *BH v The Lord Advocate (Scotland)* [2012] UKSC 24 at [30].
[36] *A v Secretary of State for Home Department* [2004] UKHL 56, [2005] 2 AC 68.

sovereignty of Parliament over all other institutions, the majority did not rule on whether the government was right to derogate from the ECHR (under Art. 15) on the basis that there was a 'threat to the life of the nation' allowing such derogation. The judges were careful to implicitly acknowledge that they are unelected and must not make or be seen to make policy. Lord Hoffman, in a stinging dissent in the case, argued that the power of indefinite detention was fundamentally contrary to the British constitution because it was both unlawful and there was an impermissible derogation from the ECHR:

> "In my opinion, such a power in any form is not compatible with our constitution. The real threat to the life of the nation, in the sense of a people living in accordance with its traditional laws and political values, comes not from terrorism but from laws such as these. That is the true measure of what terrorism may achieve. It is for Parliament to decide whether to give the terrorists such a victory" (A v SSHD, para. 97).

The case of *A v SSHD* demonstrates the difficulty of interpreting constitutions as well as rights. Given the nebulous nature of the British constitution a helpful starting point would be to identify precisely what it is or means today, as precisely as is possible, before moving to consider its origins.

In simple terms, the British constitution is a miscellaneous collection of flexible conventions, practices and rules governing political behaviour. Britain is a constitutional monarchy which means it is a State headed by a sovereign who rules according to the constitution which puts at its centre a sovereign Parliament (Bogdanor 1997, 1). Britain and New Zealand are the only two constitutional monarchies in the world where the constitution remains unwritten. It might be more accurate to say the British constitution is 'uncodified' as large parts of the body of law that would ordinarily form the constitution is written down. Its written elements appear in the form of primary legislation, delegated legislation, common law precedent produced by court judgments, and government guidance. Britain is also only one of two States, proper, in the world which have unwritten or uncodified constitutions. Israel, Saudi Arabia and Sweden's constitutions might also be considered as relatively uncodified although they do have significant Basic Laws comprising constitution-like fundamentals.

The British constitutional arrangement, with Parliament at its centre, has endured for over 350 years since the 'Glorious' or 'Bloodless' Revolution of 1688-1689. The origins of parliamentary sovereignty lie in the Bill of Rights 1688 and the Coronation Oaths Act 1689. Whilst the constitution has remained in place, Britain's underlying institutional structure has undergone gradual change as have the nations which comprise the 'United Kingdom'. Britain today comprises four nations — England, Scotland, Wales and Northern Ireland — which are held together in an uncodified, non-federal arrangement. There is no legal document in Britain identifying the country as 'a State' to which rules and principles can be ascribed or attributed. Historically, its public law has developed from interaction between parties arguing in the courts over what are the responsibilities of government over something in the public realm (as opposed to disagreements between private persons) (Turpin and Tomkins 2012, 12-13). The nature, extent and reach of the State, and its officials, organs and bodies, has developed over time. Not unlike Britain's democracy this development has been in a partial and piecemeal fashion.[37] Britain though is undoubtedly recognised as a State under international law.

Britain's political institutions are constituted as follows. The executive is comprised of a Prime Minister and Ministers from the majority party who sit in 'Cabinet' as Her Majesty's Government. They run the administration of the State supported by an a-political and professionalised bureaucracy called the Civil Service. The party with the next largest majority forms Her Majesty's Opposition. Parliament is the legislative body which has the power to make and un-make any law it wishes through primary legislation — Acts of Parliament — or related delegated legislation such as regulations, instruments and orders in council. Parliament is supreme over all other sources of law and indeed the monarch herself. Parliament

---

[37] There is extensive case law on this. See, for instance, *D v NSPCC* [1978] AC 171, *Foster v British Gas* [1991] 2 AC 306, *Chandler v DPP* [1964] AC 763 (HL).

has two chambers: an unelected upper chamber, the House of Lords, and the elected lower chamber, the House of Commons. Parliament creates law and the monarch is expected to adhere to it and has been expected to since the late seventeenth century. The judiciary is composed of judges who, since 2006, have been appointed by an a-political commission. Courts adjudicate on private disputes between legal persons as well as public disputes between the government and its citizens by way of judicial review and/or application of domestic or international human rights law incorporated into domestic legislation. Judges are also an important source of uncodified 'common law' which they create by applying or interpreting past precedent or creating new precedents where past practice is not instructive. The institutional structure under the British constitution mirrors the 'separation of powers' principle. That principle is often a formal feature of presidential and other modern systems of government: ensuring a strict division between the executive, the legislature and the judiciary. In reality, however, the British system may be better characterised as having a fusion of powers which are, in theory, finely balanced—how finely and whether the scales have tipped in favour of one institution over another is an issue addressed in Chapter 4.

As Parliament is supreme, no Act of Parliament may bind a subsequent Parliament. No single piece of legislation, therefore, may be entrenched giving it priority over any other. It is for this reason that no legislation has a special, constitutional status, conferred on it *per se*. Some fundamental constitutional conventions, rules or laws, however, may only be repealed or abrogated, if Parliament makes its intention to do so explicit. A number of fundamental pieces of primary legislation may be identified, as have the courts over time, including:

- Magna Carta 1215 (as amended and reissued in 1225)—set out that the sovereign is subject to the rule of law and provided some basic rights to free men including no taxes without common consent or imprisonment without cause.
- Charter of the Forest 1217 (as amended and reissued in 1225)—now largely forgotten and superseded only in 1971,

this instrument was a radical document on land rights. It was a statute that remained in force longer than any other in England (Standing 2019). It granted free men (commoners) access and use to increasingly vast royal landholdings and unlike the Magna Carta did not only deal with the grievances of the barons. It complemented and evolved from the Magna Carta.

- Petition of Right 1628 — reinforced two principles from the Magna Carta — no taxation without parliamentary consent and no imprisonment without cause. It prohibited quartering of soldiers or subjects, and abolished martial law in peacetime.
- Habeas Corpus Act 1679 — directed judicial inquiry into the legality of detention of a person.
- Act of Settlement 1701 — created judicial independence.
- Parliamentary Acts of 1911, 1949 — deprived the House of Lords of its absolute veto on legislation and allowed, in essence, delay rather than veto powers.
- Crown Proceedings Act 1947 — allowed civil actions to be brought against the Crown albeit with certain limitations.
- Reform Acts of 1832, 1867, 1884 — expanded the electorate of the House of Commons and made representation more democratic in that body.
- Other Acts relating to voting rights in the 19th and 20th centuries — led to parliamentary democracy and universal suffrage (most men received the vote in the 19th century and women in the first half of the 20th).
- European Communities Act 1973 — UK became subject to European Community (EC) law.
- Human Rights Act 1998 — obliged public bodies to give effect domestically to the European Convention on Human Rights ("ECHR").

The exercise of identifying constitutional statutes is always fraught. Blaustein and Flanz (1992) offered a list almost 30 years ago which listed over 300 statutes. The most recent versions of *Blackstone's Statutes in Public Law and Human Rights* rarely list more than 30 statutes out of over 100 that predate 1975 (Turpin and

Tomkins 2012, 5). The difficulty of separating out party political issues and issues of fundamental constitutional importance is neatly seen in the issue of Brexit. David Cameron, who as Prime Minister called the referendum on membership of the European Union (EU) in 2016, did not appear to appreciate that Britain leaving the EU would generate a constitutional crisis. Neither did his party. His pledge to hold a referendum in 2013 was to see off the challenge from an increasingly popular UK Independence Party and influential critics of the EU within his own party (Emerson 2020, 100-103).

The withdrawal process from the EU, as the government has found, has put at risk peace in Northern Ireland, possibly hastened unilateral Scottish secession from Britain, and curtailed the fundamental rights of the British electorate. Cameron called, foolishly, and contrary to the British constitutional tradition of representative democracy, a crude and binary referendum (Emerson, 2020, xiii). A referendum whose outcome was said to constitute the "will of the people" but clearly could not if the people only represented, as they did in fact: only 37 per cent of the electorate once non-voters (27.8 per cent) were accounted for or 51.9 per cent as a simple majority of those who voted. It was only the third such national referendum, as it happens, in Britain's entire history. The outcome of that referendum has seemingly jeopardised Britain's constitutional underpinnings or may yet still. It is an issue further considered in Chapter 4.

The 'Crown' is the title given to the monarch as the Head of State and she is also the Head of the Church of England, Head of State for assenting countries within the Commonwealth of Nations, and Commander in Chief of the armed forces. The monarch's constitutional role today is almost entirely symbolic although she nominally retains some residual powers of royal prerogative. These powers confer on her authority to take certain 'privileged' actions without requiring authorisation from any other institution. Prerogative powers are, in reality and by convention, exercised by the monarch acting through her Prime Minister and Ministers in Cabinet. She would almost never exercise those powers on her own initiative unless the circumstances were extreme and without precedent. That very remote possibility remains, and some had called for her to oppose the Prime Minister on some aspects of the Brexit withdrawal proposals as well as his advice on proroguing Parliament (Evans 2020). That was on the basis that although the Government had the confidence of Parliament (because no motion of no confidence had been passed under the Fixed-Term Parliaments Act 2011) it did not preclude the Queen, by convention, in not following the advice of the Prime Minister if that conflicted with the express will of Parliament in the form of a Bill presented for royal assent i.e., in relation to refusing a particular form of an EU withdrawal bill (Bowen 2019). The monarch also exerts some indirect influence on the Prime Minister through her weekly private consultations, which occur as of right, with him/her.

The prerogative powers of the monarch are theoretically very expansive[38] and have developed over time. They have undergone significant restriction in scope by Parliamentary convention or legislation including, for instance, expressly in the Bill of Rights 1689.[39] The courts, under common law, have made clear that the Crown is subject to the law but is immune from civil suit or criminal prosecution. The prerogative powers today include all manner of actions including: conduct of foreign affairs including declaring war and peace; signing international treaties; annexing or ceding territory; grant or withdrawal of British passports; appointment of bishops and archbishops in the Church of England; grant of pardons or commutations in sentence; appointment of the Prime Minister—theoretically anyone the monarch wishes although he/she has always sensibly decided on someone who would be best

---

[38] There is a debate and controversy surrounding the exact scope of prerogative powers and case law is supportive of both maximalist and minimalist claims as to the scope of the powers. See, Blackstone, William, *Commentaries on the Laws of England*, 1765–1769; Dicey, A.V., *Introduction to the Study of the Law of the Constitution*, 10th ed., 1959.

[39] Article 1 provides that the "power of suspending the laws or the execution of laws by regal authority without consent of Parliament is illegal"; Article 4 provides that the "levying money for or to the use of the Crown by pretence of prerogative, without grant of Parliament, for longer time, or in other manner than the same is or shall be granted, is illegal".

positioned to command a majority in the House of Commons; royal assent to legislation passed through Parliament; prorogation of Parliament; and the calling and dissolving Parliament until those powers were set out in the Fixed-Term Parliaments Act 2011.

Some prerogative powers are directly exercised by the Prime Minister, acting through Cabinet, without the approval of Parliament. In the past, this has included the powers of declaring war and peace, the issuing of passports, and the granting of honours. The Queen's or relevant Prince's consent, by convention, is required before Parliament can debate a bill affecting prerogatives or interests of the relevant Crown, such as hereditary revenue or personal property (Sumption 2020, 109). The Queen ordinarily grants or withholds consent on the advice of her Cabinet (Guardian 2013).

The power to declare war was exercised by the Cabinet in both world wars. Since then, the prerogative power has arguably been altered on the basis that Tony Blair sought symbolic and non-binding parliamentary approval for going to war with Iraq in March 2003; this has meant all subsequent Prime Ministers have sought approval. Notably, David Cameron failed to achieve support for air strikes on Syria in August 2013 and he honoured Parliament's decision. A new constitutional convention has, arguably, been created that requires Parliament to approve deployment of troops abroad other than in an emergency (Mills 2018). That new convention sits uneasily with the prerogative power to declare war, which in law rests squarely with the monarch as opposed to Parliament. Whether by practice that changes over time remains to be seen. In April 2018, Prime Minister Theresa May, launched airstrikes on Syria without parliamentary approval citing the 'element of surprise' and 'national interest'. As it happens, President Donald Trump had warned President Bashar al-Assad of the incoming missiles four days before via the medium of Twitter (Kentish 2018; Peck 2018). In Britain, the lack of parliamentary scrutiny or consultation for armed action abroad reignited a debate about whether Parliament should formally legislate on such matters to provide clarity (HoC 2011; Mills 2018).

1.3 Overview of the Bosnian constitution

The Bosnian constitution—set out in Annex IV of the 1995 Dayton Peace Agreement—is a relatively short document comprising only twelve, mainly functional, articles and two annexes. It was drafted in the English language, which is not the official language of the country, and has never been officially published in Bosnia's three official languages. The Bosnian constitution administratively divides Bosnia into two federal 'entities': the Federation comprising 51 per cent of the territory and Republika Srpska (RS) comprising 49 per cent of the territory, while reiterating the sovereignty and territorial integrity of Bosnia as a whole. Both entities have their own constitution which are required to be read, and be in conformity with, the Bosnian constitution. There is also the self-governing independent district of Brčko. The district's status was contested as each entity claimed it was theirs. Its ultimate status was settled by international arbitration.

The Bosnian constitution sets out the responsibilities of the institutions of Bosnia *vis-à-vis* the entities. Only certain exhaustive and enumerated powers are given to the State; all others are vested in the entities (USIP 2006, 3). The collective head of State, and the executive, is the three-member rotating Presidency comprising: a Bosniak and a Bosnian Croat directly elected in the Federation and a Bosnian Serb member directly elected in the RS. Bosniaks, Bosnian Croats and Bosnian Serbs constitute the three official 'constituent peoples' of Bosnia. 'Others' and 'Citizens' who are referred to in the Preamble to the constitution are left out of all of the substantive provisions in the constitution itself and are, therefore, excluded from the central governing structures. The Council of Ministers ("CoM"), acts as a *de facto* Cabinet government with one Chairperson. It is collaborative in nature and roles are divided among the three constituent peoples (although not exclusively so). Decisions by the CoM must be unanimous or be approved by the tripartite presidency. The legislature, the Parliamentary Assembly, is bicameral. The upper chamber, the House of Peoples, has 15 delegates: five Bosniaks and five Bosnian Croats chosen by the Federation Parliament and five Bosnian Serbs chosen by the RS

National Assembly. It has equal power to the lower chamber, the House of the Representatives, making it unusually and uniquely powerful (Išerić 2016). Decisions of the House of Representatives require approval of a majority which must include one third of members from each entity. Only two thirds of members of the House of Representatives may emanate from the Federation. Any parliamentary decision can be declared destructive of a 'vital national interest' by a majority of one of the constituent peoples (USIP 2006, 3). International human rights law is directly incorporated into the constitution and the ECHR has supremacy over domestic law.

The Bosnian constitution was primarily drafted with a view to ending the armed conflict of 1992-1995. Secondary to the cessation of hostilities was the idea of a fully functioning and viable State that would regulate ethnic conflict and overcome the hostility (exponentially multiplied by the war) to the very idea of a multi-ethnic Bosnian State. Franjo Tuđman, President of the newly independent Croatia, and Slobodan Milošević, President of the Socialist Federal Republic of Yugoslavia ("SFRY"), both denied many times having control or being the minds behind the armed conflict in Bosnia[40] yet both were key negotiators and signatories of the Dayton Peace Agreement.[41] As signatories, Tuđman and Milošević together on behalf of their respective States, agreed to act as guarantors of the Agreement *vis-à-vis* Bosnia.

Tuđman and Milošević, however, had no specific obligation to *ensure* compliance by the RS or the Federation (or compliance between them) except in respect of two Annexes seen as 'critical' for peace: the Agreements on Military Aspects and the Agreement on the Inter-Entity Boundary Line. That was important. Milošević was always very clear on the right of any Serb entity to have

---

[40] In June 1992 Milošević remarked to a reporter: "We are not supporting any military action in Bosnia Herzegovina. We are only supporting our people to survive there with the humanitarian and civilian help." See also Gaeta (1996, 156).

[41] Milošević headed a unified delegation (comprising representative of the Bosnian Serbs and the FRY) on behalf of the Bosnian Serbs (or more properly on behalf of the SDS/VRS (Vojska Republike Srpske) forces).

essentially a mandate to conduct foreign policy by having "parallel relationships"; Tuđman had helped negotiate a similar mandate for Bosnian Croats. As Bob Owen, a principal US peace negotiator, candidly revealed: "[..]it was quite obvious to us that he—although he never said secession—regarded that as a sort of slippery slope down which the Bosnian Serbs could slip into the hands of Serbia" (USD Jun 1996, 29). Whenever Milošević was challenged about whether he would ever push the Bosnian Serbs to secede he would always say he would not do it, but he would never commit to "giving up the right to it" (Ibid, 30).[42] Tuđman and Milošević were not signatories to Annex IV, which was the Bosnian constitution, and had no commitments to protect it. Perhaps, that indicates the importance that was given to the future of Bosnia as a sovereign and viable State (Gaeta 1996, 156).[43]

In tandem with the cessation of hostilities, a specific objective of the Dayton Peace Agreement was the return of displaced persons and refugees[44] to reverse the ethnic cleansing and territorial separation of ethnic groups that occurred during the armed conflict (Article II.5, Bosnian constitution and Annex 7, Dayton Peace Agreement). The wording of Annex 7, however, precluded complete unreserved return to pre-war homes; an inevitable outcome of negotiating with the perpetrators of ethnic cleansing. Displaced persons and refugees have, in practice, been unable to return to their pre-war homes and many remain in parts of the country to which they were displaced. Some of those displaced may now feel a sense of security around people of the same ethnicity; people who form a majority in the areas in which they have made their new homes (Kasapović 2005, 7). This feeling may reflect the fact that a consequence of attack can be defensiveness: "a desire to

---

[42] Almost all of the recent Peace Implementation Council communiques (which are issued twice a year, following two-day sessions) state and reiterate that no entity has the right to secession as they exist solely due to and within the sovereign territory of Bosnia as per Dayton.

[43] What this meant in practice is that whilst the violent conflict had ceased the 'non-violent' conflict between the RS and Federation elites resumed.

[44] Annex 7 (Agreement on Refugees and Displaced Persons), Dayton Peace Agreement.

reify that aspect of the self that is being targeted" (Carmichael 2015, xiv).

The result was anticipated and, therefore, the Bosnian constitution allowed a human rights framework, as some form of protection, to be drawn up around the demographic realities that war crimes, crimes against humanity and genocide had created (Toal and Dahlman 2011, 7).[45] The viability and reconstruction of an independent democratic State has, accordingly, been severely compromised with almost one million out of the two million displaced (out of a population of four million overall) not returning to their pre-war homes. Bosnia's legacy of ethnic cleansing has not been reversed to return it to pre-war ethnically mixed municipalities but neither has Bosnia been completely 'unmixed' into unchanging ethno-territories (Toal and Dahlman 2011, 9). Enough damage, however, has been done to challenge the legal, political and social continuity of a unified Bosnian State under the constitutional structure negotiated at Dayton.

---

[45] See, for instance, Riga and Kennedy (2013) for State Department thinking at the time.

A CONSTITUTION OF THE PEOPLE AND HOW TO ACHIEVE IT   57

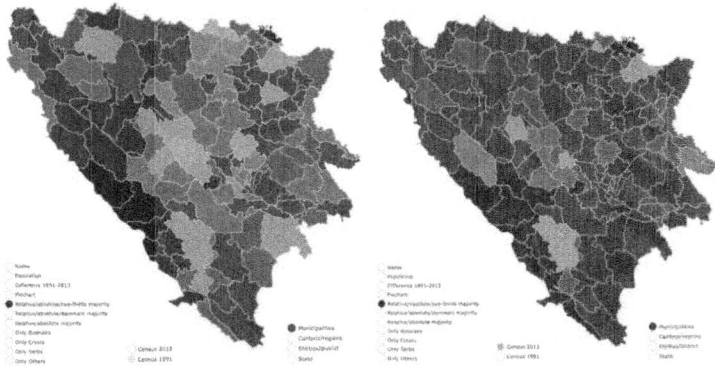

Figure 1.3A — *Ethnic composition according to the 1991 census — before the armed conflict — and ethnic composition according to the, contentious, 2013 census, by relative/absolute/two thirds majority and sub-divided by the 143 municipalities*

Source: Bosnian Statistics Agency

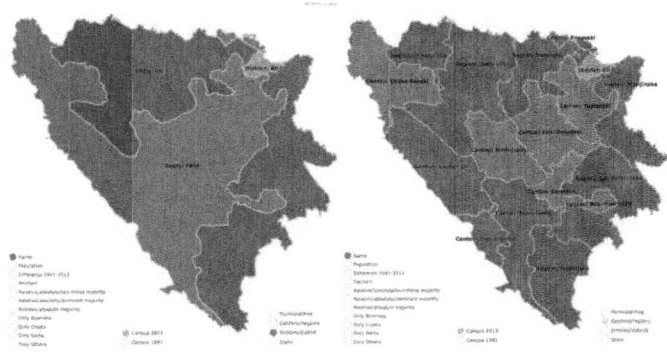

Figure 1.3B — *Bosnia by entity sub-division and by canton sub-division*

Source: Bosnian Statistics Agency

Despite the new demographic realities that created the distinct ethno-territorial borders (see Figure 1.3A), the principles of group autonomy and power sharing were worked into the Bosnian constitution. By 'power sharing' Lijphart (2004, 96) denotes the "participation of all significant communal groups in political decision-making, especially at the executive level. 'Group autonomy' means that communal groups have authority to run their own internal affairs, especially in areas of education and culture" (Ibid). The two aforementioned features are characteristic of 'consociational democracy'. Consociational features, in favour of Bosniaks, Croats and Serbs, are found in all the institutions of the State including: the Presidency, the Council of Ministers, the Parliamentary Assembly (House of Representatives and House of Peoples), and the Constitutional Court (See Chapter 4). In summary they include: decentralised asymmetric federalism to give wide autonomy to the two territorial entities; proportionality of representation of the three ethnic groups within the executive, legislature and judiciary; grand coalitions for the Presidency and Council of Ministers representing all major ethnic groups; and minority vetoes in the executive and legislature (DPA 1995; Bieber 2006; Keil and Hulsey 2013, 2020).

All territorial units in Bosnia, which largely coincide with electoral units (in the form entities, cantons in the Federation and municipalities in the RS), are based on ethnic criteria with the exception of two cantons in the Federation and the self-governing independent district of Brčko in Northern Bosnia (Keil and Hulsey 2020, 2). According to the most recent census in 2013, Bosnian Serbs make up 80 per cent of the population in the RS divided into 64 municipalities, Bosniaks have a significant majority in five of the Federation's 10 cantons, and Bosnian Croats are a majority in three cantons in the Federation and are the larger of the two in the mixed Bosniak-Croat cantons. In the Federation, the 10 cantons are layered on top of 79 municipalities. In total there are 143 municipalities across the country. As shown in Figure 1.3A, the contrast between the ethnic homogeneity today with the very heterogenous population mix in the pre-war municipalities could not be starker.

1.4 Comparative constitutional histories

British constitutional history

The precise origin of the British constitution is somewhat nebulous as might appear the constitution itself to an outside observer. Both the constitution and its origins are bound up with myth, legend and reverence that is subject to competing interpretations and historical narratives. These narratives take a distinct flavour depending on the set of circumstances Britain as a State and Britons generally find themselves in. The politics of the day are hard to separate from issues of fundamental constitutional importance.

Depending on where a political commentator stands on a particular issue of the day, they will often wish for leverage from British constitutional history to uphold their claim in being right. That is true of those seeking to uphold traditional or conservative conceptions of the British constitution or, equally, of those preferring a more modern or liberal re-imagination of the constitution. The Magna Carta of 1215 is one such constitutional document, which just 10 years after its issue acquired a symbolism associated with liberty of the individual (albeit then, only for free men). The Magna Carta is readily marshalled today to uphold the view that 'foreign' human rights standards are not required to be incorporated into UK legislation because the British gold-plate, and always have, their own laws with better standards. 'Look at the Magna Carta' they say as they point to its now famous clause 40: "'to no one will we sell, to no one deny or delay right or justice." That is notwithstanding that the Magna Carta had little to say about rights that are now recognised as universal (such as the rights to free speech, free assembly, freedom of religious belief) and offered no real means of redress when rights were infringed (other than possible war between the King and the barons). At the same time, others will say that international human rights standards are necessarily British as they derive from, and are specifically inspired by, British laws such as the Magna Carta and the Bill of Rights of

1689.[46] Most importantly, discussions in the UK are framed around a generally legitimizing centre—the constitution—however nebulous it may appear to an outsider.[47]

Most historians have traced the origin of the British constitution to the Magna Carta of 1215.[48] It was in 1215 when the first concerted attempt was made by major feudal landowners to force King John I to set out meaningful legal restrictions on his power and extract some concessions for the rights of individuals. Had he not acceded to the demands he faced the prospect of armed conflict (Hibbert 2010, 68). The Magna Carta required: consultation with the barons before imposition of new taxes; that every man be given a fair trial and be judged by his peers (other men); that no one be imprisoned without due process of law; and that the behaviour of royal officials was to be controlled (Loughlin 2013; Bogdanor 1997, 3-4).

By inference, King John I, an absolute monarch, was required to rule according to the law and take into account people other than himself namely the powerful barons and, increasingly, those lower down the wrung: knights of the shires, burgesses of the town and the gentry (Maddicott 2010, viii). The Magna Carta was almost immediately repealed by the King, but it was revived and amended a number of times particularly as the demands for money from the King came with increasingly greater demands for rights and representation (Hibbert 2010, 74). Not many years after, in January 1273, Parliament first met under King Edward I (1272-1307) with representatives from every shire and almost all major towns. Government by then was increasingly contractual between the royal and the provincial (Maddicott 2010, vii-viii). King Edward I,

---

[46] The right to a free trial and the right to be free from arbitrary detention derive from Magna Carta 1215, clauses 39 and 40 (as amended by Magna Carta 1225, Clause 29). The United Nations' Universal Declaration of Human Rights (UDHR) was hailed by Eleanor Roosevelt, chair of the drafting committee, as "the international Magna Carta of all men everywhere" (Roosevelt 1948).

[47] Even in January 2017 Britain's Supreme Court was citing the Magna Carta as containing the 'most long-standing and fundamental' rights. *Belhaj and another v Straw and others* [2017] UKSC 3 at [98].

[48] The Magna Carta was revoked and reconfirmed on some fifty or more occasions (Carpenter 2015).

for instance, was criticised for failures in his crusades abroad and he received a grant of tax on condition that he confirmed the Magna Carta (as amended) and added three barons to his regular council (Maddicott 2010, 447). At the Parliament of 1295—known as the Model Parliament because it was more representative than any great other previously—even representatives of ordinary citizens of the towns were present although they did not attend with any enthusiasm. They knew that they were wanted for their money (Hibbert 2010, 78). Nevertheless, their power and influence gradually became more prominent and eventually was formalised in the creation of the House of Commons.

The other major constitutional milestone is identified as the Glorious Revolution of 1688. After the overthrow of the Catholic King James II, the Protestant King William III (William of Orange) passed the Bill of Rights 1689 in England and Claim of Right 1689 in Scotland. Both Acts provided for parliamentary dominance over the monarchy by altering the line of succession and protected some parliamentary rights and liberties to prevent royal abuse of power. A Convention Parliament met to declare that James II had abdicated as he had fled to France fearing for his safety. Parliament invited William of Orange and Mary jointly to the Crown, by Act of Parliament, rather than by the right of hereditary process. Parliament, inevitably, presented the alteration of the line of succession as continuity rather than change; James II's son was declared illegitimate and, therefore, title naturally vested in William of Orange and Mary. Bogdanor (1997, 5) more accurately characterises this as a limit of royal power over Parliament rather than the citizen at large. William and Mary did not accept the Crown on condition that the Bill of Rights be passed but accepted it notwithstanding 'their right' to the Crown (Ibid, 6). The precedent, however, was set. The monarch now ruled with, and through, the consent of Parliament.

The Bill of Rights resulted from an earlier historical event: civil war between the Royalists supporting Charles I and the Parliamentarians led by Oliver Cromwell from 1642 to 1648. It was a war precipitated by Charles I's belief in the divine rights of kings, his financial greed and his refusal to reform the church. Those issues led him to bypass Parliament and the rights of parliamentarians (Hibbert 2010, 127-128). The mid-sixteenth century period of flux remains significant as it marks the starting point of the longest continuous constitutional, legal and parliamentary culture in the world (Sumption 2019, x; Bogdanor 1997, 8). After 1689, the monarch saw a gradual decline in power brought about largely from the severe curtailment in his/her powers due to the expansive restrictions set out in the Bill of Rights. There was, as might be expected, huge push-back by the monarchy. There was the development of the 'King's Friends' to influence the development of party politics in Parliament. The King bought Parliamentarians to support his own cause. But by the Reform Act 1832, the King's power to determine policy was relegated to mere influence (Bogdanor 1997, 10). Ministers who had previously served formal roles as advisors to the sovereign later merely informed him of decisions that had already been taken (Bogdanor 1997, 15).

Despite the perceived significance of the Magna Carta, the origins of the British constitution have been shown to go back further still. Historians have shown that the roots of the English Parliament—a precursor to the British—go back to early Anglo-Saxon times. Bogdanor (1997, 2-3) has claimed that, even as far back as the Anglo-Saxons, succession to the throne was not just a matter of descent but in reality, was determined by the leading territorial magnates comprising of what was called the *Witan*—the council of the sovereign's advisers—that retained a power to depose a sovereign who proved inadequate. Most would agree that such councils certainly played a large part in determining the royal succession even if they could not quite depose inadequate sovereigns (Maddicott 2010, 442). Maddicott (2010, vii-viii), in his magisterial account of the origins of the English Parliament, tracks the trajectory of the first truly national assemblies to the reign of King Aethelstan in 924 and documents their progression all the way to the deposition of Kind Edward II in 1327 which saw the parliamentary commons, from knights of the shires to burgesses of the town, fully engaged in a 'great national act of State'. Maddicott (Ibid) persuasively argues that, at heart, the assemblies all stemmed from a relatively primitive practice: "a leader, usually a king, taking counsel with his great men". These assemblies or Witans, a feature of Germanic political organisation, were used to confirm the accession of kings, adjudicate legal cases and give effect to royal policies and practices. These gatherings, albeit ad hoc and lacking institutional qualities, nevertheless rested on relatively broad political participation, making "them to a degree representative of peoples and places long before the days of elections and constituencies" (Maddicott 2010, 2). It was really only under King Aethelstan, following King Alfred's attempt to unify and defend England against the Danes in the late ninth century, that royal control was imposed through development of local institutions (shires, boroughs, mints, ealdormen, sheriffs) and, critically, assemblies. These assemblies dealing with affairs of the realm were periodic, large in size, had continuity in formal attendees (which came from across the social, religious and political spectrum) and meetings were recorded by charter and decisions passed as legislation (Maddicott 2010, 4-5, 441-442). The seed was planted for the constitutional monarchy and the Parliament that was to follow: the 'lineal descendant' of the Aethelstan assemblies (Ibid).

This historical overview is, of course, to ignore the vast development of Britain under the Roman Empire until 410 when the Romans fully packed up and left; leading to complete civilisation decline and preparing the way for Anglo-Saxon invasions after a period of local Romano-Britain rule (Wood 2010). Even with the Norman conquest of 1066 — which decimated the country — over time, some 150 years after the conquest, the assemblies of Aethelstan and specific features of its operation returned. One form in which it did was the *Commune Concilium*. Landowners' obedience to the monarch was contingent on royal protection and the reintroduction of national taxation meant that some of the representational qualities of earlier *Witans* were reintroduced (Maddicott 2010, 444). Whilst absolute royal power still prevailed, William the Conqueror (1066) and Henry I (1100) had promised in their coronation charters to observe the laws of Edward the Confessor in return for obedience of their subjects (Maddicott 2010, 452). In no other European State, as Bogdanor (1997, 3) argues, did the local or provincial interest and royal government interests become so tightly enmeshed as they did in the couple of centuries following the Conquest.

The cursory overview of British constitutional history provided here, is not to suggest or imply any sort of evolutionary linear progression or the untrammelled march of rights and democracy in England and then, later, in Britain. The Magna Carta like any other charter, or bill or act was not entrenched, and parts were often expressly repudiated. Oftentimes it was completely ignored by powerful monarchs. The fact that the Magna Carta led directly to the beheading of the Charles I—who repeatedly bypassed Parliament and in 1629 decided to rule without Parliament entirely—shows precisely how far monarchs abused what were considered to be enforceable rules whether tacit or express in a charter. Monarchs purported to suspend legislation all the way up to the early 18th century (Loughlin 2013; Sedley 2013).

Charting the history of the English Parliament from 924 to 1327, Maddicott (2012, ix) notes that parliamentary history was far from steady or purely evolutionary but was "subject to happenchance at every stage". What this book does attempt to show is that certain milestones in British history acquired a symbolism and the principles which were derived from them became entrenched by practice, custom and later still in accepted political culture. As Bogdanor (1997, 4) notes, the Magna Carta was used by Parliamentarians as a weapon against the divine-right theory of the Stuart Kings that led directly to the confrontations culminating in the Glorious Revolution. Sir Edward Coke claimed that the Petition of Right of 1628, which limited the royal prerogative, was derived directly from the principles of the Magna Carta: "enabling reformers to declare that it was they who were the genuine conservatives since they were acting in conformity with long-established principles" (Bogdanor 1997, 4-5). Even today, political stakeholders consider it worth their while to petition for change whilst identifying themselves with the institutions of State — symbolic or otherwise — and its interests.

Bosnian constitutional history

Bosnia, like Britain, has a rich and varied historical tradition stretching back to at least the 10th century. It was then when its name — without hyphenation or sub-division — is mentioned for the first time in writing, as a geographical entity, by an Eastern Roman Emperor, Constantine VII Porphyrogenitus, in his work *'On the Governance of the Empire'* (Malcolm 1994, 10). Bosnia is known for its breath-taking beauty and vastly diverse landscapes symbolised by mountain ranges, salt lakes, flood plains and virgin forests. It is not surprising, given its geographical richness and biological diversity, that it has been settled since, at least, the Palaeolithic age, and permanently since the Neolithic. Some of Europe's oldest cave paintings (dating to between the 12th and 16th centuries BCE) are found at Badanj Cave, near the town of Stolac in Bosnia's region of Herzegovina (Clancy 2013, 13). In recorded history, Bosnia, which would have formed part of Illyria, was taken over by the Romans in 168 BC. The region frequently switched hands between Byzantium and Rome in the centuries that followed. Christianity reached Bosnia in the seventh century following the work of Greek missionaries. Bosnia, whose then borders overlapped with those of Montenegro, Serbia and Croatia, was to remain ostensibly Christian until the 16th century when Islam began to be adopted *en masse* at the height of Ottoman rule (Carmichael 2015, 11).

Bosnia's present borders are largely consistent with its administrative boundaries under the later period of Ottoman rule from the 15th to the 19th century. It had similar borders under King Tvrtko who secured independence from Hungary in 1353. Bosnia was occupied and administered by the Austro-Hungarian Empire from the 1878 Congress of Berlin through to WWI. In 1910, under the Austro-Hungarians, Bosnia's first written constitution was promulgated; a constitution that expressly mentioned the Serbs, Croats and Muslims as the "native peoples" (IDEA 2016). On 4 December 1918, after the defeat of the Austro-Hungarians, Bosnia became part of the newly created Kingdom of Serbs, Croats and Slovenes, dominated, as the name suggests, by the Croats and Serbs (less so the Slovenes). A so-called 'Vidovdan'[49] Constitution, generally agreed between the Bosnian Muslim parties and Serbian radicals in 1921, initially allowed administrative autonomy. King Alexander, however, annulled it in 1929 and replaced it unilaterally with a new constitution in 1931. The country's name was changed to the Kingdom of Yugoslavia in an attempt to develop a wider Yugoslav patriotism and to prevent, as he saw it, local ethno-nationalism to flourish (Džankić 2015). Bosnia retained a Parliament but no independent governance structure. After 31 January 1946 and until the armed conflict in 1992, Bosnia was one of six constituent republics of the communist regime of the Federal People's Republic of Yugoslavia (and then the Socialist Federal Republic of Yugoslavia ("SFRY")) together with Croatia, Macedonia, Montenegro, Serbia and Slovenia. The constitution was largely developed from the Soviet constitution of 1936 and recognised five nationalities save for the Bosnian Muslims. Amended constitutions followed in 1952, 1963 and 1974 but it was not until 1963 when Bosnian Muslims were mentioned in the constitution alongside Serbs and Croats (IDEA 2016). It was only in the 1974 SFRY constitution that equal rights were stipulated for all nationalities living in the SFRY.

Bosnia's religious and cultural milieu was one of its distinctive characteristics even as far back as its early royalist foundations in the 12th century (notwithstanding its shared heritage with its neighbours or its status sometimes as a vassal of foreign powers). The medieval Bosnian Church, for instance, was unique and regarded itself as the true successors of Saint Peter. It was seen as heretical by its dominant Catholic and Orthodox neighbours who vied with one another to wipe it out. It was said to present an existential threat to orthodox Christianity, but that was most likely a justification for other motives including annexation of territory.

---

[49] Vidovdan is the memorial day to Saint Prince Lazar and the Serbs who fell during the Battle of Kosovo against the Ottoman Empire on 15 June 1389 (Julian calendar). It is an intrinsic part of Serbian ethnic and national identity.

Bosnia had a long stretch of independence from the 12th century to the Turkish conquest of 1463 and that period (until a time long-after) saw Bosnia emerge as a meeting place for different faiths whatever the dominant political power (Dizdar 2009, 113). Islam spread along the Adriatic sea-routes. Muslims travelled inland from Dalmatian ports decades before the Ottoman conquest when Islam was formally introduced as the State-religion to part of Bosnia's population (Dizdar 2009, 114). The Bosnian Church was outlawed by Bosnian King Stefan Thomas in 1450, prior to the Ottoman conquest, as a condition of the Pope's help against the Ottoman threat. Help which was not forthcoming in any event (Dizdar 2009, 118). The loss of Bosnia's native faith arguably made acceptance of the new Muslim faith that much easier.

As a Yugoslav Republic, Bosnia was the most heterogenous and the only one where no ethnic group formed an absolute majority.[50] As Džankić (2015, 2) explains, Bosnia was not dissimilar in this respect to other post-Yugoslav states although it was unique in the extent of its diversity:

> "The post-Yugoslav states, despite being small in terms of inhabitants and territory, are populated by a wide variety of different groups exhibiting an incredible spectrum of, and variation in, intergroup relations. As such, they represent a true laboratory for understanding people's attitudes towards post-communist, post-partition and post-conflict states and the rights they have within them."

Bosnia's Muslims lived largely side-by-side with its large numbers of Catholic, Orthodox Christian and Jewish (minority) communities as shown by a highly heterogenous constellation of cities, towns, villages and hamlets across the country. The majority of its Muslim and Christian populations were, and still remain, closely related genetically or 'ethnically'. The three constituent groups have been found by Marjanovic (2005) to "share a large fraction of the same ancient gene pool distinctive for the Balkan area." That is, they are descended from folk living in that region before the arrival of the Slavs, Christianity or Islam (Carmichael

---

[50] US Congressional Research Service, Bosnia and Herzegovina, Background and US Policy, 15 April 2019, 2.

2015, xiv, 4). Bosnia also always had significant minority populations which included among them Roma, Hungarians, Turks, Jews, Germans, and Vlachs among others.

Bosnian then has historically encompassed manifold diversity in identity and heritage. As Carmichael (2015, xiv) notes, 'essentialism' about who belongs and who does not is a long-term symptom of violence and "rejection of the very notion of overlapping identities and shared heritage."

When armed conflict broke out in 1992, popular accounts (as noted in Chapter 3) depicted the conflict as having emanated from "ancient ethnic hatreds" implying that neither could the country's ethnic groups coexist, nor had they co-existed previously. The conflict was seen as a natural by-product of un-natural diversity. The very argument used by the ethno-nationalist elite protagonists of the war who broke apart Bosnia's communities and pitted them against one another in conflict.

Glaurdić (2012) documents how this "ancient hatreds" narrative was deliberately co-opted by numerous Western governments who knew it to be wrong but found it a convenient excuse, for various policy reasons, to not intervene in the Balkans. This was before the armed conflict in Bosnia broke out. British foreign secretary, Douglas Hurd, for instance, in June 1991 justified the then government's policy of supporting Yugoslavia's continued existence by wrongly claiming that: "Yugoslavia was invented in 1919 to solve a problem of different peoples living in the same part of the Balkans with a long history of peoples fighting each other" (Glaurdić 2012, 175-177). This view persisted in many policy, political and media circles throughout the armed conflict in Bosnia and persists still to the present day. The New York Times, even on 14 August 1994, was still writing about the impossibility of an inherently diverse Bosnia: "But Bosnia is a land with no clear ethnic identity—like the former Yugoslavia, the former Czechoslovakia and the former Soviet Union—and all such countries have proved prone to fragmentation in the post-Communist world [...] But in the end a country unwanted by its inhabitants cannot survive. It may be thus, too, with Bosnia" (Cohen 1994).

The notion of ancient-ethnic hatreds, most likely lost on contemporary commentators, did have local precedent. Nobel prize winning author Andric (1920) often found it difficult, in his great literary works, to resist the orientalist narrative as a simplistic answer to complicated questions; negating what he found to be Bosnian's 'tenderness' and 'love' with an underlying darkness largely emanating from its experience with 'Turkishness': "But in the secret depths underneath all this hide burning hatreds, entire hurricanes of tethered and compressed hatreds maturing and awaiting their hour" (Andrić 1993, 115).[51] Countless experts on the region, however, and many Bosnians themselves (as demonstrated in Chapters 2 and 3) reject that thesis. A thesis that impacted the drafting of the Bosnian constitution and the Dayton Peace Agreement that brought the conflict to a *prima facie* conclusion.

Whilst Bosnia has experienced violence and bloodshed seen as inter-ethnic and communal—most notably in the Second World War and the 1992-1995 conflict—those conflicts were not without very specific contexts. The crude labelling of conflicts in Bosnia as 'inter-ethnic' or communal conflict is unjustified. The Croatian Ustasha movement, for instance, almost completely wiped out the Jewish and Roma populations and attempted to annihilate the Serb population of the Independent State of Croatia which included modern-day Bosnia. These were Jewish citizens who sought and were given shelter in Bosnia after expulsion from Spain during the Inquisition. It came about after Hitler's Third Reich invaded Royalist Yugoslavia in April 1941 and the fascist Croatian regime of Ante Pavelić allied itself with Nazi Germany and combined their coinciding interests (territorial annexation and ideological homogenisation for that purpose) with devastating effect (Carmichael 2015, xiv). In retaliation, Chetniks, extreme Serb nationalists, perpetrated atrocities in Bosnia against Croatian Catholics and atrocities against Muslims (Carmichael 2015, xviii). It was only with the victory of the left-wing Partisans, led by the Yugoslav Communists, that the nationalist bloodshed was brought to an end and not without bloody reprisals against the Chetniks and

---

[51] "Letter from 1920" in Andrić (1993, 115).

Ustasha—reference to whom would frequently arise in the conflict in the 1990s.

Between 1992 and 1995, as set out in <u>Chapters 2 and 3</u>, the conflict was largely elite led. Before the referendum on independence in 1992, as SFRY was breaking up, Bosnia had not been a fully independent State since the Middle Ages. Possible rule from Istanbul, Vienna and Belgrade was ever present (Carmichael 2015, 2). It was in this context, of outside interference and long-term instability, that domestic political elites have easily manipulated historical memory to their own advantage, or external powers have manufactured the conditions allowing their own rule in Bosnia or direct annexation (Karl 1993; Noel 1996; Majstorović 2004; Gagnon 2004).

Despite the two devastating conflicts in the 20th century, Bosnia's population for the vast majority of its history has belied the European trend in seeming self-destruction: the most recent manifestation of which was the fascist-ideology driven Holocaust under Hitler and the sweeping communist purges under Stalin. Bosnia has tried to resist the trend to wipe out its diverse populations in favour of homogenisation driven by exclusive ethno-nationalism. Bosnia's heterogenous population has lived coterminously and harmoniously for centuries (Sells 1998, 3-5). The irony is that the extremist nationalists targeted for destruction the very essence that demonstrated tolerant and multi-confessional living: the national library containing records of inter-religious dialogue and living, the oriental institute with the largest collection of Jewish and Muslim manuscripts in Europe, and religious and cultural buildings and monuments imbued by cross-ethnic and inter-religious symbolism (Ibid).

It was a multi-confessionalism that survived serious suppression under communist Yugoslavia and indeed flourished later in some ways. For instance, before the start of the 1992 conflict, approximately one third of marriages in Sarajevo were mixed—this was not because of communism but in spite of it (Crosby 2017). Prior to the siege of Sarajevo, a majority of the capital—hand in hand with those of different religions—came out to oppose the war. As Carmichael (2015) has succinctly put it:

> "This embrace of tolerance, which has sometimes been described as the Bosnian spirit (*bosanski duh*), was not just the forced repetition of the Communist regime's mantra of brotherhood and unity and it came from the heart. If Bosnia came late to nationalism, then it suffered the most for its tardiness and the belief of its citizens that a multi-faith society was possible, even preferable."

Even during the devastating conflict during the 1990s—manipulated to pit Croat against Serb against Muslim—scholars of Bosnia have accounted for the intermediate space of co-existence, harmony and acceptance that would be seemingly impossible in such a context. Carmichael (2015, 3) records the bottles of alcohol stored by Bosniaks for their Catholic neighbours; Christians refraining from eating pork in Ramadhan; the ringing of the Orthodox church bells *in lieu* of the Muslim call to prayer; a heterogenous fighting force (comprising Bosniaks, Croats and Serbs) at the start of the war and in particular in Sarajevo although it later became homogenised as the war dragged on (Perry 2019); the multi-ethnic human chains formed to try and rescue thousands of ancient and priceless Christian, Jewish, Muslim manuscript collections deliberately targeted for destruction by the HVO and Bosnian Serb forces in Sarajevo, Mostar and other besieged cities (Sells 1998, 2); the protection of the Sarajevo Haggadah which was written in Barcelona around 1350 and has been in Bosnia since the 19th century (Mašić 2020); snipers calling old classmates across the front-line to warn them that they were in the crosshairs of their guns (Sadinlija 2020).[52]

Bosnia is a living embodiment of what some have concisely characterised as 'unity in diversity' (Mahmutćehajić 2003). Whilst a whole generation has grown up, as a consequence of war, without the shared and lived experience of 'unity in diversity', (and even an active denialism of the past), the idea of a Bosnia transcending

---

[52] A colleague, Dalila Sadinlija, reminded the author that there were many such incidents, and that the sniper story is one known by many who were besieged in Sarajevo during the armed conflict.

religious, linguistic, cultural or national division is less chimeral than presumed.⁵³ Chapter 2 on political culture will address the existence or otherwise of this chimera, in detail, by examining political culture of the people in Bosnia today. Given, however, what we know of Bosnia's history, how exactly was Bosnia's constitution drafted? Did it take into account the historical, cultural and societal development of Bosnia? And did any people who had lived in the distinctly diverse cultural milieu of Bosnia have a say?

The Bosnian constitution is not conventional in any sense drawn up as it was merely as an Annex (IV) to the General Framework Agreement for Peace in Bosnia and Herzegovina ("Dayton Peace Agreement"). The Constitution, as well as the Dayton Peace Agreement, was initialled following intense negotiations over 20 days at the Wright-Patterson Air Force Base in Dayton, Ohio on 21 November 1995 and signed in Paris on 14 December 1995. The peace conference at Dayton was led by then Assistant US Secretary for European and Canadian Affairs and Chief US peace negotiator, Richard Holbrooke, and co-chaired by then Special Representative of the European Community ("EC"), Carl Bildt, and First Deputy Foreign Minister of Russia, Igor Ivanov. The location was unconventional but was chosen to reduce the ability of participants to negotiate via their local power-base or the media.

The context, of course, was also far from conventional. There was a brutal conflict that was ongoing in Bosnia with direct involvement of the newly independent Croatian State as well as the two remaining States of the former SFRY, Serbia and Montenegro. The predominantly Bosniak enclave of Srebrenica had fallen in July 1995 to the Bosnian Serb forces. Forces who were responsible for horrific atrocities which were later held, by international bodies, to have amounted to the crime of genocide (UN IRMCT 2020).⁵⁴ US policy makers faced pressure to take stronger action and bolster

---

[53] Carmichael (2015, 189) has argued for this proposition by assessing the culture, language, and the history of Bosnia. This book seek to do so more practically by looking at the difference between elite and popular preferences.

[54] By the International Criminal Tribunal for the Former Yugoslavia (UN ICTY) and the International Court of Justice (ICJ).

what were, until then, largely EC or UN led peace talks; the atrocities in Srebrenica only confirming an ineffectual and muddled response to three years of conflict (Rohde 2012).

In late August 1995, following an attack by Bosnian Serbs on Sarajevo, in violation of an international fire-free zone, NATO conducted air strikes on Serb positions. On 1 September 1995, Holbrooke announced that all the parties would meet in Geneva for talks. When the Bosnian Serbs did not comply with NATO's conditions, NATO air strikes resumed. By September 1995, NATO airstrikes, under US command, were in full-swing and quickly running out of targets although they were only one month into the campaign (USD Jun 1996, 18). A cease-fire, following NATO bombing, was agreed in Sarajevo on 14 September 1995, negotiated by Holbrooke and signed by Radovan Karadžić and Ratko Mladić. The cease-fire precipitated the end of the longest siege in modern history: 44 months and resulting in over 10,000 deaths (USD Jun 1996, 12; Morrison and Lowe 2021). By November 1995, the tide in the war was also turning. The Bosnian Serb Forces had started to lose earlier gains with their control of the territory shrinking from some 75 per cent of Bosnia to around a 50-50 per cent split between the Bosnian Serb forces and the Federation forces (comprising the Army of the Republic of Bosnia and Herzegovina ("ARBiH") which had re-allied itself with the Croat Defence Council ("HVO")). The Serbs by then had also lost the Krajina, a self-proclaimed Serb proto-State with a Serb majority, within the newly independent Croatia (USD Jun 1996, 12).

Pressure was mounting on all sides, and in particular on the US Government, to bring the war to a conclusion. The Croat and Bosniak armies were 20 km from taking Banja Luka, a majority Serb city, and the possible future capital of a Serb Republic. The US had given express orders to the Bosniak and Croat leaders that it must not be taken (USD Jun 1996). Holbrooke, claimed that Milošević "begged us to stop the offensive before it reached Banja Luka" (USD Jun 1996, 14). Holbrooke stated they stopped the offensive not because of Milošević's request but because the repercussions of continuing the offensive were assessed to be enormous due to:

possible infighting between Bosniaks and Croats over war spoils and territory, leading to a break in the alliance; humanitarian concerns relating to further vast movement of refugees particularly Bosnian Serb refugees; and concern that Banja Luka would become the centre of anti-Karadžić Serb activity and, therefore, would no longer be a credible alternative to Pale (Serb Sarajevo) as the Serb centre of Bosnia (USD Jun 1996, 15-16). The US, however, as Holbrooke stated, "let the offensive roll" [...] "we wanted the Croatians and the Bosnians to make as much military gain as possible" (USD Jun 1996, 13).

It was a moment of maximum leverage. The US was saying to the Bosnian Serbs that unless they agree to peace, they would lift the arms embargo on the Bosniaks, continue NATO airstrikes against them, and allow the Bosniaks and Croats to run them out of Bosnia completely (USD Jun 1996, 13-14, 221). To the Bosniaks and Croats they were saying that unless they end the conflict now and accept the US agreement, they are on their own other than benefiting from a possible lifting of the arms embargo (USD Jun 1996, 13-14, 221). For the Bosniaks that meant fighting again on two fronts and for the Croats it meant further instability on its frontier having just seized the Krajina. Croatia would also have to fight to defend areas in which there were no, and never were, Bosnian Croats. It was in this context the Bosnian constitution was being drafted which might lead one, understandably, to say the circumstances were difficult to reach a comprehensive settlement to a terrible conflict. But the *process* of its drafting raises all manner of questions. The most important of which was whether the process was conducive to setting up the foundation of a nation's constitutional and political structure as well as facilitating long-term nation building.

The war began in 1992 with heavy international and US involvement from the beginning. There were numerous failed peace attempts. At least four peace conferences were brokered by either, or both, the EC, as it was then, and the United Nations.[55] If an inevitable part of any peace process would have been a constitution then it makes one wonder, firstly, why it would have been inevitable as there was little to no precedent for it and, secondly, why the idea came so late. Even by 23 August 1995, Holbrooke, the principal senior negotiator was saying that nobody had given any thought to constitutional issues (USD Aug 1996, 9). To be fair, the State Department legal advisers, including Jim O'Brien, were in fact working on some so-called constitutional principles in the Summer of 1994 in preparation for the Contact Group meetings between the US, Russia, France, Britain, and Germany to bring the Serbs to the dialogue table. But clearly there was nothing being prepared that filtered to the upper levels or that was perceived to be of any great significance (USD Aug 1996, 10).

On one view, the drafting history of the Bosnian constitution can be described as utterly remarkable in almost every respect: from the modest expertise that was drawn upon, the lack of any formal procedure or process, and its lack of timeliness in planning and preparedness. On another view, and those of its principal drafters, it was the best that could be done in difficult circumstances and that hindsight is a luxury. No one, they would say, could have foreseen the difficulties and only so much could have been achieved in negotiating a constitution in a war context.

The actual drafting history might aid in getting off the proverbial fence. The Bosnian constitution was drafted largely by the US State Department lawyers. The State Department had substantial influence on post-war settlements including in: WWI and WWII Europe; Israel-Palestine; Bosnia; and then subsequently in Northern Ireland, Afghanistan and Iraq. In Bosnia, by mid-1995, the US—in particular the US Congress—had concluded that the Europeans were unable and unwilling to intervene meaningfully in Bosnia to end the conflict and so decided that its State Department should take a much firmer lead under then Secretary of State,

---

[55] The plans were the: Carrington–Cutileiro EC plan from February to March 1992; Vance–Owen Peace UN and EC Plan from January to June 1993; Owen–Stoltenberg UN plan from August 1993; Contact Group (US, Russia, France, Britain, and Germany) plan from February to October 1994.

Christopher Warren, and then Ambassador to the United Nations, Madeleine Albright. The US lead came in the context of many European and NATO allies being unwilling to lift the arms embargo on Bosnia and conduct air strikes on Serb forces; European States argued that lifting the arms embargo will prolong the war although in reality it was only the Bosniaks who were practically impacted by the embargo and the war had already gone on for three years. On 27 July 1995, the US Senate, with the atrocities at Srebrenica vividly in their mind, voted 69-29 to unilaterally lift the arms embargo (Mertus 2005, 167).

The shape of the American lead is really what was important for the purposes of drafting the future Bosnian constitution. Riga and Kennedy (2013) have found that, by 1995, South East Europe and Balkan experts, with decades of experience on Yugoslavia, were firmly embedded within the State Department's bureaucracy "on the Seventh Floor" (Riga and Kennedy 2013, paras 1.4, 4.10). Staff involved in the drafting process or in any major constitutional discussions were, however, limited to the human and civil rights lawyers in the State Department's Legal Advisor's Office working outside of formal State Department channels (Riga and Kennedy 2013, paras 1.4, 4.10). Academic expertise was seen as too deliberative and impractical. The dominant perception was that the Balkan experts were too institutionally embedded in the State Department. Therefore, they were obstacles to be deliberately bypassed as sources of possible policy impasse (USD Aug 1996, 29-30). As Riga and Kennedy (2013) note "nation building came to be conceptualized as a generic policy problem, whose solution lay in universally and widely applicable formulae, rather than as a contextually contingent, political or localized problem, requiring specialist, substantive knowledge" (Ibid, paras 1.4, 4.10). The lawyers, who by 1995 were seen to have already conducted vast amounts of work on war crimes related issues in Bosnia, thereby, simply became the "relevant policy experts" (Ibid, paras 4.5-4.6).

As far as can be deciphered from the available primary records, the lead lawyers holding the pen on the draft constitution were James C. O'Brien, Miriam Shapiro, Gro Nystuen and some work was undertaken by Carol White, and Laurel Miller (USD Jun 1996; USD Aug 1996, 66). The chief negotiators, leading the talks from the US side were Robert 'Bob' Owen, Senior Legal Advisor at the US State Department (in place from 23 Aug 1995),[56] and above him Holbrooke. Holbrooke was the link to the 'higher-ups' in Washington (USD Aug 1996, 110-111). The higher-ups here were John C. Kornblum, Ambassador to the OSCE (1991-1994) and then Assistant Secretary of State for European Affairs and Special Envoy to the Balkans (1995-1997), and Warren Christopher, 63rd Secretary of State, who was succeeded by Madeleine Albright in 1997. At the time of the Dayton negotiations, Albright was the US Ambassador to the UN. She was instrumental in getting in place NATO airstrikes that ended the siege of Sarajevo and put the Bosnian Serb and other paramilitary forces on the back-foot (Rubin 2019). Above them all sat the President, Bill Clinton.

Two lawyers who were lead drafters of the Bosnian constitution have made remarkable admissions in interviews conducted post-Dayton. James C. O'Brien, principal lead drafter from the State Department, remarked "we haven't grasped how to construct policy around democratic nation-building where there is diversity, in part because we do not understand the underlying [contextual] power structures" (Riga and Kennedy 2013, para 4.12). Gro Nystuen, Senior Legal Adviser for the EC, said: "we didn't get this right and didn't quite understand it in Bosnia; one could have imagined a lot of different arrangements, but that would have required knowledge on a very detailed level about the persons involved and their interests and constituencies [...] 'where was the specialist?" (Ibid).[57] It is of little help now but, evidently, the specialists were on the Seventh Floor!

In fact, in some cases, they were on the opposite side of the negotiating table—the Bosniaks had a wide team of largely legal experts including at Dayton Dr Paul Williams from Public International Law and Policy Group. The European Community

---

[56] The US State Department records also mention Bob Merrell although the author did not find further information on him in the records.
[57] Gro Nystuen was the Senior Legal Adviser to Carl Bildt.

had their own legal teams, led by Carl Bildt, to push through a 'European constitution', apparently at the impassioned request of the Bosniaks who feared that an 'Americanised constitution' might make them somewhat of an exception within Europe and, therefore, imperil possible future European Integration (USD Aug 1996, 52-53, 79-83, 92-94). Some European amendments, such as the creation of a Central Bank, went into the draft after tough negotiations although the Europeans never proposed an alternative constitution (USD Aug 1996, 52-53, 79-83). Even then, however, there is much doubt about the expertise or thoughtful local knowledge that went into the *process* of drafting. There are also considerable questions over who exactly had formative influence over the mechanics of the negotiations. For instance, US Ambassador Swanee Hunt recalls an astonishing account of preparations being made for the Washington Agreement, brokered by the American administration, which saw the Bosnian Croats and Bosniaks settle the "war within the war" which culminated in the creation of the constitution of the Federation:

> "Ambassador Swanee Hunt recalls walking into a room in her Vienna embassy and seeing a blurry-eyed Bosnian hunched over a computer. "Do you have any material that would be good for a constitution?" he asked. It was the spring of 1994 and the height of the American-brokered negotiations between Bosnian Croats and Muslims. Hunt's staff quickly phoned up the Swiss embassy and obtained a copy of their constitution on disk. "That might be why the Federation of Bosnia is carved into cantons," she sighs, remembering the somewhat quirky and extremely personal nature of diplomacy. One thing that really stood out in Hunt's experience was the absence of women. "Out of all of the negotiators that came through Vienna while I was ambassador, zero were women," she remembers. "With Yugoslavia having the highest percentage of women PhDs in central and eastern Europe, I wondered, how is this possible?" (Mertus 2005, 168).

Whether apocryphal or not,[58] there is an undeniable truth underlying that account; both the piecemeal nature of the work that

---

[58] There was a peace plan jointly proposed in August 1992 by the Bosniak Party of Democratic Action (SDA) and the Croatian Democratic Union of Bosnia and Herzegovina (HDZ BiH) political parties calling for the establishment of 12 cantons of Bosnia and Herzegovina, with autonomous rights. Some form of cantonal representation pre-dated the 1994 Washington Agreement. They also featured in the Carrington–Cutileiro plan.

went into the drafting and that Bosnian women, and women generally from the region, were absent from the peace process or negotiations at Dayton. Not a single person from forty, multi-ethnic, women's associations operating in Bosnia to try and end the war (united under one umbrella—the Union of Women's Organisations) was invited to the Dayton peace talks (Mertus 2005, 168). Representatives of multi-ethnic peace organisations or general grass-roots civil society were absent from Dayton; and much was done (and often is) in such pressured circumstances by those policy experts, who happen to be on hand, on a hunch and a whim. In this case, and often in conflict cases, it included the instigators of the war. As Hunt says, "we didn't have any conduit to reach into those communities, to engage them in what we wanted to do ... that is what needed to change" (Mertus 2005, 168).

The Bosnian constitution, of course, did not miraculously appear, in its entirety, in 20 days of negotiations at Dayton. But large parts of it did not emanate until the Dayton negotiations themselves or very close to the negotiations. Even by 23 August 1995, as noted earlier, Holbrooke, *the* principal senior negotiator was saying to his State Department legal teams that nobody had given any thought to constitutional issues. The earlier work had clearly not filtered up to the 'higher-ups' and in any event, as O'Brien noted that work was "so sketchy and incredibly thin model of what the constitution would be" [...] "an extremely thin central government with very limited powers and thus no real separation of those powers because that would be splitting an amoeba. It was essentially a Presidency" (USD Aug 1996, 10, 18, 28). Real discussion around some rudimentary options for the constitution took place around 25 August 1995 with the Bosniak delegation (USD Aug 1996, 10). Whatever the earlier work alluded to by O'Brien, in declassified documents, released under Freedom of Information by the US State Department in 2016, O'Brien explains exactly how significant it was by the August 1995 meeting:

> "SE: What guidelines were you operating on here for these meetings? What was—was—[sic] the contact group constitution from 1994. They were the late talking points. They were pretty vague in terms of any internal political structure. What were you relying on in these discussions? JO: We just made

this up. MS: Yeah. We -- it's funny actually to go back and read these papers and you realize how much of it really did make into the constitution and the rest of [inaudible] agreement. I guess at that point we had two goals. One was trying to figure out what kind of governmental structure to develop that would keep certain essential things there like the continuity of the state. The borders of the state, have common institutions that could exercise. [sic]" (USD Aug 1996, 13-14).

There was, however, some actual initial documentation that was the starting point for negotiations. The documentation included the Agreed Basic Principles ("Geneva Principles") of 8 September 1995 and later some further Agreed Basic Principles of 26 September 1995 ("New York Principles") (OHR 1995). By November 1995, the Federation—established by the Washington Agreement of 18 March 1994—was in place with its own constitution. Republika Srpska was also very much in place having been proclaimed by Bosnian Serb leaders in 1992. The Geneva Principles essentially confirmed that Bosnia would remain within its original borders when it was a Republic of the SFRY. The Geneva Principles established the starting point to Dayton. Bosnia was to be comprised of two entities, split 51:49 in favour of the Federation although the starting point was to be subject to negotiation. Each entity was to have a right to establish parallel relations with neighbouring countries so long as they maintained Bosnia's territorial integrity. It was also taken as a given that there would be some respect for human rights and a right to return for "dislocated" people.

One might expect that the Geneva Principles had regard to the vast experience of the State Department and other world experts on constitution drafting. In recently declassified documents, there are a series of interviews—entitled the 'Dayton History Project'— which were conducted purely for posterity in 1996. Those interviews were with some of the principal architects of Dayton. The Geneva Principles were drafted by Bob Owen in late August 1995. In the declassified interviews conducted by James O'Brien with Holbrook and Owen, Owen was asked how the Geneva Principles came about. He replied that Holbrooke and he felt that a very basic starting point was needed to see what the parties would accept: "Holbrooke said go ahead and prepare something, so I sat down and started writing it out in long-hand on the airplane" (USD Aug 1996, 23, 25-26). When asked whether he was looking at historical precedents like Camp David or "back at models of similarly complicated negotiations for this" when drafting, Owen replied without hesitation: "No, right off the top of my head." Whichever way the Principles were drafted, however, they were presumed effective as they were quickly agreed by the Bosniaks and by Milošević on 1 Sep 1995 in a hunting lodge in Belgrade at what Owen described as "a day of bonding with the Godfather [...] where in a span of twelve hours he was both drunk and sober and, over cigars and wine, you got him to agree to this" (USD Aug 1996, 28). The spelling mistake, still in the current published draft, presumably, was a transcription error. The quickness with which the Principles were agreed could equally, however, be seen as reflective of insufficient thought and preparedness.

Holbrooke confirms that during negotiations they stuck to the 1994 Contact Group (US, Russia, France, Britain, and Germany) plan to divide Bosnia 51:49 despite criticisms. The basis for that were a number of assumptions. He believed that departing from the 51:49 ratio would lead to: infighting between the Croats and Serbs, future refugee flows that would lead to a big concentration of Serbs in the East such that there would be partition, and concerns over the viability of any 'Serb Republic' without Banja Luka as the capital (USD Jun 1996, 16, 19-21, 33). The State Department also appeared to proceed with the assumption—pushed by Milošević—that Karadžić would lose any election after the war (USD Jun 1996, 16, 19-21, 33). The view was that reducing Republika Srpska to a rump part of Bosnia would not be possible. They had by this stage also got Izetbegović and Milošević to accept two entities and Warren Christopher, as Holbrooke noted, felt "personally attached to the Contact Group plan as he had negotiated it" and "did not wish to reopen it." The Bosnian Serbs could also press for parallel relationships to be established with Serbia because the Croats had already secured such a carve out in the Washington Agreement creating the Federation. Both Croatia and Serbia wanted to hold out for future separation and annexation or return, as they saw it, to the "motherlands" (USD Jun 1996, 31-32).

Holbrooke, however, considered that he may have made a mistake: for not bombing the Bosnian Serb forces further than the US did, for not taking more decisive action against Republika Srpska, for accepting the name 'Republika Srpska', and for not negotiating harder on the 51:49 split (USD Jun 1996, 13-17). These reflections, with hindsight, are instructive. Muhamed Šaćirbey, Bosnia's foreign minister who resigned during the Dayton talks in protest at the pressure being applied on the Bosniaks, has said: "He [Milošević] understood that Holbrooke was very eager to get a deal, and much of this eagerness was very personal, for recognition and further political ambition [...] In the end, I realised that much of what happened in Dayton was about the personalities" (Borger 2015).

Aside from the Geneva Principles, emanating from some musings on the back of an envelope, by late September 1995 there was no formal document about what powers would flow to the two entities under any possible settlement or what a constitution would look like (USD Jun 1996, 22-23). What did follow was what Holbrooke saw as the need for a "central connecting structure" between the entities which resulted in the New York Principles of 26 September 1995. Those ensured that the two entities would honour international obligations, that elections would take place as soon as possible, and that there would be the creation of a parliament, presidency and constitutional court.[59] The presidency and parliament was to have two thirds representation from the Federation and one third from the RS. The first language in relation to ethnic vetoes also began to appear—in relation to the presidency—which would later be locked in at Dayton despite the State Department's apparent attempt to reopen discussion of it

---

[59] In hindsight, many argue that the early election was the biggest mistake by the international community; it cemented Bosnia to the rule of the same three ethno-nationalist parties and the same ethno-national politics. The early elections merely formalised the role and gave a platform to the instigators of the war who could now continue the fight within the Dayton peace framework.

(USD Aug 1996, 52-53). Much of the flesh on the constitution was added in late September 1995 (USD Aug 1996, 64).

What this loose chronological account shows is that the events leading up to the signing of the Bosnian constitution can be characterised in two ways: at best, they were extremely elite led, confined to specialist lawyers, and prescriptive in nature; at worst, they were superficial and abstract with little or no regard to the demonstrable political culture, history, sociology or religion of Bosnia which were the presumed source of the conflict. This is not to say anything by way of criticism of any individuals involved in the drafting who were clearly accomplished, with vast and demonstrable track records in law, diplomacy and negotiations. But the process belies an environment where men — and almost exclusively men, as noted earlier — emanating from a very particular legal and political clique decided upon the fundamental governance structure of a diverse European nation with a thousand-year history. There was perhaps no time but there was, either way, limited thinking about inclusion, representation and legitimacy.

Comparing Britain and Bosnia

Why would it be worthwhile or even necessary, one might rightly wonder, to compare such radically different constitutional arrangements as those to be found in Britain and Bosnia?

The comparison in this book is between the polar opposite *processes* of constitutional creation, development and amendment in Bosnia and Britain. It is much less a comparison of the two countries' constitutions *per se*. This book is concerned not with the content of Bosnia or Britain's constitutions but something far more fundamental:

- How was the content of the constitutions determined?
- Who had a say on the constitutional negotiations and why?
- If the content of the constitutions is problematic, then why is it so and who decides?
- How might the problematic aspects of the current constitutions be remedied?

There are a number of reasons both practical and principled why the comparison between Bosnia and Britain is important but two are particularly relevant. First, the comparison is backward-looking to allow consideration of inclusion, legitimacy and representation in constitution-making and, in particular, the pre-eminence of political culture. Second, the comparison is forward-looking so that the opportunities and dangers presented by both evolutionary and revolutionary constitution-making processes can be assessed.

Bosnia and Britain sit at the very opposite ends of a spectrum that includes constitutional creation, development and amendment. Britain's constitution is unwritten or uncodified and has endured for over 350 years as a miscellaneous collection of flexible conventions, norms and rules governing political behaviour. It had no single foundational moment, it has no formal amendment process, and its development has been evolutionary. It allows a possibility of realising the idea of a social contract between the people and the State although, in practice, any such realisation cannot happen without *some* formal step. Bosnia, by contrast, has a written, rigid and imposed constitution being as it was merely an annex to an international peace agreement. It is devoid of any particular cultural, societal, or historical connection and, in practice, has a strict amendment process which means, for reasons set out in Chapter 4, it cannot undergo slow and gradual evolutionary change. No one among the existing Bosnian political elites is incentivised to do that within the current system.

Understanding the two polar opposites of the *process* of constitutional creation and amendment allows us to glean important lessons relating to: inclusion and legitimacy in the creation and amendment processes as well as on future opportunities and threats. The process of constitutional design in Britain is considered first and then in Bosnia second.

On one view, there appears in Britain a closer union between culture, shared history, and geography of its people and its constitutional arrangements. The past and the present are said to gravitate along a general trend line. Although the people have never really had formal involvement on the question of constitutional design in Britain they have, or can, indirectly shape it over time through engagement in politics. The fight for universal suffrage, the ending of slavery, movements for social and civil rights, and devolution being cases in point (Hennessy 1995; 2017). This school of thought, would say that there is a great deal of disagreement about the day-to-day of politics but until relatively recently (see Chapter 4) there was not a great deal of fundamental disagreement about the State and its general constitutional structure.

Sumption (2019, 26-27) believes that there are two characteristics which demonstrate people's acceptance of decision-making processes in Britain: representative democracy through the operation of Parliament and the rule of law. Ardent supporters of the British system, what Hennessy (1995) calls "deep traditionalists" consider it a success. Hennessy argues that the current system has seen Britain through the "acquisition and disposal of the largest territorial empire world has ever seen, saw us through two great total wars in the 20th century and a 40-year confrontation with the Soviets and their allies, so why would it not see us through now" (BBC 2017). In fact, his contention is that the current system is not flexible enough because the British constitution has become too prescriptive, too bureaucratic and too much power has been handed over to "unelected people". That is a presumed reference to judges and civil servants. Outside of a coterie of intellectuals, lawyers and politicians, this trend of thought, would say that there is a great measure of generalised trust among the people indicating tacit consent or legitimacy for the structure as a whole. As one commentator has put it, "an unshakeable belief in the efficacy of our political system" (Birnberg 2012). Their detractors would argue the opposite.

On that other view, Britain has lost its way and the decision-making process is no longer legitimate. Britain's constitution could be said to have been loosely attuned to history, society and culture but today it is more remote than ever. This view says that given

Britain's uncodified constitutional arrangements, the presumption that elites will always play by the "rules of the game" and honour unwritten rules of behaviour is misguided. The government, it is said, can successfully utilise or engineer populist or nationalist sentiment to push the rules to breaking point and have. The most recent examples of that would include: the disapplication by the government of long-standing conventions which led, for instance, to the unlawful attempt by the Prime Minister to advise the Queen to prorogue parliament in 2019. That advice, the British Supreme Court found, conflicted with the conventions of parliamentary sovereignty and parliamentary accountability.[60] The government, unhappy with this sort of 'judicial interference', has sought to undermine the rule of law by attacking judges who have reviewed government decision-making and found against them.[61] More recently, the government has launched a host of 'independent reviews' including into: judicial review (the implicit agenda of which appears to be a radical curtailment of judicial scrutiny of government decision-making), the application of the EU labour laws and the Human Rights Act 1998 (to fulfil a long-standing manifesto commitment by the Conservative Party to disapply the application of the European Convention on Human Rights). These reviews apparently have nothing to do with judicial decisions that have found the government to have violated constitutional rules.

The executive, unhappy with legislative scrutiny as much as judicial, has gone even further by bypassing minority views through the use of blunt state-wide referenda (that have no basis in the British constitution) and even the views of entire nations from issues as fundamental as Brexit to managing the coronavirus pandemic (Emerson 2020). This has been supplemented by curtailing parliamentary scrutiny of bills through use of obscure and arcane procedural rules and delegated legislation (Russell 2021). The executive, also unhappy with the interference of 'foreign

---

[60] *R (on the application of Miller) (Appellant) v The Prime Minister* (Respondent), [2019] UKSC 41.
[61] For instance, the issue of which institution of State was entitled to trigger Article 50 for withdrawal from the EU was subject to scrutiny in the Supreme Court too. See further, Chapter 4.

laws' has proposed to unilaterally disapply or violate obligations under international law (such as in the Internal Markets Act 2020 or the Overseas Operations (Service Personnel and Veterans) Bill 2019–2021).

Within the context of these recent issues are long-standing constitutional problems which have come to the fore. Long standing problems include: an unelected House of Lords, inequality amongst the regions, lack of adequate representation of the people in Parliament, and poor legislative scrutiny over the actions of the executive. These examples, it is argued, are all said to show that Britain is in a real constitutional crisis and business as usual is no longer sustainable. Whichever view is correct, and this book express a clear opinion in Chapter 4, there appear to be two prior considerations relating to political culture and about people's inclusion in decision making.

First, are the British political elite representing the best interests of their constituents in Parliament when it comes to constitutional decision-making? Is that representation attuned to the political culture of the British people? Is political culture ever properly gauged or assessed in Britain? Chapter 2 discusses the issue of political culture in detail.

Second, how much say do the people have, or should they have, in constitutional questions? What form, if any, should greater inclusion take? Can and should the people have a say in what is fundamental about their constitution? If the people have a view should that be considered? Chapter 4 begins to address the processes of constitutional change in Britain. Chapters 5 and 6 consider these questions head-on and provide tentative answers.

Bosnia, like Britain, has a rich and varied historical tradition stretching back a thousand years. It is a living embodiment, some have argued, of 'unity in diversity'. The diversity existed before much of Europe was that diverse. It also remained so after much of Europe was no longer diverse having carried out horrific atrocities against minorities during the Second World War including in occupied Bosnia itself. Yet, Bosnia's current constitutional arrangements do not, in any way, take into account historical co-existence and diversity. The international principles that were seen as inviolable—preservation of borders, the right of people of different religions to live together, the refusal to reward brutal aggression—were all arguably betrayed.

The Bosnian constitution is not based on individual political rights but instead on group or collective rights. The Preamble to the constitution identifies three main categories of people: Bosniaks, Bosnian Croats and Bosnian Serbs as 'constituent peoples', 'Others', and 'Citizens'. The Bosnian constitution is premised on the collective equality of the constituent peoples as ethnic groups affording them special vetoes, ethnic quotas in State institutions and power-sharing within a decentralised government. 'Others', which today comprise some 3 to 7 per cent of the population were not defined by the Constitution but rather by the ECtHR following legal claims against the State for discrimination.[62] The ECtHR defined them negatively as minorities that do not declare themselves as members of constituent peoples due to mixed marriage, parenthood or any other reasons.[63] Similarly, the ECtHR defined Citizens as those who declare themselves as such.[64] Others and Citizens who do not identify as constituent peoples cannot serve in the Presidency or the House of the Peoples. A Bosniak and Croat representative in the House of the Peoples or the Presidency cannot come from the RS and a Serb cannot come from the Federation (Išerić 2016).

Criticisms at the time and ever since (particularly by those who felt the full brunt of war crimes) have focused on the idea that the division and segregation sought by certain wartime leaders was institutionalised and deplorable crimes rewarded through the ill-thought out consociational model.[65] It was seen as a compromise

---

[62] Estimates of population figures by ethnicity are extremely contentious and difficult to verify in Bosnia. These figures come from the Statistics Agency of Bosnia and the academic Bahtić-Kunrath (2011, 919).
[63] *Azra Zornic v BiH*, App. no 3681/06, ECHR, 15 July 2014, para 8.
[64] Ibid.
[65] In fact, Milošević as negotiator on behalf of the Bosnian Serbs confirmed as much.

predicated on the outcome of military territorial gains and ethnic cleansing,[66] which handicapped, at its infancy, much hope of a unified multi-ethnic State and much socio-economic development with it. That outcome betrayed, in essence, a tradition of 'unity in diversity' at a critical juncture; when Bosnia's multi-ethnic milieu happened to be severely punctured by that "counter current of persecution and slaughter" attempting to destroy it (Malcolm 1996; Agee 2002; Mahmutćehajić 2005, 2011). There are critical aspects of the Bosnian constitution which, therefore, require reform including, *inter alia*, ensuring compliance with obligations under international treaties, such as the ECHR.[67] If a constitution is seen to form part of a body then in Bosnia's case, arguably, it was the yoke on its body politic, the people.

Detractors of this view will argue that a peace was made, and that peace has, in fact, proved durable to date. On that view, there is still plenty of time, within a peaceable framework, to achieve meaningful outcomes through constitutional tinkering and the constitution's development as a 'living instrument'. Some would point to Germany as an example that has made hundreds of amendments over the years to its Basic Law (despite being imposed by the victors of the Second World War) and has by all accounts accepted and made its own an imposed constitution. This book accepts that constitutional tinkering or evolution is a *possible* pathway out of constitutional crisis even if an imprecise and uncertain one.

The difficulty with the latter view (some of which emanates from historical revisionism by drafters or negotiators) is that a durable peace is only durable until it is not. In any case, it is difficult to argue against a contention that there is a frozen conflict in Bosnia as it satisfies, as Perry (2019) has set out, all the criteria for one:

---

[66] For which both Franjo Tuđman and Slobodan Milošević bore responsibility. See further Bose (2002, 53-55) and Toal and Dahlman (2011, 4).

[67] See, for instance, European Court of Human Rights. *Sejdic and Finci v. Bosnia and Herzegovina, (27996/06 and 34836/06)*, Council of Europe: 22 December 2009; or Art. 70(1) obligations under the *Stabilisation and Accession Agreement between the European Communities and their Member States, of the one part, and Bosnia and Herzegovina, of the other part*. Luxembourg, 16 June 2008.

- core issues going back to the violent conflict remain unresolved and salient including territorial control, population return, and ethno-national appropriation of the civic, social and cultural space;
- core disputes are at the forefront of mutual relations between groups including exclusive ethno-national institutional representation, identity, education, and patronage networks; and
- credible threats of the renewal of violence is ever present particularly in the context of parallel structures being maintained by secessionist-oriented leaders supported by outside powers such as Croatia, Serbia, and Russia (Hamilton 2020).

The *probable* pathway for Bosnia is collapse. Bosnia cannot afford to wait for evolutionary outcomes given the external pressures emanating from predatory neighbours and the internal pressures emanating from nationalistic—or secessionist—elite impulse. If Bosnia is to lapse into conflict, much soul-searching in policy circles will follow as to the root causes of that future conflict. What Bosnia needs are evolutionary outcomes, locally led, in the short term but that is only possible if there is genuine support for outcomes tending towards democratic outcomes premised on values conducive to democracy.

Just as there were two prior considerations for Britain set-out above the same two are relevant to Bosnia and they relate to political culture and people's inclusion in decision making.

First, are political elites representing the best interests of all their constituents when it comes to constitutional decision-making in the post-Dayton framework? Is that representation attuned to the political culture of the Bosnian people? Chapter 2 methodically assesses the issue of Bosnian political culture.

Second, how much say do the people have, or should they have, in constitutional questions? What form, if any, should greater inclusion take? Can and should the people have a say in what is fundamental about their constitution? If the people have a view how should that be taken into consideration? Chapter 4 addresses the necessity of constitutional change in Bosnia. Chapter 5 models where Bosnian political elites and the people stand on the issue of constitutional reform. Chapter 6 provides possible answers to these fundamental questions. ✺

> "Look a shoot is sprouting from
> the white stone
> Sprouting from an ancient hand a
> dark face
> From it a white flower has painfully
> budded and grown
> And from its hidden nest a bird
> has already flown
> Into the lonely ring of someone's
> gleaming dream"
>
> - Mak Dizdar, *The Stone Sleeper* [68]

2. "Look a shoot is sprouting": measuring culture

The refrain is as common to Bosnia and its neighbours as it is to the well-established democracies of Western Europe such as Britain: 'I am not interested in politics,' 'nothing will change if I vote', or 'politicians only care about themselves.'[69] What causes an individual to determine that their own political participation has no value or that their engagement will be met with indifference by those that represent them is one of most complex and perplexing aspects of democratic government. In theory, people are *able* to engage—by law, practice or convention—and are *capable* of engaging—by having the time, money and inclination to do so— those that make political decisions on their behalf. In practice, however, people who have that ability or capability *choose* not to engage.

It is in the context of increasing political apathy, in both developed and developing democracies, that it is particularly interesting to consider falling political engagement in Bosnia. While political apathy is problematic for any democratic government it is far more problematic for countries with new democratic

---

[68] An extract of a poem called "Krajina: Ending" by Mak Dizdar [1917-1971] in Buturović 2002.
[69] As noted in the Introduction, Bosnia and Herzegovina is referred to throughout as "Bosnia".

constitutions which are seen to be in transition.[70] The project of democratisation itself can be fundamentally undermined.

This book seeks to identify whether the explanation for political apathy, or more accurately *political resignation*, in Bosnia since the independence of the country from the former Socialist Federal Republic of Yugoslavia ("SFRY") is connected to political culture.

- Is political apathy in the case of Bosnia a result of non-participation in politics, as one marker of political culture? There are two corollaries to that question.
    - If political culture is to blame, then how is relatively higher political participation in its close neighbours, which share a great deal in common with Bosnia, explained? (Assuming participation is better in neighbouring countries).
    - If political culture is not an adequate explanation, then what causal variables explain higher political apathy in Bosnia in comparison with its neighbours? (Assuming apathy is worse in Bosnia than it is in neighbouring countries).
- Critically, if political culture in Bosnia is 'as good' or 'as bad' as Britain's political culture, what does that mean for the process of creating or amending constitutions? If Bosnia and Britain both have good political cultures then there may be some synergies between, and common approaches to, the process of constitutional design in both countries.

This book's claim is that political culture, in so far as it is a product of historical circumstances, cannot be the main cause of political apathy in Bosnia. If historical circumstances explained the development of a non-participant orientation, then surely those same circumstances must manifest themselves in other former

---

[70] By 'democratic transition' this book is referring to 'a political regime in which democracy as a complex system of institutions, rules and patterned incentives and disincentives has become 'the only game in town'' (Linz and Stepan, 1996, 3). In other words, the democratic process prevails as the forum in which the objectives of governance are achieved in contrast to non-democratic processes.

Yugoslav countries. Unless, that is, we adopt the idea of exceptionalism with respect to Bosnia, or the other former Yugoslav countries. The reason that political culture is often attributed to be the cause of all of Bosnia's ills is because it is convenient to blame something as nebulous as culture rather than search for the root causes.[71]

A far more nuanced narrative is required for Bosnia. To the extent that non-participation in politics *is* to blame it is because the constitutional structure and the economic market created largely by the international community after the war have helped create an environment that has inhibited, and continues to hinder, participation. Academics, international politicians and pundits that blame political culture have misidentified the variables that cause political apathy. The root causes of political apathy are the same root causes engendering an indifferent and non-participant orientation. The root cause is the constitutional structure; apathy and non-participation are manifestations of one another. And the cycle is, of course, vicious. Precisely because there is a belief that nothing can be done, nothing is done.

In the case of Bosnia, the precipitant danger is that a set of circumstances may present themselves that galvanise all the discontents, troubles and grievances of the people into a push against an incumbent government. If that happens, it could fundamentally call into question the legitimacy of the entire democratic project set up under Dayton. This may be a particular risk if we identify a groundswell of opinion that suggests that the population harbours latent political participation; the capacity for future political engagement or involvement (which will be explained later in this Chapter).[72] With the various revolutionary 'Arab Springs', starting in December 2010 in Tunisia and escalating from 2011 across the Arab world, Bosnia also saw rioting in areas

---

[71] To first blame communism, then ethnic hatreds and if that fails to fall back on Orientalist ideas of the 'backward' Eastern modes of behaviour which had dominated the region for five hundred years.

[72] See, for instance, the work of Kuntz and Thompson (2009).

where all three constituent peoples form majorities.⁷³ Common to them all was a deep and accumulated frustration with the State institutions and the entrenched political elites which run them (Judah 2014). Those riots have died down, but the underlying issues remain unresolved. What are the alternatives that could be tentatively suggested for Bosnia? What can we learn from the Croatian experience and what is required for people to engage?

In the case of Britain, the challenge is that the country is currently going through a period of rapid constitutional change. As outlined in Chapter 1, the present constitutional settlement is under unprecedented strain. As the figures set out below show, Britain has grappled with increasing apathy and decreasing participation, as much as Bosnia. The question is whether the changes that are taking place will do anything to address this and, indeed, whether they are legitimate when viewed in the context of the interests and beliefs of the wider public.

There are a number of related questions for both Bosnia and Britain. What is 'good' and 'bad' political culture and how can it have an impact on constitutional design? Why might it be important that both countries cultivate and pay heed to 'good' political culture? How might constitutional design impact culture? In order to address these issues, a deeper understanding of the political cultures in the two countries is necessary.

2.1 Political culture in theory

The "political culture" of a given society has long been framed as the context in which the potential for constitutional reform can be understood (Welzel and Inglehart 2008, 131).⁷⁴ In their classic study of the concept, Almond and Verba, define political culture as the set of "specifically political orientations—attitudes toward the political

---

[73] The majority of the rioting was in the Bosniak majority areas and to a limited extent in the three Croat cantons and the RS. This is largely explained by differing methods of coercive and monopolistic control wielded in these areas by Croat and Serb elites respectively. There is less monopolistic means of control available to Bosniak elites in the Federation (Bassuener 2020).

[74] For an overview of the development of the concept, see Welzel and Inglehart (2008, 131).

system and its various parts, and the attitudes toward the role of the self in the system" ([1963] 1989, 12). Political culture is not dissimilar to the way in which one might refer to an economic culture or a religious culture. That conception of political culture may be supplemented by the idea that political culture can be the product of complex historical experiences that create norms of behaviour in society.

The literature on political culture asserts that certain mass attitudes are conducive to democracy. That societies with certain characteristics and views are more likely to be successful in establishing and sustaining democratic institutions (Welzel and Inglehart 2008, 131). This thesis has been taken further in countries deemed to have a "poor" or "bad" political culture such as Bosnia.

In Bosnia, some scholars have concluded that certain mass attitudes are *not* conducive to democratic structures which means that there is a limit on the democratic reforms that are possible. For example, a report by the European Stability Initiative concluded:

> "At the heart of the Bosnian governance problem [...] lies the lack of engagement by Bosnian citizens and interest groups in the practice of government [...] public institutions which are not subject to constant pressure from citizens exerted through the democratic process will not respond to the needs of the public effectively" (European Stability Initiative 2004, 48).

Such views, however, are hard to sustain when one considers that political culture is not a fixed variable but one that is highly dynamic and constantly in flux. Political culture is and will be. Political culture influences political outcomes. But the political context is constantly reshaping and influencing the supposed culture of which the context is supposedly a product. Data shows that a wide variety of factors can influence the propensity of a population to engage with political institutions, including socioeconomic conditions, which are created or maintained by the institutions themselves (Welzel and Inglehart 2005, 150).

This idea of political culture, as a non-fixed variable, serves as the basis for analysis of civic attitudes and behaviour towards democratic institutions within Bosnia and Britain, including the way in which the institutions might themselves autonomously impact political culture. As a critique of existing work explaining political participation in Bosnia, this book attempts to challenge the commonly held assumption that poor political culture is the bane of Bosnia's political life and the root cause of the political apathy seen in the country since independence. Political apathy, which in reality in Bosnia is resignation, is not synonymous with poor culture.

In Britain, differing views on the "health" of its political culture have been put forward in relation to the willingness of the populace to engage in the democratic process, particularly in recent years as commentators have "blamed" the outcome of the EU referendum on mass disengagement with the political system (Curtice 2016). This book aims to interrogate common assumptions about Britain's political culture and examine what this tells us about the potential for constitutional reform.

In addition to outlining key markers for political culture of Britain and Bosnia and giving a broad commentary on the respective political cultures of the two countries, this book will compare, systematically, Bosnian culture with its close neighbour, Croatia. Clearly there are considerable differences between Bosnia and Britain impacting on political culture and political participation rates. Given the shared histories of Bosnia and Croatia, the comparison allows us to ascertain to what extent, if at all, Bosnia genuinely has a politically apathetic populace, by drawing out the similarities and differences (if any) with its culturally and geographically close neighbour.

The rationale for comparing political culture in Croatia and Bosnia is threefold. First, having two comparator States with shared history and norms allows us to challenge path dependent explanations of why democratic participation in Bosnia is allegedly so much worse than in its neighbouring State, Croatia. Second, given the different paths Croatia and Bosnia have taken following the armed conflicts in the 1990s and the relative political success of Croatia (as it is now an EU member State) the comparison is immensely useful in analysing variations, if any, in political culture.

Third, moving away from anecdotal evidence (and an exclusive focus on post-war Bosnia) to using time series statistical data—pre-war and post-war—from two neighbouring countries is a helpful way to comprehensively and comparatively measure two features of culture: (i) long-term political participation as a marker of political culture *versus* short-term political apathy; (ii) the root causes of political division in Bosnia by eliminating irrelevant variables such as a *belief* in a long-term non-participant orientation among the people rather than its actual existence.

The comparison between the Bosnia and Croatia is, therefore, helpful to challenge the commonly held assumption that current non-participation in politics is an insurmountable impediment to political life in Bosnia rather than the autonomous impact of its imposed constitutional structures. The statistical analysis discussed shortly in this Chapter will seek to demonstrate that political participation in Bosnia is as, or more, favourable than in Croatia. That is notwithstanding that trust in institutions continues to fall in Bosnia as it was falling in Croatia under President Franjo Tudman who was Croatia's first post-communist leader and its only war-time leader. Addressing the issue of participation then allows a more meaningful comparison between the processes of constitutional reform and amendment in Britain and Bosnia respectively to resolve any doubt about whether political culture in Bosnia is conducive to democratic practices and processes. By contrast, the latter is almost a given in Britain.

A myriad of contemporary literature and scholarship focuses on the importance of political culture for democratic practice. The very idea of liberal democracy, quite aside from a simple electoral democracy, is "based on mass voice in self-governance [and] therefore depends on social preconditions such as the wide distribution of participatory resources and a trusting, tolerant public that prizes free choice" (Welzel and Inglehart 2008, 126).

The literature on political culture is rich and varied and the typology for analysing participation in a country dauntingly disparate. Approaches taken by scholars to conceptualising political culture can be divided into the following categories: (a) value based models that use people's self-expression values across time and focus on the essential value preconditions for liberal democracy (Almond and Verba 1963; Hakansson and Sjoholm 2007; Welzel and Inglehart 2008; Kuntz 2011); (b) social capital models that focus on how social interaction between people leads to greater trust, reciprocity and participatory habits (Putnam 1993);[75] (c) more complicated modernisation and post-modernisation hypotheses which suggest that the absence of material need in communities propels people into the democratic arena—that view is countered by theories that suggest democracy first 'happens' as a precondition and is then subsequently sustained by socio-economic development (Lipset 1959; Inglehart 1997; Acemoglu and Robinson 2001); and (d) alternative or 'new politics' hypotheses which assert that less formal associational behaviour in the civil (non-political) sphere can have important potential consequences for conventional political practice (Ekman and Amna 2009; Ekman 2009).

Value-based models maintain that democratic politics requires more than just democratic institutions. In *The Civic Culture*, Almond and Verba dispense with the idea that electoral participation is the sole measure of political participation. The effectiveness of democratic government, which is by definition participatory, depends essentially on an allegiant political culture (a civic culture) that is also participatory in nature (Almond and Verba [1963] 1989, 26). Crucially, however, 'parochial' or 'subject' orientations in society that are non-political in nature—such as a limited interest in politics and little appetite for dissent—are important for a balanced political culture. Where the parochial or subject culture is predominant then democratic institutions will find it difficult to be legitimate. Conversely, if there is no parochial or subject culture at all then populations will become completely unruly and will never accept any decision by authorities as legitimate. In Bosnia, therefore, if the culture is largely one of

---

[75] Although others argue that social interaction can both increase or decrease trust depending on the conditions under which association takes place (Pettigrew 1971; Knack and Keefer 1997. See further Håkansson and Sjöholm (2007).

deference and disinterest then it should have an impact on democratic institutions (following Almond and Verba).

Social capital models focus extensively on why political culture is a key explanatory variable to good political government and political participation. Putnam (1993, 167) explains why the North of Italy has a far better regional government than the South. The key variable is not wealth, but the civic community of the North characterized by horizontal, rather than hierarchical, networks embodying values of solidarity, civic-engagement, cooperation and honesty—"social capital" in short. Social capital refers to "features of social organization, such as trust, norms and networks that can improve the efficiency of society by facilitating coordinated actions" (Putnam 1993). Voluntary cooperation is easier in a society with an inherited supply of social capital, in the form of networks of reciprocity and civic engagement. Acknowledging the usual problems of collective action (such as the tragedy of the commons, credible threats, and prisoner's dilemma) Putnam outlines that institutions can reduce the transactions costs of co-operative behaviour. But why do collaborative institutions work in some places and fail to work in others? Putnam links this difference to the civic community: there is a conducive political culture in the North but not in the South. Cross-sectional data showed that, due to the political culture, the North of Italy puts new institutions to better use in four ways: civic engagement; political equality; solidarity, trust and tolerance; and social structures of cooperation. His statistical inferences show that all the regions with high institutional performance and high scores on the civic community index are from the centre-North. Happiness, concludes Putnam, "is living in a civic community" (1993, 113).

Carlo Trigilia (1995), however, has pointed to the growth in associational activity in the South of Italy "in part political, but above all cultural, which is shaping new possibilities on the level of democratic growth and the positive use of civic resources" (Tarrow 1996, 392). In fact, 6400 cultural associations were found in the South, two thirds of which were created after 1980. Putnam fails to account for the growth of such activity and why it does not appear to correspond to improved political participation or governance. A salient criticism of Putnam is that his concept of civic engagement includes all manners of behaviour which may be far removed from influencing political behaviour. Not all civic engagement has consequences for politics (North 1991, 97-112). Ekman (2009, 4) rightly notes that to explain declining levels of civic engagement we need to be clear about what exactly is declining otherwise we stretch the concept to be completely meaningless.

Putnam (1993) also conveniently leaves out the successive 'explosions' as Tarrow (1996, 392) calls them in Northern Italian associational activity which are far removed from developing social capital—organised corruption, far-right separatist movements, mafia organisations and the "collapse of Marxist and Catholic subcultures with their assortment of mass organisations giving way to a party system whose entrenched structures have all but disappeared" (Ekman 2009, 4). Not all associational activity is 'good' activity towards the health of political institutions. Associations themselves can have conflicting objectives to those of other associations which can promote rivalry and possibly conflict (Walzer 1999, 89 and Walzer 1980). The democratising and anti-democratising impact of associational behaviour is important when analysing political participation in Bosnia and increasingly in Britain, as will be discussed further. The forging of associations presents an opportunity for participation, but that participation can be disastrously anti-system. They may serve to undermine rather than reinforce existing political and economic structures and institutions. That is particularly so when associations receive the patronage of narrow-minded, self-interested governing elites with little interest in deepening political engagement and democratisation.

No doubt, horizontal ties and the forming of associations can help counteract the effects of individualism and build trust among people through mutual assistance: all very valuable for democratising and developing participant political orientations. But such developments must not leave out the influence of governing elites and the systems and structures in which they operate (an issue considered further in Chapter 4). For Putnam, the State suffers as a result of poor political culture, but he does not appear to consider that the State itself may be the cause of poor political culture. Tarrow's (1996) critique, very cogently elaborated by Skocpol (1996, 20-25), is that States, via political elites within institutions, can carry out autonomous actions with political and civil consequences.

Alexis de Tocqueville (1863, 121), described by Putnam as the 'most relevant social theorist' on this issue, believes the role played by civil associations is crucial in a democracy as "democracy... confines him [man] entirely within the solitudes of his own heart." De Tocqueville believes democracy can be dangerous because it breeds individualism, where people are concerned only with themselves and leave society at large to itself, causing public life to be stifled and excluding large parts of society such as the poor. In contrast to this, civil society, and the forming of associations, helps to counteract the effects of individualism by addressing issues through voluntarily helping one another, rather than through compulsion by a governing class. The argument, however, that individualism is prone to be used by the governing class to enforce actions in the community can be also true of associations. In defence of de Tocqueville, though, Walzer (1996, 89) notes that "this is probably as close as we can come to that 'friendship' which Aristotle thought should characterise relations among members of the same political community" (See also, Walzer 1980). The democratising and anti-democratising impact of associational behaviour is important when analysing political participation in Bosnia and Croatia—they present an opportunity for participation, but that participation can be disastrously anti-system. That institutions and political elites can have such autonomous effect, both good and bad, is no clearer than in Bosnia. The autonomous impact of institutions is an issue further elaborated on in Chapter 4.

2.2 Political culture in practice

The typology for analysing culture is less developed than the rich literature underpinning the concept. The term political culture is often used as a 'catch all' explanation when it is used to describe political outcomes, so readily available indicators can be elusive.

In order to make operational the concept of political culture, in a practical sense, this book builds on Inglehart and Welzel's (2008, 132) studies based on data in the *World Values Survey*. Those studies show that countries in which certain attitudes are more widespread have more successful democracies than those in which those values are less prevalent. It is possible to use those studies to create a typology with which to assess whether societies have the preconditions for successful participation in democratic life. Political participation is a marker of sorts for political culture, but it is only one among many. Voting at the ballot box may be the most obvious indicator for a pro-participation culture, but there are numerous markers that indicate the willingness or potential capacity to participate in democratic processes. Clearly, political culture can manifest in many different ways. The terms 'participant' and 'non-participant' must, therefore, be unpacked from 'political culture' so as to help us understand and make operational the vigorously debated concept of political culture.

'Political participation' denotes "action by ordinary citizens directed toward influencing some political outcomes" (Brady in Ekman and Amna 2009, 7). The latter is wider in scope than Verba's (1978) popular definition: "those legal acts by private citizens that are more or less directly aimed at influencing the selection of governmental personnel and/or the actions that they take" (Verba, Nie and Kim 1978, 1). Widening the definition gives prominence to the notion that: participation is manifest and observable; ordinary people are the participants and not political elites; and those being influenced are people in power. The people in power refers to powerful actors, groups or businesses capable of influencing government and not just political elites alone (Ekman and Amna 2009, 7). Political participation though is not limited to action specifically directed toward influencing political outcomes. We must account for *latent* forms of political participation. These are observable civil actions which may have important future consequences in relation to political outcomes, what could be termed 'capacity action' or 'capacity building' (Ekman 2009, 19). This tends to capture social involvement (i.e., attention to and interest in political and societal issues) or civic engagement which combines attentiveness and action (Ekman 2009, 19).

Political cultures which are conducive to successful democracy tend to have societies with 'participant orientations'. Conversely, societies which demonstrate values which are not favourable to democracy tend to have long-term 'non-participant orientations'. 'Participant orientation' refers to norms, values, orientations tending towards engagement with politics and high levels of trust towards, or participation with, others. Participation — and, conversely, non-participation — is defined as such by building on Inglehart and Welzel's (2008, 126-140) aforementioned studies showing that self-expression values (of tolerance, interpersonal trust, participatory habits) demonstrate a commitment by people towards democracy because they value freedom and autonomy, in and of itself, rather than pledging a practical commitment to democracy. Their thesis is that 'survival values' (driven by economic need) are replaced by 'self-expression values' (giving priority to the environment, tolerance of diversity and demands for participation in decision making in politics). A growing emphasis on self-expression values increases the demand for responsive government, helping to establish and sustain democratic institutions. Societies which rank high on self-expression values also tend to rank high on interpersonal trust—this in turn leads to a high value for freedom and autonomy which leads to political activism—all essential to the endurance of democratic practice (Inglehart and Welzel 2008, 132).

But some expression of commitment to democracy is important too and, therefore, it is essential that a participant orientation is allegiant to the political structure to which it is oriented, namely to the idea that democracy is "the only game in town" ([1963] 1989, 30) Systemic disengagement from the State, therefore, is an extremely non-participant orientation. Non-participant orientations deserve particular attention in the context of the challenges to constitutional reform in Bosnia. As Matthew

Gutmann (2002, 21) has noted, "we gain a far better understanding of why some people participate sometimes in some forms of political activities if we understand why others do not."

Building on Inglehart and Welzel, and Verba's works above, non-participation in politics (or *non-participant orientation*) can be modelled by two values: absence of interpersonal trust i.e., generalised trust towards others and in particular other ethnic groups; and negative orientation towards political behaviour. Negative orientation towards political behaviour can be *"a-systemic"* — engendering a total lack of interest in politics, no importance of politics in life, no confidence in government — or it can be *"anti-systemic"* — capturing majority views that having a democratic system is bad, the economy in a democracy runs badly or the political system as it was before was much better. If Bosnian society is non-participant, as many have claimed, it would fall easily within such a model, as attitudes towards others would be characterised by mistrust and attitudes towards the democratic system *per se* would be acutely anti-systemic. The typology for *participant or non-participant orientations* may be further understood by also taking into consideration and modelling *latent* participation using two variables: interest in and awareness of political and societal issues (following politics in the news, discussing politics with friends), and self-reported activities within the civil society sphere (membership of groups).

Related to the concept of non-participation is that of *political apathy*, which is concerned with a present state of political inaction amongst citizens. Political apathy might traditionally be lumped together with a non-participant orientation, but the evidence suggests that it is a little more complicated than that. Political apathy may be defined as ordinary citizens' disinterest and indifference to political outcomes manifest by measurable inaction (i.e., there being no attempt to have their voice heard) or action (i.e., the attempt to make their anti-political stance vocal and public). This inaction and indifference appear to be far more short-term and variable than more longer-term markers of political culture made operational, as above, by measuring participant or non-participant orientations.

The measurable action (or inaction) constituting some degree of political apathy in a population can, therefore, be modelled by inverting and adapting a five-dimension typology used by Teorell *et al* (2003) to analyse what might better be considered as only short-term markers of political participation. Political participation, therefore, is characterised by *electoral participation* (voting), *consumer participation* (donating money to charity, boycotting, signing petitions), *party activity* (being a member, donating money or volunteering time), *protest activity* (taking part in demonstrations), and *contact activity* (contacting politicians, civil society organisations or civil servants) (Ekman 2009, 7). Inverting this would be a marker of political apathy. For instance, a lack of protest activity or a lack of party activity would indicate apathy. These are not markers of political culture *per se* but may be a manifestation of that culture or not as the case may be.

2.3 Political culture applied to Bosnia and Britain

As set out above, participant orientation refers to norms, values, of orientations tending towards engagement with politics and high levels of trust towards, or participation with, others. These values tend to be conducive to successful democracies: they indicate that individuals in society at least have an interest in democratic processes or the capacity to engage with them in the future.

Better understanding whether Bosnian and British societies broadly have either a participant or non-participant orientation is one of the central aims of this book. Moreover, in Chapter 1, the question was posed as to whether political elites in Britain and Bosnia are attuned to the political culture of the people in the two countries when they make constitutional decisions. In order to assist in answering that question, a broad understanding of the political culture in the two respective democracies is needed. This book investigates Bosnia's political culture in more detail in Chapter 3, including by way of comparisons with its close neighbour Croatia, but the following will serve as a broad overview using the markers for political culture outlined above.

Almond and Verba ([1963] 1989) describe the historical political culture of Britain as "a deferential civic culture," with a highly developed participant role for the public in which exposure to politics, and an interest, involvement and a sense of competence in politics are relatively high in society. They find that there are accepted norms supporting political activity, and emotional involvement in elections. People have a general pride in the system as well as "satisfaction with specific government performance" ([1963] 1989, 315). Almond and Verba contrasted the deferential culture in the Britain with a "strongly participant culture" in the United States. The British they believed "have maintained a strong deference to the independent authority of government." The implication of this is that there is an understanding and acceptance of the "rules of game" in democratic and constitutional terms amongst the general population as a product of the gradual evolutionary history of Britain's political system" (Ibid, 316). If this analysis still holds, one expects high levels of interpersonal trust, as well as strong positive orientations towards political behaviour. More recently, however, it has been suggested that the vote to leave the EU marked a rupture with that long-established tradition of popular acceptance of the system (suggesting a greater proportion of a-systemic or anti-systemic views). Marsh (2018) suggested that the vote represented "an almost total rejection of the idea, which, historically, was at the core of the British democratic settlement, that the 'government knows best'."

Bosnia, on the other hand, has been described variously as having a "passive", "undemocratic" or an "intolerant" political culture (Taniyici 2008, 88). In November 2011, the High Representative for Bosnia told the UN Security Council that his Office had to remain in place because of the "continued negative trends and political instability" and challenges to the Dayton Peace Agreement. He remarked that "one of the basic reasons for those challenges *lay at the core of the nation's political culture* [emphasis added]" (United Nations Security Council 2011). Some international stakeholders have called the political culture in Bosnia a 'kafana culture,' meaning that it is indifferent and uninterested. The blame for low levels of political participation was squarely put on the lack of engagement by citizens, describing the "passivity of large parts of society" (European Stability Initiative 2004, 1). As noted above, if Bosnian society fitted these stereotypes, it would exhibit markers for an extremely non-participant orientation, as attitudes towards others would be characterised by mistrust and attitudes towards the democratic system would be acutely anti-systemic. As this book, however, noted at the outset, it is not clear that such views stand up to empirical scrutiny and recent events.[76]

Recent data from the *European Values Survey* and *World Values Survey* on key systemic indicators for political culture shows that people in both countries have similar appetites for a democratic system of government (94 per cent and 92 per cent of those surveyed in Britain and Bosnia respectively). On other markers, survey data (Figure 2.2A) indicates a greater interest in Britain (than in Bosnia) in politics and a greater appreciation of the importance of politics in people's lives overall.

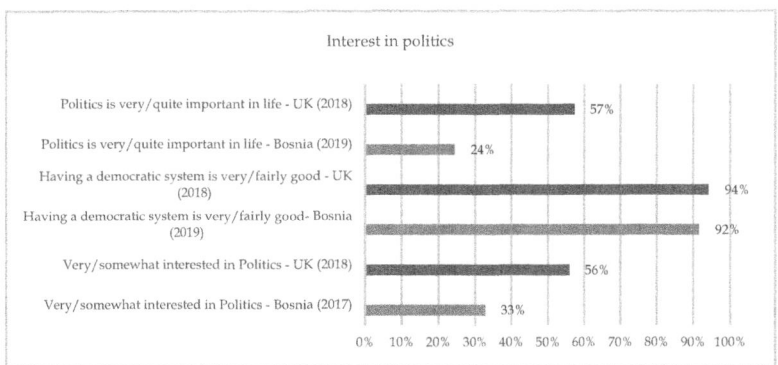

Figure 2.2A

The a-systemic measures of confidence in political structures and political representatives follow similar trends in both Bosnia and Britain (Figure 2.2B). British surveys demonstrate higher levels

---

[76] See, for example, Monitor (2018).

of confidence, although the gap is narrowing in most areas including on confidence in the EU. The proportion of Bosnians sampled who say they have a great deal or quite a lot of confidence in the EU is 17 points higher than in Britain. Furthermore, confidence in political parties is similarly low for both countries, with only 16 per cent and 13 per cent of those surveyed saying that they have a great deal or quite a lot of confidence in Britain and Bosnia respectively.

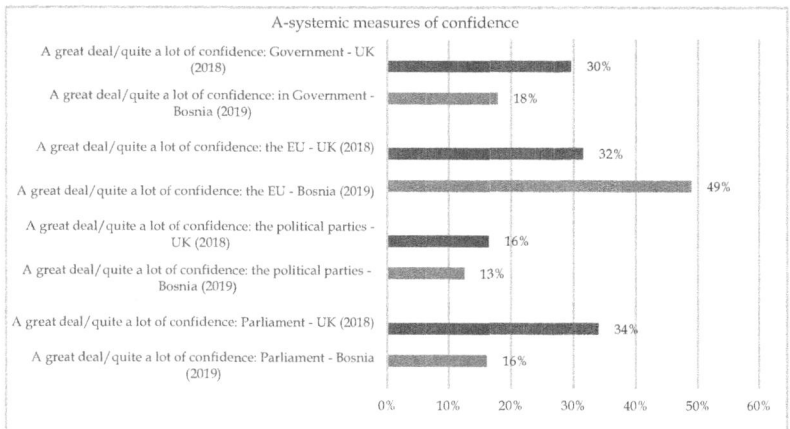

Figure 2.2B

Low levels of trust in political parties in Bosnia is a trend that is replicated across studies. A survey carried out in 2015 found that political parties were the least trusted institutions, with 62.3 per cent of citizens saying they did not trust the political parties "at all" (Analitika 2015). The next least trusted institutions were the cantonal parliament, cantonal government, State government and State parliament, in respect of which a majority of respondents said they had "no trust at all" in each of the institutions (Analitika 2015).

The British Social Attitudes survey asks a similar set of questions on confidence in institutions.[77] This allows us to break down a-systemic sentiment in terms of the institutions people are

---

[77] Albeit with slightly different possible answers so can't be cross-referenced with the European Values survey.

most negatively orientated towards. Given recent constitutional developments in Britain, what is particularly interesting is the way in which confidence in the courts and the legal system compares with political institutions like Parliament (Curtice *et al.* 2019). Figure 2.2C shows that the courts and the legal system were the second most popular institution after schools and the education system, with 75 per cent of respondents selecting the three positive options. Parliament was narrowly the institution in which people had the least confidence, with 45 per cent selecting the positive responses and 16 per cent expressing no confidence.

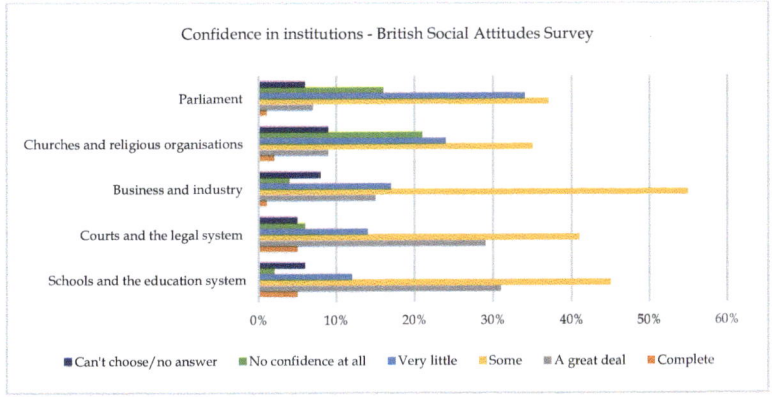

Figure 2.2C

There are many possible explanations for the differences between the two countries—discussing these will be a further focus in subsequent chapters. As the short political and constitutional histories set out in Chapter 1 demonstrate, Bosnia and Britain sit at the very opposite ends of the spectrum in terms of their recent political contexts. It is, therefore, perhaps surprising that there are not more marked differences between the two countries in terms of some of the key a-systemic and anti-systemic indicators (and, therefore, overall participant orientations). The relative stability of democratic structures in Britain can be contrasted with Bosnia's turbulent history and clearly, such factors shape societal views on the role of government and politics in people's lives and the level of confidence people have in those who are supposed to represent them. For example, higher numbers of people stating that politics is very/quite important to their lives in Britain may be demonstrative of the longer established provision of State services at both a national and local government level. The public health care system, public pensions and insurance programmes have been in place in Britain from the early decades of the 20th century (Montgomery and Baglioni 2018).[78] In addition, as discussed in Chapter 4, what is often most interesting about such data is what it shows about how well the actions of elites and entrenched democratic structures reflect and are responsive to popular belief systems.

In Britain, it is interesting to note that key markers for a participatory political culture (both systemic and anti-systemic) have remained fairly high throughout the last 20 years, with most indicators steadily increasing (as shown by Figure 2.2D). There has been extensive commentary suggesting that the results of the EU referendum in 2016 represented widespread political disillusionment and dissatisfaction with the existing political system. The data suggests, however, that there was no sudden drop in society's positive view of the political system.[79] In fact, the proportions expressing a-systemic or anti-systemic views appears to be relatively stable. British society does broadly appear to have the markers of a long-term participant orientation. If disaffection explains the result for a minority of the voting population, it is clear that it has been a problem for a long time prior to 2016 and that the constitutional developments that have followed were not a product of any kind of clear sea-change in popular political culture. Perhaps, most surprisingly, the proportion of those surveyed expressing "a great deal" or "quite a lot of confidence" in the EU reached its highest level in 2018 at 31.5 per cent, whilst the proportion of those who expressed "no confidence at all" in the EU fell from 30.4 per

---

[78] Montgomery, Tom & Baglioni, Simone, "Britain" in Federico, Veronica and Lahusen, Christian in *"Solidarity as a Public Virtue? Law and Public Policies in the European Union"* (2018), Baden-Baden: Nomos Verlagsgesellschaft mbH.

[79] It is beyond the scope of this book to discuss how the views of particular demographics contributed to the EU referendum result. This book merely suggests that, when the population is taken as a whole, there was not a sudden drop in key markers for a participatory political culture.

cent in 1999 to 25.2 per cent in 2018. It is important to note, however, that those who had "not very much" confidence in the EU represented the largest proportion of respondents, at 43.3 per cent in 2018. This was broadly in line with numbers in previous years (45.2 per cent in 2008 and 43.0 per cent in 1999).

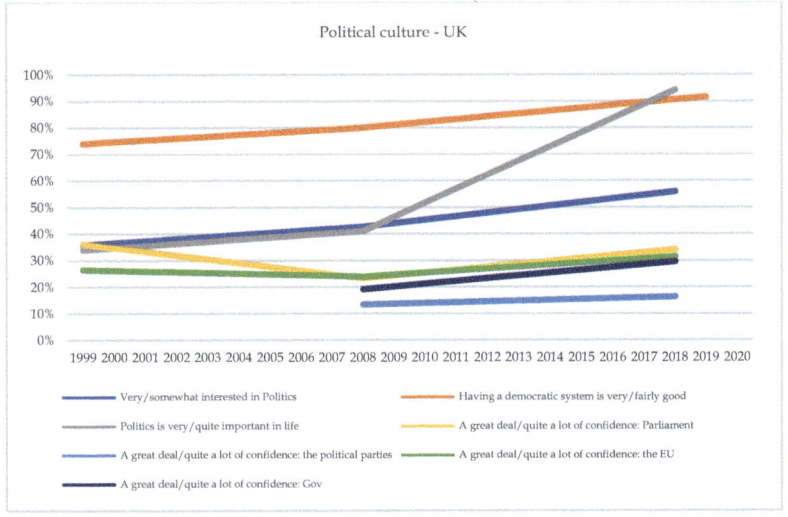

Figure 2.2D

In terms of interpersonal trust, it is important to note how changeable societal beliefs and values can be. Reference to measures of interpersonal trust for Bosnia and Britain show significant changes to a number of indicators over a 20-year period. For example, the proportion of those surveyed in Britain who stated that they would not be happy to have Muslim neighbours fell from 14 per cent in 1999 and 13 per cent in 2008 to 6 per cent in 2018. An opposite change appears to have taken place in Bosnia, with the figure rising from 13 per cent in 2009 to 26 per cent in 2020.[80] In

---

[80] There are complicated reasons for this disturbing and destabilising new development, linked to media and educational polarisation, which are beyond the scope of this book. These polarisation efforts have been elite-led: with people being fed a diet of Islamophobia built on fear and amplified by elites co-opting wider unrelated international narratives (connected to migration in

Britain, those who said they would not be happy to have neighbours of a different race has fallen from 9 per cent in 1999 to 6 per cent in 2008 and to 2 per cent in 2018. In Bosnia, the proportion has varied from 24 per cent in 1998, 13 per cent in 2001, 14 per cent in 2008 and then back up to 23 per cent in 2019. Those taking the view that most people cannot be trusted in Britain has varied between 40 per cent at its lowest to 71 per cent at its highest proportion, whilst in Bosnia the figure has ranged from 72 per cent in 1998 to a peak of 90 per cent in 2019. It is important to note that the rising proportion of people in both countries with generalised mistrust of others is concerning and potentially threatens participation.

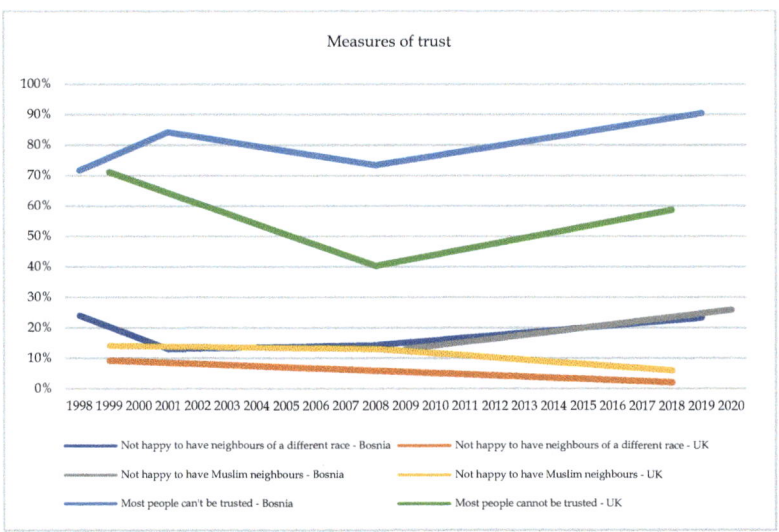

Figure 2.2E

On the question of what people think about the constitutional structure in Britain, a Parliamentary Committee found that trust in ministers, parliamentarians and civil servants has been in a state of

---

Europe from the Middle East and efforts to tackle terrorism, by so-called Islamic groups, in other countries). The fact that there is a correlation with people expressing a desire not to live with people of "another race" points perhaps to a need for further study.

decline and suggested a written constitution in order to bolster public confidence in existing structures (HoC 2014). The referendum for Britain to leave the EU and the constitutional implications of that have clearly prompted people to think about constitutional rules. For example, a poll of 3,000 representative voters carried out by Politico (2019) found that 40 per cent thought that it was acceptable for the Prime Minister to suspend Parliament "in order to deliver no-deal", whilst 41 per cent did not think it was acceptable (the remainder did not know). Approximately 68 per cent of "leavers" thought it was acceptable compared to 16 per cent of "remainers" (Cooper and Pagel 2019). Remain voters were also asked if blocking Parliament would be acceptable to achieve the opposite result (revoking the Article 50 trigger for Brexit), but 59 per cent of remain voters thought that this scenario was unacceptable (and 59 per cent of overall voters with only 21 per cent who thought it would be acceptable).

Does this demonstrate that remain voters are more constitutionally minded than leave voters, or, have the views of remain voters on the importance of constitutional rules been shaped by a prime minister who has repeatedly committed to taking any measures necessary including, apparently, breaking the law to realise Brexit? (Ibid) Clearly, the need for such protections is most apparent in the context of a binary referendum when the rights and interests of different groups are at stake and the Prime Minister is content to privilege the rights of one of those groups at the expense of others. Interestingly, when leave voters were reminded that the unconstitutional measures like the suspension of parliament could be used to achieve an outcome they did not prefer (such as revoking the Art. 50 trigger for Brexit), more people had second thoughts about it being a good idea (Cooper and Pagel 2019). The order of the questions also made a significant difference to leave-voter responses. Approximately 72 per cent of leavers who were presented with the no-deal scenario first thought that it would be acceptable, but that figure dropped to 63 per cent if they saw a scenario that countenanced a remain-Prime Minister unilaterally revoking Art. 50.

British respondents were also asked if they were worried about the state of democracy in Britain (Cooper and Pagel 2019). Around 84 per cent of remain-voters said they were "fairly worried" or "very worried" about the state of democracy, and 66 per cent of leave voters also said they were worried about democracy in Britain, demonstrating a level of dissatisfaction with present structures albeit likely for different reasons (i.e., the Prime Minister's breaking of constitutional conventions *versus* Parliament's perceived role in hindering Brexit). Similarly, in Bosnia, survey data suggests that few people feel satisfied with the current political and democratic arrangements. There are high levels of overall dissatisfaction with the direction in which the country was perceived to be moving, with 87 per cent saying that the country was moving in the wrong direction at a State-wide level; 86 per cent for the Federation and 81 per cent for the RS. Since 2015, the proportion of Bosnians reporting that things were going in the wrong direction has remained over 85 per cent (NDI 2019, 5). Support for EU accession remains strong among Bosniaks and Croats (at 88 per cent and 75 per cent respectively) and is slightly favoured among Bosnian Serbs (54 per cent) (Ibid, 10). When asked if they believed that political leaders and parties are working in good faith to achieve EU accession, only 9 per cent responded "yes", with the rest saying either "some are/some are not (50 per cent) and 39 per cent simply saying "no".

The political settlement in Bosnia is seen to negatively impact many areas of life. When asked about media freedom, 66 per cent see "political influence" as the greatest obstacle to freedom of media in Bosnia (whilst 81 per cent said that public broadcasters' editorial policy should be independent and impartial). Around 81 per cent agreed that corruption in Bosnia "begins with the political parties, and that we need to reform the way parties work if we are going to address public corruption in Bosnia" (NDI 2019, 31).

Interestingly, there was some degree of optimism about the potential for reform measures to reduce public corruption in Bosnia (NDI 2019). A majority of people thought that every possible measure suggested to them would be either "very effective" or "somewhat effective" in reducing corruption, including: reducing or eliminating party funding through State and entity budgets (44 per cent very effective, 34 per cent somewhat effective); implementation and enforcement of transparency requirements for party spending (36 per cent very effective, 38 per cent somewhat effective); regulation of the party registration process (32 per cent very effective, 39 per cent somewhat effective) and increasing the number of signatures required to get on the ballot (29 per cent very effective, 40 per cent somewhat effective). Similarly, 36 per cent said they would support political party reform and only 16 per cent said they would not (the rest responded "maybe").

What does this data tell us combined with the *European Values Survey* data highlighted above? Broadly speaking, there are high levels of dissatisfaction about the way in which Bosnians are governed and little faith that things will get better under the present arrangements. A 2012 study on local election voters in Bosnia found that the most popular reason for not voting is that "it will not help me" (Puhalo and Perisic 2013). There is, however, clearly appetite for change and, in particular, a feeling that better regulation of, and legal control over, political parties would improve the situation. In this context, it is understandable that, whilst citizens express a desire for things to change, they do not see participation in conventional political processes as the best route to that.

2.4 Problem of political apathy

The broad analysis of Britain's and Bosnia's respective political cultures above shows that, while both countries clearly face various challenges, they appear to have broad markers of a long-term participant orientation. Yet, as noted above, it has commonly been suggested that low levels of voting turnout and other political problems in Bosnia are a product of fundamental or intrinsic anti-democratic or non-participant orientation "at the core of the nation's political culture" (United Nations Security Council 2011).

Clearly, many, if not all, modern-day democracies encounter the challenge of significant apathy among their populaces, so why is Bosnia particularly associated with the label in comparison to other nations, both within and outside of the region? It is true to say that political participation in Bosnia has not been particularly high. All the conventional measures of democratic participation in the last 20 years show low electoral turnout, low levels of political protest/activism, decreasing social participation (i.e., membership in civil society organisations) and low party membership.

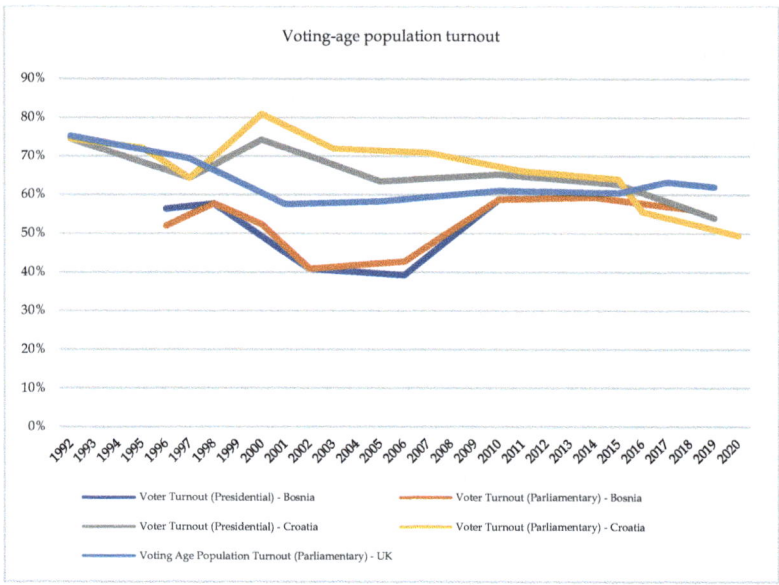

Figure 2.2F

Appendix 1 shows that voter turnout in the last 20 years has consistently been under 60 per cent, although as Figure 2.2F shows, Bosnia, Croatia and Britain have all experienced falling voter turnout over the last 20 years; with the most recent parliamentary elections producing a turnout amongst the voting age populations of 56 per cent, 49 per cent and 62 per cent respectively (IDEA, n.d.).[81]

---

[81] There seems to be widely varying figures for turnout in Bosnia for the 1996 presidential election. The International Crisis Group (19966) put the figure at 103.9 per cent. IDEA places the figure at 60.32 per cent (56.35 per cent if considering voter age population). I wish to highlight the discrepancy without going into detail behind it. See International Crisis Group (2007) and Belloni (2007, 91).

Data from the *European Values Survey* and *World Values Survey* (Appendix 2) demonstrates that active political participation has generally been low in Bosnia in the last 20 years. Between 1998 and 2008, for example, except for signing petitions, no more than 10 per cent of people had joined in boycotts, lawful demonstrations, unofficial strikes, or were active members[82] of political parties. Although the most recent data from 2019 does show an uptick in conventional measures of participation. What could explain the apparent political apathy and, in particular, the seemingly apathetic Bosnian population? Do the figures actually show a crippling politically apathetic populous?

Following almost £5.1 billion in pledged aid for post war reconstruction (ICG 1999), deep international involvement in the political process through the High Representative, and thousands of internationally funded civil society projects, the explanation for Bosnia's failure to have democratised sufficiently quickly (and have accountable political elites) has been put squarely on political culture. At its extreme, the explanation is a kind of historical determinism whereby Ottoman influence split the region between the European Habsburgian States (Croatia and Slovenia) from the Balkan Ottoman States—the latter being characterised by political fragmentation, bitter 'tribal' feuding, archaic social structures and corrupt habits.[83] It was in a sense that very clash between Huntington's enlightened West and the backward East and is a legacy which apparently persists in Bosnia (Batt 2007, 74).

Some have sensibly dismissed certain such views outright: "Indeed, we cannot identify with the ethnocentric view of the Balkans as a territory where 'Turkish dominance caused permanent retardation'" (Cabada, Ladislay, and Hösch 1998, 80). The

---

[82] Party membership has declined from a high of 11 per cent in 1998 in Bosnia to 4.4 per cent in 2008 although the figure in Croatia has increased from 2.8 per cent in 1996 to 6.9 per cent in 2008.

[83] This can be dismissed outright for the Habsburgians could equally be charged with leaving a legacy of the kind of ethnic tribal nationalism that has become a feature of Balkan politics. In addition, Greece and other former Ottoman States (Romania and Bulgaria) have acceded to the European Union as functioning democracies.

persistence of the view, however, endures. Kasapović (2005) confidently surmises that

> "In more than five centuries of shared history, the members of the three major religious and ethnic communities never permanently, unitedly [sic] and massively stood behind one State. Only one community would do so, while the members of the other two would be adversaries or enemies of the incumbent ruling power. This centuries-old division was also manifested in the 1990s in the different attitude of the three communities to the idea of an independent Bosnian State" (Kasapovic 2005, 3).

The enduring legacy of socialism is a more salient factor for other academics, who note the particular hardship in developing a rich civil society due to an apparent inherited civic passivity from the socialist regime (Vozab 2012, 2). Jasiewicz (2007) more coherently argues that the communists replaced 'natural' horizontal ties of civil society with vertical ones whereby the State had a controlling influence in both public and private social relations. The mass upheavals in Eastern Europe in the 1990's and in Yugoslavia could only partially restore long-lasting grass roots level bonds and permanently destroyed formal organisations creating vertical ties. The result, he argues, is that East-Europeans are apt at getting organised in times of crisis but "seem indifferent, if not helpless, when it comes to managing their day-to-day affairs. Social atomization and anomie, induced along with the introduction of communist regimes decades ago, remain in place" (Jasiewicz 2007, 208). The absence of strong formal organisations he believes helps the proliferation of cronyism and corruption as only informal, personal ties can help get things done.

Mudde (2007) has gone deeper into the associational aspect noting that trust is the crucial cultural component that has been impacted by communism. He argues that 'generalised trust' (trust in people generally both known and strangers) has been undermined at the expense of small-scale experience-based trust, for instance, by the economy of favours and 'particularised trust' (trust of one's own kind).[84] Eastern European States show

---

[84] See further, Håkansson and Sjöholm (2005) on 'partial trust' or 'particularised trust'.

apparently high levels of particularised trust far more than Western States especially when it comes to ethnic bonds which would suggest that "civic engagement may create a less civil and less trusting society" (Mudde 2007, 223).[85]

Path dependent explanations about democratic participation are highly suspect especially where a concept as nebulous as culture is apparently the main causal variable. They raise many unanswered questions—how far do inherited political cultural legacies last? What does it take for inherited legacies to be dislodged? How quickly can new political culture emerge? The analysis below uses Croatia as a comparative case study. Given the different paths Croatia and Bosnia have taken following the war and the relative political success of Croatia as an EU member State the comparison is immensely useful in analysing variations, if any, in culture.

The statistical data on Bosnia demonstrates that: people are not as apathetic as they seem although they are slightly more apathetic (on conventional measures) in Bosnia than in Croatia (See Appendices 1, 2 and 3); measures of non-participant orientation are very similar in both Bosnia and Croatia, therefore, the higher apathy in Bosnia cannot be explained merely by referring to 'culture'; if anything the cultural measures are more promising in Bosnia than in Croatia (See Appendices 4a and 4b); non-participant orientation is split by attitudes towards political structure or systemic measures and a-systemic measures. A-systemic measures concerning current politics and the government have become increasingly anti-government since 1996 (See Appendices 4 and 5). Systemic measures have remained constant since 1996 in terms of general attitudes towards democracy but in terms of attitudes towards Bosnia as a unified State views remain complex and disparate.

Appendix 1 demonstrates that, until the most recent elections, turnout has generally been higher in Croatia than in Bosnia yet there is no clear downward trend in participation in Bosnia since the late 1990s. Additionally, the 2018 parliamentary and

---

[85] See further, UNDP (2009).

presidential elections in Bosnia saw voting-age population turnouts of 56 per cent, whilst the 2019 presidential election and 2020 parliamentary elections in Croatia saw only 54 per cent and 50 per cent respectively. Croatia almost had 80 per cent turnout in 2000, the highest since independence, partly due to the death of President Tuđman in December 1999, increasing media plurality and the growth of civil society organisations encouraging voter participation (Fisher 2006). Bosnia in 2010 had higher turnout figures in both the presidential and parliamentary elections than the first post-war elections. Appendix 2 shows that over the last 15 years measures for active political participation have all increased in both countries and at the most recent survey are now very similar. Most measures show less than one percentage point difference between Bosnia and Croatia on the proportion joining in boycotts, attending lawful demonstrations and joining a strike. Signing petitions is the only exception, in which a far greater proportion in Croatia responded positively. In Croatia, after sharp falls in participation in signing petitions and unofficial strikes during the Tuđman years (probably explained by intimidation and reprisals) the trend has since been increasing.

That is not the full picture, however. Measures of latent participation (i.e., building capacity for political participation in the future) when the relevant questions were last asked by the European Values Survey (2008) would suggest that Bosnia has higher latent participation rates than Croatia which is seeing rapidly decreasing levels of latent participation. This means that it is more likely for a Bosnian to frequently discuss politics with friends or belong to some kind of community, political or religious group. Remarkably, people who stated that they are *not* a member of a voluntary organisation were 17.6 per cent in Bosnia whereas the figure in Croatia was 58.5 per cent (See Appendix 3a).

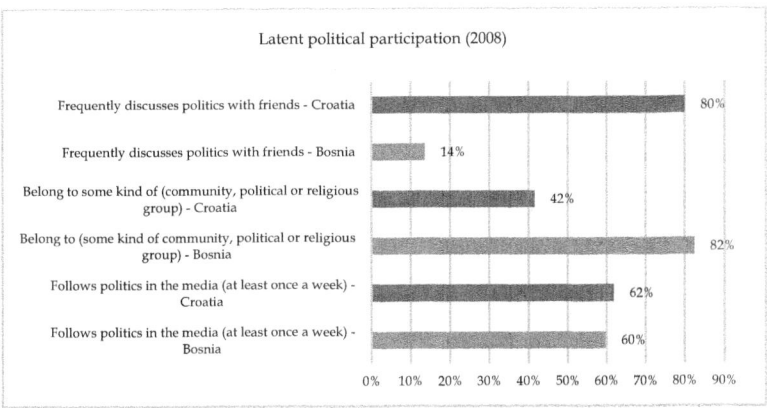

Figure 2.2G

In the most recent European Values Survey, instead of asking a general question about whether or not individuals followed politics in the media, the question was broken down by different news platforms (See Appendix 3b). It is notable that across every platform (radio, social media, TV and newspapers), a higher proportion of Bosnians used the relevant platform to follow politics. Again, this suggests that the population maintains an interest and engagement with politics, harbouring the capacity for future political engagement or involvement. This included almost half of Bosnians following politics on social media at least once a week, and 67 per cent following politics on TV with the same frequency.

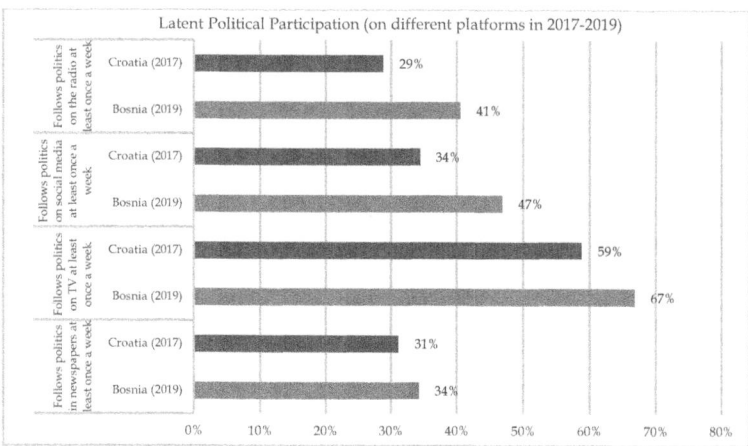

Figure 2.2F

In Croatia, following the demise of Tudman, politics has focussed on bread-and-butter issues. As Appendix 3 shows, people are increasingly less inclined to join voluntary groups, follow politics in the news, or discuss politics with friends. Under Tudman with little prospect of change the "public granted increased approval to whatever means necessary to bring about change" (Kuntz 2011, 233). They are not as Kuntz (2011) suggests "engaging increasingly with society, but not with the political sphere." In fact, the data shows that Croatians are actually taking an increasingly active part in the mainstream political processes — party membership, signing protests, joining boycotts are all on the increase. But the propensity to engage (i.e., the desire and will to engage) is on the wane — it is a case of a developing indifferent culture maybe because 'things aren't so bad'.

In Bosnia, the inclination to participate, though not in mainstream political action *per se*, actually seems to be increasing in the past 10 years but trust in government is falling. Those saying they have a great deal or quite a lot of trust in the government has fallen from 69 per cent in 1998 to 17.8 per cent in 2019. Similarly, in Croatia that proportion has fallen from 50 per cent in 1996 to 8.7 per cent in 2017 (See Appendix 4a). As Kuntz (2011, 238) notes "In Croatia, participatory habits surged in a nationalist regime lacking democratic institutions yet declined under more democratic institutions. Institutions alone, it appears, cannot prevent nor sustain participatory habits." But institutions *do* impact conventional forms of participation and attitudes towards participating.

The fact that the measure for latent non-participation is not increasing sharply for Bosnians would suggest that Bosnians have very promising potential for political action if we are to consider awareness of political issues and membership of voluntary organisations as indicators of possible future mobilisation. But could, perhaps, the relatively higher levels of political apathy of Bosnians, which is really political resignation to mainstream political participation, be because of culture?

> "I dissolved
> And streamed
> Streamwards
> Riverwards
> Seawards
> Now here I am
>
> Now here I am
> Without myself
>
> Bitter
>
> How can I go back
> To whence I sprang?"
>
> - Mak Dizdar (2009), *The Stone Sleeper* [86]

3. "Going back to whence I sprang": assessing apathy

The discussion in Chapter 2 demonstrates that understanding the true nature of Bosnian political culture is a more complex exercise than some have assumed.[87] It is certainly true that, according to all the available evidence, there are strong anti-government feelings and a severe lack of trust in political parties. That, however, does not necessarily mean that Bosnians are not interested in politics. It also does not mean that they do not have a latent potential to participate more in formal processes in the future. The problem for many people may be that the political system is genuinely incapable of providing for meaningful policy change or improving their lives. The reason for this is political elites' failure to compromise on policy issues, endemic corrupt practises and divisive ethnic-nationalist rhetoric which means that progressive action on pressing socio-economic issues is unlikely. This Chapter considers the key markers for Bosnian political culture in detail and, in particular, whether the people have a participant or non-

---

[86] A poem called "A Text About Spring" by Mak Dizdar [1917-1971] (2009, 35).
[87] As noted in the Introduction, Bosnia and Herzegovina is referred to throughout as "Bosnia".

participant orientation. It will explain some of the institutional underpinnings of the problem of political apathy. By doing so it challenges the assumption that the inherent culture of the people or an (unavoidable) historical legacy causes the poor political engagement that we now see.

3.1 A-systemic orientations

Negative orientation towards political behaviour, as discussed in Chapter 2, can fall into two categories. The first is an *a-systemic* orientation that engenders a total lack of interest in politics; the markers of which are people expressing no importance of politics in life and no confidence in government. The second is an *anti-systemic* orientation that challenges the fundamental system; the markers of which are people believing that having a democratic system is bad *per se*, the economy in a democracy runs badly or the political system as it was before was much better. If Bosnian society is fundamentally non-participant in nature, one would expect attitudes characterised by a total lack of interest in politics and a belief that democratic systems are inherently bad.

In this context, the key *a-systemic* measures of non-participant orientation are interesting and demonstrate that Croatia has a far more non-participant orientation (and growing) than Bosnia, and this is despite the reform measures taken by Croatia prior to acceding to the EU. People expressing no confidence in political institutions has increased in both countries, as shown by Appendix 4b, although the proportion has remained higher in Croatia for every institution in every year surveyed. For example, the proportion of people expressing no confidence in the political parties has been rapidly increasing in both countries, from 14 per cent in 1998 in Bosnia to 53.9 per cent in 2019, compared to 20 per cent in Croatia in 1996 to 63.8 per cent in 2019. Fascinatingly, the number of people saying that politics is not at all important in their lives was rapidly declining in Croatia during the Tuđman years declining from 33.3 per cent in 1996 to 20.2 per cent in 1999 and has since been slowly rising again. It rose to its highest level in the last survey of 2019 and stood at 41.9 per cent. In Bosnia, from 1998 to

2001, the figure rose from 21 per cent to 28.6 per cent but has fallen since to 20.6 per cent in 2008 and then to 25.5 per cent in 2019. People expressing 'no interest in politics at all' increased in Croatia from 23.1 per cent in 1996 to 39.1 per cent in 2017 despite the demise of Tudman's anti-democratic legacy. In Bosnia, it has increased from 16.6 per cent in 1998 to almost exactly the same proportion as Croatia (39.2 per cent) in 2017.

Appendices 4a, 4b and 4c show that the markers of political culture are constantly changing, and these changes are likely shaped by the political environment. It is evident that Bosnia enjoys a slightly more favourable participant orientation (when considering *a-systemic* issues) than Croatia but the difference between them is not considerable. If that is the case, then it is difficult to argue that higher levels of apparent political apathy in Bosnia, than its neighbours in the region, can be explained by a non-participant culture. That is simply not the case. Batt (2007) astutely recognises that "political weaknesses conventionally attributed to the 'Balkans' as a region are by no means immutable; nor are such defects unique to the region" (Batt 2007, 74).

In fact, if we are to look at political culture historically, any supposed apathy induced by communism would be hard to substantiate in the case of former Yugoslav countries such as Bosnia. Distinguishing Yugoslavia from the USSR was the economic system of self-management. Kuntz (2011, 223) notes that self-management was designed to produce a highly decentralized economy, in contrast to the central planning of the Soviet Gosplan. In Bosnia, this partly meant placing decision-making in the hands of the workers. Elements of civic and economic responsibility were introduced as long term commitments: 20 per cent of people had served in workers' councils, 7 per cent in local community councils, 6 per cent in apartment/house councils, and 4 per cent in municipal councils (Ibid, 224). People from Yugoslavia freely travelled to Europe and Europeans frequently travelled to Yugoslavia which led to cultural exchange and the exchange of political ideas. Civic society, however, of the type described in Chapter 2, was restricted largely to those of higher socio-economic status. Membership of communist bodies, like the League of Communists, was restricted by criteria such as being atheist. Any legacy which was inherited in Croatia and Bosnia was, therefore, mixed but we can confidently surmise that they were not the usual 'communist' basket cases (Ibid, 226). That Yugoslavia was indeed an exception is demonstrated by pre-war data collected by Hodson, Sekulic and Massey (cited in Kuntz 2011) showing a direct correlation between levels of diversity and levels of tolerance on a republic-by-republic basis; measures which on paper are very conducive to democratic practice (See further sub-chapter 2.1).

Krajnc's (2012) work supports the findings of this book by identifying that the post-Yugoslav population is almost as protest oriented (i.e., inclined to signing a petition, joining in boycotts, attending lawful or peaceful demonstrations) as citizens in western countries, and more so than many of today's EU member States. For example, the narrow differences between Bosnia and Britain on key markers of political culture, as set out in sub-chapter 2.3, despite their vastly different democratic histories, shows that poor governance and democratic fragility does not necessarily correspond to non-participant orientations amongst the general population. Krajnc (2012) also observes that within post-Yugoslav States protest participation is positively associated with pro-democratic orientations—again confirming the findings of this book. Krajnc (2012, 13) verifies that, in the post-Yugoslav context, levels of political participation have a weak association with levels of socio-economic development. Therefore, political apathy in the post Yugoslav States must be explained by something other than economics and political culture.

While the inclination to protest declined in the first decade following the collapse of communism, it is on the rise in almost all the post-Yugoslav States other than in Bosnia.[88] So why is Bosnia an

---

[88] As will be noted in sub-chapter 3.4, there are two factors which are relevant to the issue of protest in Bosnia. The only substantial country-wide protest, post-war, took place in 2014. The reason for this exception, as explained by Dalila Sadinlija (2020) in a conversation, is because of two simple reasons: 1. People are still traumatized that any major protest would lead to violence and then

exception? It is safe to say that the usual aspects of political culture cannot be the prime reason for relatively higher political apathy in Bosnia. What then can persuasively explain the democratic deficit in Bosnia? Is it that Bosnia as a multi-ethnic State is the problem?

3.2 Anti-systemic orientations

Appendix 5 shows that non-participant attitudes towards the democratic system have remained fairly constant and are not particularly *anti-systemic* in either Bosnia or Croatia. The proportion of respondents who said that having a democratic system was very bad has fluctuated from 2.2 per cent in 1998, 1.9 per cent in 2001, 4.1 per cent in 2008 and 3.2 per cent in 2019 in Bosnia. The figures have remained between 0.2 per cent and 2.4 per cent in Croatia during the same period.

The figures for whether the economy runs badly in a democracy are below 7 per cent in both countries with marginal difference, although in 2008 the figure was higher in Croatia than in Bosnia. An analysis based on the socialist legacy might have expected much higher figures given the very poor economic situation in Bosnia, but people's views are not extreme at all. The key structural figure of whether people thought 'the system as it was before [under Yugoslavia] was very good' shows that in Croatia the figure increased from 1.3 per cent (1996) to 2 per cent (1999) and in Bosnia from 5.2 per cent (1998) to 19.5 per cent (2001). This massive increase indicates that people in the first decade following independence in Bosnia hardened their views about the democratic system relative to the system under Yugoslavia as a result of their practical experience of "democracy" in the intervening years; although their views about democracy *per se* are

---

violence to armed conflict (the "as long as there's no shooting" or "samo nek' ne puca" mantra); 2. The only attempt at protest demonstrated that nothing could be changed with protests so they people do not see a point in them anymore. Sadinlija notes: "the only recent notable protests were tied to the two unsolved death cases of two young men (Dragičević in Banja Luka and Memić in Sarajevo), with the protests in Banja Luka taking a political overtone."

not anti-democratic as noted earlier. That the relative difference was not a product of inheritance is clear.

The logic of the civil war of 1992 to 1995 which pitted Bosnian Croat against Bosnian Serb against Bosniak and the consequences of widespread ethnic cleansing has meant that the three constituent peoples have been segmented geographically; if they were not, as some argue, already segmented by historical processes (Kasapović 2005) The latter view claims that relations between the three peoples has always been characterised by political competition always in some imposed form of consociational agreement either the millet system under Ottoman rule, or proportional systems under the Hapsburgs or the Yugoslavs. Another consociational agreement has been put in place today under Dayton.

There is no doubt that it is possible to gauge, or more precisely poll, secessionist sentiments amongst citizens of the three communal groups. The authenticity and endurance, however, of such sentiment is highly suspect. It is dependent, as such sentiments are, on many factors including elite manipulation, group preferences, or recent societal or communal group conflict. The Dayton Peace Agreement could be seen one in a series of concessions (to ethno-nationalists) that sought to protect the territorial integrity of Bosnia at the expense of having a State consensually legitimised by all the people. In fact, if the people were to have had a referendum after the war it would have been likely (and likely still) that at least the Bosnian Serbs and Bosnian Croats would want separate independent mono-ethnic States. Kasapović (2005) speculates that that risks of a constitutional referendum is "incalculable" and "must remain under the international military and political protectorate" (Kasapović 2005, 5).

The outcome, therefore, is political impasse, inefficiency and intractability as foundational division, instigated by the Dayton Peace Agreement, is replicated at a day-to-day political level.

Gallup polls indicate that 87 per cent of Serb respondents would support the creation of an independent State *if* a majority of its citizens voted that way (Gallup Balkan Monitor 2010, 4). More recent polls suggest that the number of people supporting secession has declined to around 50%.[89] Aside from the fact that knowledge about how the majority might vote can significantly skew individual choices (see Chapter 5) it is clear that some degree of support for secession is readily available or can be rapidly mobilised. That support is particularly forthcoming when others are perceived to support that choice and especially if others are seen as belonging to the same ethnic group. Incidentally, a majority of both Bosnian Croats and Bosniaks (63 per cent and 80 per cent, respectively) did not agree with a potential secession of the RS in the event of a referendum. In general, a majority of Bosnian Croats (56 per cent) and Bosniaks (86 per cent) do not agree with the idea of dividing up Bosnia any further, although 61 per cent of Bosnian Serbs state that they would be in favour (Nezavisne Novine 2015). Alarmingly, a 2015 survey found that approximately two out of three respondents stated that they do not believe that that Bosnia could "break up peacefully" (Office of the UN Resident Coordinator 2015, 50).

The conclusion that some academics would reach is that there never was, and never will be, the will to create a single unified State of Bosnia and it is fruitless to try and do so (Economist, "T.J.", 2011). Parish (2011), coming dangerously close to endorsing the outcome of ethnic cleansing, remarks that "the future of Bosnia without heavy international oversight is inevitable disintegration. The international community should now be focused upon managing the side-effects of this ugly process rather than striving to keep alive a discredited vision" (Parish 2011). This view, however, is morally and politically indefensible (Bassuener 2011).[90]

---

[89] For instance, a poll of 1,414 respondents in July 2015 in the RS found that only around 54 per cent would support independence. When asked "should the independence of Republika Srpska be a political goal for the future?", 54 per cent of respondents circled the answer "yes", 15 per cent answered "no", while 31 per cent "no attitude on this issue" (Nezavisne Novine 2015).

[90] See further remarks in this respect by Bassuener (2011): "...Parish's prescription — the internationally managed dissolution of the State — would be a disastrous failure, as well as demanding far deeper and more risky international engagement than would be required to prevent State dissolution. There is no way that the country could be divided in a consensual, nonviolent fashion. A deceptively simplistic solution, it would create more problems than

What might separation mean, for instance, for the 30 per cent of the Bosnian Croat National Assembly (Sabor) that did not vote for independence in 2000 or the remaining Bosnian Serbs or Bosniaks in a future 'Croat entity'? Should they also be entitled to 'independence'? What had Croatian independence meant for Croats living in the Republic of Serbian Krajina many of whom were expelled when that Republic was proclaimed? What did it then mean for the Croatian Serbs living in that same 'Republic' 240,000 of whom who had fled or were expelled following Croatia's Operation Storm towards the end of the war? Might the Muslims of Sandzak in Serbia also obtain independence? And what of the Muslim populations of Macedonia and Montenegro and the Serbs in Kosovo? Horowitz (2003, 5-6) is right to suggest that secession is never an answer to the problem of apparent ethnic conflict or violence particularly for the minorities that will inevitably be created by the division. Without ethnic cleansing, assimilation, forced or voluntary population transfer, mono-ethnic States, at least at face value, are not possible to create (Arendt 1948; Mann 1998; Derrida 2002; Taylor 2002).

The appropriate prescription is the one elaborated by the Badinter Commission on 11 January 1992, namely that: "that the Serbian population in Bosnia and Herzegovina and Croatia is entitled to all the rights concerned to minorities and ethnic groups [...]" and "that the Republics must afford the members of those minorities and ethnic groups all the human rights and fundamental freedoms recognized in international law, including, where appropriate, the right to choose their nationality" (Pellet 1992, 178). One might substitute the name of the relevant ethnic group so that the prescription applies to any State. Indeed, that prescription in some ways was partly built into the Bosnian constitution (as noted in Chapter 4), namely that individual human rights and freedoms cannot be amended by any future constitutional change (Art. X.2, Bosnian constitution). But following the war achieving such a State based on the consent of all of the people was and remains the

---

it would solve, further destabilize the region, and fuel nationalist politics in neighbouring Serbia and Croatia."

ultimate challenge as is prescribing the right medicine for the particular malady.

3.3 Absence of interpersonal trust

Hayden (2007, 2020) has gone further than most and says that the war if anything was an extension of a deeper tradition in Bosnia of segregation, intolerance and division.

> "The international imagining of a single Bosnian community despite the efforts of large, non-random segments of the population to reject it actually delegitimizes the beliefs of many of "the natives" themselves [...] Indeed the whole enterprise of the international community in postwar Bosnia may be seen as an attempt to create a single society in a setting in which a large portion of the natives successfully fought a war to prevent just that result" (Hayden 2007, 105).

Hayden (2021) 25 years after the war, and after countless studies on multi-confessionalism in Bosnia, continues to maintain his stance: "Bosnia isn't the way it is because of Dayton; rather, Dayton is the way it is because of the nature of Bosnian society."

Hayden's arguments are not persuasive for both historical and cultural reasons. On the historical context, the independence referendum which was held on 29 February and 1 March 1992 was required by the Badinter Commission as a condition of European Economic Community recognition of Bosnia and indeed recognition of all other Republics seceding from the former Yugoslavia (Pellet 1992, 178-185). Before the referendum and independence, Bosnia faced being dominated by Belgrade: Slovenia and Croatia were already independent, and the Bosnian Serbs in January 1992 (encouraged by Belgrade) held a referendum to secede—cleansing had also already begun (Serwer 2019). It was following those events that the state-wide referendum was held, and the people voted in favour of an independent Bosnia, as confirmed by the Parliamentary Assembly on 4 March 1992 with 63.37 per cent of people voting "yes" to independence. Even assuming, however, that each and every Bosniak entitled to vote turned up and said yes, that would only amount to 43.47 per cent which must have indicated support amongst other groups. In fact, at a political level, both the HDZ and SDA the two major parties supported independence. The majority of Serbs in Bosnia, in particular in the then non-segregated 'Serb areas', were led and encouraged by elites of the SDS to boycott the independence referendum (as did the Muslims and Croats in the January 1992 Bosnian Serb referendum). It is not as clear-cut as concluding that all "the Bosnian Serbs and Herzegovinian Croats" rejected the idea of a Bosnian State at its inception (Bieber 2006, 42; Imamovic 2006, 389; Mahmutćehajić 2011) or that a groundswell of popular feeling propelled ordinary people into war. Rather the conflict was instigated, planned and orchestrated by the ethno-nationalist elites suing for power and control as Yugoslavia dissolved; a dissolution that occurred because of a nationalist attempt, led primarily by Milošević, to recentralise control in Belgrade (Duijzings 2007; Serwer 2019).

With regards to the cultural context, Bosnia was a highly intermingled society even if one is to accept the debateable position that Bosnian society was not 'imagined' as a nation by its constituents at the time. In fact, with "very few exceptions (notably Drvar), the municipalities were not mono-national, but had at least two of the three communities living in close proximity" (Bieber 2006, 31). Bosnia demonstrated a tradition of tolerance and co-existence against which a war was waged (for complex reasons) in an attempt to create mono-ethnic nation-states (Mahmutćehajić 2003, 2005; Bieber 2006). It was not in fact until the late 1980s that exclusive ethno-nationalist perspectives took root in Bosnia. Even as late as 1990 the electoral law banned political parties organized along ethnic lines; a decision that was widely supported in opinion polls at the time (Bieber 2006, 16, 19).

The war in itself was a reason for intervention by the international community. It was this intervention that challenged the behaviour of those elites willing to support the use of ethnic cleansing (directly or indirectly) to create mono-ethnic States.

It would be unsurprising if large sections of the population rejected co-existence during the war and may continue to do so not least because genocide, war crimes and crimes against humanity on a large scale may not have made pluralism particularly appealing (Håkansson and Hargreaves 2004). Borneman (2007, 110) rightly notes that "we might lessen the incidence of such behaviour not by replicating but only by changing the understandings of the people involved."

People's preferences are not stable and are constantly shifting, shaped as they are by time, space and circumstance. Whilst people may have been inclined to reject cultural pluralism at particular points in time, such as during a war, they need not do so for time immemorial. Studies suggest that trust is fragile in that it often requires time to build and sustain but it is also easily broken (McGregor 1967).[91]

That division and segregation is far from engrained in Bosnian political culture is amply demonstrated by statistics today on trust, tolerance and reciprocity which are all measures of participant political cultures. The commonplace view is that the lack of interpersonal trust (particularly generalised trust) in Bosnia is the key hindrance to future reform and accommodation amongst the people. That view is widespread even amongst international NGOs: "There is no agreement on the future, and elite mistrust reflects a genuine absence of social trust" (ICG 2009, 2). Many such views rely on surveys showing that generalised trust is very low in Bosnia. As Appendix 6 shows, in 2019 approximately 90 per cent of Bosnians said that "most people can't be trusted." This figure is little different from the figure in neighbouring Croatia (82.4 per cent) and, in fact, in 2008 the figure in Croatia was a full seven per cent higher than in Bosnia.

The relevant measures of trust, however, are not so much generalised trust but partial trust which relates to trust between different ethnic groups. It is the failure of inter-ethnic accommodation which is the problem. If generalised trust was the only salient variable, then there should be political paralysis in Croatia too. But here too the studies are instructive and actually counterintuitive.

---

[91] See further, Hakansson and Sjoholm (2007).

Hakansson and Sjoholm (2004), (2007), for instance, convincingly demonstrate that people in Bosnia, aside from regional differences, tend to show low levels of trust in all other people irrespective of their ethnic belongings. In addition, there is a strong correlation between trust for one's own ethnic group and corresponding trust for people from other ethnic groups. People, therefore, unlikely to trust their own are unlikely to trust others notwithstanding their ethnic group. Hakansson and Sjoholm (2007, 972) suggest that the strong effects of ethnicity on trust is likely to be explained by the fact that those regions that were ethnically heterogeneous were also the worst hit by the war as seen in countless areas across Bosnia including, among many others, Una-Sana, Goražde, Drina Valley, Prijedor, Srebrenica, and Brčko. Those regions, therefore, are likely to suffer from low trust both partial and generalised.

What the available figures show is that the underlying population is not averse to cross-ethnic political compromise because their mistrust of other ethnic groups is paralleled by mistrust of their own. In any case, figures for ethnic accommodation and trust between groups have been very variable—as demonstrated at Appendix 6 and below. Gallup polls confirm respondents showed more trust in members of the other religious groups than they had in 2006; each ethnic group was inclined to trust another either 'a lot' or 'somewhat' between 60-70 per cent which was around 10 per cent more than five years prior (ICG 2009, 2).

Yet such figures should not come as a surprise unless there is a fixation with anecdotal evidence and an exclusive focus on *post-war* Bosnia. Studies by Hodson, Sekulic and Massey (1994) confirm a direct correlation between levels of diversity/integration and levels of tolerance on a republic-by-republic basis in the former Yugoslavia; measures which on the face of it are very conducive to democratic practice on a non-ethno-nationalist basis. They found that Bosnia—the most diverse of the Yugoslav Republics—had the highest average tolerance score of 3.88, while the province of Kosovo—the least diverse part of Yugoslavia—had the lowest score of 1.71.⁹² Croatia came second after Bosnia. In addition, Bosnian citizens generally do not feel that their ethnic groups are particularly threatened today, and concerns are going down over time. According to research from the UN, the proportion responding that their ethic group is "fairly" or "a lot" threatened has fallen from 24.3 per cent in 2013 to 12.8 per cent in 2015. Those saying that their ethnic group is "a little" or "not at all" threatened has risen from 34.7 per cent to 59.3 per cent in the same period (Office of the UN Resident Coordinator 2015, 23).

The results demonstrate that despite increasing tolerance or willingness to accommodate the 'Other' among the people, paradoxically, there are sentiments existing within society, for a myriad of reasons, that can reinforce division and separation. Inter-ethnic accommodation is precluded by design because of the structures imposed by the Bosnian constitution and the failure of the Dayton arrangements to have ensured full refugee return. Growing political apathy, or more accurately resignation, in Bosnia and the persistence of secessionist sentiment is primarily explained by the behaviour of political elites performing in the institutional framework created by the supposed international guarantors of Bosnia's fledgling democracy (Perry 2015; Bassuener 2020). The statistics indicate that poor political institutions are not only responsible for the cause of the growth in a non-participant orientation but may also be the principal cause of political apathy in the country (when looking at conventional measures).

Culture, unexplained, cannot be the primary reason for relatively higher apathy in Bosnia. What follows is an analysis which suggests that the ethno-nationalist territorial divisions occurring as a result of the war are certainly problematic but far more so are the ethno-nationalist divisions within State institutions created by the Bosnian constitution. Institutions which give preference to a model of representation based on exclusive ethno-territorial control by the political parties (Hulsey 2017).

---

92   See further, Kuntz (2011, 223, 226).

3.4 Institutions as an explanation

Recognising that there is no wide acceptance or consensus on the institutional structure created following the Dayton Peace Agreement, elites endorse extreme anti-systemic positions. As Chapter 5 demonstrates using rational choice models, politics in Bosnia is characterised by elites making maximalist claims that favour one's own group at the expense of the legitimacy of the State. Elites have proven unable and unwilling to compromise on many issues (Koneska 2014, 56). Whilst the people are not anti-democratic, they are forced in many ways to support anti-democratic and anti-State political elites, as this sub-chapter will highlight.

Whilst the Dayton Peace Agreement has undoubtably helped to secure relative peace and stability in the short run, it has failed to discourage threats of secession or secure a stable or participatory decision-making political process (Koneska 2017). For instance, in June 2011, the RS threatened a referendum to secede as a way of extracting concessions on reforms to the judiciary—international actors duly obliged (International Crisis Group 2011).[93] The precedent, however, was set much earlier. The HDZ, in 2000, convened a National Assembly (Sabor) of all Croatian parties to pass a referendum on independence of the 'Croat cantons' unless the reform of electoral laws (implemented by the Office of the High Representative) which would reduce Croatian influence in the House of Peoples was revoked. The referendum went ahead with high turnout and 70 per cent of the voters were in favour of the establishment of a Croatian entity in the Federation. The impasse only ended when the international community caved in on the electoral law reform and the HDZ rescinded the Croatian self-rule referendum (Kasapović 2005, 18).

---

[93] More recently, Milorad Dodik, SNSD leader and Serb member of the Bosnian Presidency, proposed a law to replace foreign judges on Bosnia's Constitutional Court with domestic ones, threatening secession if his proposal was turned down and warning that RS was "on a path towards leaving Bosnia and Herzegovina" (N1 Sarajevo 2020). It followed four weeks of boycotts by RS representatives of the Parliamentary Assembly, Council of Ministers and the Bosnian presidency (Kovačević 2020).

Furthermore, Suljagic (2020) has persuasively argued that Serbia and Croatia pursue "tribalization" of Bosnia in the interests of their own regional dominance, "through intelligence and diplomatic operations as well as cultural and educational policies", aiming ultimately to "co-opt the Serb and Croat ethnic populations in the country," dividing the three major ethnic groups further.

One must caution, though, that the potential for secessionist sentiment is far from a wholesale endorsement of secession or secessionist government, notwithstanding the highly unfavourable economic, political and social circumstances for making secession viable. For instance, elected leaders in the RS openly talk of secession or greater autonomy despite increasing disavowal from NATO and the EU (and on occasion Serbia).[94] Yet, the electorates in both federal entities, at the same time, are generally highly dissatisfied and disillusioned by elites representing them. People who stated they have no confidence in the government at all has rapidly increased from 6 per cent in 1998 to 33.9 per cent in 2008 and 45.8 per cent in 2019 (See Appendix 4). In terms of government performance at a State level the assessment of respondents in both entities has remained negative—92 per cent of respondents in the Federation and 82 per cent in the RS said they thought that the government's work was poor or only fair: a level that, in aggregate, has been rather stable since 2008.[95] Around two-thirds of Bosnian Serb respondents (64 per cent) were convinced that the RS government was doing a poor or only a fair job although there was an increase of 13 percentage points saying it was doing a good job (Gallup Balkans Monitor 2010, 5). A UNDP (2013) poll found only 37 per cent of Serbs trusted the RS government. In the Federation, respondents had a much more negative assessment of their entity leaders with 91 per cent (roughly stable since 2008) saying that their

---

[94] Statements made by the current President of the RS and leader of SNSD, Milorad Dodik, are noted in sub-chapter 3.4.
[95] There is some cause for optimism as this dissatisfaction has softened in past years: while in the Federation, in 2008, 70 per cent of interviewees stated that the government's performance was poor, that figure has decreased to 57 per cent in 2010. In RS, this same figure dropped from 56 per cent to 26 per cent in the 2008-2010 timeframe (Gallup Balkans Monitor 2010, 2).

performance was poor or only fair (Gallup Balkans Monitor 2010, 10). Bassuener (2020, 223) captures these dynamics which may lead to real conflict perfectly:

> "despite pooh-poohing of the actual risk by peace brokers and their successors in the EU (who wish to avoid responsibility), the dynamic in the country could be shifted completely with the violent conflict potential in-country at present. Citizens from all standpoints are aware of the risk. The instability is not a mirage conjured solely for extortion and blackmail purposes (though it is used in this fashion). This is an *actual*, not fraudulent, hostage situation. The difference in BiH's case is that the Western peace brokers have made *themselves* hostages and can free themselves, while BiH citizens have not willingly (and wilfully) subjected themselves to the peace cartel. Nor can they singlehandedly change the dynamic."

As noted in Chapter 4, the political agenda is largely focused on maintaining the status quo (Bahtić-Kunrath 2011). Until the 2010 elections, Bosnia was governed by Bosniak, Bosnian Croat and Bosnian Serb parties with exclusionary nationalist agendas, with one exception between 2000 and 2002.[96] However, demonstrating that cross-ethnic political compromise is possible, 2005 marked the formal integration of the Bosniak Army of the Republic of Bosnia and Herzegovina, the Bosnian Serbs Army of Republika Srpska ("VRS") and the Croatian Defence Council into a single national army following years of intensive informal negotiations (Koneska 2014, 93).[97] As a result, in 2006, Bosnia joined NATO's Partnership for Peace programme in 2006, allowing Bosnia to build a relationship with NATO which could help support future accession. The integration of the armies demonstrated that change driven on a cross-ethnic basis is possible even for such a symbolically significant institution (Basta 2016, 965).

Furthermore, the October 2010 elections saw the election of a compromise-oriented Bosniak President[98] and the re-election of a non-nationalist Croat President, Zeljko Komšić. This was partly

---

[96] This coalition between multi-ethnic parties was called "Democratic Alliance for Change."
[97] For further discussion of the conditions allowing for successful military reform see Koneska (2014, 91-96).
[98] Bakir Izetbegović, member of SDA against the relatively hard-line Haris Silajdžić.

because of high numbers of Bosniak votes who voted in the Croat List instead of their 'own' Bosniak List but also because the two major Croat parties, HDZ and HDZ 1990 split due to personality politics. Komšić was re-elected to serve his third term in 2018. The SDP which campaigns on a non-nationalist ticket, although its political base is largely Bosniak, also won the largest number of seats in 2010. At the same time, however, a senior member of the SNSD,[99] campaigning on grounds to secede from Bosnia, was re-elected as the Serb representative of the State Presidency. Importantly, none were the leaders of the strongest parties in their communities (SDA, HDZ and SNSD, respectively), which weakened their policymaking ability and link with the entities.[100] Just as critically, it took almost fourteen months to form a State government after the elections; then the fledgling coalition broke down less than six months later, on 31 May 2012. Belloni has remarked that:

> "Since the early twentieth century Bosnians have often voted along ethno-nationalist lines when given the opportunity, and it is not startling that they continue to do so in the aftermath of the 1992–95 war, particularly given that constitutional and electoral norms favour ethnic voting."

The elections in 2010, however, show just the opposite in the Federation; Bosnians (at least in the Federation where there is greater plurality) are happy to vote on non-ethnic lines. The constitutional and electoral norms, however, encourage anything but especially when moderates in the Federation are met by intransigent elites in the RS and reciprocally intransigent opponents in the Federation. Keil and Hulsey (2020, 4) have shown that ethnic parties only can compete on ethno-territorial lines because ethnic cleansing created homogenous electoral districts — the entities serve as electoral districts for Bosnian central institutions and the cantons for elections in the Federation. In the RS, there are no cantons but

---

[99] Nebojša Radmanović.
[100] The International Crisis Group suggests that the Presidency is now overshadowed by the leaders of the six ruling parties who since September 2011 have been meeting behind closed doors to agree on policy (ICG 2012, 15).

there is no diversity because 80 per cent of the population is now Bosnian Serb largely because of ethnic cleaning.

The picture since 2010 has been more mixed. On the one hand, it is clear that there are numerous self-declared non-nationalist or civic parties which consistently receive about a quarter of the vote in the Federation (Hulsey and Keil 2020, 5). They tend to compete with ethnic parties for votes. The main civic parties are the long-established SDP, a successor to the Bosnian League of Communists, NS and the recently created DF which split from SDP. On the other hand, just as the support for non-nationalist parties has been stable in the Federation so has been the support for ethno-nationalist ones (although not for the same ethno-nationalist parties). In the RS there is stability in support for ethno-nationalist parties because there is little ethnic diversity any longer. The consequence of this is paralysis. For instance, civic parties such as the SDP, which have been part of several governing coalitions, have been unable to push for wider constitutional change because of severe competition with ethnic parties over access to resources and assets. That competition has been in the context of institutionalised ethnic division and strict power-sharing mechanisms all of which has led to state capture by the ethno-nationalist parties (Hulsey and Keil 2020, 5, 8).[101]

For example, in 2018, despite broad voter dissatisfaction, entrenched ethnic parties won the largest vote shares (CRS 2019, 10). Analysis of the results shows that the country remains "dominated by ethnic parties who are mainly focused on their own patronage networks" (Hulsey and Keil 2020, 17). Inter-ethnic divisions "continue to dominate political life" (Koneska 2014, 25) and the electoral system "discourages a shift from nationalist to inter-ethnic interest parties, as it draws the constituencies around ethno-territorial lines" (Bahtić-Kunrath 2011, 918). The dominant

---

[101] Keil (2018) defines 'state capture' as "efforts by either groups or individuals in the public and private sectors to influence, manipulate and shape laws, policies, regulations, decrees and other government policies to their advantage. This can take place for the private gain of individuals (often through corruption), but it can also occur on a wider scale in which actors take control over large parts of the institutional set-up in order to push a certain policy agenda and promote their own interests." (See further, Hellman, Jones and Kaufmann 2000).

parties in the RS are almost non-existent in the Federation and *vice versa* (Keil and Hulsey 2020, 4, 8) and there are no state-wide elections for any of Bosnia's central institutions.

But why has support for the ethnic-national parties been relatively stable? Electoral rules with strict criteria for ethnic representation favour the ethno-nationalist parties because the electoral districts themselves are homogenous. That is coupled with low barriers to entry to becoming a party[102] at cantonal and entity level (Hulsey and Keil 2020, 6). This creates a perverse incentive to gain power for personal reasons leading to fragmentation of parties but also a bigger incentive for parties with big bases to wield power and money to keep control of their pool of electors. This is seen with the dominance of the same parties competing with one another for only the votes of one ethnic group.

The parties have developed strong patronage and clientelist networks with links to businesses, banks, and the public sector which has essentially resulted in party capture of the state (Perry and Keil 2018; Keil 2018). At a regional level, there is a fight between powerful parties of the same ethnicity largely to access key resources, budgets, employment opportunities and control over state assets (Hulsey 2018, Piacentini 2019). To that is added the (still) explicit efforts to stoke hostility and exploit ethno-nationalist tensions for political gain. Ethnic party leaders are regularly accused of inflaming nationalist tensions and manipulating historical memory to distract from corruption and win elections (Touquet 2015; Mujanovic 2015; OHR 2018, 2020).

In the face of this crippling paralysis, it is hardly surprising that party membership is rapidly declining, and trust in government is at an all-time low. Distrust in political parties is immensely high—62.3 per cent of Bosnian citizens surveyed in 2015 said they did not trust the parties at all, which, combined with those who said, "I do not have much trust" (14.9 per cent) amounted to 77.2 per cent who do distrust political parties (Analytika 2015). In another survey by the UN Resident Coordinator (2015), 88.2 per cent of those asked said that political elites "represented a

---

[102] A 3 per cent threshold sometimes applies.

problem." This was the institution seen as most problematic, followed by the judiciary at 66.5 per cent and then the Bosnian constitution and the current structure of the country at 46.3 per cent (UN Resident Coordinator 2015, 15). A majority in each of the three ethnic groups do not feel that somebody was speaking for them at a political level (Gallup Balkans Monitor 2010). There is cross-entity and cross-ethnicity dissatisfaction in how political elites represent people's interests, for instance, when it comes to the issues of corruption, economic management, political representation and justice (Raduta 2015).

Significant majorities are willing to accept changes to the Bosnian constitution, for instance, to support EU accession yet elites are unable to agree on such reforms (Toal and Maksić 2011, 70) despite the fact that EU and NATO integration is one of the few areas in which there is a general convergence of attitudes amongst political elites from across ethnic groups (Koneska 2014, 85). As discussed in Chapter 2, survey research documents people's anger towards the political classes and their deep distrust of parties and politicians. A vast majority believe the country is heading in the wrong direction, and an estimated 170,000 individuals (disproportionately the young and the skilled) emigrated between 2013 and 2019 (CRS 2019, 9). Dissatisfaction with education and healthcare, insecurity, and nepotism have been cited as key motives to emigrate (Oxford Economics 2018).

Aside from the paralysis that ethno-nationalist politicians induce, other institutional explanations for political apathy can include among other things: the frequency of elections—there have been nineteen electoral races between 1996 and 2006 and frequent changes to the electoral rules (Toal and Maksić 2011, 70)—for instance, the changes to the parliamentary electoral rules in 2000 were proposed by the OSCE just a month before elections;[103] a complex electoral system that encourages centrifugal outcomes—it encourages ethnic competition and extreme party fragmentation at

---

[103] In fact, since its introduction in 2001, the Electoral Law of Bosnia was amended 18 times, often within a few months or even days before the election (OSCE). See also Kasapović (2005, 17).

the expense of accommodation and compromise—due to political gridlocks, the previous State-level Parliament adopted only twelve new laws over the course of its 2014-2018 term (Ivkovic 2018); and the widespread perception that the role played by international organisations has made political participation and the election of local politicians redundant (Belloni 2007, 92). This has arguably been further exposed by the coronavirus crisis (OHR 2020).

We may in some ways have come full circle, as Denitch (1993, 5) writing about the death of Yugoslavia remarked: "The fragmentation in the 1980s of a relatively successful State and economy (compared to the rest of Eastern Europe) exacerbated an already excessive dependence on international and transnational institutions remote from the citizens and unaffected by democratic control." This does not appear to be something that those in power are interested in addressing. The European Commission's 2020 Report on Bosnia found that "no progress had been made in ensuring an enabling environment for civil society. Meaningful and systematic consultations with civil society remain to be ensured" (EC 2020, 10).

As Koneska (2014, 8) notes in her study of Bosnia's (and Macedonia's) post-conflict recoveries, institutions matter and are crucial to shaping the behaviour of political actors: "they constrain or enable certain actors' identities and thus their interests." Moreover, political elites can work to undermine any strong organized interests from outside entrenched systems of party-political control, fearing that organised interest groups could threaten their political power (Kapidžić 2019, 2).

Recent examples show that where civil society *has* mobilised to influence those in authority, there has been a failure by elites to listen or to act in response, and evidence of efforts to shut down opposition.

The first example is the rise in the number of non-nationalist and civic parties particularly in the bigger cantons such as Sarajevo and Tuzla. For the first time they successfully formed a coalition in 2018 to exclude the SDA (although it later broke down due to personality politics). In Tuzla, in 2014, there were also protests by industrial workers who went unpaid for several months (Hulsey and Keil 2020, 14-15). These protests quickly spread across the Federation and the RS and forced cantonal governments to resign before the protests dissipated. As Keil notes, these were remarkable cross-ethnic protests that threatened those in power and were the largest, most organised symbol of dissatisfaction with the status quo since the end of the war in 1995 (Ibid, 15). More importantly, these protests led to the formation of several plenums in the Federation in which people from all backgrounds came together to structurally discuss the country's problems and possible solutions (Keil 2014).

The second striking case study of civil society mobilisation, is the "Justice for David" movement in Banja Luka. Following the suspicious death in March 2018 of a young Bosnian Serb, David Dragičević, and allegations of an institutional cover-up of his murder, thousands of protestors took to the street to demand a new investigation into his death. By July 2018, campaigners had carried out at least 100 protests (Monitor 2018). A "Justice for David" Facebook group currently has around 240,000 members (Pravda Za Davida n.d.). What began as a campaign by Mr Dragičević's father became "the largest anti-government demonstration in Bosnia in decades" and supporters come from across the three majority ethnic groups (Surk 2019).

Yet the scale of the campaign has not been matched by the political will to address the case. The National Assembly of RS formed an inquiry May 2018 which found that there was more than enough evidence that Mr Dragičević was murdered and that the police had not performed their duties properly. The report called on the public prosecutor to respond to its findings. The report, however, was rejected by a majority in the National Assembly and over two years later no official prosecutorial decisions have been made. In addition, in 2019 and 2020 there appears to have been increasing attempts by police to restrict the freedom of assembly of "Justice for David" activists, who have been subject to intimidation, fines, and judicial prosecution (European Commission 2020, 11).

Activists are on trial in Banja Luka for, among other things, shouting 'justice' on the streets (Ibid, 30).[104]

Today, international intervention is the one of the main reasons used by elites to excuse their policy and personal failings. A case of missing opportunities and attributing blame elsewhere; elites have no incentive to be accountable to their populations and populations have no legal means of forcing them to be so. Greenberg (2010, 52) observes that international conceptions of participation, and certainly those espoused by the European Union, have some ideological assumptions at work. They ignore heterogeneity in respect of class, education, region, but most significantly ethnicity which means that they do not take into account local circumstances and preferences.

International organisations now require cross-ethnic participation amongst citizens in Bosnia to be considered successful, yet the institutional structure imposed on Bosnians belies that goal. We must return ultimately to the socio-psychological underpinnings of many theories of participation: people's deep-seated desires, fears and needs. Withdrawal from, and apathy towards, political institutions and structures particularly in Bosnia are a way of distancing oneself from what is seen as failure, corruption and compromised political processes (Ibid, 61). Both the plenum movement and the Justice for David campaign distanced themselves from party politics (Hulsey and Keil 2020, 17) and that shows the real opportunity for action by the people: they may be empowered from below but not directed from above.

Bosnia is experiencing an increase in political apathy as a result of poor governance primarily caused by the institutional framework. It is the kind of poor governance that galvanised people into action upon the death of Tuđman in Croatia. What this might mean is that latent political participation that is on the rise in Bosnia can be channelled into the political domain or risk that such latent

---

[104] Johannes Hanh, then European Commissioner for European Neighbourhood Policy and Enlargement Negotiations, described the long delays in the judicial follow up of this and similar cases as unacceptable (European Western Balkans 2020).

capacity becomes dangerously anti-systemic. In the UN Resident Coordinator's study in 2015, almost two out of three respondents (65 per cent) said it was "likely" that "further deterioration of the situation in Bosnia could lead to some kind of social unrest." Only 7.6 per cent said it was not likely at all, and 23.4 per cent said, "not very likely." Compared to the same survey carried out in 2013, respondents predicted social unrest more frequently — only 46 per cent said it was likely previously. It seems that the threat is real and growing. Worryingly, they also predicted that violent protests (44.3 per cent), followed by an increase in criminal acts (31.7 per cent) would be the most probable manifestations of the further deterioration of the situation in the country (UN Resident Coordinator 2015, 47).

What is required is not a moral lesson to Bosnian citizens on the power of democratic political practice; for such practice (in the current institutional set-up) ultimately reinforces non-participant modes of behaviour. Also, political participation itself, as this book has demonstrated can be disastrously anti-systemic especially when structures are imposed from outside. Rather people and their representatives must be left, and their neighbours too, to face the hardships, dilemmas and difficulties of political life on their own terms. The successes, failures and compromises by those attempting to address those hardships will help build on what is already, in a non-conventional sense, an environment conducive for vibrant democratic life: Bosnia is indeed a land of tolerance of difference, reciprocity and trust. The international community may now help but they must not lead. For future constitutional reform, locally led and agreed initiatives will be critical if a sustainable, democratic, unified Bosnian polity based on citizen rights is to be achieved. It might be worth listening to the people. When asked in 2015 "who do you believe may be the catalysts for positive changes in the country?" the top response was "youth" (65.7 per cent), followed by "citizens" (42.8 per cent), and then "authorities" (31.2 per cent), "intellectuals" (29.1 per cent) and finally the "international community" (26.5 per cent) (Office of the UN Resident Coordinator 2015, 23).

What are then the options for Bosnia in breaking the political impasse? Constitutional reform and linking such reform to the willingness amongst the population for ethnic accommodation and tolerance is the obvious answer, yet elite intransigence and the logic of the institutional structure provides no incentive for such reform (CRS 2019, 8). Playing the ethnic card in elections pays dividends and, sometimes, quite literally. ✥

> "Past time's thorns and switches
> past wizards and witches
> Our hands are still here but we still
> haven't clasped each other's hands
> We're still not free of their sorcery
>
> For we've still not found a cure
> Except this ancient lore
> Except this curse this prayer
> Except from river to river
> From Drina to Ukrina and Sava
> from Una and Sana to Rama
> and Neretva"
>
> - Mak Dizdar, *The Stone Sleeper* [105]

4. "We've still not found a cure": constitutional rules

4.1 Constitutional choice and change

This book began by considering the origins of constitutional theory and the fundamental disagreements which frame ideas about what a constitution is and what purpose it ought to serve. That is, if a constitution should have any instrumental purpose at all. Chapter 1 considered the imposition of a top-down constitution on the people and contrasted that with having a more inclusive, bottom-up, process of constitution-making. A more inclusive process would be where elements of the spirit of the people and their political culture could be summoned *in addition* to the people's approval of the letter of the constitutional rules (which become law). In this Chapter, the focus is on contemporary thinking about creating or changing constitutions.

Some constitutional scholars have moved beyond the philosophical fundamentals—rightly or wrongly—to analyse the impact of institutional systems, structures and rules on political elites and the people. Political elites are seen as embedded in

---

[105] An extract of a poem called "Madderfield" by Mak Dizdar [1917-1971] in Buturović (2002).

broader institutional structures or constitutional rules.[106] These institutional rules help determine outcomes (March and Olsen 1989, 2011). More importantly, institutional rules are seen as critical in mitigating or regulating ethnic conflict in divided societies (Horowitz 1991, 1993; McGarry and O'Leary 1993).

Formal institutional rules, however, are not the only way to mitigate or manage conflict. Others have considered that more effective strategies might be to change political elites or create exogenous shocks to the system that could make cooperation between elites necessary (March and Olsen 2011). Exogenous shocks might emanate, as they have in Bosnia, from the international community. It is arguable, in theory, that elites could be incentivised to act differently within the same set of institutional rules but, in practice, such policies have produced very mixed results as this Chapter will attempt to demonstrate.

Institutional rules, however, need not be formally written in a constitution. Informal rules and conventions of association can be equally important and institutionalised in a society through practice (North 1990; Foley 1989). Much of the analysis in <u>Chapters 2 and 3</u> was essentially concerned at gauging how receptive informal norms in Bosnia are to the Dayton-imposed institutional structures.[107] Successful political systems, as North (1993) puts it, "have evolved flexible institutional structures that can survive the shocks and changes that are a part of successful evolution. But these systems have been a product of long gestation. We do not know how to create adaptive efficiency in the short run." In more simple terms, the most successful political systems have had a long evolutionary history where there is some general acceptance of the "rules of the game" such that they have been internalised by most major political elites and the people.

Changing the formal rules and institutions when societies' underlying beliefs remain rigidly opposed will result in failed institutions. A failure, however, to change the formal rules and

---

[106] Political elites are often referred to in the literature as 'political agents'.
[107] As noted in the Introduction, Bosnia and Herzegovina is referred to throughout as "Bosnia".

institutions when belief systems are conducive to change imperils formal institutions. In summary, successful constitutional design is endogenous and from within (Voigt 2011; Dougherty and Julian 2011). The choices made by individuals when the status quo is abhorrent (for instance, during a war) is very different from the choices made when the status quo is agreeable (for instance, during peacetime) (McGann 2006).

Bosnia is seen as a case in point. The initial design of the Bosnian constitution at Dayton was formal and geared towards creating power-sharing, and in particular *'consociational'*, institutions to incentivise political elites to cooperate. Stability was the operative aim. The institutions, however, created at Dayton have not been adaptive to change at all and are far from cooperative. They are unresponsive to changes in society, which is all the more critical given that political culture is rarely fixed.[108] The Bosnian people have not had a choice on their constitution outside of conflict or at all. It is unarguable that they should, at least, have the possibility of that choice in the near future. Britain's constitutional arrangements, despite its flexibility, may also be considered for reappraisal as much as any other country's constitution. That is particularly imperative, if the current arrangements are found to be far removed from, or inattentive to, the political culture of its people.

The literature on *consociationalism* is predicated on the idea that elites co-operate and work together despite a lack of a political consensus or 'sharp plural divisions' within society (Lijphart 1977, 2; 2004; 2008). Constitutions, accordingly, in the consociational model, are imposed on the electorate with provisions for institutions inclined towards accommodation between political elites. Civic involvement in constitutional choice or locating constituent power in the people is seen by consociationalists as a grave mistake if there are historical divisions within society and there is a propensity towards despotism or entrenched group conflict (Arangio-Ruiz 1895; Elster 2012, 29-30).

---

[108] This is an issue addressed in Chapters 2 and 3.

As deep political cleavages are seen as unfavourable to democratic governance generally, consociational theory suggests that power sharing and group autonomy may moderate cleavages and allow democratisation (Lijphart 2004, 97).[109] Both consociationalists and non-consociationalists agree that constitutional choices creating rules and institutions for power sharing and autonomy are critical (Lijphart 2008; Horowitz 1993). The fierce disagreements, however, focus on which choices are optimal to help manage possible conflict.

Lijphart (2008) prescribes the following institutional choices in a constitution for divided societies, notably, regardless of their particular circumstances: parliamentary over presidential regimes; proportional representation (closed list) electoral systems (over majority rule); collegial executives that allow for coalitions; multi-party federal systems with bicameral legislatures; and high thresholds for amending a constitution. Constitutional rules and institutions are said to allow political elites to accommodate one another despite the intransigence of their divided people. Elites, according to the theory, co-operate for a number of reasons including external threats or international pressure (Cameron 1978), long term concern for the political system if divisive politics are pursued, or self-interested behaviour to extract rents from the system (Lijphart 1977, 182; Tsebelis 1990, 162).

When successful, consociational States should demonstrate high degrees of institutional trust amongst citizens, multiple and complementary identities among citizens, a high degree of identification by people with the State, and reconciliation and reciprocity amongst different communal groups (Kavish 2012, 7). The failure of consociational model is often attributed to shallow constitutional prescriptions having either insufficient grounding in either the interests of politicians or in careful diagnosis of what is likely to go wrong (Horowitz 1993, 35-38). For instance, sometimes consociational designs develop a preoccupation with numerical

---

[109] 'Power sharing' denotes the participation of all significant communal groups in political decision-making, especially at the executive level; 'group autonomy' means that these groups have authority to run their own internal affairs, especially in areas of education and culture.

balance rather than workability (Bahtić-Kunrath 2011). Power sharing is also universally applied with direct involvement of international actors which raises questions about the agency of the people who have to live with the arrangements as well the legitimacy of those imposed arrangements (Keil 2015). Those questions need to be balanced with the security and stability guarantees that those international actors might play in intervening and creating constitutional structures (Ibid, 354).

Power sharing may provide a convenient short-term mechanism for ending hostilities, but it may become a source of long-term tension. It can institutionalise the conflict that gave rise to the arrangements (Rothschild 2008; Murshed 2010). The reasons for this could include, *inter alia,* the following: asymmetric information about a peace agreement or a constitution and their interpretations; perceived group strengths between elites may differ and, therefore, may encourage opportunism; spoiler groups may hijack the new institutions and external guarantors of peace may not be sufficiently credible (Murshed 2010, 154). Roeder and Rothschild (2005, 12) propose 'power dividing' institutions as an alternative to power sharing in the long term. In summary, they prescribe fewer veto powers and more decentralised governance structures that act as checks and balances on executive powers. Many such prescriptions are either applied in Bosnia or are proposed as reforms. The challenge, though, is how to successfully implement such structures in a particular State and how power-dividing structures could receive the approval of political elites in post-conflict, deeply divided societies.

Other critics of consociationalism have argued that the prescriptions mandated in its models leave out the role of the people or the electorate. This can be problematic for three reasons. First, the people may not be as polarised as the literature might make out (Keech 1972; Barry 1975) and this is critically important in the case of Bosnia as the analysis in Chapters 2 and 3 sets out. Second, political elites may become completely unaccountable to the electorate and, therefore, their behaviour may stop being influenced by popular will and opinion (Barry 1975, 406). Third, elites may initiate conflict themselves or help to perpetuate it (De Ridder 1978). Indeed, cleavages may be mobilised by political elites to generate support for an elite issue arising from other sources of political competition (Tsebelis 1990, 163). This Chapter will consider whether the any of these features are common to both Britain and Bosnia.

The behavioural aspect of elite decision making is also critical in understanding the success or failure of consociational models with their emphasis on institutional design (Konig, Tsebelis and Debus 2010). The literature relates to how political elites maximise their chances of winning office by presenting their proposals in the electoral arena (Downs 1957; Strom 1999). In order to win, political elites must fulfil the wishes of, and remain faithful to, the median voter (Konig 2010, 272). Preferences of voters, however, may not be faithfully represented or translated by elites in the parliamentary arena because of the design of the electoral system, the legislative structure, and/or the nature of executive power. In fact, preferences of voters may not exist at all or voters may not be rational utility maximising agents they are assumed to be (Thaler and Sunstein 2009; Tversky and Kahneman 1974).

The literature on elite behaviour and decision-making is instructive for modelling the failure of the current institutional arrangements in Bosnia and lack of constitutional reform (Tsebelis 1995, 1999, 2000). It also allows us to see whether Britain does any better at the opposite end of the spectrum of constitutional design. How exactly does Bosnia fit into the consociational mould and how far might Britain be an exemplar?

4.2 Recurrent crisis and rarefied reform in Bosnia

Chapter 1 set out the basics of the Bosnian constitution as well as its unusual drafting history. It noted that without major reform in Bosnia a *probable* pathway out of its evident constitutional crisis is collapse. Some might dismiss such a view as being naïve and prone to hyperbole. They might say that there are many States, such as Japan or Germany, which had imposed upon them codified constitutional frameworks which have worked perfectly fine. On that view, all Bosnia needs is time, sensitive handling and incremental development. The current Bosnian High Representative, who is the guarantor of all civilian aspects of the Dayton Peace Agreement, said in October 2020 that: "For the past ten years I have talked about local ownership and not used my Bonn powers. It is logical if [Bosnia] is to be grown up and if you want to throw away the clutches and if you want them to walk on their own. We need to give locals chance to walk on their own."[110] There are two points that can place the High Representative's remarks into context.

The first point is about the success of imposed constitutions. The constitutions of Germany and Japan are not relevant comparators with Bosnia. Germany had by the end of the WWII no significant ethnic, religious, or other cleavages. Its then fascist government had committed heinous crimes to eradicate difference and create a homogenous society. That made acceptance of a constitutional settlement somewhat easier if difference of diversity is seen as a problem requiring a 'solution'. Imposition of a constitution was also easier as both Japan and Germany had lost catastrophic international armed conflicts. In contrast, Bosnia was emerging from a non-international armed conflict with no clear winner and with major architects of the war actively working to undermine the legitimacy of the constitution they had just agreed.

Using Germany as a comparator, one might wonder whether RS's Entity Constitution may indeed be considered, in a perverse sense, a success. In some ways, its institutions are far more streamlined and efficient than anywhere else in the country. That was easier to achieve as a result of large numbers of Bosnian Croats and Bosniaks being ethnically cleansed or forcibly displaced during the war from the RS. The whole region was previously highly mixed down to the village and hamlet (See Marko 2000, 95-97).

The second point is that divided or post-conflict societies do not necessarily have the luxury to wait for evolutionary processes to unfold. The High Representative's comments, therefore, whilst

---

[110] Pax, Webinar, 25 Year Anniversary of the Dayton Peace Agreement with Paul Williams and Valentino Inko, 15 Oct 2020—Pax—Meeting, 14:30 to 16:00 CET.

on the face of it seem to be arguing for Bosnian agency is setting them up to fail. That is particularly the case when the imposed structures from outside are not at all amenable to change. A major pathway from power-sharing arrangements like those in Bosnia is through collapse as seen, for instance, in Lebanon or Burundi or Iraq. The markers of a successful consociational State are trust amongst citizens, multiple and complementary identities, identification with the State, and reconciliation and reciprocity amongst different communal groups. Bosnia, however, demonstrates anything but despite the fact that consociational characteristics, establishing equality and proportional representation of Bosniaks, Croats and Serbs, are found within all the structures and institutions of the State (as set out below).

In Bosnia the decentralised asymmetric federation gives wide autonomy to two territorial entities (Art I.3, Bosnian constitution).[111] The Federation is highly decentralised with key features designed to ensure equality and power sharing between Bosnian Croats and Bosniaks within the executive and legislature.[112] The institutions were designed to ensure that the less numerical Croats (and decreasing ever since the war)[113] are not outvoted by the majority Bosniaks.

By contrast, the RS is highly autonomous and centralised. It has no cantons and no intermediate layer between the entity government and municipal governments and few consociational prescriptions given the homogeneity engineered during the war.[114] This is perplexing as the Dayton Peace Agreement allowed for the full return of refugees to pre-war homes but did not then require consociational prescriptions (for instance, cantonisation) in the RS

---

[111] The term 'federalism' is used as Dahl (2007) defines it: "a system in which some matters are exclusively within the competence of certain local units — cantons, states, provinces — and are constitutionally beyond the scope of the authority of the national government; and where certain other matters are constitutionally outside the scope of the authority of the smaller units". See further, Stepan (2011, 5).

[112] See further, Bose (2002, 241).

[113] Estimates suggest the figures are far below the 17 percent recorded in 1991 and could be as little as 10 per cent (ICG 2009, 10).

[114] See further, Bose (2002, 68-75).

to manage the ethnic heterogeneity which would have returned to the RS. Federal territorial autonomy in Bosnia necessarily entailed political autonomy to ethnically pure areas. (See Figure 1.3A).

The competencies of common State institutions are fairly limited, even excluding defence. These competencies are expressly set out in the Bosnian constitution (Art. III.1). Anything not specifically falling within the competency of the State is within the competency of the entities (Art. III.3.a, Bosnian constitution). The discrepancy on most policy issues between the two entities and the relatively weak powers accorded to State institutions makes unified, central government highly dysfunctional particular when minority vetoes are considered (See 4.2.4 below). Furthermore, the stability of Bosnia is constantly threatened by the failure of the entities to cooperate with one another within the joint institutions. Bosnian Croat and Bosniak elites challenge the legitimacy of the RS and the elites in the RS challenge necessary moves towards greater political integration or the expanding of critical State competencies (under Art III.4, Bosnian constitution).

Proportionality of representation within the executive, legislature and judiciary is a key feature of the Bosnian constitution. Seats in the Parliamentary Assembly are allocated on the basis of ethnic group membership. The House of Representatives must have two-thirds of the members from the Federation and no less than one-third of its members have to come from the RS through proportional representation. Strict parity rules apply to allocation of seats in the House of Peoples to the three constituent peoples and members are elected by proportional representation on a territorial and ethnic basis (Keil 2015). Similarly, there is a collective, rotating, three-member Presidency consisting of: a Bosniak and Bosnian Croat directly elected from the Federation and a Serb directly elected from the RS (Art. V, Bosnian constitution).[115] The Council of Ministers (CoM), which conducts most of the operational work of the government, must also have at least one member of each constituent people and one minority (Art. V.4.b, Bosnian constitution), however, the constitution generally does not stipulate

---

[115] See further, Bose (2002, 64-65).

from which ethnic group other representatives have to come. Quotas and parity rules, in general, apply to all State level institutions (Article IX.3, Bosnian constitution).[116]

There is a requirement in the Bosnian constitution for grand coalitions, representing all major ethnic groups, in order for a government to be properly constituted. Both branches of the government, the Presidency and the CoM, must be ethnically proportional and represent both entities. The CoM[117] is comprised of ministers drawn from both entities with a two thirds proportion from the Federation and one third from the RS but there are no ethnic quotes which makes the CoM (as well as the House of Representatives) unique among the Bosnian state institutions (Keil 2015). The chair and ministers within the CoM must each though be of different nationalities. There is a perception that the functioning of the CoM is as a reflection of the disunited governance between the entities as demonstrated by its inability to always propose jointly-agreed-upon policy to the Parliamentary Assembly (See further, sub-chapters 4.4 and 5.2). In reality, however, it is the only institution that presents the vast majority of legislation to the Parliamentary Assembly (approximately two thirds of all bills). The lack of formal veto mechanisms within the CoM means cross-party agreement is easier to reach. It is only later in the process that these bills fail because of other political elites from the same ethno-national parties vetoing the legislation in the Parliamentary Assembly.

Decisions are largely made by consensus or by qualified majorities in the Parliamentary Assembly subject to veto rights accorded to the three ethnic caucuses (See further Table 4.4A below). The Presidency decides by consensus although "if all efforts to reach consensus fail", decisions may be made by two members subject again to an ethnic veto (See further Table 4.4A below).[118] In essence mutual veto mechanisms are extended to all significant political groups, which are the three constituent peoples, in the

---

[116] See further, ICG (2012, 11).
[117] Functions of the Council of Ministers are set out at Art V.4, State Constitution.
[118] Article V.2c and 2d, Bosnian constitution.

executive and legislature. Majoritarian voting is, thereby, checked by essentially a requirement for consensus of all ethnic groups on 'important' issues. As elaborated on in sub-chapter 4.4, what precisely is important is of great contention.

Although consociational institutions and rules were prescribed at many levels of government there has been an acute failure to create the kind of accommodation that elites are meant to be interested in. The failure of consociation, as noted in sub-chapter 4.1, is attributed sometimes to an "insufficient grounding in the ongoing interests of politicians or in careful diagnosis of what was likely to go wrong" (Horowitz 1993). In Bosnia, however, the constitutional prescriptions in Annex IV would seem to have identified the "ongoing interests of politicians" very well; precisely encouraging and incentivising the pursuit of nationalist conflict by non-violent means now that the war had ended. What was likely to go wrong was ignored.

Criticisms at the time and ever since, particularly by those who felt the full brunt of war crimes, have focused on the idea that the division and segregation sought by certain wartime leaders was institutionalised and deplorable crimes rewarded. It is true that peace was only secured by obtaining the signatures of men who denied being behind the conflict, but all of whom were either indicted (and convicted) or would have been indicted (or convicted) for international crimes (Gaeta 1996, 152-161). These included President Slobodan Milošević who represented the Bosnian Serbs together with Momčilo Krajišnik; and President Franjo Tuđman who represented the Bosnian Croats (Gaeta 1996, 156, 161).

What has been done to try and remedy the institutional failures? Can political elites, at least, agree to create better accommodating institutions for the future? If not, why are elites unable to agree?

Previous proposals for reform

Bearing in mind the failure of the Bosnian constitution to produce sustainable and working central institutions without international intervention, there have been a number of constitutional reform proposals largely driven by the international community (Kavish 2012, 8). Many of these initiatives have been American or European led. This book does not consider executive actions, imposed actions as they are, by the Office of the High Representative ("OHR") even though the "vast majority of successful reform to date has come through direct intervention by the Office of the High Representative, who has final say on all legislative matters in the country" (Kavish 2012).[119] This book is concerned with proposals to revise the constitution with the involvement of local actors in a way that is inclusive, transparent and sustainable.

Annex IV, it should not be forgotten, was seen by its international progenitors as the interim Bosnian constitution with a view that substantial aspects of the constitution would be negotiated and agreed by political elites at a later date. Just the fact that it is still definitive in only its English form due to an unwillingness of elites to agree on its publication in the official languages of Bosnia is cause for amazement and despondency in equal measure. The substantial expanding of State competencies, given the general and somewhat limited competencies prescribed in Art. III.1 of the Bosnian constitution, are clear examples. The expansion of competencies allowed, *inter alia*, the: setting up of a court at the State level; transfer of responsibilities to the State in the fields of defence, intelligence, justice, indirect taxation, immigration and asylum; and State competency in electoral matters (Venice Commission 2005, 4, 7). The key caveat though is that the transfers or assumptions of the new competencies would have been highly unlikely without the direct leadership or intervention by the High Representative; very few were local initiatives which Art. III.5.a envisaged would be the case.

---

[119] The Dayton Peace Agreement established the OHR (Annex 10) and granted it considerable powers over implementation of civil aspects of the Agreement. The Peace Implementation Council ("PIC") is a group of 55 countries and international organizations "that sponsor and direct the peace implementation process." The 1997 PIC Conference in Bonn provided executive powers to the High Representative enabling him/her to impose legislation and remove any official obstructing the Dayton Peace Agreement.

Intervention from the international community in the face of elite intransigence is indicative of the precariousness of the reforms that have already been made to the Dayton-imposed system. Ethno-nationalist groups, least inclined to reform, try and rollback reforms or remove existing State competencies whenever they feel the international community is distracted, or otherwise unable or unwilling to intervene. The threatened actions of Milorad Dodik, leader of the SNSD and the Serb member of the Bosnian Presidency since 2018, are a case in point: the Indirect Taxation Authority, the State Court, State control over extradition policy, the intelligence agency, the Presidency of which he is part of, and the powers of the High Representative have all come under vociferous attack in an attempt to extract extra-legal concessions from other domestic actors or the international community (Parish 2011; Edwards 2019).

For consensual amendment of the provisions of the Bosnian constitution, agreement of the respective elites of the constituent peoples within the Parliamentary Assembly would be required with at least a two-thirds majority in the House of Representatives (Article X.1, Bosnian constitution). Even a constitutional decision of the House of Representatives could be subject to the 'vital interest' veto in the House of the Peoples. Essentially three people from the same ethnic constituency, in the House of the Peoples, can veto any amendment. The veto is not an easy hurdle to pass in Bosnia. It is the very definition of 'entrenchment'. Critically, however, any such constitutional amendment is subject to the ultimate safeguard for all of Bosnia's peoples: that no amendment could be made such that any of the guarantees of individual civil and political rights extensively detailed and incorporated by Annex IV could be diminished (Article X.2, Bosnian constitution).

There have been three major reform proposals as well as two important missives that have recommended reforms. All of these proposals failed either to garner sufficient support (at inception) or when put to a vote in State institutions: the Venice Commission recommendations in March 2005; the April Package of 2006; the Prud Agreement of 2008; the Butmir Process of 2009; and numerous attempts at implementation of the decision of the ECtHR in

December 2009 in the *Sejdic-Finci* case. A summary of the reform proposals and the reasons for failure are set out in Table 4.3A below.[120]

---

[120] A detailed comparison of constitutional reform provisions proposed by various institutions can be obtained from the Public International Law and Policy Group (PILPG).

TABLE 4.3A: SUMMARY OF REFORM PROPOSALS TO THE BOSNIAN CONSTITUTION

PROPOSAL OR MISSIVE NAME, DATE, INITIATOR	MAJOR FOCUS OF REFORM	CIVIC ROLE	STAGE OF FAILURE	NOMINAL ACCEPTANCE BY	REASON FOR FAILURE
Venice Commission Recommendations,[121] March 2005, International: Council of Europe Parliamentary Assembly	Articles II, III, IV, and V - Define 'vital interest' with narrow scope - Transfer presidency responsibilities to PM - Single indirectly elected weak president - Abolish House of Peoples	No civic role at procedural level or substantive level – i.e., either during reform process or as a focus of reform as considered desirable but unworkable	No wholesale adoption but many elements incorporated in April Package	SDA, SNSD Rejected by: SBiH, HDZ 1990	Only recommendations (elements of which incorporated in April Package)
April Package Proposals, Autumn 2005–April 2006, International: US[122]	Articles II, III, IV, and V - Transfer presidency responsibilities to PM - Indirectly elected weak president - Limited powers for HoP - State has competency over EU integration	No civic involvement at procedural or substantive level – during reform process or as a focus of reform effort	Parliamentary Assembly: House of Representatives	SDA, SNSD Rejected by: SBiH, HDZ 1990	Lost by two votes. Perceived failure to address Croat concerns (2 HDZ 1990 and 1 SDA MP defected). Bosniak hardliners wanted centralisation (SBiH). Smaller parties

[121] Also known as the 'European Commission for Democracy through Law'. It is the Council of Europe's expert body on constitutional affairs. It delivered an "Opinion on the Constitutional Situation in Bosnia And Herzegovina and The Powers of the High Representative" (Venice Commission 2005).

[122] In March 2006, under US pressure, three major ethnic parties (SDA, HDZ, SDS) and four smaller parties (SDP, SNSD, HNZ and PDP) signed the plan for constitutional reform and ushered it into the parliamentary procedure.

				refused to give consent[123]
Prud Agreement Proposals, November 2008–February 2009, Domestic: Three major political parties—SDA, HDZ, SNSD	Restructuring of State into four units between the central State and the municipal level and incorporation of Brčko into jurisdiction of State institutions	No civic involvement at procedural level – during reform process	At discussion stage	SDA Rejected by: SBiH, ultimately all parties.	Each group wanted own entity unit based on ethnicity. Croats wished to create exclusive entity (despite non-contiguous dispersion of population) and RS wished to maintain the RS as an undivided canton.
Butmir Process Proposals, October 2009–December 2009, International: Joint US/EU	- Presidency powers to PM with strong CoM - Indirectly elected weak president - HoP converted into HoR committee - Expand HoR - More State powers[124] - State competency over EU integration	No civic involvement at procedural or substantive level – during reform process or as a focus of reform effort	At discussion stage	SDA Rejected by: All major parties by 2009	Widespread rejection amongst most major parties across a number of issues (seen as being far too radical)

---

[123] See further, ICG (2009, 2011, 2012).
[124] Including inter alia defence, intelligence, and external security and the establishment of a single indirect system of taxation.

Sejdic-Finci[125] Implementation Recommendations, December 2009–Present, International: Judgment of ECtHR in a case brought before the court	Article IV and V. Election to HoP and State Presidency should be open to all ethnic groups[126]	Limited civic role at procedural level and no civic role at substantive level (as a focus of reform effort)	At discussion stage	All parties accept principle but not specifics[127]	Proposal A: All Croat parties rejected - insistence on Croat president elected by 'Croat electorate' though not case since 2006.[128] Proposal B: Still outstanding

---

[125] European Court of Human Rights. *Sejdic and Finci v. Bosnia and Herzegovina* (application nos. 27996/06 and 34836/06)

[126] Proposal A: Open run for Presidency but 2/3 allocation for Federation, 1/3 for RS. Proposal B: Direct elections but no member of same ethnicity nor from 'others'. Split districts.

[127] Proposal A: SDA, SNSD – Rejected by: HDZ BiH and HDZ 1990. Proposal B: SDA, HDZ, SNSD – Rejected by: SBB, SBiH, SDP

[128] ICG interviews, Bakir Izetbegović, member of presidency of Bosnia (SDA), Sarajevo, 2 March 2012. All Croat parties rejected it. ICG interviews, leading Croat politicians, Mostar and Sarajevo, March-May 2012 (ICG 2012, 5).

A remarkable feature of each of the major reform proposals are the lack of *any* civic involvement in the reform process or any willingness on the part of political parties to include the people. That is despite civil society groups in Bosnia trying—despite short-term, piecemeal and limited international support—to become more involved in constitutional reform debates since at least 2009 (Perry and Keil 2015, 44). The proposals themselves present few, if any, institutional structures providing for greater civic involvement in the political process let alone civic involvement not based on narrow ethno-nationalist interest (Perry and Keil 2015). The reason for this is predicated on the received wisdom that there are deeply engrained ethnic hatreds in society that must be regulated by elites (as set out in sub-chapter 3.3 above) and that the people are not democratically mature. Even on the 25th anniversary of the Dayton Agreement, in 2020, the High Representative was talking about "removing the training wheels" from the Bosnians; elites, therefore, are presumably best placed to ensure co-operation, compromise and stability.[129]

Reform processes are led by ethno-nationalist elites, decided (or more accurately vetoed) by ethno-nationalist elites and would seem largely beneficial to ethno-nationalist elites. These political elites would contend that their actions are in favour of protecting their ethnic group. Yet, all the objective evidence shows that they are responsible for creating, fomenting and exploiting ethno-nationalist division that they claim to represent (Belloni 2001, 173).

In March 2005, the European Commission for Democracy through Law ("Venice Commission") issued a report at the request of the Bosnian government to facilitate future constitutional deliberations in Bosnia. The 2005 report noted that "there is a powerful wish [among the citizens of Bosnia] for the country to participate in European integration with the final aim of becoming a member of the EU" but critically found that "it is unthinkable that

---

[129] See further, Caspersen (2004) who argues given the deep division in society, the maximalist positions of elites and the numerical balance between groups (all of which are exogenous) it would be premature to sacrifice the 'stability' induced by consociational institutions in Bosnia.

[Bosnia] can make real progress with the present constitutional arrangements" (Ibid).

The Venice Commission report, and the April 2006 Package that followed it, made recommendations, for instance, that attempted to introduce stronger parliamentary processes (a strong prime minister, a strong effectively uni-cameral legislature,[130] and a weak indirectly elected single State President) for all the consociational benefits for power sharing such an arrangement *should* entail. Both failed to garner sufficient support notwithstanding that they would still have meant much continuity for elite-led decision making. It was just that they were not accommodating enough to ethno-national interests. In that respect, it should be noted that the Presidency is the only State level institution directly elected and accountable to the electorate and has worked relatively well in Bosnia without the extent of deadlock seen in the other State institutions although it excludes election of anyone who is not Bosniak, Bosnian Croat or Bosnian Serb (ICG 2012, 4; Kavish 2012, 13).

The Prud Agreement proposals, from November 2008 to January 2009, failed to generate concrete proposals other than some high-level political principles for reform (See Table 4.3A; Perry 2015). The Butmir Process proposals followed, as the US and the EU attempted to resuscitate some of the amendments in the April Package. These included greater powers for the House of Representatives and the Council of Ministers, decreasing the powers of the Presidency, limiting the role of the House of Peoples, and creating a stronger prime minister-led executive (Perry 2015; ICG, 2009). The Butmir Process also failed to earn support among political elites and ended without agreement.

In December 2009, the ECtHR issued its judgment in the case of *Sejdić and Finci v Bosnia and Herzegovina*, which established that certain aspects of the provisions of the Bosnian constitution — prohibiting the election of 'Others', such as Jews and Roma, to the House of Peoples and the Presidency — were in contravention of the

---

[130] Although the April package suggested a House of Peoples with very weak powers limited to consideration of VNI only.

ECHR.¹³¹ The Council of Europe, NATO, the OSCE and the European Commission have made it clear that the constitution must undergo reform to provide for greater equality (Weber and Bassuener 2014).¹³² The judgment in *Sejdić and Finci*, however, has still not been implemented a decade later. In simple terms, non-implementation of this decision, together with related decisions, means that around 12 per cent of the population cannot run for president or parliament because of their religion, ethnicity, or where they live (HRW 2019).¹³³ Other constitutional discrimination cases since *Sejdic-Finci* have followed and remain unimplemented.¹³⁴ The Venice Commission is right in saying that "constitutional reform is indispensable since the present arrangements are neither efficient nor rational and lack democratic content."¹³⁵ Every serious proposal, however, for implementation of *Sejdic-Finci* at the time of writing focused on indirect elections to the House of Peoples or the Presidency despite all the problems that entails in terms of legitimacy and inclusion of the people.¹³⁶

Parliamentary systems have often been proposed for divided societies as they reduce the harshness of 'winner takes all'

---

[131] The ECtHR found both to be discriminatory; the first under Art 14 read in conjunction with Art 3 of Pr. No.1; and the second under Art 1 of Pr. No. 12.
[132] See further, Resolution 1725, 2010; SEC [2009] 1338, October 14, 2009
[133] It should be noted that other domestic court decisions also remain unimplemented. In 2016, for instance, the Constitutional Court declared that the election procedure for the second chamber of the Bosnian-Herzegovinian Federation unconstitutional (Case No. U-23/14, Decision upon Request of Dr Božo Ljubić, the Chairman of the House of Representatives of the Parliamentary Assembly of Bosnia and Herzegovina, 1 December 2016). This ruling, at the time of writing, had not been implemented and elections have continued as usual.
[134] *Zornic v Bosnia* 2014; *Pilav v Bosnia* 2016, and *Baralija v Bosnia* 2019.
[135] Constitutional reform tending towards individual rights and greater democratic content, however, has suffered significant setbacks and it is clear the international community now considers such reforms unrealistic. See, however, Venice Commission (2005, 25).
[136] Opposition RS politicians (SDS, PDP) actually prefer direct election though the SNSD is prepared to accept indirect election (so long as the RS National Assembly selects). Opposition parties (SDS, PDP) insist on direct election partly because it gives them a greater chance at winning. Nebojša Radmanović, the SNSD candidate, won by fewer than 10,000 votes out of 604,370 cast against Mladen Ivanić, the joint opposition candidate. See further, ICG interview, Mladen Bosić, SDS president, Sarajevo, April 18, 2012 (ICG 2012, 12).

presidential systems, reduce executive-legislative deadlock by having grand coalitions for government, and remove majoritarian elections for personality-oriented presidents who may overshadow party political decisions (Linz 1990; Mainwaring and Shugart 1993). In Bosnia, however, an indirectly elected executive, with possible closed list elections for the legislature (as a number of major parties have vowed to reintroduce)[137] would further reduce citizen identification with the State and accountability for political decisions.[138] This dilemma is addressed in the game theory model introduced in Chapter 5.

What non-implementation of the ECtHR decisions demonstrate is that addressing very high political apathy (set out at Chapter 2 above), making leaders accountable and increasing representation of the electorate to include minorities are not significant objectives of political elites; if anything, further insulation of elites from the electorate is the goal. On one view, elites would argue that this is to ensure peace and stability. But as the ECtHR itself stated in *Sejdic-Finci* that position becomes untenable in the long-term. What would have been a national security issue in 1995 clearly is not a relevant issue in 2020. Bosnia has established a single military force, has readied aspects of the Bosnian military to join the NATO alliance through activation of the Membership Action Plan, has signed the Stabilisation and Association Agreement with the EU and has become a formal member of the UN Security Council and General Assembly (Išerić 2016). Protection of power-sharing interests of the elites as a collective are the real reason for inaction. Whilst proposals such as indirect elections for the Presidency will allow the letter of the law will be met, they are far removed from the spirit of the ECtHR judgment. The same is true of requirements that suggest that

---

[137] These include but are not limited to the SNSD, SDP, HDZ and HDZ 1990. (See sub-chapter 5.1 below).
[138] The 2006 proposal to transform the presidency into a weak, indirectly elected president (mentioned above) has been dropped largely due to Croat and Serb objections. ("RS leaders reject transferring powers to a new prime minister, and argue the presidency needs the legitimacy that comes with direct election to exercise its powers." ICG (2012) interviews, Banja Luka and Sarajevo, 2011-2012. Croats want to retain a secure seat).

representatives of a constituent people must be of the same ethnicity.

In respect of possible EU accession, the policy from Brussels has been fungible, incoherent and too willing to bend to the ethno-national demands of political elites in Bosnia (Perry 2019; Hamilton 2020). The promise and hope of eventual accession have led the EU to focus on economic and social issues rather than address, what it considers, complicated and risky constitutional issues (Hamilton 2020). The EU's conditionality criteria, for instance, for financial support is weak and most of the money goes to the public sector: "precisely the parts of the economy that are captured by kleptocratic, ethno-nationalist elites" (Ibid). Ambivalence to further enlargement within the EU, and the increasingly distant promise of accession, simply emboldens local ethno-nationalist instigators. The EU has long said constitutional change is a necessary pre-condition for accession and socio-economic development, but the EU Commission and EU member states refuse to commit to putting pressure on ethno-nationalist elites and resources in favour of the those advocating reform (Ibid). Without structural change the problems of corruption, patronage and ethno-national intransigence has to be reckoned with at every turn by EU interlocutors as well Bosnian elites open to progressive change.

Ethno-nationalist political elites who benefit from the status quo know the international community's position very well and, therefore, operate in an environment without external (EU) incentives and internal disincentives: no one can hold them to account and there is no pressure for reform. In fact, reform suggestions have tended towards entrenching political elites' monopoly even further.

What explains the intransigence of elites to meaningful constitutional reform? What explains the inclination to maintain the status quo and why is exclusive ethno-nationalist politics rewarding in the context of constitutional reform? In sub-chapter 4.4 some answers are suggested. Before those answers on Bosnia the next sub-chapter considers the recent crises, instabilities and reforms under the British constitution.

4.3 Rising strain amidst weak reform in Britain

Chapter 1 set out the basic structure and origins of the unwritten or uncodified British constitution and it posited two questions. Was the British constitution working as intended and was the flexibility inherent in having an uncodified constitutional arrangement being used well by those who had control of its levers? Or was the British constitution and its fundamental arrangements under threat? Are Britons living in an exceptional era where its democracy itself is in jeopardy?

Britain, as one of seven constitutional monarchies in Europe, has had longevity, evolutionary continuity and constitutional stability despite tumultuous events affecting the State, its Empire and the world at large over the past 350 years (Bogdanor 1997, 2, 298). This book, though, is less concerned with something possibly special about constitutional monarchies *per se* but more with the processes of constitutional development in such systems that may allow them to better align with historical societal, cultural and economic norms. The existence of monarchies within modern Europe may well be one feature of a political culture that has been malleable and accepting, generally speaking, of democratic modes of government.[139] Largely because the absolute monarchical systems gave way to democracy and, in particular, to universal suffrage did the monarchies themselves survive. But *stability*, in particular short-term stability, is not sole determinant of constitutional success as evidently demonstrated in Bosnia.

In Chapter 1, we came across those who argue that the British have always been a "'back of the envelope type race" (Ziegler 1996) and "organic checks and balances will see us through" rather than formal ones because we have a free press and judiciary (Hennessy 1995). The idea goes back to the war time spirit that "we'll cope because we always have" (Hennessy 2017) and that constitutional flexibility allows easy absorption of societal tension. Others argue that even if some of that may have been historically true, it is not

---

[139] Bogdanor (1997, 299) focuses on political culture being a factor for *stability* and retention of monarchy rather than the constitutional structure although they are of course closely related in Britain.

true any longer. They would say that: the rule of law is under attack, representative institutions including the devolved administrations are being undermined by politicians taking advantage of the flexible constitutional arrangements, there are few checks and balances on government decision-making, and the constitutional protections on rights are being rolled back by populist sentiment whipped up by the executive in the name of sovereignty, tradition or nativism.

The suggestion is that Britain is following a trend that is being witnessed across European States such as in Russia, Ukraine, Turkey, Poland and Hungary. President Viktor Orban, in Hungary, provides a textbook lesson in how to break-up democracies and facilitate state capture. His strategy follows what is now becoming a familiar pattern: weaken executive-legislative relations; attack state institutions and courts; 'reform' the civil service and stuff it with allies; reform local government to favour the incumbent party; and finally change the constitution to lock in the piecemeal changes previously made (Keil 2018, 8).

Britain arguably *is* at a crossroads. The legitimising protections in the British constitution have arguably been bypassed and neither the people in the regions nor the devolved nations are properly engaged in constitutional decision-making: the people are dissatisfied (see Chapter 2 and 3). Furthermore, over the past 20 or so years, major constitutional change has not tended to occur on a bi-partisan basis and certainly not with the long-term interests of the British people a core consideration (it might be argued they never were). Changes to fundamental constitutional provisions or people's rights either: emanate from piecemeal and short-sighted constitutional change in Parliament that is largely advantageous to the party to the day; or is relegated to determination by judges within a justice system that is being repeatedly and systematically undermined by the executive.

King has suggested that the term "constitutional crisis" is overused. His view is that they are rare, and that Britain has often avoided them because of its flexible constitutional structure allowing it to absorb socio-economic and even political tensions particularly where they emanate from the public at large; tensions which in more formal written constitutions would necessitate regime change (King 2007; Flinders 2010). If that is true, then when Britain has had crises it has either just weathered them well through absorption or they have not yet completely materialised into great public discontentment with the status quo; if Britain has not absorbed them completely, then it begs the question exactly how severe the crises are.[140] There is, however, a fierce disagreement among commentators on where Britain is exactly positioned along a path beginning at constitutional continuity and ending at constitutional crisis.

Turpin and Tomkins (2012, 6) suggest that profound changes in society and politics in the past century have created stresses in Britain's historical constitution, but they allude to two relatively simple reasons to explain lack of radical constitutional reform. The first reason they give is that there is a general lack of consensus on what to do amongst British elites due to official inertia and the second is that people are satisfied with the status quo (Ibid).[141] In either of those contexts, politicians consider it better to tinker with the problems without deliberation or debate rather than embark on complete redesign — the classic British fudge.

One aspect of that tinkering has been a whole host of unrelated and uncoordinated constitutional changes, particularly during the Blair years, that were said to deal with the complexity of modern life, intense media scrutiny and the need for efficient government (Norton 2007; Flinders 2010). These issues have meant increasingly more of the constitution is being written down. Examples include the Civil Service Code; the Freedom of Information Act 2000, and the Ministerial Code. A written constitution may well incorporate significant rules from each of these documents into its provisions.

---

[140] Flinders (2010, 63) believes that only where there is public clamour for change can there truly be a crisis but there was no public clamour for Brexit, and it led to a massive crisis.

[141] An academic and author on constitutional issues (Kurt Bassuener) alerted the author to an apt line from Pink Floyd's "Breathe," *Dark Side of the Moon*: "Hanging on in quiet desperation is the English way."

A more persuasive and alarming explanation is that the constitutional tinkering, of the past decade in particular, has been deliberately designed to accumulate power by the Westminster executive at the expense of the two other branches of the State — the legislature and the judiciary — as well as the devolved nations and local governments: people's remoteness from the constitution has made it easier.

The use of the State-wide referendum in 2016, on whether the people wished to remain in the EU, is a case in point. The 2016 referendum was only the third State-wide referendum in Britain's history but one that has uncovered many festering constitutional wounds.[142] The referendum on withdrawal from the EU, posed a question which, all the objective evidence said, the people cared little to nothing about and which many people knew very little about. In fact, it was a fringe issue being pushed by Conservative Party backbenchers and the UK Independence Party — neither of which would ever have been able to effect the change they sought as a self-standing political party (Emerson 2020, 100).

Since 1997, the polling company Ipsos Mori has asked about 1,000 British voters every month which issues were the most important, in their minds, facing the country. When David Cameron became Prime Minister in 2010 only 1 per cent of British voters listed Europe as an important issue (BBC News 2019). Although the figure increased over time, even by May 2014, the month of the European elections, only 8 per cent identified Europe as a concern (BBC News 2019). Immigration was the biggest concern in the public's mind between 2014 and 2015 and that was often conflated with the EU (BBC News 2019). Whilst immigration does have some connection to membership of the EU, the referendum debate was never framed as a debate on immigration. Figures for long-term international net migration show that, since 2004 to the present day, there are always more non-EU migrants coming to the UK per annum than there are EU migrants (ONS 2020). A referendum on immigration from outside the EU would

---

[142] The others being a state-wide referendum on membership of the EEC (1975) and the referendum on changing electoral rules (2011).

have been more apt than a referendum on the EU itself. Public concern about the EU in fact remained very low until *after* the referendum vote in 2016.

The outcome of the Brexit referendum is undoubtedly problematic from a constitutional perspective. The nation was divided by age, area and critically nationality. Around 62 per cent of those voting in Scotland, and 56 per cent in Northern Ireland, voted to remain in the EU, while 52.5 per cent of voters in Wales wished to leave, as did 53 per cent in England although major cities like London did not (Douglas-Scott 2018). When one accounts for those who did not vote, only 37 per cent of eligible voters actually voted to leave (Douglas-Scott 2018). Critically, however, the process that was pursued — a bare and binary referendum, formally non-binding, and without consideration of the wishes of the nations or regions — betrayed both the failure to understand Britain's changed political system and the inevitable constitutional problems that awaited political elites. Elites wished to crudely gauge but not really understand, interpret or apply the "will of the people" in full. But this approach to a fundamental constitutional issue is not necessarily new.

Supposed constitutional reforms, as individual political parties have characterised them, were taken by the Blair government (1997–2007), the Brown government (2007–2010), the Coalition government (2010–2016) and the Conservatives (2016 to date). In contrast with Bosnia, there has been no shortage of avowed constitutional reform in Britain. At the time of writing (January 2021), in fact, the terms of the constitution were seemingly changing on a day-by-day basis. The sheer volume of executive decisions, which included the passing of hundreds of pieces of delegated legislation — unscrutinised and unamendable by Parliament — has raised serious constitutional issues about the legitimacy, accountability and scrutiny of government decision-making (Sinclair and Tomlinson 2020). Some 44 years' worth of EU directives, for instance, were being converted into domestic law[143] with very limited to no oversight after the decision to leave the EU.

---

[143] Jones and Norton (2019).

Bogdanor (2009, x, 276-285) has called the developments since the Blair era as amounting to no less than a "new British constitution" and "a radical discontinuity" given that the new rules have allowed the decentralisation of power among institutions and the diffusion of power to the regions and nations. King (2007, 349) also says that Britain has a new constitution as a result of the supposed reforms. He believes this is not because of power dispersal but because Britain now has a chaotic ensemble of rules, practices and conventions (as a result of both intended and unintended consequences); a "mess" as he puts it. Norton has been more acerbic than both King and Bogdanor and has dubbed the Blair-era reforms as "vandalism" to the traditional British constitution (Morrison 2001, 509-510). On all these views, the developments in Britain cannot be explained by constitutional inertia or the classic British fudge.

Others suggest that really much of the old, especially the institutional structures, remains even if more has been written down and some powers re-distributed due to devolution or Brexit (Jones and Norton 2019; Turpin and Tomkins 2012, 36).[144] That view is well-articulated by Douglas-Scott (2018) who, whilst disagreeing with the status quo, finds that successive Conservative governments have seen Britain as a "unitary, centralised State with an omnicompetent Parliament" no matter the views, pleas or demands of Holyrood, Stormont or the Senedd (Douglas-Scott 2018). On that conservative interpretation, the UK-wide referendum on Brexit was non-binding—"of no constitutional significance"—so it makes little difference to ask what the nations thought about it. Whilst devolution legislation such as the Scotland Act 1998 devolved powers, again on that view, they derive from Westminster. Parliamentary sovereignty means that the Westminster Parliament can in theory legislate on any matter it sees fit (Douglas-Scott 2018). Conventions, such as the Sewel Convention—now placed on statutory footing in the Scotland Act

---

[144] Flinders (2010) characterises much of UK Parliamentary politics as follows: "[...] the core power-hoarding components of the Westminster Model (that is, a simple plurality electoral system, executive dominance within the Palace of Westminster, and executive vetoes and opt-outs in relation to other measures)."

2016 and Wales Act 2017 — or the Joint Ministerial Committee which were thought to control intra-governmental disputes are not legally binding notwithstanding their codification into statute.[145] As in matters such as foreign policy or treaty making, the British government may consult the devolved administrations, but it need not do more.

Whatever the extent and nature of the supposed constitutional reforms in the past two decades, they lay bare the largely piecemeal and partisan nature of constitutional change. A few of these reforms were indeed bipartisan — such as peace and reform in Northern Ireland which were widely commended (Turpin and Tomkins 2012, 26). Some reforms are now contentious where perhaps few would have originally envisaged them to be — such as giving domestic effect to the European Convention on Human Rights 1950 through the passing of the Human Rights Act 1998. Some reforms seemed thoroughly sensible at the time but shallow legislative prescriptions, and a lack of genuine popular participation in the process, have opened up unforeseen consequences. The Scotland Act of 1998, for instance, devolved powers to Scotland (in a similar fashion to devolution in Wales and Northern Ireland) but has given rise to a largely elite-led national campaign for secession; where the day-to-day of politics interlocks with the existential matter of continued union between the rest of the UK and Scotland.

The key piecemeal and partisan changes that could lend credibility to an argument that Britain is in a severe constitutional crisis are the following live constitutional issues: the apparent strain on devolution arrangements in Scotland, Northern Ireland and Wales; the perceived accumulation of power by judges disguising an attack by the executive on the justice system; and the supposed erosion by the executive of the rule of law generally, including mechanisms for parliamentary oversight and scrutiny. Are each of these three issues demonstrable? Could it be said that Britain is in an exceptional period where there is a fundamental risk to the evolutionary mechanisms that have allowed constitutional

---

[145] *R (on the application of Miller and another) v Secretary of State for Exiting the European Union* [2017] UKSC 5 at [136-151].

stability, unity and cohesion? Is the government seeking to undermine Britain's long-standing unwritten constitution?

Devolution

The devolution arrangements for Northern Ireland, Wales and Scotland (all incidentally different) have led to inherent tension between various competing ideologies and designs for a future Britain. As Douglas-Scott (2018) has noted, this tension is largely due to a largely Conservative attempt to hold onto the idea of Britain as a unitary and centralised State—with the Westminster government attempting to retain as much power as it can—no matter what the formal authority of devolved administrations (Douglas-Scott 2018). That has been laid bare by Brexit (since 2016) and the coronavirus pandemic (since 2020): the executive ignoring the wishes and delegated competencies of the devolved nations and regions. In contrast, the Labour Party, generally, and the devolved administrations which have not been Conservative led, firmly see the constitution as creating a union of nations whereby Westminster may only exercise certain devolved powers with their consent. That historical development is traced back in Scotland to the Treaty of Union 1707 which created the Great British Parliament as opposed to the English Parliament with its, Douglas-Scott suggests, English conception of parliamentary sovereignty (Douglas-Scott 2018). More recently we trace this back to the Claim of Right in 1989 and the Scottish constitutional convention of the early 1990s: declaring that that "the people of Scotland are sovereign and that they have the right to determine the best form of government for Scotland's needs" which in 2018 was read aloud and passed as a non-binding resolution of the House of Commons. It is, of course, paradoxical that the Treaty of Union 1707 which suggests a union of equals would today be a reference point for Scottish 'independence' or 'secession'.

One may rightly ask, as of Brexit as much of Scottish nationalism, secession from what and independence from whom? These are all matters that go back to the now disputed Union of 1707—were the Scots and their Parliament merely subsumed into

Greater England and the English parliament? (Kidd 2014). In legal terms, Kidd (2014) is right that there is: "still no special recognition of the Treaty of Union which created the British State; no guarantee respecting the status of the component nationalities of the current United Kingdom or—in the event of Scottish independence—the unbalanced rump ensemble of England, Wales and Northern Ireland." There is, however, no such recognition of the English who happen to comprise 85 per cent of the UK by population, although the arithmetical majority of the English may well justify some specific protections to those less numerous. The issue is less to do with law and more to do with political practice whereby inequality and democratic deficits within the nations and, ultimately between the nations and Westminster has become the norm. Kidd (2014) mentions how the Scots became the "guinea pigs" of Thatcher's poll tax, introduced in Scotland a year earlier than in England (although many Scottish Conservatives, it is suggested, welcomed the poll tax to avoid another—more expensive—property-based levy or a rates revaluation).

In Northern Ireland, devolution stemmed from the Good Friday Agreement 1998 which is uniquely modern given its "complex provisions regarding cross-community consent, self-determination and a role for the Republic of Ireland and the EU" (Douglas-Scott 2018). Not unlike Bosnia, Northern Ireland's written constitution was introduced as part of a peace agreement which brought into "existence a consociational, pluralist system designed to ensure that major change happens only with broad support in both parts of the community" (Douglas-Scott 2018). The domestic effect of EU and Council of Europe instruments (such as the ECHR); and developments to leave those institutions have served to entrench appeals for further devolution as Northern Ireland did not wish to leave the EU. This is compounded by the nature of the consociational model adopted in Northern Ireland. Assessing the success and failures of the consociational model, in the Bosnian and Macedonian forms, Bassuener (2020, 14) has persuasively argued that: "these deals effectively create an ideal ecosystem for oligarchical, rent-seeking political and economic power, indeed in cartel form, as Lijphart had envisioned: captured states." Political elites form essentially a new class: "peace cartels with a common interest in maintaining their political and economic dominance, as well as legal and political impunity" (Ibid, 221). This centrifugal force in Northern Ireland meeting the centripetal, and centralising, tendency of the Westminster government is a recipe for conflict.

The devolved nations have lost, against their will, the protections that were once offered by EU rights instruments and free movement of people, goods and services. Even though Britain and the EU had secured a free trade deal at the time of writing, Brexit still leaves open the following possibility: a hard border between the Republic of Ireland and Northern Ireland; secession of Northern Ireland and union with the Republic of Ireland; or that Northern Ireland remains in the customs union and single market. All those options are mutually exclusive and two of those options threaten the long-term peace in the island of Ireland and particularly cross-border cooperation. In relation to Scotland too, there has been ongoing tension between Westminster and Holyrood about which of the powers controlled by Brussels pre-Brexit will be returned to Scotland and indeed Wales and Northern Ireland; the particular concerns relate to industrial subsidies, agriculture, and fishing (Ascherson 2020). Strong views have been presented as a solution. Here is one that is particularly memorable:

> "The conceit that Westminster is a British parliament must be jettisoned: it is, and always has been, an English parliament to which representatives of the Celtic regions have been invited to attend. With Westminster reverting to its original role as an English parliament, a new federal settlement should be established in which only national aspects of defence, foreign affairs, taxation, pensions and social security are retained, and new federal institutions should be created—in Manchester" (Loughlin 2016).

Cardiff, Belfast and Edinburgh have increasingly complained that their civil servants are cut out of conversations in Downing Street and the Cabinet Office and Joint Ministerial Council meetings are said to be just mere formalities (Ascherson 2020). Given the tensions and difficulties it is not hard to understand why calls for dissolution, further devolution in the form of federalism, or unilateral secession (or 'independence') grow louder as the centre fights to retain control.

Judicial intervention in politics

King (2007, 346) believes that during the processes of constitutional reform, over the past two decades, judges have accumulated greater power and authority by virtue of accession to the EU among other things. Sumption (2019, 34-37), a former Supreme Court Justice, has frequently gone beyond this to suggest that the judges have impermissibly strayed into debateable public policy issues under the guise of the 'rule of law'. He believes judges are answering questions which were always reserved for reasoned political deliberation in Parliament (not the zero-sum environment of judicial determination). On that view, some have suggested, that issues such as punishing the public expression of racial hatred, the rights and wrongs of abortion, gay marriage, the death penalty, limits to the right to bear arms, and limits of privacy and so forth are not to be left in the hands of the courts (Waldron 2006).

The idea of reasoned and democratic deliberation, however, is a function of political culture, rules and practice. That function was seemingly long lost when political elites, in particular within the executive, themselves stopped observing the rules of the game in a sovereign Parliament where only the House of Commons is elected (Kennedy 2020).[146] Political action today is characterised by a failure to honour—in that classic British sense—unwritten rules of procedure and practice. In fact, there is now open and flagrant opposition to written rules including accepted international rules and norms as well as increasing hostility to the idea of 'unelected judges' deciding on a whole host of issues. The executive arguably is no longer exercising the self-restraint that Sumption (among

---

[146] An example is provided by Sumption (2020, 111) himself: minority governments, including Theresa May's, tried to bypass parliament (using standing orders) by controlling the parliamentary agenda to push through unpopular Brexit proposals. In fact, a majority in Parliament did not want them and that was why the Speaker, John Bercow allowed private members to take control of the order papers to provide for emergency debates and passing an act to prevent a no-deal Brexit. This was what led to proroguing of Parliament.

others) have naively entrusted to them and the attacks on some rights and some judges are being taken to their logical conclusion: an attack on all.[147]

Recent events in Britain and the contestation over human rights demonstrate an increasing trend to realise an executive government free of judicial scrutiny. A Conservative Party goal, since 2010, has been to repeal the Human Rights Act 1998 ("HRA"), which gives domestic effect to the ECHR.[148] Over time, this manifesto commitment has become increasingly anti-human rights and anti-rule of law with the HRA denounced as an "undemocratic fetter on a sovereign British state and its Parliament, and a threat to the fabric of our unwritten constitution" (Sands 2015, 5).

Ideologues have to a large extent seized on a traditional interpretation of rights (consistently articulated by Sumption (2020) and Finnis (2015) over the years) which essentially argue that debateable policy issues should not be subject to legal contestation or, indeed, adjudication. This is usually justified on the following basis: policy matters are for elected politicians; the Strasbourg court has interpreted rights in a manner that goes far beyond what those rights were originally intended to cover, and such interpretations should not apply in the UK; the UK courts are subordinate to Strasbourg and unelected foreign judges; and that human rights law is foreign to, irrevocably taints, or arrests the development of the common law in the UK (Sands 2015, 24).

Yet, Britain's membership of the ECtHR, as others have argued, allowed the common law to adapt and take into account human rights in light of the changing socio-political norms of the people. The HRA, they would say, has enabled a continuing dialogue between the Strasbourg court and the UK courts through subsidiarity and the margin of appreciation afforded to the UK courts in interpretation. It has also ensured that where there is any fundamental incompatibility between UK laws and the rights enshrined in the HRA, ultimately Parliament retains the final say

---

[147] See an insightful discussion on this in Turpin and Tomkins (2012, 9-10).
[148] "To protect our freedoms from State encroachment and encourage greater social responsibility, we will replace the Human Rights Act with a UK Bill of Rights" (Manifesto 2010, 79).

(Sands 2015). This is just a reflection of how judicial, legislative and executive powers are separated. But this debate still continues and there remains vociferous, and oftentimes irreconcilable, views among political elites on the issue.

Elsewhere, Sumption (2019) has reduced his position in respect of the judicialization of politics to this: "the only effective constraints on the abuse of democratic power are political."[149] This claim however is incorrect. First, the law may be fundamentally unjust because of who a person is or what their life circumstances happen to be (Sedley 2019). We need only think of the constitutionally-sanctioned and widespread civil rights violations in the US for many decades. These legal and moral violations and inequities persisted, in particular against minorities, because of a permissive political environment but also because of a lack of sufficient constitutional protection (combined with complicit courts and judges).

Second, issues which are designated by the executive as being in the 'national interest', or the 'public interest' often escape the purview of the courts, for instance, when the House of Lords found a discontinuance of a Serious Fraud Office investigation into the BAE/Al-Yamamah arms deal with Saudi Arabia unlawful.[150] Courts often have to respect policy dimensions and balance rights against policy decisions; this often precludes any form of protection for the individual or the minority.

Third, the executive in Britain, unchecked, has almost unlimited power. Sumption himself has argued this in a recent paper (2020) arguing that in pursuit of Brexit the government has overridden key constitutional conventions and bypassed parliamentary scrutiny. Where the government commands a big majority there are very few checks on its legislative agenda if it chooses to curtial parliamentary processes and whip MPs into line. In theory, the House of Lords may delay, *in extremis*, a bill for two parliamentary sessions over a one-year period[151] — under the

---

[149] See further, the brilliant review of Sumption's (2019) book by Sedley (2019).
[150] *R (Corner House Research) v Director of the Serious Fraud Office* [2008] UKHL 60
[151] From the original second reading to its final third reading in the House of Commons.

Parliament Act of 1911 (as amended in 1949) — after which the government may pass the Bill in the House of Commons, if it commands a majority, without amendment. Select committees may also scrutinise prospective legislation but they may not strike it down. And the government has very significant power over what MPs get to discuss, which is has frequently abused over the past two years contrary to wishes of key select committees, backbenchers and large numbers of MPs (Russell 2021). The possibility of unchecked majority decision-making persecuting minorities or even a minority tyrannising the majority is more than just academic without extensive legal protections for the individual.[152]

As it happens, Sumption frequently mixes the two separate State institutions — the executive and the legislature — when he criticises judges for foraying into matters of policy. Sedley has rightly noted that judicial review is of executive decision-making (Sedley 2012).[153] In some instances, such as where an individual's fundamental rights are engaged, a court may also scrutinise government acts passed by parliament which violate rights, as such, set-out in other instruments (such as the HRA) or other common law rights. But, ultimately, where there is an incompatibility with primary legislation judges revert the matter back to Parliament, as it reigns supreme.

The idea, therefore, that the only effective constraints on abuse of democratic power are political depends on the very institutions of politics being able to withstand the abuse Sumption speaks of.

---

[152] The Parliament Act 1911 truncated the powers of scrutiny afforded to the unelected, and partisan, appointees to the House of Lords. The House of Lords has not threatened a serious veto since 1914 (Mclean 2012, 322). The government also largely controls Parliamentary business including the order papers and time allowed for scrutiny of legislation which restricts the ability for the elected MPs of the Commons to scrutinise legislation (Ibid). As for the monarchy McClean (2012) notes: "The monarchy is unelected in the same way as it has been since 1714. It was elected then (and in 1689 and in 1660), but all these dates are a long time ago." It should be noted that there is now roughly party balance in the House of Lords but there is nothing to stop the government from packing it with its supporters as the government attempted to do, despite much criticism, in December 2020.

[153] See further, *Belmarsh*, 2004; *A v SSHD*, 2005; Kennedy (2020).

All three strands of the state play a part: the executive, the legislature and the judiciary. Convention does dictate, for instance, that where a government cannot pass legislation and has lost the confidence of the majority of the Commons it ought to resign. As one academic has rightly put it "for [it] to do otherwise would amount to a *coup d'état* destroying the democratic basis of the government" (Franklin and Baun 1995, 22). But, throughout the Brexit crises, and in particular in 2019, the government (comprising a minority in parliament) suffered repeated defeats in Parliament, its party whips had no control and its coalition partner (secured with billions of pounds in promised money for Northern Ireland) was in open revolt. The government did not resign (Sedley 2019). The government was perhaps deploying the Edward Heath and Harold Wilson 'fudge' that a government only really loses confidence of the House should it fail to win a formal vote of confidence or censure although there is little doubt it would have failed had one been held (Franklin and Baun 1995, 22).

In practice, the judiciary, seemingly, is the last true bulwark against unchecked majority rule. Judges address the deficit in government decision making (because decisions are irrational, illegal, improper or contrary to fundamental laws) in all manner of areas such as immigration, prison policy, housing, and crime, as they always have done. Notwithstanding their constitutional role, they are under attack from an executive that feels they are a policy impediment. Sumption desires reasoned political deliberation in Parliament. He accepts it has not been forthcoming. Those in power who have seized upon his (and other anti-rights) sentiments have long desired something else. It is not clear what exactly but developments of late suggest untrammelled power over the rule of law.

Erosion of the rule of law

Constitutional processes that have evolved over time are, arguably, being replaced by revolutionary, and partisan, executive decision-making. Sumption recently accepted that the consequences of the referendum to leave the EU has led to Britain having a "more authoritarian style of government" considering that governments since 2016 have bypassed parliamentary scrutiny and centuries old conventions (2020, 108).[154]

In September 2020, this trajectory appeared to hit a new low when the Conservative Party 2019 manifesto promise to launch a Commission to, apparently, address a broad range of constitutional issues was replaced with a so-called "Independent Review of Administrative Law." The terms of reference for the Review raised the prospect of drastic restrictions on legal oversight of government decision-making through reducing legal grounds of challenge, limiting remedies available to successful litigants, reducing government disclosure obligations and limiting ways judicial review can be initiated in the first place (Elliot 2020). The public announcement that followed and remarks previously made by the newly appointed Chair, Lord Faulks, suggested a desired outcome: the executive having an unrestrained "right to govern"; and the "need for effective and efficient government" when "balancing against citizen's rights" (Elliot 2020). The agenda implicit in the Review, betrayed by the appointment of a Chair who has been consistently critical of human rights and judicial review, is to seemingly up-end fundamental rules and conventions that stipulate that the government is: subordinate to Parliament; and is allowed to do only what is prescribed to it in law (subject to adjudication of the courts in the event of challenge).[155]

The context in which the Review came about is instructive. In September 2019, a year before the announcement of the Review, Boris Johnson took the decision to prorogue Parliament for five weeks. At the time the Attorney General had told the told the House of Commons that it had "no moral right to sit" (Sumption 2020, 109). It was the decision to prorogue parliament that was subject to

---

[154] Sumption (2020, 12) distinguishes his criticism of judges deciding on policy issues with recent judicial intervention on issues such as the prorogation of parliament: "The Supreme Court intervened not to claim decision-making powers for judges, but to safeguard the decision-making powers of Parliament."

[155] See further, Elliot (2020). See also the definition of 'parliamentary sovereignty' and 'parliamentary accountability' in R (on the application of Miller) (Appellant) v The Prime Minister (Respondent), [2019] UKSC 41.

judicial review where 11 judges of the Supreme Court, in the case of *R (Miller) v The Prime Minister and Cherry v Advocate General for Scotland* [2019] UKSC 41 ("*Miller II*"), unanimously held on 24 September 2019 that the advice by the Prime Minister to the Queen to prorogue Parliament for that length of time, at that particular moment, was unlawful.

It was following *Miller II*, that the manifesto commitment for a Commission on the constitution came about alongside a warning that judicial review should not be "abused to conduct politics by other means" (Dean 2020). The Prime Minister's chief political advisor Dominic Cummings was reported to have said that he wanted to "get the judges sorted" (Dean 2020). The now Chair of the Review stated that MPs should "limit the courts' incursion into political territory."[156]

The Supreme Court in the judicial review case of *Miller I* held that parliamentary consent was necessary for the triggering of Article 50 (which would notify the EU that Britain would cease to be a member); the executive could not bypass Parliament.[157] In both the *Miller I* and *Miller II* cases, the Supreme Court reasserted the primacy of parliamentary sovereignty over the executive improperly exercising prerogative powers rather than saying anything about public policy. This, of course, was in the wider context of the Daily Mail's front page following the High Court decision in *Miller I* in November 2016, with its characterisation of the senior judiciary, including the Lord Chief Justice, as "Enemies of the People," simply because they decided that Parliament, not the government, had to trigger Article 50 to initiate a departure from the EU (Kennedy 2019). Notably, Sumption was with the

---

[156] Some facts are helpful to bear in mind about judicial review: the costs of pursuing and losing judicial review are very high; only approximately five per cent of claims for judicial review ever reach the High Court for substantive hearing; and even in those cases the government wins fifty percent of cases (Hogarth 2020). Furthermore, applications for judicial review have fallen by nearly half between 2015 and September 2019, as a result of massive legal aid cuts, higher court fees, and a 'merit' test that is applied *before* a court can determine whether there is merit in the case or not (Bar Council 2020; MoJ 2013).

[157] *R (on the application of Miller and another) v Secretary of State for Exiting the European Union* [2017] UKSC 5.

majority in *Miller I* and expressed his support for *Miller II* explaining his position as an ordinary exercise of the function of English judges in line with judicial restraint and an "orthodox application of the long-standing constitutional rule that only Parliament can change the law."

The final point here is that the terms of reference for the Review (MoJ 2020) are apparently set by the Lord Chancellor who, without any hint of irony, declared when launching the Review that it formed part of his "duty to defend our world-class and independent courts and judiciary that lie at the heart of British justice and the rule of law" (MoJ 2020). The terms are set without consultation, without any rational explanation as to why they are designed in the manner that they are, or how their expansive or restrictive scope decided. At the time of writing, the Review had completed its mandate and the Chair had submitted its report to the government; none of the consultation submissions were published and the government refused to publish the report it had received.

The decision to hold the Review was quickly followed with the publication of the Internal Market Bill 2020 which, if it had been enacted in that form, would have authorised Ministers to place the UK in breach of its international legal obligations which it had agreed to be bound by in the EU Withdrawal Agreement 2019 just one year prior on 17 October 2019 and its associated obligations under the Northern Ireland Protocol 2019 (with consequences for the Good Friday Agreement). The Bill also sought to immunise itself from judicial review (Elliot 2020). The Bill was making its way through parliament whilst another was having its second reading in the House of Commons on 23 September 2020, the Overseas Operations (Service Personnel and Veterans) Bill. If adopted, in the form proposed, it would introduce a presumption against prosecution for alleged crimes committed by UK service personnel in overseas operations if five years had elapsed. That Bill is another which directly contravenes UK obligations under international law including: the right to life and prohibition against torture; as well as undermining international rule of law by signalling to other countries that limitations may be placed on absolute prohibitions such as those against genocide and torture (Cubbon 2020).[158]

Incidentally, this Bill was followed by the Covert Human Intelligence Sources Bill which authorizes, if passed in its current form, informants of the security services to break the law including the commission of murder, torture and other serious crimes. These Bills came together with a report that Ministers were "drawing up proposals to severely curb the use of human rights laws in areas in which judges have 'overreached'" (Elliot 2020). At the time of writing, indeed, another 'independent review' was launched on whether HRA was fit for purpose with a consultation end date for March 2021. Lord Faulks, the Chair of the supposed independent review (on judicial review) has himself written on the subject: "'leave the Council of Europe altogether, repeal the Human Rights Act and allow our own courts and Parliament to protect human rights" (Faulks 2017). The proposal would remove a critical check on government which currently obliges it to follow widely accepted international human rights law and norms. As it happens, norms and laws largely developed by the British after WWII.

Developments in contravention of the rule of law in the UK in 2017-2021 have not magically manifested; and they go back to at least 2010. Since then, there has been a proliferation of criminalisation of people's conduct, rights to legal aid have been cut, and the socio-economic rights of large numbers of people have been curtailed such as these relating to work, housing and health. The debate around the Human Rights Act 1998 in the UK, as noted earlier, has been swirling in certain circles in the past decade in this context. It originally revolved around: whether rights were situated domestically or internationally (by virtue of where they originated from, where they are applied, who interprets them and who ultimately fulfils or guarantees them); and whether the proper form

---

[158] In 2015, the Conservative government quietly dropped reference in the 2010 Ministerial Code, in line with party policy, to the principal that members of the government should be bound by international law. On the same day that the 2015 code was issued, the Attorney General, Jeremy Wright QC, gave a keynote about the importance of international law to an audience of government lawyers at an International Law Conference held in London (Taylor 2020).

for adjudication of certain issues is the judicial or political forum. What started as a questioning of the role of international judges has now morphed into questioning the role, in its entirety, of the justice system in the democratic process.

4.4 Reform dilemmas and deadlock

British proposals for reform

In Britain, there have been numerous constitutional crises this past decade and they have led to calls, commissions and inquiries looking at the issue of reform (Kidd 2014). Some of the proposed reforms are competing and some are complementary. Some of the enacted reforms, where they have been insincere or partisan, have precipitated further crises. Nevertheless, the major proposals for reform have included calls for: a written or codified constitution; further devolution to the regions and nations; secession or independence of the devolved nations; a republican settlement for Britain; a greater internationalisation of protections for the rule of law and democracy; and other forms of domestic entrenchment of fundamental rights to protect citizens and key institutions and offices of the State that are critical for democracy (with a possibly greater role for judges).[159]

Bogdanor (1997, 300) clears up the misnomer that radical, egalitarian and socially progressive change cannot occur under constitutional monarchies by pointing to Denmark, Norway and Sweden, each of which are more socially progressive than Britain. There are also countries that are no longer constitutional monarchies, like Italy, which are less egalitarian. Republicanism is not a cure all, although something might be said of the symbolism perpetuated by monarchies and unwritten conventions: they reinforce and complement hierarchical and deferential modes of behaviour and thinking. That is true of Japan and possibly of Britain but, then again, it is not of the Scandinavians. There has never been a great urge for Republicanism in at least three of UK's four

---

[159] There are simply too many to list. See Kidd (2014).

nations—the last time it was seriously up for discussion in Parliament was in 1936 where a motion on the issue received only five votes in the Commons. Furthermore, a constitutional centre—albeit a royalist one—within which the 'game' of politics and elites, in particular, operate could paradoxically help to legitimatise radical policymaking. This is in contrast with policy making where a head of State is also a party-political figure. The Queen, as the royalist centre has to maintain her social base and accommodate herself, as Bogdanor (1997, 303) persuasively argues, to changes in society. Such a head of State who presides impartially over a constitutional structure, and who is careful to remain above the political fray, may make radical policymaking (that does not challenge the system itself) more amenable and possibly more legitimate. There is a debate to be had. Where arguably there is little debate to be had, any longer, is whether the constitutional underpinnings of Britain which make it democratic are working as intended for the reasons set out earlier.

Writing down the British constitution in full is, of course, a *possible* route out of the current constitutional crises.[160] It could present a comprehensive and coherent settlement and allow for entrenchment of key rules. Only one major party in the UK, the Liberal Democrats have made this a serious and consistent manifesto commitment (since 2010) although Labour leaders have also advocated for a written constitution. In the Conservative Party, the most serious calls for a written constitution came from its former party chairman and Lord Chancellor Lord Hailsham in the 1970s (HoC 2014) but, today, the Conservative Party remains firmly opposed to a written constitution. Hailsham is oft quoted in criticising the 'elective dictatorship' of government in Britain; yet when he made that famous remark, he, of course, was criticising the

---

[160] The HoC (2014) Political and Constitutional Reform Select Committee produced a report making a possible case for a codified constitution. It presented three possible models: Constitutional Code—a document that does not have legal force, but which would set out the existing principles of the constitution and the workings of government; Constitutional Consolidation Act—a document which would consolidate existing constitutional laws in one place; Written Constitution—a document of basic law by which the UK would be governed, setting out the relationship between the state and its citizens.

then left-wing government (McClean 2012, 316). He never criticised or did anything to challenge the 'dictatorship' of the Thatcher government he joined in 1979 (Ibid).

The Liberal Democrats have also proposed a constitutional convention to determine the contents of a constitution although they have not set out much detail on either.[161] Gordon Brown, who is currently championing a commission on constitutional reform, similarly proposed an ambitious and comprehensive reform program upon becoming Prime Minister although nothing meaningful materialised for reasons discussed in Chapter 6. Bingham (2011) argued, even before the recent crises, that the absence of a written or codified constitution means that "constitutionally speaking, we now find ourselves in a trackless desert without map or compass." But the path along this route is not without impediment at all. There are many codified constitutions around the world that are progressive, and in theory paradigmatic, but are frequently bypassed in the absence of free and fair judicial systems to enforce their provisions and/or strong media and civil society organisations to hold elected officials accountable for violations.

There is also the difficult problem of identifying: what should be codified and what should remain outside the purview of the constitution, what necessarily is fundamental and what is clearly less-so, and who exactly should decide and when. Another consideration is that, historically, the flexible British arrangements have left off the political agenda complicated and possibly divisive issues of belonging to the State, identity, citizenship and formal political associations (Loughlin 2016).[162] If the approach to a written constitution is unthoughtful, partisan and misguided, then the divisions within society—generated by Brexit, revealed by long-standing socio-economic inequality, and garnered by populist attacks on democratic institutions—risk being amplified manifold.

---

[161] Liberal Democrats, Liberal Democrat Manifesto 2010, 88; Liberal Democrats, Manifesto 2015, 133. Labour were considering similar proposals at the time of writing.

[162] The question of what the State even is a matter that has only come up in the jurisprudence.

Another pathway is a form of federalisation (which may form part of a written constitutional settlement) or unilateral secession of nations or an agreed dissolution of the four nations. A number of politicians are countenancing the idea of federalism in Britain. Federal arrangements are those in which "certain groups are granted autonomy within their territory, while at the same time enjoying participation in central decision-making, either through representation in second chambers, or through more complex power-sharing arrangements" (Keil and Alber 2020, 4). Federal arrangements are different and more formal to the self-rule and autonomy afforded to three of the four devolved nations in Britain. The formality usually relates to sharing of power between the centre and the federal unit. Whilst there is no empirical evidence to suggest that federal arrangements are doomed to fail (Schulte 2020) ill-conceived arrangement have resulted in political and armed conflict; with minorities and majorities wrestling over the nature, scope and extent of autonomy and self-rule. The two major considerations to a federal solution, as noted by Keil and Alber (2020), is that the arrangements need to be carefully adapted to the country and territory in question, which means considering political culture and history, and the arrangements must be arrived at through an inclusive process, which means having on-board key actors and spoilers (Ibid, 5). Arrangements must also necessarily be flexible and adaptable and move beyond the issues that gave rise to the impulse to reach for a federal solution and anticipate future contestation. Indeed, we see the problem of contestation already in the UK with the devolution arrangements. The real dangers of shallow prescriptions for ailments are plain to see. As voices in the UK grow louder for a quick federal fix, as Chapter 6 cautions, some deep thinking is required about longer-term consequences and how such an arrangement might be arrived at, if at all.

Other routes out of the crises are possible: for instance, greater entrenchment of human rights and clearer delineation of the rights of devolved administrations. When the 2010 Conservative Party manifesto argued for a UK Bill of Rights there was some suggestion that the Bill could in fact gold-plate or bolster existing protections for individuals. A Commission was set-up in the summer of 2010 to assess whether a Bill of Rights was necessary and to provide a solution to a split within the coalition government about the future of the Human Rights Act 1998 (Sands 2015, 26). The Conservatives wished to leave the ECHR and the Liberal Democrats wanted to remain within it. Two of the four members appointed to the Commission by the Liberal Democrats found that that the four members appointed by the Conservatives had a pre-conceived agenda: to withdraw from the ECHR altogether. One of those members was, Lord Faulks, the now Chair of the 'independent review' on judicial review (Sands 26-27). This agenda was, in part, also a confirmation of the traditional hostility of the Labour Party to a Bill of Rights for fear that its provisions would be designed to allow conservative judges to hinder progressive or 'socialist' policy making (Ewing and Geary 1990).[163]

Kennedy and Sands (2015), who were members of the Bill of Rights Commission wrote a minority opinion disagreeing with the majority that did, in principle want a Bill of Rights. In that opinion, they said that there was no appetite whatsoever to change the current arrangements: "amongst anyone." They commissioned two surveys and in both some 88 per cent of respondents to the simple question "retain or repeal the HRA?" replied retain. Some 98% of people also answered that the ECHR should continue to be incorporated in British law (Sands 2015, 28). Sands and Kennedy found abhorrent the suggestion, by Conservative members of the Commission, that fundamental rights, which are universal, might be curtailed for 'foreigners'. Furthermore, Sands noted that repeal of the HRA, which is incorporated in the devolution arrangements for Scotland, Wales, and Northern Ireland, could jeopardise those arrangements. The one thing relating to a Bill of Rights on which there was some consensus within the Commission was that "the subject raised sensitivities, should be addressed gradually, and ought to be addressed in a forum such as a Constitutional Convention that also addressed wider constitutional issues,

---

[163] See also, summary and analysis in Turpin and Tomkins (2012, 25).

including devolution" (Sands 2016, 26). This is an issue returned to in Chapter 6.

Others in response to the crises have advocated more of the classic British fudge. Kidd (2014) whilst lamenting and highlighting the inadequacies of the current constitutional arrangements and the inconsistent devolution settlements reaches for the very prescription—shallow and ill-thought through—that have led to the intractable impasse that is unfolding or is yet to come. He suggests that the House of Lords be transformed—"without any violence to the *coherence* of the British constitution"—[emphasis added] into a German-style Bundesrat. The reformed House of Lords would have the following features: its members would be drawn from the devolved administrations and regions, the Parliamentary Acts of 1911 and 1949 would be repealed, and a supermajority threshold would be introduced for decision-making. The new body would act as a check on the House of Commons. The prescription is shallow not just for the reasons of illegitimacy, non-inclusion and non-deliberative process by which such a reform should occur but a practical one highlighted by Kidd (2014) himself. First, England still does not have regional institutions though the Mayoral systems have proved popular and have proven their credentials by challenging the Westminster government's impositions of rules—delegated to them—during the coronavirus crises. Second, the West Lothian question would be introduced into the House of Lords as well as the lower House: Scots voting on English laws on English matters but not the other way around.

In essence, constitutional reform in Britain has been disparate, disorderly and disconnected from its peoples and nations. There is little coherence in methodology let alone a master plan. There is a dearth in dreams let alone a vision. Although the British constitutional system, inherently, retains the capacity and flexibility to help realise dreams should they be had. No one, for instance, has seriously suggested that the Blair to Cameron constitutional reforms (1997-2016) were ever intended to be: inclusive of all major political elites, civil society or the people generally; rooted in or engaged with any broad-based popular movement; or pursuant to the meaningfully assessed preferences of the people. As an example, Flinders (2010) finds that none of the Labour reforms were rooted in public pressure for change—this is an issue that the book considers in Chapter 6—although the Blair-era reforms did have some very serious academic thinking, analysis and strategy behind some of its key reforms (Turpin and Tomkins 2012).

In Britain, the question then, is whether public pressure for change of constitutional structures is often demonstrative of 'too little too late'—is it that only when it seems the system is at breaking point do civic and national power centres attempt to appeal to the centre for reform? Is really radical systemic reform necessary in Britain? How might future constitutional reform look like and should it be inclusive? Before tackling these questions further in Chapter 6 for Britain, it is necessary to compare and contrast the current reform dilemmas in Bosnia.

Bosnian proposals for reform

In Bosnia, the general deadlock and lack of consensus can be attributed to the exclusive ethno-nationalist attitudes of political elites to policy even when such policy is important for the political and economic welfare of the people. A significant problem is that the positions of the majority of the elites of the three constituent peoples are almost all anti-systemic and envisage competing ethno-nationalist visions for Bosnia.[164] As highlighted in Chapter 3, elites are elected in ethno-territorial districts with power-sharing rules that allow those elites to monopolise control over the electorate particularly through maintaining patronage and clientelist networks (Perry and Keil 2018). Elites within the same group of ethno-nationalist parties compete with one another for power but cross-ethno-national competition is precluded because of the rules. That is why ethno-nationalist elites are insufficiently interested in reform although each of three main party groupings do have some common themes on reform *within* their groupings.

---

[164] See further, ICG (2012, 12); ICG (2009, 4-12); Kasapović (2005). Bahtić-Kunrath (2011, 903).

Bosniak elites advocate a unitary-civil State premised on the equality of individuals or on simple majoritarian electoral rules. Proposals for centralisation differ but, generally, their detractors say that attempts at centralisation are really attempts at forced assimilation of others using narratives of multiculturalism or Bosniak victimhood (Basta 2016, 957). Essentially, the detractors feel that if people vote along non-ethnic lines then the State would become dominated by the group with the biggest ethnic majority: the Bosniaks (Belloni 2008, 55; Perry 2015). Supporters, however, note that a State based on plurality protected by individual human rights can only be conceived of as a State unified and de-entitised.[165] Indeed, moderate Bosniak political elites are avowedly for greater centralisation with appropriate safeguards for the other constituent peoples. Again, detractors would say that this is their public position only (Bieber 2006).

Civic or non-nationalist parties, such as the SDP, DF, NS focus largely on policy issues (Hulsey and Keil 2020). Their position on constitutional reform largely coincides with the moderate Bosniak position. They envision greater State centralisation and a State based on the equality of individuals rather than the equality of ethnic groups. As non-nationalist parties are only able to compete in the Bosniak cantons or mixed Bosniak-Croat cantons in the Federation—because of the way the electoral rules and electoral districts are designed—this means their position is often conflated with the Bosniak position. Inevitably, this leads to the charge that they are insincere in their non-ethno-nationalist position even though their policies, leadership and practices may objectively be identified as non-ethno-nationalist.

Serb elites advocate for the exclusive status of the RS as a nation-state of the Bosnian Serbs and propose its separation from the rest of the State (Basta 2016, 960). Indeed, comments by the

---

[165] Manfred Novak (former Austrian member of the Bosnian Human Rights Chamber) and Zoran Pajic (Bosnian constitutional lawyer) among them (Belloni 2008, 56).

current RS President, Milorad Dodik, and leader of the SNSD[166] are instructive on this point.[167] Political elites in the RS present any reforms, short of secession, as potentially depriving the RS of political power and resources without getting anything in return (Perry 2015, 42). Recognising that secession cannot be achieved without cost, elites in the RS prefers to maintain the status quo under the Bosnian constitution and nominally accept, as a necessary evil, the federal arrangements under the Dayton Peace Agreement granting the RS wide autonomy. They also routinely deploy narratives of historic victimhood of which the current Bosnian State is a manifestation: designed to hobble and handicap the Serbs rightful greater nation (Basta 2016, 961). Meanwhile, the elites continue to take steps to build institutions for future secession (ICG 2009, 7).

Croat elites advocate the elimination of entities to be replaced by a number of cantons or see the State as a union of three national entities (ICG 2009, 56). In the absence of a large demographic, cultural or economic base that is becoming increasingly smaller as young Croats leave for the EU, the Bosnian Croat elites work towards cementing their territorial and political resources with a view to push for further autonomy in the future (Basta 2016, 964). Bosnian Croat parties insist that seats guaranteed for them are being used by other ethnic groups to field candidates that do not genuinely represent their 'ethnic interests' and rather represent party interests (for instance, Bosniaks voting for Bosnian Croat seats in the Presidential elections). This situation, of course, hinders the effective functioning of the Federation. Bosnian Croats are also unhappy about not having the possibility to employ significant

---

[166] Which commands majorities in both the Parliamentary Assembly (i.e., a majority in respect of delegates from the RS) and the RS National Assembly at the time of writing.

[167] Milorad Dodik has separately and repeatedly said of Bosnia as: "a nightmare" (Oslobodenje, 23 July 2010); "makes him sick" (Večernji List, 17 September 2012); "has a future only in case a third, Croat entity is set up, so there is the Serb Republic, Herzeg-Bosnia, and Bosnia, so that only foreign policy, foreign security and foreign trade decisions are made on the state-level" (Večernji List, 17 September 2012); "a failing state" (Politico, 29 June 2017); "an impossible state" (The Atlantic, 2 January 2019).

vetoes (including an entity-voting veto in Parliament without Bosniak support). This Croat veto grievance is elaborated on further in sub-chapter 5.2 as is the increasing desire by Croat political elites to create their own, exclusively Croat, 'third entity' in Bosnia.

Bahtić-Kunrath (2011) accounts for the failure to change the status quo primarily by looking at the use of veto mechanisms built for power sharing and stability within Bosnia.[168] She outlines that legislation which was planned by the government (particularly the Council of Ministers) but not then adopted by the legislature was because policy change was inhibited by elites with veto powers adopting exclusivist or nationalist positions. Vetoes are the essential safeguard against majority decision-making, but maximalist positions by ethno-nationalist elites (operating in silos) inevitably lead to deadlock and indecision. Both prevent reform for only one reason: protection of ethnic interests over any other consideration (Bahtić-Kunrath 2011).

In terms of mechanisms to address the deadlock, Bahtić-Kunrath's proposals for reform are prescriptive and look to extra-institutional means to resolve the conflict. Primarily, reform, she concludes, must come from pressure from the outside: the EU, Bosnia's neighbours, and/or a change in political leaders (Bahtić-Kunrath 2011, 914, 918). The veto player approach can be developed much further though, as this book does in Chapter 5, in an attempt to reach some meaningful conclusions as to how Bosnian constitutional reform can come from within so that change is enduring.

---

[168] The approach (although not on constitutional reform specifically) is a refreshing addition to the literature and analyses the significant points of veto that lead to deadlock at a legislative level. Her statistical analysis between 2006 and 2010 is very insightful.

TABLE 4.4A: SUMMARY OF VETO MECHANISMS UNDER THE STATE CONSTITUTION

VETO NAME	STATE INSTITUTION WHERE EXERCISED	RELEVANT PROVISION OF STATE CONSTITUTION	VETO PLAYERS	INVOCATION	ETHNIC USE
Vital national interest presidency veto (VNIP)	State Presidency	Article V (Presidency) 2.c and 2.d	Each of the three members of the Presidency	Only for issues of 'vital interest' Note: no prescribed definition of vital interest	Any member (solely Bosniak, Croat or Serb) may invoke VNI subject to ratification by relevant caucus in the entity parliament
Vital national interest house veto (VNIH)	House of Peoples	Article IV (Parliamentary Assembly) 3.e and 3.f	A majority of a national caucus present and voting (so any three members or two if quorum of caucus is three)	Only for issues of 'vital interest' which is ultimately and definitively decided by the Constitutional Court. Note: no prescribed definition of vital interest.	Any caucus (Bosniak, Croat or Serb) may invoke VNI if a quorum of three members of the HoP is met
Entity-voting veto (EVV)	House of Peoples and House of Representatives	Article IV (Parliamentary Assembly) 3.d	Support for decision of at least one-third of the delegates (present and voting) elected from each of the RS and the Federation in both houses. If decision	No rules governing use. Can be used to veto any decision (including draft laws, conclusions, requests, initiatives, and proposals)	Federation. A single caucus can pass a bill. Majority Bosniak support will pass a bill in either House. Majority Croat support will pass a bill in the HoP but not at the initial stage in HoR – they could be outvoted by Bosniaks (i.e., by abstaining). To ensure the veto works, both Croats and Bosniaks

TABLE 4.4A: SUMMARY OF VETO MECHANISMS UNDER THE STATE CONSTITUTION

VETO NAME	STATE INSTITUTION WHERE EXERCISED	RELEVANT PROVISION OF STATE CONSTITUTION	VETO PLAYERS	INVOCATION	ETHNIC USE
Constitutional amendment veto	House of Representatives	Article X (Amendment)	harmonised, then 2/3 majority from either entity can still veto		must neither support a bill in the HoP to trigger the veto. RS. Delegates can deploy entity-voting in all stages of law making uninhibited given that the majority are Serbs. RS in best position[169]
			Two thirds majority in House of Representatives	No rules governing use. Can be used to veto any amendment	Any caucus may decline to give support thereby vetoing the amendment. Note: other vetoes could still be deployed
Inter-entity coordination veto (IECV)	State Presidency	Article III (Responsibilities of and relations between the institutions of Bosnia and Herzegovina and the Entities) 4 and 5.b	Simple objection or absence of consent for a decision by either entity	No rules governing use. Can be used to veto any decision of the Presidency. Note: there is an entity veto in this respect vis-à-vis the State but only so far as such an area actually falls outside of State competencies	Either entity (via members of the Presidency) may decline to give support thereby vetoing a decision

[169] Essentially, 10 of the 14 delegates elected to the House of Representatives from RS territory must agree for the entity veto to operate i,e., to block legislation.

TABLE 4.4A: SUMMARY OF VETO MECHANISMS UNDER THE STATE CONSTITUTION

VETO NAME	STATE INSTITUTION WHERE EXERCISED	RELEVANT PROVISION OF STATE CONSTITUTION	VETO PLAYERS	INVOCATION	ETHNIC USE
Simple majority-voting[170]	House of Representative or House of Peoples	Article IV (Parliamentary Assembly) 3.d	Not technically a veto: Insufficient support by the delegates from either entity in the HoR, or rejected by more than one caucus in the HoP	No rules governing use. Can be used to veto any legislation	Any caucus may decline to give support thereby vetoing legislation

Source: derived from the provisions of the Bosnian constitution unless otherwise stated.

---

[170] Although this is not technically a veto mechanism it is included within this table though for completeness.

Table 4.4A above sets out the five primary ways the three constituent peoples are able to cripple legislation using vetoes under the Bosnian constitution either as caucuses in the Parliamentary Assembly or members of the Presidency.

The most talked about is the vital national interest vetoes (VNI) which can be exercised either by each of the Bosniak, Bosnian Croat or Bosnian Serb members of the Presidency (VNIP) or a Bosniak, Bosnian Croat or Bosnian Serb caucus of the House of Peoples (VNIH). The procedure has been used relatively infrequently partly because any declaration of VNI is either definitively determined for procedural regularity by the Constitutional Court (for VNIH) or by a substantial majority of the upper house in Entity Parliaments (for VNIP).

In fact, the VNIP was invoked only four times in 11 years and only once between 2006 and 2010 (Bahtić-Kunrath 2011, 22). The Constitutional Court has also started to interpret objectively the notion of 'vital national interest' although there is no constitutional definition at the State level (Venice Commission 2005, 9). The other major reason for VNI's infrequent use is that opponents in the political process will anticipate its use (in an objective sense) and become more intransigent—the veto emboldens intransigent actors and dissipates moves towards cooperation even though the potential for abuse of the veto is not great. Although its day-to-day use may be minimal it is relevant for constitutional amendments as many aspects could, given the absence of a definition, fall within a caucuses' vital national interest.[171]

Of the veto mechanisms, the most powerful mechanism is the 'entity-voting veto' (EVV) which is often abused to protect exclusionary ethnic interests without any objective way to determine whether it is really deployed to protect vital interests (unlike a decision of the Constitutional Court). Contrary to the view of the Venice Commission which considers it 'redundant' (Ibid, 10), it would be correct to say that it "threatens the consociational

---

[171] The Venice Commission believes in a curtailment and narrowing of the vital national interest to essential issues concerning language, education and culture but no broader scope (Venice Commission 2005, 9).

system of checks and balances, and inhibits the adoption of reforms, which makes Bosnian politics highly status quo–oriented" (Bahtić-Kunrath 2011, 3).

Only 30 per cent of the planned legislation during the period between 2006 and 2010 was actually adopted.[172] The majority of that legislation was proposed by the Council of Ministers which represents all ethnic groups in coalition government. The EVV in the House of Representatives was responsible for most of the failures to adopt legislation and, in particular, vetoes emanating from RS delegates.[173]

Contrary to popular opinion, the House of Representatives, in effect, has become an ethnically divided institution primarily due to electoral rules (ICG 2012, 5). There have been no Serbs among the 28 Federation representatives since 2006, and no Bosniaks or Croats in the RS delegation since 2010 although one member of the SDA (Bosniak) was in the RS delegation in 2014 and again in 2018 (CEC; See Table 2A, Appendix B). Entity voting was less frequently used in the House of Peoples but, where it was, RS delegates tended to use it most frequently.[174] This belies a particular failure of the institutional set-up. In an attempt to get broad consensus, there is no real government nor opposition. The same parties which are meant to be in government and propose legislation via the Council of Ministers are the ones that veto the legislation in the Parliamentary Assembly. There is no consequence as in an ordinary parliamentary system for the failure of the government to pass legislation.[175] In any ordinary parliamentary system, a failure by the incumbent government to pass major legislation should lead to the fall of the government but in Bosnia the government is completely subsumed by party self-interest as evident in the actions of the

---

[172] See further, CCI (2010) and Bahtić-Kunrath (2011, 891).
[173] "RS entity-voting was the major reason for bills failing in the HoR, rejecting 50 draft laws, followed by majority-voting with 39 failed bills, while Federation entity-voting was applied eight times" (Bahtić-Kunrath 2011, 8).
[174] "Of 31 failed bills, RS delegates rejected 19, while Federation delegates deployed entity-voting only once, on the census law" (Bahtić-Kunrath 2011, 12).
[175] Although there is a mechanism for a vote of no-confidence in the Council of Ministers in the Parliamentary Assembly (Art. V.4.c, Bosnian constitution) it would appear unworkable.

legislature. Division in the executive is amplified by division in the legislature and agreement within the executive is undermined by disagreement in the legislature.

Studies confirm that RS delegates tend to prefer the status quo when it comes to policy changes i.e., preserve RS autonomy and interest whatever the policy benefit for the wider State including the RS itself.[176] But the ability to force such a position on the State depends critically on the RS's ability to deploy vetoes without hindrance. It is able to do so without regard to other ethnic groups (using the EVV) because the majority of the population in the RS is Bosnian Serb, by virtue of the legacy of ethnic cleansing, forcible transfer or deportation during the 1990s conflict or due to population exchange. In addition, the opposition parties are disparate and divided Belloni (2008, 71).[177] Without mass return of refugees or stronger centripetal forces amongst parties[178] that is unlikely to change; unless vetoes and vital interests are defined in the constitution very narrowly or abolished altogether.

What does this mean for constitutional reform? Any proposal for constitutional reform in the Parliamentary Assembly which might challenge Serb autonomy would come up against very strong and significant vetoes. In fact, the requirement for two thirds majority support for constitutional amendments would mean vetoes could be deployed by any caucus (See Table 4.4A above). As was evident in 2006, lack of support amongst the smaller parties and minor defections amongst Croat and Bosniak delegates scuppered the April Package by just two votes. In any case, the VNI

---

[176] See further, International Crisis Group (2009, 2011, 2012); Venice Commission (2005); Bahtić-Kunrath (2011).
[177] Constitutional Court of Bosnia and Herzegovina. *Request for evaluation of certain provisions of the Constitution of Republika Srpska and the Constitution of the Federation of Bosnia and Herzegovina*, Case No. U 5/98-III, Third Partial Decision, 1 July 2000, para 61.
[178] See Table 5.2A which demonstrates that a stronger oppositional coalition could reduce the power of the EVV significantly if the SDS/SNSD seats in the House of Representatives are reduced to 10: blocking legislation in the House of Representatives would be much more difficult.

deployed in the House of the People could scupper constitutional change by a single vote.[179]

Adopting the language of game theory, academics have prescribed that "... the elites must *a priori* renounce the intention to achieve in negotiations their exclusivist or maximalist political goals at the expense of the other parties" (Kasapović 2005, 18). The prescriptions have been many: re-cantonisation and consociational government with limited, defined vetoes for cantons (Kasapović 2005; Bahtić-Kunrath 2011); regional devolution through mayor-led municipalisation and a strong centralised government (Bassuener and Weber 2014; Serwer 2020);[180] "de-ethnization" of entity-voting (Belloni 2008); maintaining Dayton institutions but changing political actors and imposing external incentives (Bieber 2010); a "centripetalist" system, with one single constituency throughout the whole country, providing incentives for politicians to cross ethnic boundaries (Bahtić-Kunrath 2011); or creation of super-majority decision making in electoral units requiring super majorities for decisions such as elections but ensuring all major ethnic groups have a super-majority veto in certain defined issues (Keil 2015; Serwer 2020).

Yet how can this be practically and practicably achieved and what exactly would persuade elites to give up their maximalist national interests in favour of co-operation? Elites, under the current system, must not only adopt the language of accommodation but must ensure the support of their ethnic base. This has been, for instance, a recurring problem for the directly elected Presidents at State level whose conciliatory positions are undermined by stronger nationalist positions taken by indirectly elected party leaders (ICG 2012, 15). Any elite which attempts to use

---

[179] Presumably the entity-voting veto may also apply because of the ambiguous way in which the constitutional amendment clause in the Bosnian constitution (Art. X) is drafted: it essentially adds a two thirds majority requirement in the House of the Representatives in addition to the ordinary decision-making procedure.
[180] Part of this model is inspired by the success of the Brčko District, which is in essence a pre-war municipality that has had a special, autonomous status for over two decades. It has prospered while managing its ethnic tensions better than most of the rest of the country (Serwer 2020; Bassuener and Weber 2014).

the language of accommodation risks being undercut by extreme nationalists who would question their loyalty to 'their people' and cite the short-term self-interest of pursuing maximalist nationalist positions. There is always a perceived existential threat to 'us' as a people; a people distinct incidentally from 'them'. Consequently, the clamour for exclusivist and narrow ethno-nationalist policies grows louder. To circumvent the problem of deadlock and intransigence, it is first necessary to elaborate on the so-called zero-sum game that is being 'played' by elites.[181] ◌

---

[181] It is commonly assumed that the game being played by elites is zero-sum (Kasapović 2005) although only if certain conditions are met is a game zero-sum. A zero-sum game is one where it is impossible to make one person better off without making at least one other worse off (i.e., a situation which is Pareto optimal). For instance, distributing some sweets to one group of people will mean that there are fewer sweets available to distribute to everyone else (as long as each group values the sweets equally). Chapter 5 will show that the 'deadlock' game being played by elites is 'zero-sum', but the 'prisoner's dilemma' game is not.

> "We need to learn again
> to listen to the rain the rain
> We need to unstone ourselves
> and eyes straight to walk
> unwavering through the city gate
>
> We need to uncover the lost paths
> that pass through the blond grass ...
> We need to wash ourselves anew
> and dream in clean drops of dawn dew ...
> We need to meet our own hearts
> again
> that fled so long ago
> We need to unstone ourselves ..."
>
> - Mak Dizdar, *The Stone Sleeper* [182]

5. "We need to uncover lost paths": modelling change

5.1 Modelling intransigence

To propose ways to circumvent the barriers to constitutional reform in Bosnia, and explain the intransigence of political elites, it is first necessary to model the 'game' that is being 'played'.[183] In the language of game theory, at least two arenas for the game need to be considered: the **parliamentary arena** where **political elites** play the game with each other and the **electoral arena** whereby the **people** (or the **electorate**) can interact with political elites.

The people, who vote, in the electoral arena can affect the choices elites make, and therefore the resulting payoffs of their choices, in the parliamentary arena. That, of course, depends on whether the electorate remain passive observers or are active agents in the parliamentary arena. Passivity or activity of the people can be a function of institutional design as demonstrated in <u>Chapters 2</u>

---

[182] An extract of a poem called "Rain" by Mak Dizdar [1917-1971] in Buturović (2002).
[183] As noted in the Introduction, Bosnia and Herzegovina is referred to throughout as "Bosnia".

and 3. The people can be included in the parliamentary arena or can be excluded to varying degrees.

This Chapter utilises three models to explain the interaction between political elites and the people; the **nested game** model; the **veto player** approach, and finally a combination of **prospect theory** and **behavioural economics**.

The first model utilised is the nested game model. The game being played amongst elites, is said to be *nested* within the wider game being played between elites and the people (Tsebelis 1990, 161).[184] The literature on nested games, and game theory, is drawn upon to model the situation in Bosnia by explaining how two sets of elites decide to cooperate or not cooperate with one another within the State institutions (Flood 1952; Tucker 1950; Downs 1957; and Tsebelis 1990) (See sub-chapter 5.1).

The second model utilised is the veto player approach. After playing out the nested game, it is then necessary to model how elites of the three constituent peoples (Bosniak, Bosnian Croats and Bosnian Serbs) would behave in the wider game (being played in the electoral arena) when one introduces a game-changing policy question such as constitutional reform whereby the fundamental rules of the game are up for renegotiation. The literature on veto players is used in a modified form to model elite behaviour in the parliamentary arena (Tsebelis 1990, 1995, 2002) (See sub-chapter 5.2).

The third, and final, model utilised is prospect theory. This model is used to account for how political elites and the people interact in the parliamentary arena and the electoral arena *given* their real-world preferences and real-world behavioural impulses. This section models whether the adoption of particular types of rules or institutions in creating a new constitution could help break the deadlock in the constitutional reform game by modifying the underlying assumptions, incentives and disincentives of the games being played by elites and the people in the parliamentary and electoral arenas (See sub-chapter 5.3). A wide variety of inter-

---

[184] Given that elite decision making occurs in the context within which the electorate can impose significant constraints on representatives.

disciplinary literature, including *nudge theory*, is drawn upon to modify the 'rules of the game' in order to see how the 'game' of constitutional reform in Bosnia would respond (See sub-chapters 5.3 and 5.4).

Britain is largely omitted in this Chapter for three reasons. The first reason is that the major consideration here is to understand how political elites interact with one another in the formal constitutional structures of Bosnia (as mandated by its consociational system)[185] and then how they interact with the people (as the structures were largely designed to be remote from the people). A similar analysis is not needed, and will not assist, for Britain as this division between elite political decision-making and the people plays out very differently there. The second reason is that Bosnia is in a post-conflict phase and has particular structural problems due to its imposed constitution. By contrast, Britain is arguably in a 'pre-conflict' phase and is looking to make more rigid, and formal, its very flexible arrangements. The game theory and veto player models do not assist greatly in drawing meaningful conclusions where the parameters of constitutional decision-making are very broad as in Britain. The third reason is that Britain does not have the same problem of legislative or constitutional deadlock; if anything, the opposite is the case. This chapter essentially seeks to show what are some of the advantages to having a more flexible constitutional posture. Understanding these relationships, and the starkly different dynamics between Britain and Bosnia, will then allow then some broad principles to be delineated, in sub-chapter 5.4, for reform in Bosnia. This will then aid the broader comparison between Bosnia and Britain in Chapter 6.

To begin utilising the nested game model, the following basic two-player model is deployed so that the game theory concepts can be understood a little better.

---

[185] See further, a detailed discussion on consociational models in Chapter 4.

Game theory and the nested game

There are two sets of players in this game. The game being played could be between elites in the **parliamentary arena** *or* the game being played between groups of people in the **electoral arena**. The people are separated into segments (representing Bosniaks, Bosnian Croats and Bosnian Serbs) and political elites (representing the people in each segment). The players interact with one another in their own arenas: either the parliamentary arena *or* the electoral arena. Players have two different strategies: either accommodate and cooperate with other players (**A**) or be intransigent and non-cooperative (**I**) (as set out in <u>Matrix 5.1A</u> below). The outcome of choosing a strategy, given the choice by the other player, is situated in the highlighted area (these are known as the **payoffs**). Essentially, payoffs are the rewards or penalties a player receives as a result of the decision the player takes.

Players (P_i):	- 1 or 2
Strategies:	- Accommodation/Cooperation (**A**) or Intransigence/Non-Cooperation (**I**)
Payoffs:	- Mutual Cooperation Reward, R_i - Mutual Defection Penalty, P_i - Sucker payoff, S_i - Defector temptation payoff, T_i

As rational actors, players attempt to maximise their payoffs in any given situation. The choice of strategy available to each player is the same but the order of preferences for a particular payoff can differ for each. For instance, in a given situation, one player may find it preferable to cooperate with another player rather than not cooperate. The ordering of the payoffs determines the difference in behavioural outcomes between elites in the parliamentary arena or between the people in the electoral arena. It should be noted though that the elite payoffs can be influenced by what happens in the electoral arena and *vice versa* if there is significant interaction. The payoff orderings (set out in <u>Matrix 5.1A</u> below) determine the type of game is being played. There are four games here: prisoner's dilemma, deadlock, chicken or assurance. Each is explained, in summary, below.

The subscript *i* refers to the player participating in the game (either player 1 or player 2). Where two players cooperate with one another on an issue (i.e., mutual cooperation) then each player receives a reward, R_i. Where each player refuses to cooperate on any given issue (i.e., mutual defection) then each player receives a penalty, P_i. If one player cooperates while the other defects, the cooperative player receives the sucker's payoff S_i, and the defecting player receives the temptation payoff, T_i. Depending on how these payoffs are ordered, players will be incentivised to prefer one strategy over another. For instance, if in the environment in which elites operate, the temptation T_i payoff is very high (because it is a dog-eat-dog world) then an elite would be far more inclined to defect when the other elite is trying to cooperate. That other elite will, therefore, receive a sucker's payoff, S_i, (which will be relatively painful given the brutal environment in which they are in).

The story of the prisoner's dilemma is often told as follows. Two prisoners, both charged with a serious crime, are held in two different cells and they have a chance to strike a bargain with their interrogators. They cannot communicate with one another and each is offered the following deal: if you confess but the other prisoner does not confess, you will be freed; if the other prisoner also confesses you will both receive a moderate sentence. If neither of you confess, you will both receive a smaller sentence than if you both confess; if you do not confess but the other does, you will receive the maximum sentence. Cooperation means helping each other by not-confessing and remaining silent (payoffs R_1,R_2) to get the maximum reward for both: a very small sentence (See Matrix 5.1A below). Non-cooperation means defecting i.e., confessing and blaming the other prisoner (payoffs P_1,P_2). If both prisoners end up confessing, they each get a moderate sentence. Remember, however, if they both do not confess, they get a chance to get off relatively scot-free.

Matrix 5.1A: Payoffs of possible games in parliamentary arena and electoral arena		
STRATEGIES:	Accommodation (A)	Intransigence (I)
Accommodation (A)	R_1R_2	S_1T_2
Intransigence (I)	T_1S_2	P_1P_2

$T_i>P_i>R_i>S_i$ Deadlock	Nash equilibrium: (P_1,P_2)
$T_i>R_i>P_i>S_i$ Prisoner's Dilemma	Nash equilibrium: (P_1,P_2)
$T_i>R_i>S_i>P_i$ Chicken	Nash equilibrium: (T_1,S_2) and (S_1,T_2)
PAYOFFS:	- Reward for mutual accommodation, R_i - Penalty for mutual intransigence, P_i - Sucker payoff for being accommodating when other is intransigent, S_i - Temptation payoff for being intransigent when other is accommodating, T_i

In the prisoner's dilemma game (Flood 1952; Tucker 1950) the dominant strategy for each player is non-cooperation (i.e., confessing). Dominant means a strategy which leaves each player individually better off no matter what the opponent does. The temptation to confess when the other prisoner does not and, therefore, come away with the temptation payoff (T_i) is very real. So, if one prisoner confesses on behalf of both and the other does not then s/he is freed. But the dilemma is that by choosing this dominant strategy (defecting) the players risk reaching a suboptimal outcome (P_1,P_2) i.e., mutual defection in the form of two confessions: they are worse off than if they had chosen the cooperative strategy (R_1,R_2) i.e., if both cooperate to deny the crime. The ordering of the payoffs for the prisoner's dilemma can be expressed as follows: $T_i>R_i>P_i>S_i$. In simple terms, this means that the temptation payoff is higher than the reward payoff which is higher than the penalty payoff which is higher than the sucker payoff. In the absence of communication between the prisoners and playing the game a single time (single shot), the dominant strategy is the one that leaves both worse off i.e., mutual confessions (P_1,P_2,) with a moderate sentence for both. The temptation to confess and risk that your fellow prisoner does not is just too appealing an opportunity to give up as the reward is that you might be freed. That is the dilemma.

By reversing the ordering of the payoffs for payoff penalty, P_i (non-cooperation as a result of mutual confessions) and payoff reward R_i (co-operation as a result of mutual denials) so that $T_i > P_i > R_i > S_i$ a different game is generated: deadlock. In this game, defection or non-cooperation is also the dominant strategy but the outcome here is equally optimal: both players are just as better off with telling on each other leading to non-cooperation (mutual confessions) as they are in cooperation (mutual denials). The reason for deadlock is that the payoffs for telling on each other (confessions, P_i) are higher than the reward for both working together to deny the crime (denials, R_i). So, the dominant strategy is to defect always and not cooperate with one another (P_1, P_2). The self-interested strategy is also the dominant strategy and there is no dilemma.

Ordering the payoffs so that $T_i > R_i > S_i > P_i$ produces the game of chicken: here, cooperating with one another (both players denying the crime) has a higher payoff R_i than being a sucker with payoff S_i. But being a sucker is better than not-cooperating (both players working against each other and confessing) with payoff P_i. There is no dominant strategy but mutual defection (i.e., ratting on each other) is the worst possible outcome with payoff, P_i. The fear of such an outcome (P_1, P_2) leads both players to cooperate even though the individual payoff for defection (T_i) is greater and there remains the possibility that you are left a sucker (S_i). This is why it is the game of chicken; you can dare your opponent to defect but the risk for them is that you might do the same and you will both be left with the worst outcome (P_1, P_2).[186] There is, therefore, always two equally optimal outcomes leading to instability: defect when the other accommodates (S_1, T_2) and accommodate when the other defects (T_1, S_2) – the obvious risk here is both players confess leading to the worst outcome (P_1, P_2).

---

[186] Ordering the payoffs so that $R_i > T_i > P_i > S_i$ makes mutual cooperation the most preferred outcome and is called the game of assurance. As this does not apply to the games in Bosnia it need not require further explanation.

As the players maximise their payoffs, they adopt mutually optimal *strategies* which in turn become the *Nash equilibrium*. Nash equilibriums are stable outcomes which no player has an *incentive* to deviate from as long as the opponent does not change strategy (See Matrix 5.1A). Unilateral improvement, therefore, is impossible. Multiple Nash equilibriums (as in the game of chicken) can be a source of instability of outcomes because it is not clear which strategy one should take. Instability may also result if *outcomes* are not *Pareto optimal* for both players. An outcome is Pareto optimal if it is impossible to improve one player's payoff without reducing the other player's payoff. So collective improvement is impossible unless at the expense of another. When outcomes are not Pareto optimal players know if they get together, they can improve the payoffs for some or all the players, but this does not happen due to lack of communication. For instance, in the prisoner's dilemma P_1, P_2 (non-cooperation as a result of each player trying to confess and get the best outcome for themselves) is not a Pareto optimal outcome although it is the *Nash equilibrium*. If the prisoners got together then they can both avoid a long stretch in prison; but they do not have an *incentive* to change their current strategy until their opponent does.

Nested games in Bosnia

The *Nested Games* approach (Tsebelis 1990) can be applied to Bosnia. Let us assume, for now, something that many take for granted: that society *is* irrevocably polarised.

If the people are polarised in the electoral arena, they have a dominant strategy: be intransigent when others accommodate — this would result in outcome T_1S_2 with high payoff T_i for voter 1 and a low payoff S_2 for voter 2 i.e., intransigence has the higher payoff. The worst outcome for a voter is to accommodate while others are intransigent (S_1T_2) with a very low payoff S_i for voter 1 for being a sucker. The polarised environment is not kind to the accommodating voice. Two other outcomes are equally amenable to a voter — mutual accommodation (R_1R_2) or mutual intransigence (P_1P_2). If mutual accommodation is preferred to mutual intransigence, then the game is prisoner's dilemma. If mutual intransigence is just as preferred as mutual accommodation, then game is deadlock. Regardless of whether the game is deadlock or prisoner's dilemma the dominant strategy for voters is intransigence whatever strategy their opponent pursues (as outlined by the ordering of preferences in <u>Matrix 5.1A</u>). In both games the stable Nash equilibrium is mutual intransigence and in the prisoner's dilemma the Nash equilibrium is also Pareto non-optimal i.e., if voters were to get-together, then they could get a better outcome for everyone. The problem is how might that happen and what would be the incentive-changing inducement?

The literature on consociationalism, set out in <u>Chapter 4</u>, is predicated on the idea that elites co-operate and accommodate each other despite the 'sharp plural divisions' among the people (the electorate) which segments and polarises them (Lijphart 1977, 2). Following the consociation model, in the parliamentary arena, if elites are doing their job of accommodating each other, then their dominant strategy is to be intransigent when their opponent compromises with equilibrium outcome (T_1S_2). Yielding, however, to an intransigent opponent and avoiding conflict (S_1T_2) is preferred to mutual intransigence (P_iP_i); that is the whole basis for assuming elites are reasonable and more accommodating. Therefore, fearing mutual intransigence elites prefer mutual compromise or yielding to intransigence (so, cooperation over non-cooperation). Or so the theory goes.[187]

But we know that is not what happens in Bosnia and we also know that the people's (or voter's) preferences in Bosnia are not the same as the elites. As demonstrated in <u>Chapter 2 and 3</u>, and contrary to the assumptions of the consociational model, the following propositions are true of Bosnia. First, the electorate may not be as divided as made out. Second, the electorate may be more inclined to accommodation than presumed. Third, elites may not be

---

[187] Following the *Nested Games* approach, the inequalities below show the order of preferences for elites in the three possible games: Electoral arena: $T_{ei}>P_{ei}>R_{ei}>S_{ei}$ (deadlock), **(Inequality 5.1a)**; $T_{ei}>R_{ei}>P_{ei}>S_{ei}$ (prisoner's dilemma) **(Inequality 5.1b)**; Parliamentary arena $T_{pi}>R_{pi}>S_{pi}>P_{pi}$ (chicken) **(Inequality 5.1c)**. The subscripts *p* and *e* stand for the parliamentary and electoral arenas respectively.

as accommodating as they should be in institutions designed for such accommodation.[188]

What explains the inability of political elites to be accommodating and honour their voter's preferences?[189] In reality, elites must pay attention to both the parliamentary and electoral arenas and they are influenced by two primary factors:[190]

- the information the people have on the decisions of elites in the parliamentary arena and, if they have such information, whether they know the real reasons why the elites made those decisions; and
- the monopoly that elites have on the representation of the people which is often a factor of electoral competition or lack thereof (Tsebelis 1990, 168).

In relation to the visibility of decisions, high information costs would reduce the visibility of political decisions thereby reducing people's influence over elites. This would give elites greater independence — elites can do what they want where 'their people' cannot see what they are doing within the institutions. Greater information would act as a constraint on elite behaviour only, of course, to the extent the people have different preferences from elites (i.e., they disagree with what the elites are doing).

If the people are polarised, then the elites would faithfully fulfil popular aspirations (i.e., greater polarisation) because the

---

[188] The failure of consociationalism is set out in further detail in Chapter 4.
[189] Considering the literature on consociationalism, Tsebelis (1990) may explain this discrepancy by identifying two extremes: isolation of the people from politicians and faithful representation by politicians of people's true preferences. Tsebelis (1990) considers the case of Belgium and the disparity in behaviour between elites and the people. See Tsebelis (1990, Chapter 6).
[190] Elites must pay attention to both arenas and so their actual payoffs would be a convex combination of the payoffs in the two arenas (Tsebelis 1990, 166) demonstrated by the linear formula: $PO_i = kPO_{ei} + (1-k)PO_{pi}$ (**Formula 5.1d**). Where PO_i stands for the payoffs (T, R, S, or P) of player i. k lies between interval [0,1] indicating the weight of the electoral arena (or the weight of the people in the decisions of the elites). $1-k$ indicates the weight of the parliamentary arena. k is influenced by two primary factors: (a) information people have on elite decision making and if they have such information the *reasons* for elite behaviour (so costs of information); and (b) monopoly of representation (or electoral competition) (Tsebelis 1990, 168).

people have lots of information about decision making and actively punish and reward elites (Sartori 1976). Elites then would play the prisoner's dilemma or deadlock game in the parliamentary arena where the dominant strategy is intransigence.[191] This would explain elite behaviour in Bosnia very nicely and would accord with the discourse that underlying ethnic hatreds and division within society is to blame. There would be little further analysis needed and in essence the institutional arrangements would merely be prolonging the inevitable conflict between the people into the future.

There is a problem, however, in applying the model with the assumptions above for two reasons. The first reason is that it is evident that the people (as an electorate) do not have much information on, or involvement in, the decision-making process.[192] In fact, minimal involvement was built into the Bosnian constitution. This means that elites should have the incentive to choose strategies resulting in the game of assurance (mutual cooperation being the dominant strategy) or at worst chicken,[193] according to consociational models but, in fact, they do not. People's involvement (or lack thereof) cannot then explain persistent intransigence by elites. The second reason is that, if anything, people's inclination to be accommodating seems to be increasing in Bosnia (or certainly was at numerous post-war junctures) whilst elite intransigence seems to be intensifying so elites are not faithfully fulfilling people's aspirations otherwise, they would be more accommodating. These are not just conjectures; they are bolstered by the detailed analysis in Chapters 2 and 3 on political culture. If there was, therefore, greater transparency, high-visibility and plurality of independent media then there would be exchange of information and mutually 'bargained' outcomes between elites with the people's preferences in mind. That is why the endeavour of constitutional reform cannot be seen in isolation and merely as an exercise in institutional tinkering.

---

[191] Inequality 5.1a above.
[192] High political apathy and dissatisfaction as demonstrated in Chapter 2 would be evidence of such a situation.
[193] Inequality 5.1c above.

In relation to the issue of electoral choice, more choice should increase people's representation. Elites in Bosnia, however, have monopoly control on electoral choice as the people do not have a varied pool of representatives to choose from other than those from the same ethno-nationalist and exclusivist elites (Hulsey and Keil 2020; Belloni 2001, 173). The electorate, therefore, may not be able to reward or punish elites in any meaningful way. As Figure 5.1A below demonstrates, across a one-dimensional policy space for simplicity, two elites (A and B) competing for election would converge to the position of the median voter (Downs 1957).[194] Reduce the choice of leader to a single elite (say A) with an ideal position SQ', and voters can be blackmailed into accepting any position between the current status quo (SQ) and the elite's ideal position SQ'. Voters must accept a possibly very wide range of policies favoured by the elite.[195]

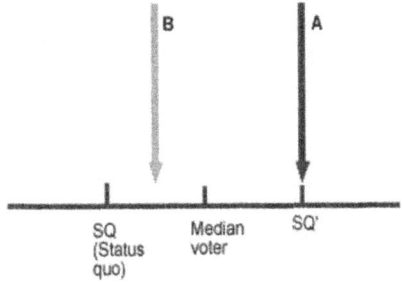

Figure 5.1A

There are a range of factors that can influence what choices are available to the people to elect elites in the parliamentary arena including the salience of issues, the costs of entering an election (set out usually in electoral laws or party structures), the resources that the elite has at their disposal, and in poor rule of law environments patronage, nepotism and corruption (Tsebelis 1990, 170). In terms

---

[194] Assuming, the usual Downsian principles, including, fixed electoral preferences and elites conducing to take policy positions that would maximise their appeal for votes.
[195] See further, Tsebelis (1990, 170).

of the resources and the environment, strong organisations and endorsements by other monopolistic institutions such as organised churches or mosques, oligarchic media barons and so on can be very strong influences.

Consociational policies have tended to reduce electoral choice to a minimum (with closed lists and proportional representation (PR)) so the supposed intransigence of the people does not spill over into the parliamentary arena resulting in intransigent elites.[196] In Bosnia, monopoly control by intransigent and ethno-nationalist political elites of electoral choice[197] is very visible particularly in the RS (Sahadžić 2009). All the major parties in the RS are nationalist vying for the most extreme policy positions which, in essence, revolves around challenging the future existence of a Bosnian State (ICG 2011, 3). In the three majority Croat cantons there is little choice other than the two major Croat parties, the HDZ and the HDZ 1990. In the five Bosniak-majority cantons the SDA remains the biggest party although it is followed closely by the SDP, SBB and DF which shows that civic parties can make inroads although seemingly only in Bosniak majority areas (Hulsey and Keil, 2020, 14;). The main issue is capture of the party and state structures by ethno-nationalist elites, as outlined in sub-chapter 3.4.

Coupled with little policy differentiation opposition moderates complain of limited media coverage of their campaigns, weak civil society (due to tight government control) and a highly-centralised entity government restricting development in municipalities controlled by the opposition (ICG 2011, 4, 7).[198] The entity separation and lack of a multi-ethnic electoral base (given the lack of large-scale refugee returns) only reinforces the monopoly of nationalist representation. Representatives can then use critical

---

[196] Questions of representation and barriers to entry in and deterrence strategies used by elites in Bosnia are not within the scope of this book although understanding how much electoral competition there is within segments of the Bosnian population is useful to the analysis. See further, spatial voting literature in Shepsle and Cohen (1998) and a discussion in Tsebelis (1990, 170).
[197] Although the elections for the 42 members of the House of Representatives are now partly through open-list proportional representation.
[198] See further, Perry and Keil (2015).

issues to provoke conflict between the constituent groups in order to remain in political office and stifle rival opponents.

Greater popular involvement in politics

In essence, because of low visibility of decision making and minimal electoral choice, the assumptions relating to the preference ordering of elites and the people are reversed: elites play deadlock or prisoner's dilemma, but people would prefer they play chicken or assurance. As the people are deliberately excluded from most decision-making processes, elites can play in the parliamentary arena alone (unconstrained by people's preferences). But elites still *choose* to play prisoner's dilemma or deadlock. Why is this? Why is mutual cooperation not appealing to elites? The answer depends on the payoff orderings for cooperation for a particular issue being fought over. In the language of game theory, as payoffs T_i (temptation payoff for defection when other accommodates) or P_i (penalty for mutual intransigence) increase, cooperation decreases and *vice versa*.[199]

The 2000 and 2006 general elections provide an excellent example of a situation where it would pay for elites (sometimes quite literally) not to cooperate with one another and be intransigent. Elites of SBiH,[200] an exclusively Bosniak party, campaigned on the platform of a 'Bosnia without entities.'[201] In response, Serb nationalists sparked alarm of a Bosnia dominated by Bosniaks and rallied support to try and defeat the SNSD leader, Milorad Dodik, who at the time was the international community's favoured and well-funded moderate candidate (Belloni 2007; Peric 2000).[202] The irony was that in 2006, Dodik deployed electoral

---

[199] See further, Tsebelis (1990). Figure 1A in Appendix B confirms that where an issue is very important for both parties (for instance, constitutional reform) the value attached to T_i will be very high and the value attached to S_i will be low: any accommodation is highly unlikely and R_1,R_2 would not be Pareto optimal.
[200] Haris Silajdžić, Bosnia's wartime prime minister in particular.
[201] Partly as a result of past positions of ethno-nationalist Serbs although it would be hard to identify when the cycle began precisely.
[202] Upon election as PM of the RS in 1998, Madeleine Albright described Dodik as "a breath of fresh air" and someone "determined to peacebuilding,

tactics that outdid the most radical Serb nationalists by championing RS autonomy and threatening again to hold an independence referendum to see off the existential threat to the RS. The SNSD won a landslide.[203] For high-importance issues a greater value attached to payoff T_i may be reasonable but even very trivial matters in Bosnia seem to fall victim to nationalist bickering at the expense of cooperation. In 2008, for instance, a law regulating genetically modified food was supported by all the parties but failed due to an inability to agree on the ethnic composition of an advisory committee which, as it happened, was powerless anyway (ICG 2009, 2).

On issues of high salience, the game in Bosnia is not iterated and there is only a single shot in which the players have to make a decision. Players cannot offer compromises in subsequent rounds or punish defectors who strike a bad agreement. That inability takes on a new meaning when the issue is as fundamental as changing the constitution and, therefore, the fundamental rules of the game. In one-shot games such as this, the ordering of the payoffs (T_i, S_i, R_i and P_i) is all critical. The dominant strategy, therefore, here will be intransigence and the equilibrium would be mutual intransigence (P_1, P_2). Congleton (2010) is right that where mutual intransigence is inevitable parties may, in fact, agree to increase the payoffs for mutual intransigence (P_1, P_2) to ensure it is not so painful and to postpone any irreparably damaging conflict.[204] Players will tend to focus on the lowest common denominator and agree on minimal or retrogressive measures. This is exactly the situation in Bosnia whereby parties agree to embed and postpone the conflict and create further division and segregation.

---

    reconciliation and connection of democratic alternative" (2018). Early on in his career he helped clean up RS corruption, turn over war criminals, normalise relations with the Federation, and facilitate the return of some non-Serb refugees (Edwards 2019; Majstorovic 2013; Washington Post 1998).

[203] See further, Belloni (2007, 54-60).

[204] Arranging a game to increase payoffs for a non-Pareto optimal outcome is common in numerous political bargains: "Insofar as conflict within political institutions tends to be less costly than on the battlefield (or within an organization's production teams), adopting such procedures tends be advantageous for both parties" (Congleton 2010. 98).

The value of P_i (payoff for mutual intransigence) is high in Bosnia due to a number of factors: there is no collapse of the incumbent government following a failure to pass policy; very basic human rights are respected and un-amendable; elites continue to be paid as elected representatives even in the absence of a government;[205] entities can continue the provision of essential services in the manner they wish free of State intervention due to the asymmetric federation; international actors cannot and will not allow collapse of the State; there is a collective security blanket at least seemingly in the form of a NATO guarantee to protect the integrity of Bosnia from outside attack; and funding, compromises or concessions can be obtained from the international community or other parties for being intransigent (such as calling for secession).[206]

Intransigent political practice in Bosnia is endemic. A clear example is the agreement of cooperation in 2012 between two almost diametrically opposed political parties (the SNSD and the SDP)[207] which if implemented would have deepened and entrenched division by entity. Measures agreed included: amending the electoral laws to closed electoral lists and abolishing the Central Vote Counting facility. HDZ and HDZ 1990 offered support to the agreement in exchange for an indirectly elected State Presidency but only if the Bosnian Croat member of the Presidency

---

[205] In fact, large sums of party funding come directly from the State. Over 80 per cent of funding for parties can be derived from various government budgets. In 2009, spending on the party financing accounted for a whole percent of Bosnia's GDP (Transparency International 2011).

[206] For instance, between 2003 and 2020 the leader of the SNSD, Milorad Dodik, called for an "independence" referendum on at least nine different policy areas: On defence reform (November 2003); preserving the RS name (March 2004); police reform (November 2006); defence against attempts to abolish RS (March 2008); NATO membership (October 2009); and OHR's decisions to extend the mandate of foreign judges and prosecutors (December 2009) ; to support the Dayton Peace Agreement (January 2010); to challenge OHR intervention in formation of Federation government (April 2011); to challenge decisions of the Constitutional Court (February 2020) (ICG 2011, 14; Toal and Adis 2011, 284; Kovačević 2020).

[207] The agreement was between Alliance of Independent Social Democrats (SNSD) leader Milorad Dodik and Social Democratic Party (SDP) leader Zlatko Lagumdžija (Tanjug 2012).

was elected by Croat votes (Jukić 2012). Dodik also supports the creation of a third Croat entity, partly because it would cripple decision making in the Federation and bolster the case for RS secession.

When it comes to the issue of constitutional reform the idea is to make accommodation in the future Pareto optimal and to decrease the payoffs of mutual intransigence (P_1, P_2). As noted earlier, a Pareto optimal outcome is one where it is impossible to improve one player's payoff without reducing the other player's payoff. Where it coincides with the Nash equilibrium players have no incentive to change their position. It is literally a win-win situation. By pushing outcomes towards the Pareto frontier, it is possible to improve the situation for all players if they come together to improve their lot. Adopting a new constitution (thereby changing the rules of the game) is fundamentally different from questions concerning everyday policy issues whose outcomes one may discern relatively easily. Given the lack of information, the uncertainty surrounding the possible outcomes from constitutional change is the critical factor. On the one hand, if there was absolute ignorance about the outcomes the position is not dissimilar as to the question facing a person under Rawls 'veil of ignorance' — the best possible result for all could be secured (Perry 2020). On the other hand, Tsebelis is right, that with complete information a player would pick the institutional arrangement most favourable to them (given their particular set of preferences). Constitution making in the real world sits in between these two extremes (Tsebelis 1990, 118).

Given the uncertainty about the constitutional reform process and having discounted any adverse role of the people in the process, the focus must be on modelling elite behaviour alone; so that as a result of analysing the positions of political elites towards reform, institutions can be created which make accommodation the dominant strategy. A three-way veto player approach would be the best way to analyse elite intransigence and lack of reform.

5.2 Modelling the failure of reform

Elites representing the three constituent peoples – Bosniak, Bosnian Serbs and Bosnian Croats – in the parliamentary arena are essentially veto players. A *veto player* is an individual or collective actor with specific preferences and intentions whose agreement is necessary to change policy. An adapted version of the model developed by Tsebelis (2002) is used here to model exactly how representatives of the three constituent peoples behave in the parliamentary arena.[208]

The veto player model is particularly useful as it succinctly demonstrates that policy change (or its opposite policy stability) is a function of three variables: the number of veto players; the distances between these players' policy ideal points (policy congruence); and veto players' internal cohesion (Tsebelis 2002, 13; Ganghof 2003, 8). Veto players may be institutions (such as parliaments or presidencies) but the rules governing that institution may determine the partisan veto players (such as parties in a coalition) who in essence hold the ability to veto.

In the case of Bosnia, the veto players would be the elites of major parties representing the electorally segmented populations of Bosniaks, Bosnian Croats and Bosnian Serbs. The model allows us to think about how vetoes can completely preclude policy change because the players simply would not agree to a change and how, within that constraint, a Pareto optimal outcome can be achieved i.e., an outcome where there is no way to make someone better off without making someone else worse off. This means that as people work towards the Pareto optimal frontier everybody can mutually benefit from any change.[209]

---

[208] The primary literature used for the model includes but is not limited to Konig (2010), Tsebelis (2002), and Tsebelis (1995).

[209] This sub-chapter, for accessibility, presents the conclusions reached as a result of applying the veto player model rather than setting out its technical basis in full.

Veto players in the constitutional change policy space

The parliamentary arena is the main veto gate through which constitutional change can occur but critically agreement depends on the three caucuses that make up the Parliamentary Assembly: Bosniaks, Bosnian Croats and Bosnian Serbs.[210] Each of these caucuses can exercise a veto regardless of party affiliation to scupper constitutional change.

The constitutional amendment veto (CAV) and entity-voting veto (EVV), explained in Chapter 4, are the most important but each of the veto players cannot deploy them as effectively as the other. The RS's streamlined governance structure and the lack of grand coalitions make deployment of the veto easier as it requires fewer parties to agree. The vital national interest veto (VNI), in the House of the Peoples, is slightly less important as the question of 'vital interest' when a proposal is vetoed can be assessed for validity by the Constitutional Court thereby changing the game dynamics.[211] Essentially, when the vetoes are considered together near unanimity is required, among political elites representing the three constituent peoples, for unimpeded constitutional change.

To clarify, the veto players here are the elites of the each of the major ethno-nationalist parties that comprise a majority in the Parliamentary Assembly (in both Houses).[212] The location of the relevant veto players in the constitutional change policy space is common knowledge and is specifically catalogued in Chapter 4 above and a summary is provided in Table 2A, Appendix B. What Table 2A suggests is that the constitutional change policy space in Bosnia has changed remarkably since the 2002 elections: party

---

[210] The institution of the Presidency can be ignored as the ability for Presidents to veto policy is via the 'vital national interest mechanism' and their ability to veto is essentially constrained by the preferences of the parties to which they belong. The veto capacity of the Presidency therefore is subsumed under the veto ability of parties represented in the Parliamentary Assembly as an ultimate veto of any decision exercised by the Presidency is exercised by the parties in the Parliamentary Assembly.

[211] The role of the Constitutional Court is not considered any further given that is beyond the scope of this book.

[212] They can be represented diagrammatically by the indifference curves Bosniak, Croat and Serb.

positions are far more extreme and single track than they were two decades ago; there are more anti-systemic party positions (greater vetoes or autonomy) than before; and use of the veto is far more feasible than two decades ago. The greater polarisation amongst parties can be compared with the data in Chapter 3 which suggests greater accommodation and tolerance amongst the population at large. In some ways, the increasing despondency and hostility towards elites and the government amongst the population may be a consequence of this discrepancy as suggested in Chapter 4.

It is assumed that Bosniaks, Bosnian Croats and Bosnian Serbs exercise their veto only on the basis of their policy preferences. As noted earlier, as the interaction between the electoral and parliamentary arenas is minimal, political elites' electoral goals and appeals to their constituency are not immediately relevant for constitutional change. The policies, statements and practices of the political parties, shows that the positions of Bosniaks, Bosnian Croats and Bosnian Serbs on constitutional change are far apart and, therefore, there are a large number of points where agreement cannot be reached due to the potential for veto.

The potential to reach agreement for change is rather small and any change will actually be incremental (no major policy change can be expected). Any change will tend towards the lowest common denominator of the most extreme political parties in power that can wield a veto; this means that change would be far apart from each of the general Bosniak, Croat and Serbs ideal party-political preferences and will not be Pareto optimal.

The ideal point in terms of reaching agreement on constitutional change — where each party must push as far away as possible from where their current self-interested ideal would allow — is not impossible to achieve. The ideal is closer to Bosniak and Bosnian Serb policy preferences than Croat preferences. Croats have far greater in common (objectively) with Bosniaks than Bosnian Serbs on the question of constitutional change. That reflects the proximity of both in the Federation.[213]

---

[213] Indicated by the substantial overlap of the Bosniak and Croat indifference curves if this is depicted diagrammatically.

Bosnian Croats though had less influence in drafting the current Bosnian constitution which is reflected in the fact they are unable to deploy the entity-voting veto (EVV) alone, and they do not have sufficient numbers in the HoR to block legislation. Their ultimate safeguard is in utilising the VNI veto or using extra-constitutional means of pressure.[214] That is precisely why Croat delegates would not accept proposals to abolish the House of Peoples ("HoP") without preserving an undefined VNI veto in a unicameral legislature together with additional safeguards such as a stronger hand in utilising the entity-veto which was one of many perceived grievances of the April Package (CoE 2006). By abolishing the HoP, any ability of Croats to seriously veto policy would be lost but it would generally allow greater scope for policy change across Bosnia. The irony is that in practice Bosnian Croat vetoes, partly because they are not extensive or significant, are not currently the issue but the abuse of Bosnian Serb vetoes is (the EVV in particular).

Dragan Čović, leader of HDZ BiH since 2005, has long advocated for a Croat-only entity in the name of "absolute constitutional equality" with all the irony that has for actual equality of individuals in Bosnia (APN 2018; Perry 2019, 7-8). But if greater Croat vetoes are awarded then policy change would become even harder and intransigence even greater. The pressure for a third Croat entity also comes from nationalists in Croatia proper who have feared losing leverage over Bosnia as the population of Bosnian Croats has decreased over time, particularly as many young people leave for better opportunities abroad. They also have designs on incorporating 'Croat areas' in Bosnia into Croatia proper in the event of any conflict as suggested by a Croatian President in comments leaked in 2016 (Less 2020). These designs have continued since, with the Croatia's current President, Kolinda Grabar-Kitarovic, repeatedly characterising Bosnia as a failed State controlled by "militant Islam" as justification for its implicit nationalist aspirations towards Bosnia (Gadzo 2020).

---

[214] Although its votes are needed for meeting the two thirds requirement for constitutional amendments.

Existing proposals for constitutional change

The vetoing ability of Bosniak, Bosnian Croat and Bosnian Serb political elites, given their extreme policy positions, significantly reduces the scope for radical constitutional change. In fact, some of the negotiation positions taken by them confirm that they are tending toward further intransigence rather than accommodation.

Agreement on such positions should be outright ruled out in the constitutional reform agenda. Providing further autonomy or vetoes to any caucus would not help with greater accommodation. If, for instance, stronger vetoes were granted to Bosnian Croats which the Bosnian Serbs currently possess (and nothing else) the effect would be like introducing a completely new veto player and completely preclude any future constitutional change or even major policy change. A number of commentators have thought further 'entitisation' may be a solution thereby ensuring that each Caucasus has a "stake in the political process" (Parish 2011; Hayden 2006, 2007 cf. Belloni 2008). But with a set of structures predicated on the Dayton arrangements, further entitisation is a recipe for deadlock, division, and ultimately separation.

Other popular proposals in the constitutional reform debate concentrate on abolishing or weakening the Presidency (Venice Commission, April Package, Sejdic-Finci Proposals) (Gavrić 2013). Yet such a measure will do very little to break the deadlock, for a number of reasons: the VNIP is rarely invoked because the Presidency makes few decisions that are of critical consequence; competencies of the Presidency are relatively narrow in scope already and the Presidency rarely submits draft laws to the Parliamentary Assembly even though it is able to do so.[215] The majority of proposals for draft laws (in fact, over 75 per cent in both Houses) emanate from the Council of Ministers (CoM) which has no effective veto mechanisms (Bahtić-Kunrath 2011, 907).

---

[215] Proponents who are authorised to submit draft laws to the Parliamentary Assembly can be any member of one of the Houses, a parliamentary committee and the joint committees of the houses, the Presidency, and the Council of Ministers (Bosnia and Herzegovina, "Rules of Procedure House of Peoples" Art. 92, "Rules of Procedure House of Representatives" Arts. 101, 102). See further, Bahtić-Kunrath (2011, 920).

Given that the CoM proposes the majority of legislation — as a grand coalition representing all party interests — one would expect almost all legislation gets passed. That is, however, not the case because it is the only major institution that does not protect ethnic interests (i.e., there are no effective vetoes) whereas the Parliamentary Assembly does. This is precisely why the CoM is able to agree and create legislation through striking informal bargains and creating cross-party alliances before an issue is voted on. The entity-voting veto, VNI or majority vetoes are deployed in the Parliamentary Assembly especially by RS delegates who can hold back any legislation they wish using vetoes. Empowering the Council of Ministers further and abolishing the Presidency may meet the technical requirements of the judgment in *Sejdic-Finci* but little policy change will occur on the ground *unless* simultaneous changes are made to parliamentary vetoes and ethno-national electoral districts that reinforce divisions created by ethnic cleansing and the consequences of the war. That is reinforced by the fact that members of the Presidency can already be side-lined by more influential party leaders.

Is there a way out of the current predicament? Can the exclusionary ethno-nationalist parties be moderated? Are there a set of points in the constitutional reform space which could allow all three constituent peoples to coalesce around?

5.3 Modelling successful evolution in the short run

Constitutional reform is often seen as extraordinary and given a constitution's importance in providing stability they are purposefully designed to be difficult to change, as noted in Chapter 4 (Dougherty and Edward 2011). The assumption, therefore, made in the models above was that any game, modelling constitutional reform, would be a single-shot game unlike models concerned with day-to-day political decisions. The other assumption, based on the design of Dayton institutions, is that there ought to be very limited civic involvement.[216]

---

[216] Therefore, k in Formula 5.3d (restated below) is very low.

In the models below, it is demonstrated that if a new mechanism to achieve constitutional reform in Bosnia relaxes these two assumptions, then it will have two significant effects. First, it would allow for greater communication between ethno-national elites over time on fundamental constitutional issues as repeated games will lessen winner-takes all scenarios. Second, involving the people will bring the position of the elites closer to the median-voter position.

If the statistical analysis (in Chapter 3) is to be believed, and neither Bosnian history nor the statistical methodology provide any basis that it should not, the preference of the median voter in Bosnia is not dissimilar to Britain's: moderate, accommodating and far more inclined to political participation than consociational models would presume them to be. People's involvement in politics, therefore, should significantly moderate elite behaviour.[217] We know from the literature on political culture in Chapter 2 that civic participation has a favourable impact on democratic culture, in and of itself, but here there is also the promise of changing political outcomes.

Greater communication and repeated interaction

Figure 1A in Appendix B outlined that where an issue is very important for both parties (such as, for instance, constitutional reform) the value attached by elites to T_i in the parliamentary arena will be very high and the value attached to S_i will be low. Any accommodation is highly unlikely and mutual cooperation (R_1, R_2) is not Pareto optimal.[218] The assumption that was made was that games were single-shot and that general actors were self-interested, rational and independent. If we relax some of those assumptions and assume that games are repeated, and actors have the ability to communicate and coordinate strategies, then the game changes in a fundamental way. These strategies are called **contingent**.

---

[217] Therefore, increasing the value of k in Formula 5.3d (restated below) and altering the veto player scenario.
[218] That is, there are a set of options where someone can made be better off without another being made worse off.

Whatever game is being played (deadlock, chicken or prisoner's dilemma), when player 1 chooses to cooperate, player 2 chooses to cooperate with probability p (probability of inclination).[219] Similarly, if player 1 is intransigent player 2 will be so too with probability q (probability of retaliation). Essentially, player 2's decision is contingent on player 1's decision before: each player would choose the strategy that would maximise her expected utility.

Although it sounds intuitive, modelling these probabilities, shows that as the probabilities p (inclination to cooperate) and q (likelihood of retaliation) increase, the choice of cooperation is more likely.[220] If one was to work through the algebraic inequalities, two propositions can be made: the likelihood of cooperation increases when the payoffs for cooperation increase (R_i and S_i) and decreases when the payoffs for intransigence increase (T_i and P_i). Those propositions apply whatever the nature of the game (prisoner's dilemma, chicken or deadlock). Critically, however, inclination to follow cooperation (p) or retaliation (q) in future rounds must be credible.[221]

Indeed, a player's perspective on the future is all important; a factor influenced by history, recent interaction and so forth. There are two extremes and an intermediate position.

The one end of the extreme is to imagine that there is no consideration of payoffs in future rounds as players (largely political elites) are concerned with immediate payoffs and are impatient (Addison and Murshed 2002).[222] The costs or consequences of today's action in the future is heavily discounted;

---

[219] This term is used because it is assumed that player 1 by setting an example inclines player 2 to follow.

[220] This is because of Inequality 5.3d. p and q allow us to consider the expected utilities (EU) of each strategy as follows: $EU(I) = T(1-q) + Pq$ **Equation 5.3a**; $EU(C) = Rp + S(1-p)$ **Equation 5.3b**. Cooperation would be the preferred strategy if: $EU(C)-EU(I) > 0$ **Inequality 5.3c**. Rearranging the three equations above results in the following inequality: $(R-P)p + (T-P)q > (T-S)$ **Inequality 5.3d**.

[221] Inequality 5.3d shows that for the variation in payoffs (T_i, S_i, R_i and P_i) to make a difference cooperation (p) or retaliation (q) in future rounds must be credible.

[222] This might apply for ordinary political decisions as much as it does to constitutional decisions.

both in terms of reputation of players (such as being non-cooperative) and their inability in future rounds to create surprises (such as strategically resorting to conflict when the opponent least expects it)[223] — these are often situations of war.

The other end of the extreme is to imagine that elites are highly concerned about the future (especially constitutional 'game rules') and, therefore, unconstrained by any outside forces they choose high-level conflict to finally determine the future — often situations of opportunity when there is multi-polarity or divergent positions by surrounding powers. You take your chances and go for broke at the opportune moment.

The intermediate position is that elites are highly concerned about the future (especially constitutional 'game rules') and, therefore, choose low levels of conflict with their opponents to ensure an outcome favourable to them in the future — given that they are unable to erase their opponents and that they will exist in the future and, therefore, must accommodate them somehow (Garfinkel and Skaperdas 2000). In the latter case, both reputation and surprises matter and it is the situation most relevant to this study if the conditions are to be created for meaningful constitutional reform.

As demonstrated in Chapter 4, in the Bosnian parliamentary arena, legislation was constantly vetoed and parties preferred intransigence precisely because there were very low payoffs for cooperation (R_i and S_i). The likelihood of retaliation (q) or inclination to follow cooperation (p) was very low. It should be noted that in a single-shot game with no communication between players the size of the payoffs cannot be varied and, therefore, preference orderings are all important. Everyone sets out their

---

[223] The discount factor, $d=1/(1+r)$, is a figure between 0 and 1. r is the indicator of time preference. d, determines the relative weight attached by a player to the future, where 0 demonstrates no concern for the future, only immediate payoffs in the current stage game and 1 a sole concern with future payoffs (demonstrating supreme patience and concern for long-term well-being). See further, Leyton-Brown and Shoham, Yoav (2008, 51); Addison and Murshed (2002, 495).

positions at the outset and they cannot conceive of shifting them under any circumstances.

What makes the game of constitutional reform different is that the rules themselves are being changed — future interaction is being determined. Introducing contingent strategies can make threats of retaliation (q) or promise of cooperation (p) very believable and real because the new rules may either reward or punish — in some cases totally and in perpetuity. The immediate objection to this might be why would elites commit to making any changes given that consent of all significant elites, more or less, needs to be obtained? Why not be intransigent in all periods? These issues will be addressed below, and it will be demonstrated that allowing repeated interaction and, in particular, involving the people can have a special and positive effect.

5.4 Modelling future co-operation and participation

Repeated interaction, in the process of constitutional reform, is in many ways critical because players become interested in maximising their payoffs during the entire period of interaction (Tsebelis 1990, 75). As a result, it becomes rational to choose sub-optimal outcomes in the single-shot game if such strategies increase their payoffs over repeated interaction (Luce and Raiffa 1957; Axelrod 1984; Tsebelis 1990). This means elites are more inclined to accept slightly worse options today in the hope of a better trade off in a certain tomorrow.

Carroll (1987) has suggested that if, in a repeated game, the number of rounds of interaction are finite then contingent strategies are impossible. By backward induction a player would rightly expect defection in the final round and, therefore, defect earlier in anticipation of future defection (Tsebelis 1990, 74). Indeed, in repeated games only the penultimate and final rounds are important subject only to a discount factor to weight the relative importance of the final (second) round; whereby a relative low importance attached to the future, or impatience, will lead to short-term decision making.

Under Carroll's (1985) model, however, agreements between opponents could never occur (because they expect defection in the final round) which is not realistic. Fudenberg and Maskin (1986) present the *folk theorem* which confirms that any individually rational outcome can arise as a *Nash equilibrium* in infinitely repeated games even with sufficiently little discounting.[224] A Nash equilibrium, as noted earlier, is an outcome from which no player has an incentive to deviate from. A player in essence cooperates until the other player fails to cooperate, which results in non-cooperation forever more. The only caveat is that the discount factor for the future needs to be sufficiently high (so that the players attach a sufficiently high weight to the future (such that the punishment will be known to be painful). If, therefore, players are sufficiently patient, cooperation can be sustained.

In addition, any outcome that gives each player at least as much as they could obtain on their own can be a stable *Nash equilibrium* in any number of finite rounds whenever there is incomplete information or uncertainty about the opponent's payoff (as would be the case in constitutional reform in Bosnia).[225] Credibility and the reputation of players and their ability to generate surprises in future rounds becomes important. As there is imperfect information, there is a probability (however small) that the opponent's payoff makes mutual cooperation rational (Tsebelis 1990, 76). Moreover, with a number of repeated games threats of punishment and promises of rewards become more credible.[226]

---

[224] Zikos, Vasileios. *Lecture Notes on Game Theory*, 29 September 2013; and Fudenberg and Maskin (1986, 533).

[225] In Figure 1A in Appendix B for any type of game, each player can guarantee themselves P_i and therefore any outcome that is at least P_i is equilibrium. Players can arrive at any point Pareto superior to (P_1P_2) and be at equilibrium: essentially repeated games help players reach the Pareto surface.

[226] For a set of payoffs $T_i>R_i>P_i>S_i$ across a number of iterations when the rewards for cooperation (R_i, S_i) increase or rewards for defection (T_i, P_i) decrease cooperation could occur under much shorter time horizons. For instance, if an opponent's payoffs are ($T_i=6$, $R_i=4$, $P_i=2$, $S_i=1$) then if she defects, she gains 2 units (6-4) in that round but thereafter will only receive 2 (a net loss of 2) in each further round — so more than two iterations are required for punishment. If the payoffs for mutual defection decrease so $P_i=1$; following defection the net loss is 3 units, so she is punished immediately in the next round.

Greater communication and repeated interaction are, therefore, in principle, important for the game in the parliamentary arena. For constitutional reform in Bosnia, because the rules of the game are being decided, punishments would be much more painful and incentives much more rewarding.

For repeated interaction to work, however, there must be a fixed and regular possibility to amend the constitution (with civic participation). A failure to amend or unilateral deviation amongst participants must lead to the threat of credible punishment and preferably a monotonic reward scheme that links choices made by players to rewards (Jihong and Hamid 2011) i.e., very exclusive and tasty carrots and memorably stinging sticks. Higher levels of accommodation should be rewarded[227] with higher payoffs so that different players have an incentive to align themselves in a way that they can be identified by their equilibrium choices (this is known as *incentive compatibility*). Credible punishment in the parliamentary arena would be an inability to form a government, dissolving of parliament, and a requirement to re-elect elites or delegates deliberating on the constitution (See further sub-chapter 6.2).

Under the current Bosnian constitution, a failure to pass policy has no consequences for the coalition government. Kavish (2012, 15) rightly notes that in the current system with no risk of government collapse, "there is little incentive for the ethnically based parties to compromise resulting in renewed emphasis on each group's "preferred solutions" and nationalist rhetoric." In the proposed model, the rewards for cooperation (R_i and S_i) would increase significantly and the threat of retaliation (with probability q) would be very credible which would encourage elites to bargain more than they are currently willing in a single-shot game. Far more important, however, than the possibility of government collapse would be the threat posed by one critical aspect of this model: the people. Civic involvement will help to ensure greater

---

[227] Such features already exist in institutions in other spheres: "For instance, many constitutions involve explicit provisions for amendment, [via voting rules] while a designer of repeated auctions or other repeated allocation mechanisms often commits to excluding collusive bidders or free-riders from future participation" (Lee and Sabourian 2011).

responsiveness of the Parliamentary Assembly to the will of an accommodating majority and ensure the stability of the State if not the government.

Spoilers of constitutional reform

There are two objections, related to stability, to repeated interaction on constitutional changes; both relate to the possibility of elite spoilers who may co-opt secessionist sentiment. First, why would political elites, who can take spoiling action in the short term (e.g. pursue conflict, secession, or even terrorism), be willing to be conciliatory and lose their reputation for being tough on the opponent especially if one makes the assumption that the future is not discounted heavily by elites?[228] Second, why would elite spoilers reveal their dominant position (i.e., to compromise) in the repeated interaction game when that could mean losing the ability to generate surprises in the future?

In relation to the first objection, spoilers can be kept in check by the guarantee provided by the signatories to the Dayton Peace Agreement which precludes any imminent violent conflict in the medium term.[229] Unilateral secession of either group is also not a viable option given the guarantee provided by the parties to the Dayton Peace Agreement although calls for it grow ever louder in the RS still dominated by Milorad Dodik; he has even attempted to find support in nationalist circles in Croatia, Serbia and Russia (Hamilton 2020). Unilateral secession would have no basis under international law and would not in the case of RS gain wide international acceptance.[230] Spoilers would be incentivised to

---

[228] See, for instance, the work of Murshed (2002, 2010).
[229] Especially given the proximity of Bosnia to the EU, the history of the violent conflict in Bosnia, and the geo-strategic considerations at play in the region with various minorities in each of the South East European States.
[230] A region's desire for independence from a State is not sufficient. The RS has not been subject "subject to alien subjugation, domination or exploitation", nor has its people been "denied any meaningful exercise of its right to self-determination within the state of which it forms a part." If anything, the RS has had quite the opposite experience with wide autonomy and the ability to exercise their rights to self-determination internally within Bosnia. See further,

compromise as, given uncertain information, they would still retain the ability to generate surprises in later stages of the game. Extremist followers of elite spoilers, with participation and incentive compatibility constraints, may mean they would defect from any conciliatory behaviour of the elites but again the international guarantee will contain such defection (which elites will recognise). In addition, under the mechanisms developed in sub-chapter 6.4 the body that would consider constitutional amendments would have electoral rules favouring centripetal positions (with minority protections) thereby restricting the ability of (minority) extremists to get elected.

In relation to the second objection, if the current institutional arrangements for constitutional change were kept intact, spoilers would have little reason to reveal their dominant position in the initial rounds given their reputation for intransigence. The current actors in the Parliamentary Arena are already those taking the most extreme positions and, therefore, there is little further scope for more extreme intransigence, short of violent conflict.

In this proposal for constitutional revolutions a non-nationalist elite taking part in repeated interaction will be encouraged to reveal their dominant strategy of compromise (which they are currently unable to do). The extreme ethno-nationalist elites will have a check on their ability to spoil the game due to new institutional restraints and rewards for higher accommodation. Also, given the smaller pool of people extreme nationalists can now call followers[231] there will be little loss to them in being conciliatory (other than losing extremist minority support). In any case, the least bad outcome would remain the status quo, which is characterised by deadlock, and elite intransigence. The

---

In the Supreme Court of Canada in the Matter of Section 53 of the Supreme Court Act, R.S.C. 1985, Chap. S-26 and in the Matter of a Reference by the Governor in Council Concerning Certain Questions Relating to Secession of Quebec from Canada, As set out in Order in Council P.C. 1996-1497, September 30, 1996. Ottawa: Supreme Court of Canada, 1997; ICG (2011, 24).

[231] Assuming, of course, there is appropriate non-nationalist civic involvement in the new institutions.

institutional mechanics that would make this possible is set-out in sub-chapter 6.4.

Civic mass involvement

The key problem identified in the games above was that insulation of the parliamentary arena from the electoral arena was a major stumbling block to reform. How might direct and greater civic participation and deliberation in the constitutional reform process affect the game being played in the parliamentary arena?

The content of constitutional reforms suggested by elites in parliament will, of course, be preferred by them over the status quo, while the content selected by the people in a participatory process (such as a referendum) will be preferred by a majority of voters. As we saw earlier, on a single-dimensional issue the outcome would be determined by the median voter. In multiple dimensions (where there is more than one issue, as in constitutional reform) a medium voter does not really exist. The preferences, however, of a large population may be very well approximated and amalgamated.[232]

Modelling people's mass preferences, allows us to consider how civic participation (such as in a referendum) on the Bosnian constitution may interact with the preferences of the elites in the parliamentary arena. One scenario (based on the analysis in Chapter 3) is that the preferences of the people identified by a referendum on the Bosnian constitution can coincide very closely with elite preferences but there is a space in which preferences do not coincide. In fact, the outcome of a referendum could fall in a space quite radically different from current elite preferences, if the people are accommodating, tolerant and democratically oriented. That would suggest that referendums could increase the possibility of policy change as the number of outcomes that can defeat the status quo are significantly increased. Greater civic participation would reduce policy stability, which has been inhibiting constitutional reform in Bosnia, especially if the evidence-based

---

[232] This is done by identifying the median position of each voter and the point at which point each voter is indifferent between two alternatives equal distance from their ideal point.

assumption in this book, that the electorate is more accommodating than the elites, is correct.

There is, however, one important aspect that could mean that referendums induce greater policy stability than currently the case. The institutions that regulate civic participation, and specifically referendums, are absolutely critical.

Bare referendums, partisan triggers and civic initiatives

There are many forms of civic participation in a constitutional design process including referendums, civic initiatives, deliberative assemblies and so forth. The person or the group that is able to trigger civic participation (such as through referendums or civic initiatives) and the person or group that can ask and frame the questions is critical in terms of the outcomes of any constitutional reform process.

We know that referendums in their simple and unrefined form can be 'blunt instruments' — both Britain and Bosnia have found that out to their peril. But the argument that referendums can never be usefully deployed in divided societies is wrong despite claims to the contrary: "It is doubtful that a form of plebiscite can be devised, let alone implemented, in divided societies that would avoid all these dangerous pitfalls [of inflaming and polarising conflicts]" (Bose 2002, 51). Bare referendums which have a yes or no option and has a simple majority threshold, *are* inadvisable. If a referendum is merely the ability to ratify a constitutional amendment of the parliamentary arena (as is usual in many countries)[233] then the outcome has to be located within the intersection of the preferences of the elites in the parliamentary arena and people's preferences.

---

[233] Suski (1993, 138, 142) confirms that out of 160 constitutions analysed 56 make reference to referendum on constitutional amendments. Of those, only 36 make explicit reference to required referendums for ratification. 47 countries allow for non-required referendums but only a minority allow civic initiatives. See further, Hug and Tsebelis (2002, 487).

Constitutional referendums which merely have a ratifying function create an additional veto player in the game: the people.[234] In Bosnia, this means the majority of the people will not be any worse off if they get to have a say on the constitution (as a simple yes or now). Even better, any decision taken would be closer to the voters' median position. But mere ratification will not really increase the range of possibilities to move away from the status quo overall although it would ensure the position of the median voter is taken into account.

Referendums that allow a kind of civic veto, allowing the people to strike down parts of a constitution, as opposed to the entire constitution, does however increase the potential for policy change.[235] However, a bare referendum (of any sort) will not really work because of the very high likelihood of boycott by one or more groups because of its crude and binary majoritarian logic. There is also the very significant danger that the outcome of a bare referendum may be interpreted as approval of the status quo when in reality it may tell us very little. Bare referendums tell us little because of the majoritarian logic, how the question is posed and by whom the referendum is championed.

Furthermore, any proposal for constitutional referendums, civic initiatives or deliberative assemblies in Bosnia cannot be partisan — that is the ability to trigger referendums or set agenda questions cannot be partisan. If Bosniaks, Bosnian Croats and Bosnian Serbs were all given equal ability to call referendums then if one player gets an outcome in the parliamentary arena outside of the preferences of the people, and the elites own ideal position, then they have an incentive to call a referendum to get an outcome closer to their own ideal points — in fact, this is exactly what happens in Bosnia with ethno-nationalist elites — they threaten secession referendums. The only possible positive aspect from partisan

---

[234] It is assumed that simple majorities in a referendum can pass a policy proposal purely for simplifying the model. The model can easily accommodate differences in majority requirements. See further, on required referendums, in Hug and Tsebelis (2002, 478); and Tsebelis (2002, 176).
[235] Referendums on this basis are allowed in Italy. See further Hug and Tsebelis (2002, 491).

triggers is that if a referendum was truly State-wide the median voter position would be better represented; the downside is that instability and short-termism would reign (Cronin 1989).[236]

A far more serious scenario is if Bosniaks, Bosnian Croats and Bosnian Serbs are also able to set the agenda question on constitutional reform. Assuming complete information between elites, the ethno-nationalist referendum agenda setter would be guaranteed to get the outcome they most prefer. If, for instance, the ethno-nationalist Serb elites had a referendum veto and agenda setting power independent of the parliamentary arena it would anticipate that a lowest common denominator position is likely to be the outcome of deliberations in the parliamentary arena. To obtain, however, a better position for itself, those elites may trigger a referendum, set an agenda question designed to influence an outcome closer to its most preferred position. It can obtain a more extreme outcome or even retreat to the old status quo; the possibility of any reform is vetoed. Indeed, the referendums used by the RS and the National Croatian Assembly (Sabor), discussed in Chapter 3, were exactly designed to have such an impact: referendums are called during an engineered crisis, leading questions are posed ("would you agree to secession if a majority agreed?"), and the inevitable success of the referendum is used as leverage to veto policy proposals that are disliked.

Giving partisan players the ability to set the agenda in a referendum would risk cancelling out other partisan veto players leading to governmental or even State instability. Just as important, the utilisation of referendums as partisan vetoes will lead to even greater policy stability (i.e., moving away from the status quo will become very difficult). The will of the people may be merely the will of one segment (Hug and Tsebelis 2002, 483).

Where the ability to trigger referendums and set the agenda is by civic initiative (where citizens trigger and ask questions) then the outcomes can significantly shake up the status quo especially if elite preferences in the parliamentary arena are not close to the

---

[236] See further, reviews by Zimmerman (1990), Engstrom (1992); and Benedict (1991).

median voter preferences. In fact, if the process of referendums or civic initiatives is completely detached from the parliamentary arena then the preferences of the elite (as veto players) can be completely eliminated and replaced by the preferences of the people. Elite veto players can be completely disregarded so it is unsurprising that very few constitutions provide for unrestrained civic initiatives.[237] Civic initiatives could lead, in theory, to a much wider pool of preferences of the people to be considered and far greater scope for change. The optimal position—in order to maintain governmental stability and ensure a check on unconstrained voter preferences—is a balanced link between the parliamentary arena and electoral arena.

What empirical evidence supports the theoretical position on civic initiatives? Tsebelis's (2002) caveat can only be echoed: there are so few civic initiatives that are built into constitutions that there are few, if any, studies showing the effect of such referendums on policy outcomes cross-comparatively. Gerber (1996), however, shows that at a sub-national level in the US and Switzerland provision for civic initiatives lead to policies significantly closer to the voters' median position (Tsebelis 2002, 492). Where civic initiatives are introduced, agenda setting powers (both triggering and setting questions) should ideally be competitive and inclusive.

Hug and Tsebelis (2002, 492) rightly note that if all the potential players (both veto and non-veto) are included in the selection process then the status quo would only be defeated if proposals are made so that they are supported by a majority: "which means that the process will converge towards the preferences of the 'median voter'." Much of the literature focuses on civic initiatives launched by broad-based citizen groups or specialist interest groups to trigger and set questions (Gerber 1999; Hug and Tsebelis 2002). Broad-based groups would collect signatures meeting a high threshold, which would indicate wide majority support, leading to moderate proposals close to the

---

[237] Only 11 constitutions provide civic initiatives but these provisions other than in Switzerland are hardly used. The countries allowing for such initiatives include Belarus, Latvia, Liechtenstein, Lithuania, Moldova, Philippines, Slovakia, Switzerland and Ukraine. See further, Hug and Tsebelis (2002, 489).

median voter. Such a system, however, relies on a homogenous and relatively harmonious population without significant cleavages. In a conventional way, signature selection could not work in Bosnia. Thresholds on signatures for reform would not be met as a result of elites mobilising support against any initiative they disliked. Lowering the threshold to encourage use would risk that elite veto players may try and initiate referendums in their own isolated segments to trigger a referendum and set questions pursuing narrow nationalist goals — far away from the preferences of the median voter.

Harnessing the power of the people

It is possible, however, to harness the power of participatory and deliberative mechanisms, including referendums and civic initiatives, for meaningful constitutional reform in Bosnia. Thaler and Sunstein (2009), following in the footsteps of Tversky and Kahneman (1974), use prospect theory or behavioural psychology to demonstrate that decision making and preference formation under risk is not simply a function of utility maximisation (as they are under rational choice models).[238]

Violations of the assumptions of rational choice models[239] generate, in particular, two biases that could affect constitutional

---

[238] From observed behaviour, prospect theory says that: people systematically make decisions which assess probabilities poorly. People tend weigh losses greater than gains (i.e., they are loss averse). People tend to be more interested in their relative gains and losses as opposed to their final income and wealth — they therefore encode choices in terms of deviations from a reference point rather than net assets. People tend to under-react to low-probability events and over-weight high-probability events (certainty effect). Because people are loss averse and are interested in relative gains and losses the identification of the reference point, or framing of a choice problem, becomes absolutely critical (Tversky and Kahneman 1974; Thaler and. Sunstein 2009; Yeung 2012).

[239] Or more accurately, violation of several of the basic assumptions of expected-utility theory in uncertain choice situations including transitivity, dominance, invariance, and cancellation (or the independence of irrelevant alternatives transitivity, dominance, invariance, and cancellation (or the independence of irrelevant alternatives).

referendums: a status quo bias and a framing effect bias.[240] The status quo *bias* refers to people's tendency not to change established behaviour given their limited time, intellectual or educational capacity and resources. People, thereby, remain passive unless compelling incentives are provided for them to be otherwise.[241] It can also mean that actors encode choices in terms of deviations (loss or gain) from a reference point rather than simply think in terms of gains and losses in the abstract (Levy 1992). What this means in simple terms is that the choices made during or immediately after a war are likely to be quite different from choices made in times of relative peace. In addition, choices made by people when they are faced with impediments to accessing information, education, or resources are likely to skew their decisions in preference of the status quo. It is for this reason that Perry (2021) argues that any constitutional changes or 'fixes' in Bosnia cannot happen successfully "without looking at the educational system that has taken root and continues to do damage to BiH's human and social capital."

Framing effects occur when two "logically equivalent (but not transparently equivalent) statements of a problem lead decision makers to choose different options" (Druckman 2001, 62). The example frequently used is that people might support an economic program when it is said to result in 90 per cent employment, but then oppose the same program when it is said to result in 10 per cent unemployment. If the status quo bias and framing effect bias hold, then, Thaler and Sunstein's work could contain some very useful suggestions for overcoming biases in the political arena. In

---

[240] On the axiomatic basis of utility theory, consider Luce and Raiffa (1957, Ch. 2). For a discussion of behavioural violations of various axioms (transitivity, dominance and cancellation, invariance), consider Kahneman and Tversky (1979), Arrow (1982), Tversky and Kahneman (1986, 252-254), and Tversky, Slovic, and Kahneman (1990). Levy's (1992) work is very instructive.

[241] Kahneman and Tversky (1979) also talk about an 'endowment effect' as an instance of status quo bias. When people value objects/services already in their possession more than items that they do not have. Preventing loss of something already owned, therefore, is far more important than gaining something extra. Studies also point to psychological discounting (Frederick 2002). People would tend to place more weight on the short term than on the long-term effects of decisions. See, Thaler and Sunstein (2009), Stoker (2012, 3), Yeung (2012, 6).

particular, designing policies with defaults that are closer to voters 'real preferences'[242] or desires. It would, therefore, be possible to nudge[243] them in a particular direction without removing voter's ability to choose. The impact of that in the Bosnian context, where people's preferences are clearly being ignored and, in fact, are impossible to consider in the current constitutional framework, could have very useful social, political and economic consequences.[244]

Framing effects in particular have enormous implications for referendums and civic initiative agenda setting, in particular, for the people. At a normative level, at its extreme, framing effects suggest that voter preferences are nothing more than arbitrary whims and completely irrelevant when policy makers are considering decisions which impact voters (Druckman 2001, 63). At a positive level, framing effects would break the connection between the normative theory of rational actors[245] and the expectation that actual human behaviour accords to rational choice assumptions about maximising utility. Framed the right way, therefore, the suggestion is that you can get voters to agree to pretty much anything.

The assumptions, however, of prospect theory (of the non-utility maximising rational actor) challenge the assumptions of the rational choice model used earlier which hold such an actor (albeit a relatively weak one) as the basis for analysis. There is some way to reconcile the work of Thaler and Sunstein to the models above. The two biases can be accounted for in the rational choice

---

[242] Which of course begs the question what real preferences are? For to 'nudge' people towards their real preferences would presumably mean to nudge them in the direction of the normative rational actor. Nudge's libertarian paternalism presumes that policy makers understand what ordinary people want better than the people themselves leaving open the possibility of policy makers' susceptibility to make mistakes. See, Leonard (2008), Farrell and Shalizi (2011).

[243] By which he means "any aspect of the choice architecture that alters people's behaviour in a predictable way without forbidding any options or significantly changing their economic incentives" (Thaler and Sunstein 2009, 6).

[244] Some examples Thaler and Sunstein (2009) consider are enrolling employees on a pension scheme or people onto an organ donation scheme automatically unless they actively opt out.

[245] In particular, the axiom of invariance.

framework. Druckman (2001, 64) demonstrates that individuals can overcome framing effects by relying on credible advice. In fact, much of the literature on framing effects (including Kahneman and Tversky's work) has ignored this possibility by forcing experimental participants to make decisions in isolation from social contact and context.

Variance of preferences as a result of framing can be addressed to a large extent by greater information and interaction amongst individuals.[246] At the very least, simultaneous presentation of choices would render framing effects more transparent and reduce the chance that decision makers are influenced by them without knowledge or desire (McDermott 1998, 27). For elites in Bosnia this would already be the case and, as demonstrated in the models above, they are driven largely by narrow self-interest. For the electorate, however, framing effects matter but only to the extent that they make choices with relatively little information and relatively little credible advice. The veto player approach analysing referendums confirmed as much. The partisan veto player was entitled to set questions which would achieve a result closer to her ideal point rather than the ideal of point of the other players.

We know, however, from Chapter 2 where Bosnians' ideal points on key institutional and fundamental values are due to extensive time-series data. Regardless, of the strength of rational choice assumptions in individual decision-making some insight on constitutional referendums can be gained from the effects of framing and status quo bias: in particular, 'nudging' outcomes amongst the population at large in Bosnia towards accommodation rather than intransigence in line with their clear underlying preferences.

---

[246] Although, the advice giver themselves must be credible and believed to be so. In any case, "... preference formation is consistent with a conventional rational choice model where people base their preferences on their prior beliefs as well a credible signal (e.g., Lupia and McCubbins, 1998) — preference invariance is not violated because preferences are not based on arbitrary features of the problem description (See Arrow 1982, 7; Bartels 1998, 7). Moreover, from a normative perspective, preferences based on the systematic integration of credible information are much more meaningful as a public policy instrument." Druckman (2001, 66).

One such device would be to make constitutional referendums, civic initiatives and deliberative assemblies a default, fixed and regular feature of Bosnian politics; what may be termed a *revolving constitution*. The procedural rules of such a constitutional regime would be set out in a constitutional covenant widely agreed and adopted.[247] The constitutional covenant would form the legal basis, both procedural and substantive, for the process of revolving the constitution and ensure the rules for setting the 'rules of the game' are clear, transparent and themselves ratified by the public at large. Auer (2008) considers such a covenant (although he refers to a 'charter') as a way to initiate a democratic process of autonomous constitution making in Cyprus. He does not consider anything similar to a revolving constitution but his work on trying to increase civic participation as a way to break the deadlock and give legitimacy to any future constitution in Cyprus is both instructive and innovative.

Based on the models set-out in this Chapter, a revolving constitution would have four principle accommodating effects.

First, it would introduce into political life the possibility of iterated games with the consequent effect that cooperation and accommodation become much more likely. This is not entirely exceptional. For instance, in the Ohrid Framework Agreement, which brought the inter-ethnic armed conflict in Macedonia to an end in 2001, the text of the agreement is clear that a modern state: "must continually ensure that its Constitution fully meets the needs of all its citizens and comports with the highest international standards, which themselves continue to evolve." Whilst no mechanisms were prescribed for this it has been suggested that Bosnia was very heavily on the minds of the parties and negotiators to the agreement. It was for that reason power-sharing arrangements were less strict and arrangements for reaching cross-ethnic agreement between Albanians and Macedonians more lenient (Koneska 2016, 46).

Second, the process of agenda setting (triggering and asking questions) by the people would be made possible but critically

---

[247] See further, Auer (2008).

removing status quo bias or the possibility of the process being hijacked by narrow ethno-nationalist goals. Furthermore, mechanisms for referendums or civic initiative would become a possibility without partisan framing effects (See sub-chapter 6.2 below). Such mechanisms may help avoid the pitfalls of blunt, Brexit-style, binary referendums.

Third, political elites would be forced to consider the preferences of the median voter which are more accommodating when making decisions in the parliamentary arena (as Chapter 3 demonstrated). People's incentive incompatibility and participation constraints are removed by virtue of active participation in the constitutional reform process. In fact, elite vetoes can be completely eliminated should agenda setting (asking questions) be determined solely by the electorate.

Fourth, although there may be formal barriers to institutional change, with sufficient incentives or disincentives, it is possible to bypass those barriers through "institutional layering" — adding new rules to existing ones — or "conversion" — changing the interpretation of existing rules (Mahoney and Thelen 2009). A constitutional convention could be created as a regularly convened body, with representatives of popular parties being selected or elected to the convention (at regular intervals) for the specific purpose of settling the terms of a new or amended constitution (See Chapter 6). A covenant creating a convention can be transposed onto the existing structure as a means to achieve future constitutional change. Therefore, elite's and people's preferences could be reconciled, and people's political culture cultivated rather than ignored. The popular vetoes in the parliamentary arena, of course, would be eliminated but replaced by elites being selected or elected (as party representatives) for the specific purpose of constitutional reform; ensuring that such elites are far closer to the position of the median voter. If a constitutional convention can amend the existing constitution and have it widely ratified, then the political elites in the Parliamentary Assembly would have no grounds or basis to reject it under the current provisions relating to constitutional change in the Bosnian constitution.

There are, of course, a large number of factors to consider in trying to make operational a revolving constitution. Countries like Cyprus, Ireland, Canada, Chile, Iceland, South Africa, Germany, Poland which have considered or used participatory or deliberative methods of constitutional reform (including constitutional conventions) can provide instruction in developing and implementing such a model. Chapter 6 provides the theoretical and practical basis for a revolving constitution for Bosnia and outlines exactly how participatory and deliberative processes may be instructive to possible constitutional reform in Britain. ☼

> "And here is written
> A prisoner which rejoyceth not
>
> May he be the last prisoner
> Whom hope forgot"
>
> - Mak Dizdar, *The Stone Sleeper* [248]

6. "A text about hope": lessons from Bosnia and Britain

6.1 Debate, deliberation and participation

One of the underlying premises of this book is that countries rush into designing restrictive written constitutions, in a single constitutional moment, without formally assessing people's true political preferences towards a future constitutional settlement. The consequence of both is a lack of legitimacy, stability and durability.

Restrictive constitutions can mean a number of things. A constitution can be non-representative, exclusionary, prone to manipulation by narrow partisan interests, and/or difficult to adapt to needed change. An obvious, and perhaps understandable, criticism might be that there are many deliberative or participatory processes for creating or amending written constitutions in numerous countries. Deliberative or participatory processes — whereby the public have some form of involvement in constitution making — include referendums, commissions on constitutional change, and exceptionally active public participation in conventions which deliberate on constitutions. Some scholars have even suggested that some form of public participation in constitution making may be approaching the status of an international legal rule (Hart 2010).

---

[248] A poem called "A Text About Hope" by Mak Dizdar [1917-1971] (2009, 85). The notes to the poem state that: "The wall of the Treasurer's Gaol in Mostar bore until recently the message: 'Vrsan Kosaric was here, a prisoner who does not rejoice' — at which the sentence is broken off."

It may well be argued, therefore, that given participatory or deliberative processes are apparently ubiquitous then this book proceeds on a false presumption: most constitutions could be said to reflect well the preferences of the people. Bosnia, on that view, simply does not work because maybe the conventional wisdom is right:[249] Bosnia was, is and will remain divided because the constitution merely reflects the reality that exists among the people. Britain, on that view, has little to glean from the extreme Bosnian example. It should merely cast its eye towards the various deliberative or participatory processes elsewhere and follow the well-trodden path to a written constitution to resolve some of the current problems. There are three responses to this.

The first response is that participatory processes need not be genuine and there are plenty of examples of rubber-stamp referenda or deliberative processes that are wholly insincere. Those processes are sometimes partisan, conducted in poor rule of law environments, and often have built-in framing or status quo biases.[250] For instance, the March 2020 referendum proposals to reform the Russian State constitution—which successfully extended the current term of President Vladimir Putin by another 12 years to 2034—had bundled within the proposed amendments: pension and minimum wage reform; emphasis on traditional values; and restrictions on officials who had material links with foreign States. All these popular policy issues were mixed up with major constitutional changes and indeed the changes passed by a large majority when put to a simple (yes or no) vote in a referendum. Can this really be considered as truly deliberative? It is the pretence of deliberation under the façade of democracy: "a world of appearances trying to pass for reality" (Havel 1978, 20).

The second response is that formal assessment of true political preferences consists of much more than a one-off binary referendum. That is the case whether a referendum ratifies the decision-making of political elites, who largely designed the

---

[249] As noted in the Introduction, Bosnia and Herzegovina is referred to throughout as "Bosnia".

[250] Chapter 5 explains what is meant by framing or status quo biases and their relevance to participatory and deliberative processes.

constitution, or reaffirms a constitution which followed from deliberation at a convention of wider stakeholders. Measuring people's true political preferences is the kind of in-depth, cross-time and interdisciplinary assessment of political beliefs and values that this book has attempted.

Constitutions and institutions, in and of themselves, are insignificant. It may be a truism to say that constitutions are supported, bound and constrained by the people even if only tacitly through their representatives. That is because their beliefs, customs and norms reflect a confidence and acceptance of the status quo (Wenzel 2012, 2). It remains somewhat surprising, therefore, that measurement of people's preferences has no formal or structural relevance in the constitutional design question. The case can, therefore, be made for a more comprehensive, interdisciplinary and genuinely representative approach. This would mean assessing people's preferences and designing institutional structures that allow for a truly deliberative and inclusive constitution-making process.

The third response is that the *belief* that truly participatory or deliberative processes are the norm is not borne out by the analysis and is, especially untrue of States with power-sharing arrangements. O'Leary (2019) and Wallis (2019, 207) identify the primary forms of power sharing as multiculturalism, consociation, minority or group rights, territorial pluralism found in pluralist federations, systems of territorial autonomy, and federations. In fact, within these arrangements participatory or deliberative processes are minimal to non-existent partly because they are still largely seen as crude and blunt instruments. Horowitz (2013) has warned they may hinder democratization or political secularization and can exacerbate existing tensions. As Chapter 5 noted, participatory processes such as referendums, if unrefined, can be divisive and if applied without careful calibration they may reinforce and help perpetuate existing divisions or create new ones. If such crude methods are used, however, they betray a failure in *thinking* as well as *practice*. Widner (2005, 503) has found that among

194 instances of constitution making since 1975 only a third had a deliberative process involving the public.

Where deliberative processes do exist, they are so variable in nature that it cannot be said there is any agreement on principle or practice (Saati 2017). Public input may be *substantive* if people play a role in drafting the constitutional text itself or *procedural* if people merely ratify existing proposals in a referendum. Referendums can be at the start or the end of the creation or amendment process. Processes can be exclusionary due to majoritarian voting rules or inclusionary by providing for mechanisms to protect minorities. And public involvement can be extensive or mere 'window-dressing' (Lerner 2019). Even progressive and innovative forms of public involvement, such as the civic initiative which allows the electorate to propose questions for legislative deliberation, are very rare. Only 11 constitutions, worldwide provide for civic initiatives and, even then, these provisions other than in Switzerland are hardly used.[251] More modern consultative processes where the public can suggest provisions of the constitutional text and be guaranteed consideration by the constituent or deliberative body — what might (fashionably) be termed *hive-mind* constitutions — are rarer still.[252]

6.2 Lessons for Bosnia and post-conflict societies

There are three major insights we can obtain from this book for Bosnia. The first is that not only is there a workable suggestion for a peaceful departure from the debilitating constitutional status quo, there is one that can and should involve the Bosnian people. A *revolving constitution* is one such method. The second is that whilst a revolving constitution *prima facie* appears utopian or revolutionary in reality it would put in motion and help catalyse evolutionary processes. The third is that it is possible to introduce flexibility into constitutional design even in supposedly deeply

---

[251] See further, Chapter 4.
[252] An excellent overview of such deliberative processes, termed by Bernal (2019, 235) as 'constitutional crowdsourcing', can be found in *Comparative Constitution Making* edited by Landau and Lerner (2019).

divided countries without fundamental drawbacks. A staged and carefully calibrated process that is based on the objective evidence can incentivise the major international, domestic and civil society actors through practical deployment of inter-temporal incentive or disincentive constraints.[253] These three insights are considered further below.

Public involvement and inclusion

The first insight is that a revolving constitution in the form of fixed and regular constitutional referendums, civic initiatives and deliberative assemblies, properly institutionalised and with procedural safeguards,[254] will make people no worse off than the status quo. A revolving constitution, to be clear, is not a new constitution for Bosnia. It is merely a *process* (or mechanism) for allowing people to have a meaningful say, and role, in assessing whether to amend the existing constitution. It is 'revolving' because that process can be iterated every new generation, according to a fixed and regular schedule. Over time, with enough revolutions of the constitution, a new constitution for Bosnia may result.

The procedural rules of a revolving constitutional mechanism would be set out in a constitutional covenant widely debated, agreed and adopted which would lead to a constitutional convention (where deliberations on the existing constitution will take place).[255] The constitutional covenant would bypass the current institutional impediments for reform as it would be outside the Dayton framework although it would take as its starting point the current Bosnian constitution and subject it to debate, deliberation and determination by the people within a

---

[253] Some of the detailed discussion about these incentive and disincentive constraints was in Chapter 5.
[254] Cronin (1989) suggests a number ranging from: "details of petition requirements (number of signatures, geographical distribution, certification) through campaign regulations (fairness doctrines, mandatory financial disclosures, public financing), to scheduling (general elections only)." See further, Engstrom's review of Cronin's book (Engstrom 1992).
[255] See further, Auer (2008).

constitutional convention. It would not in any way replace the constitution as it would only be a document to start a process.

If anything, just the mere possibility of such structured referendums, civic initiatives and deliberative assemblies on the current Bosnian constitution guarantees that any outcome in terms of constitutional reform would accord with the median voter, whether accommodating or intransigent. If the median voter is intransigent, as suggested by political elites operating in the current Dayton framework then they have nothing to fear. The median voter in both entities (in the cantons and municipalities) would simply vote for the status quo. Imposing high thresholds, in terms of voter turnout and the majority threshold required, will ensure the status quo is preserved and, in fact, be given some public legitimacy. Multi-option referenda (Emerson 2020) allowing the population to rank their preferences on amendments to a constitution or keeping the existing one or proposing an alternative set of amendments, would give a clearer indication on where people stand. No one could then argue that the elites are in it for themselves only, if the existing structure is endorsed by the people at large. In Bosnia, that is progress in itself notwithstanding the significant benefits that participation would bring: increase in popular legitimacy for reform (if any), increase in public trust in institutions, and empowering citizens to discuss and debate key issues with a sense of ownership in a future State constitution either amended or created afresh.

If, however, the analysis in Chapters 2 and 3 of this book is correct, and people are not as intransigent as their ethno-nationalist political representatives make them out to be, then they will have an opportunity to amend the provisions of the constitution in accordance with their true preferences by participating in a constitutional convention. Features of that convention—constitutional referendums, civic initiatives and deliberative assemblies—would allow an outlet for policy change currently being completely overlooked by policy actors.

The median voter—accommodating, tolerant and democratic—will be empowered to amend the constitution notwithstanding ethno-nationalist elites, segregated educational systems and a polarising media. People do relate their fear of the coercive force of political elites and the dominant role of patronage in the public and private sector economy (Bassuener et al. 2021, 3). Eliminating that fear, and the consequences for people that cut against elite monopoly interests, requires critical international support: "Reducing the valence of these two primary levers is a prerequisite for creating functioning, popularly legitimate governance in BiH. This fundamental post-Dayton change needs to be done from above" (Ibid). There will also need to be consideration of practical incentives to encourage people to participate in a convention such as adequate funding, time off work, comfort in deliberation settings, insulation from intimidation and so forth. The literature on conventions provides important policy guidance on what works to increase engagement and what does not (as set out later). In any case, elite policy decisions about the fundamental game rules would become firmly located in the set of preferences of the electorate as whole rather than single elite-led ethnic silos in parliament.

A constitutional covenant in Bosnia—far from imposing any normative prescription of the majority on the various groups— would open up the potential for civic debate and changing a constitution that has institutionalised ethnic division, discrimination, and exclusion (Stojanović 2011 cf. Bochsler 2011). Critically, mechanisms can be introduced to ensure that State stability is maintained, overriding concerns scholars have raised about preferring an incremental approach (Behnke 2008; Lerner 2011 cf. Doyle 2011).[256] The approach in this book is, paradoxically, about actively making operational the *opportunities* for an evolutionary outcome in the short term in place of a naïve and passive hope that the 'future will be better'. It could allow the implementation of Stojanovic's (2011) call for 'direct democracy' in Bosnia but avoiding the pitfalls that his approach would entail, such as: the risk that referenda outcomes permanently exclude

---

[256] Discussion about spoilers, the risk of violent conflict and unforeseen crises as a result of implementing a revolving constitution appears in Chapter 5.

certain minorities leading to instability; the erosion of human rights; and the risk of further dividing communities.

In relation to minority protections, an inclusive constitutional covenant would achieve two things. First, it would remove questions of partisan agenda setting i.e., the status quo and framing biases as explained in <u>Chapter 5</u>. Second, it would set the revolving constitution into motion by deliberating on constitutional issues which require key stakeholder agreement which by definition includes minority rights protection (this is dealt with in more detail in <u>sub-chapter 6.3</u>). Protection of minorities can be achieved by providing for strict for cross-entity, cross-municipality or cross-canton agreement in referendums, allowing civic initiatives and ensuring principles of internal autonomy and internal self-determination are built into the Covenant. People would be encouraged to reach across to their peers across cantons, municipalities, and entities and be incentivised to do so because the constitutional covenant will ensure that those issues will be debated and deliberated upon in the guaranteed future convention assembly.

In relation to the erosion of human rights, the current Bosnian constitution does not allow any dilution of specified human rights protections. A reformed constitution may add to rights but may not subtract or compromise them; that is a given. In any case, this book's argument is premised on the fact that certain universal rights are not up for negotiation, and least of all by majority decision-making, in the 'revolving constitution' model. There is, however, a debate to be had here. A debate, which is very much alive in Britain too, about what rights over and above universal rights should be accorded special protection in a constitution. The debate centres on whether, when a constitution is created, there should be a wide, unconditional, and national conversation about rights, their scope and their enforceability; it goes without saying that revocation of accepted international laws, customs and norms as to fundamental rights should not be up for bargaining particularly where minorities in a State already fear negative majoritarian impulses. This matter is discussed in more detail in the sub-chapters below.

One aspect of the history of the Bosnian constitution that a constitutional covenant offers the opportunity to put right is the inclusion of the women of Bosnia in the design process. Between 1992 and 2019, women constituted, on average, 13 percent of negotiators, six percent of mediators, and six percent of signatories in major peace processes around the world (Bigio 2019). This confirms that few women participate in leadership roles as negotiators, guarantors, or witnesses. At Dayton, Bosnian women had no say whatsoever. As there was no subsequent constitution-building process in which to broaden inclusion, "women and wider civic actors had no role or opportunity to influence constitutional design since the document was negotiated at a high diplomatic level" (Grebäck and Zillén 2003). Analysis of consociational arrangements—based on single-case studies—demonstrate that a focus on community identity can undercut and distract from the inclusion of women, making it difficult for the strategic interests of such groups to gain political traction (Bell 2015; Byrne and McCulloch 2018; Kennedy et al. 2016).[257] This clearly requires redress not just in Bosnia but around the world.

In relation to the risk of further dividing communities, the constitutional covenant would be careful to require concurrent and simultaneous decision-making and ratification among major community ethnic groupings roughly identified by entities and cantons (in the Federation) and municipalities (in the RS). Therefore, joint-entity-civic-initiatives, concurrent-joint-entity referendums, concurrent-joint-assembly deliberation and even cross-entity discussion and exchange would ensure greater accommodation as would consideration of accommodating electoral-district voting mechanisms.

---

[257] See further, Houlihan (2019, 32).

Catalysing evolution today over revolution tomorrow

The second insight is that, whilst the adoption of a revolving constitution would seem like a polemical revolutionary moment, in fact, its practical operation would tend to speed-up constitutional evolution. Incremental change in Bosnia is not an option for the reasons set-out in Chapters 4 and 5. The possibility of amending the Bosnian constitution with civic involvement (under the stages set out below) could lead to a whole raft of moderate proposals which could change the shape of Bosnian politics far sooner than currently possible.[258]

Lerner (2011) writes about the value of incremental constitutional change in divided societies so that difficult issues are deferred for resolution in a more settled political climate in the future. She uses the examples of India, Ireland and Israel as 'deeply divided societies', where societal schisms involve competing visions of the State as a whole. The shortcoming of her approach is that such a future may never arrive in Bosnia under the status quo. In fact, the analysis in this book shows it is highly improbable if not impossible under the existing constitution. As Perry (2019) has persuasively argued, Bosnia is in a frozen conflict. This means that violent conflict is being deferred into the future; violence which may happen before any resolution of difficult constitutional issues.[259] Furthermore, incremental change presupposes that the divisions that currently appear in the political or public spheres reflect deep divisions within the political culture of the people. We know that is not true of Bosnia from the analysis in Chapters 2 and 3. That makes change imperative and pressing.

It should be noted, that on the incremental model, temporary constitutional measures (for instance, the non-adoption of a written constitution in Israel) may become permanent features leading to entrenchment of divides both within institutions and without. In Bosnia, the features of deferral mechanisms such as an avoidance of clear decisions, use of ambivalent or vague legal language, or the

---

[258] See further, for instance, Lerner (2011).
[259] The choices and framing of constitutional reform in a conflict context will be very different from in peacetime, as noted in Chapter 4.

inclusion of contrasting provisions are all present in the Bosnian constitution (O'Brien 2010). In Bosnia, deferral has lasted long enough especially given the imperative for reforms to protect the rights of those discriminated against and to ensure a viable, self-sustainable State. Deferral has created a polarized media, a divided education system and elite-led entrepreneurial initiatives to separate and divide people further. There is also the further complication, that the Bosnian constitution has never had a civic mandate. In fact, that has been precluded precisely because the false assumptions of deep and ancient ethnic-hatreds among the people clouded the thinking of the principal drafters.

Incentivising detractors and disincentivising spoilers

The third insight concerns how to get elites to agree to a revolving constitution given their current intransigence. The issue of spoilers, and how to curtail their possible anti-constitutional or anti-democratic behaviour, was addressed in Chapter 5. There could be three potential first movers or 'champions' of a revolving constitution: international actors who might force the start of a process; civil society actors who may, and certainly should, lead any reform movement; or a domestic political elite-led initiative. Each is taken in turn.

International actors could, coordinating with the PIC, EU, US, UNSC and other stakeholders of Dayton, agree to force political elites to agree to a constitutional covenant, setting out the procedural rules, for a revolving constitution prior to any proposal for a new constitution — to 'start the ball rolling' to speak. The EU, for instance, could insist on reforms that ensure implementation of the ECHR and in particular to ensure non-discrimination and equality as individual rights. This ought to be a given as accession to the EU requires adherence to the ECHR and compliance with even stronger human rights protections under the EU Charter on Fundamental Rights. What this would mean is that the EU would have to depart from its current policy position which is essentially that "anything is negotiable, that conditionality is flexible and that any notion that EU membership might force politicians to make uncomfortable reforms is misplaced" (Perry and Keil 2015, 62). But in order to depart from its logic of inaction it must confront anti-democratic trends both in the EU and outside (Keil 2018, 14). As Bassuener (2020, 227) has rightly pointed out the choice is not between stability and reform it is between reform and conflict especially where citizens are aching for change:

> "While seeking external policy support from the Western peace brokers makes sense, the case is far more convincing when citizens demonstrate their ability and will to leverage fear against peace cartels—and effectively against the peace brokers' attachment to stability. Only a recognition that there will be no stability unless it is generated on terms that citizens can accept, can shift the defaults in Western chancelleries for stability and the status quo."

Furthermore, as Perry (2019, 11-12) has identified, every country has had to reform its constitution to prepare for EU membership (with the exception of Cyprus). There has been much criticism of the OHR and rule by decree; some of the criticism is legitimate and there is some validity in suggesting it has removed agency from Bosnians. But it is not the primary problem. Merdzanovic (2015), for instance, argues that the strong influence of the OHR has meant elites have no responsibility to govern and rather focus on mobilising their respective groups to extract rents and concessions from the international community. Whilst some of that is true, the 'ethnic entrepreneurship' is largely because of the institutional logic of the whole Dayton structure accepted and negotiated by indicted, or indictable, war criminals: the OHR is merely keeping that entire structure together (or was until 2006). As Bassuener (2020, 231) succinctly puts it, this was a "co-production".

It might be time for the OHR to truly put their Bonn powers to long-term strategic use based on evidence-informed decision making. The US, EU and other guarantors must also be prepared to sanction those threatening the integrity of the state, enforce human rights, and support investigations into corruption and illegal practices. This must be complementary to ensuring predatory neighbours Croatia and Serbia stop working to break Bosnia apart and that Russia is put into check by stopping it providing financial, military and intelligence support to parallel state institutions in the

RS (Hamilton 2020; Serwer 2020). The EU can leverage its considerable economic and political clout in this respect particular in terms of the accession process for Serbia and Bosnia. It also has leverage over Croatia given the structural funds and other support it provides to the government (Hamilton 2020). Ghai and Galli (2006) have helpfully set out some useful criteria in disaggregating the component of international engagement:

> "engagement *of what kind* (providing finance, technical assistance, documentation, etc.); engagement *by whom* (the UN, regional powers or one superpower); engagement *for what purpose* (giving voice to local people, privileging particular groups or leaders, or serving the interests of the interveners); and engagement *by what means* (laying down the procedures for the process or enabling local leaders to design it)."

Whilst some international involvement will be necessary it ought to be facilitative and supportive of local initiatives. A solely international-led movement and one that is not multilateral is the least attractive option given that forced adoption of such a constitutional covenant would defeat the purpose of incentivising elites and may lead to a rejection of the concept at its inception. Other powers excluded from any process may also encourage spoilers.

Local groups and civil society could take up the concept and raise awareness about the need to reform the Bosnian constitution and the necessity for it to have democratic legitimacy and civic involvement; the statistical analysis that proves the people prefer a settlement that accords with their demonstrable preferences would be a great advantage (see Chapters 2 and 3). Pressure for a constitutional covenant—allowing a form of revolving constitution—could be a prime focus for building 'broad church' coalitions that could pressure the elites in both entities and in each of the ten cantons and the RS municipalities. Cross-entity, cross-canton and cross-municipality cooperation by civil society groups and ordinary people themselves would genuinely cut against ethno-nationalist led politics.

Elites themselves could lead support for the idea of a revolving constitution. If elites are playing the rational game in an institutional structure encouraging intransigence (but they would actually prefer to cooperate should the rules allow) then they themselves would acknowledge the advantage of introducing some flexibility and civic involvement for constitutional amendments particularly where the beginnings of any process would be outside the ordinary parliamentary framework. Being the prime mover — risky, bold, innovative though it may be — could hold the possibility of solving an intractable conflict. That in itself is a preference-altering incentive in a game that will have a clearly defined structure allowing for repeat interaction: an opportunity to amend the constitution every generation. As this avoids a single constitutional moment with all the risks such moments entail, it could open up the possibility of changing the rules of the game for the elites' own benefit and for the benefit of society as a whole. The logic of the revolving constitution would be self-fulfilling. Those inclined to accommodation and non-nationalist politics could be the concept's first champions.

In reality, co-opting each of the relevant actors — international, civic, and domestic actors — would be the most practical way to encourage the idea of an inclusive, fair and just constitutional framework of which the idea of a revolving constitution is a manifestation. Pressure emanating from both the people who seek change and the international community willing to support that change — a "pressure sandwich" (Bassuener *et al.* 2021) — is the only realistic way to challenge the dominance and monopolies of the elites.[260] But those from below must be the leaders and champions for any process to be authentic, genuine and durable.

6.3 Lessons for Britain and pre-conflict societies

A premise of this book, set out at the very beginning, was that Britain has as much to learn from the Bosnian *process* of constitutional creation and change as Bosnia has to learn from Britain. Britain is far from paradigmatic. Chapter 4 highlighted the

---

[260] The practical basis and means for implementing the 'pressure sandwich' have been set out by Bassuener et al. (2021, 4-5).

constitutional crises in Britain of late, the policy instability and the risks to the 'good' elements of its constitutional framework. Not least the flexibility that has allowed accommodation, without violence, for centuries; at least at Britain's political centre as opposed to its outer dominions of its once expansive empire.

What, however, are the lessons for Britain and how might future constitutional design or amendment processes look if they are to be reconciled with Britain's increasingly polarised politics? This book is not concerned with the *outcome* of any process only with the *process* itself so that general outcomes might be fairer, more just and more inclusive.

There are four major insights that emanate from this book for Britain. The first insight is that revolutionary constitutional moments are rarely satisfactory. As constitutional statutes are of such significance in Britain this book finds that there should be more political discussion, popular engagement and bi-partisan agreement prior to their creation or amendment. The second insight is that whilst Britain has had hundreds of years to evolve its flexible parliamentary arrangements, recent events demonstrate that nothing should be taken for granted. Without care, political culture can regress to an extent where we might talk about a 'pre-conflict' society (Perry 2019).[261] There must, therefore, be efforts to constantly renew, reinvigorate and reinforce a democratic, inclusive and rights-oriented political culture. That is true of Britain as much as it is of Bosnia. The third insight is that the temptation to resort to short-sighted shibboleths and politically partisan practices must be resisted. The lack of meaningful inclusion in constitutional decision-making of the devolved administrations and Britain's diverse communities is no longer sustainable. The breakdown in good political practice is because of partisan and piecemeal constitutional change by elites. This poor political practice sits in contrast with the political culture of the British people, and it fails them because the consequences cause apathy and alienation. The

---

[261] I am grateful to Dr Valery Perry for a fruitful discussion about the challenges Britain faced as a result of Brexit and devolution in 2019; she had referred to the idea of 'pre-conflict' States and what might be the warning signs of such a risk materialising.

fourth insight is that, in Britain, there is no need for a revolving constitution as many such features are in-built into the constitutional structure of the unwritten constitution. A reset, however, is required perhaps with a new constitutional statute which may resolve current constitutional problems. Such a statute could form a new centre ground around which the people and politicians can coalesce in a not dissimilar fashion to the way people coalesce around the *idea* of the Magna Carta of 1215. Comprehensive change is possible in Britain whilst maintaining its political traditions and the admirable political culture of its people. Without that underlying political culture, the rules, norms and practices of its uncodified constitution mean nothing. These four insights are each taken in turn.

Be wary of revolutionary constitutional moments

The first insight is that revolutionary constitutional moments are fraught with uncertainty, unpredictability and danger. In Britain, the Westminster Parliament is both a representative body, deliberating and passing ordinary legislation and in the scholarly terminology also the 'constituent assembly' deliberating and passing legislation that has constitutional importance. Legislation with constitutional importance, in theory, can be repealed just as simply as an 'ordinary' piece of legislation, if *expressly* desired by Parliament.[262] A 'constitutional moment' is when the rules of the game are formally up for negotiation or re-negotiation (Ackerman 1991). Britain has largely resisted such moments, as a parliamentary democracy, after its brief and bloody experience with republicanism under the 'Lord Protector', Oliver Cromwell, between 1653 and 1658.[263]

The reason constitutional moments can be so dangerous is that, when the fundamental rules are up for negotiation, they create the potential for cutting out key stakeholders from the game, forevermore. Britain has been reminded of that as a result of the

---

[262] Speech of Laws LJ *Thoburn v. Sunderland City Council* [2002] EWHC 195 (Admin) [2002] 3 WLR 24 at [64].

[263] As well as the turmoil leading up to that, including the execution of Charles I.

consequences of Brexit, devolution for the nations and nascent secession or dissolution processes in Northern Ireland, Wales and Scotland. Bosnia is still living with a crisis, following a devastating war, after going ahead with its own controversial plebiscite in 1992 following the dissolution of the SFRY; although it was the external designs of elites in Serbia and Croatia that forced its hand and the international community that recommended and required the plebiscite process (Serwer 2019). As Chapter 4 outlined, there are numerous reform proposals and designs for a future constitutional settlement or moment for Britain. They include many prescriptions: a codified constitution, federalism, greater devolution, greater centralisation, reform of Parliament, reform of the electoral rules and so forth.

Paradoxically, in Britain, there have been examples of what some have concluded to have been *ex post facto* constitutional moments whereby acts of Parliament other than the great historical acts, are seen as having such fundamental constitutional significance that they amount to a new constitution. Those that hold that view maintain it, notwithstanding that the 'new constitution' can be uncreated, by simple majority, just as easily it was created.

These constitutional moments may include the passing of the: Devolution Instruments (including the Government of Wales Act 1998, Scotland Act 1998, Belfast "Good Friday" Agreement, Northern Ireland Act 1998); Fixed-Term Parliaments Act 2011; Human Rights Act 1998, European Communities Act 1972 and Constitutional Reform Act 2005. Arguably others may include the Equalities Act 2010, the European Union (Withdrawal Agreement) Act 2020 and additional legislation that will follow from the free trade agreement with the EU. All of these statutes are seen either by the incumbent government or the opposition parties as the target of possible unilateral repeal, amendment or reinterpretation in Parliament. There is a partisan constitutional reform agenda with often a purpose to cement party or ideological objectives at the expense of others and their interests. This makes reform not just partisan but piecemeal.

The matter comes back to constitutional tradition, convention and culture which is less about the law and more about political practice. There are two general principles which *should* be amenable to political elites across the spectrum. The first being that the rule of law requires that some special respect be accorded to certain common law principles and constitutional statutes that go to the heart of an individual's rights or the workings of Britain's democratic institutions. The second being that certain constitutional conventions, rules and practices are critical although their *raison d'etre* may have been forgotten over time. In fact, to ensure a harmonious political community the locus of political action must be within the institutional framework of a representative parliament rather than extra-legal or extra-constitutional instruments such as the bare referendum or executive *diktat*.

In relation to respect for the rule of law, this ought not to be particularly controversial. There must be some distinction and special treatment accorded to constitutional fundamentals over ordinary legislation otherwise the system would collapse. As Laws LJ in the case of *Thoburn* said:

> "This development of the common law regarding constitutional rights, and as I would say constitutional statutes, is highly beneficial. It gives us most of the benefits of a written constitution, in which fundamental rights are accorded special respect. But it preserves the sovereignty of the legislature and the flexibility of our uncodified constitution. It accepts the relationship between legislative supremacy and fundamental rights is not fixed or brittle: rather the courts (in interpreting statutes, and now, applying the HRA) will pay more or less deference to the legislature, or other public decision-maker, according to the subject in hand."[264]

The line between what is a constitutional statute and an ordinary statute, as set out by Laws LJ, has been subject to academic criticism for both its over- and its under- inclusiveness (McClean 2019, 331). Generally, however, there is an acceptance that the principle itself is a check on the executive and purely majoritarian

---

[264] Speech of Laws LJ *Thoburn v. Sunderland City Council* [2002] EWHC 195 (Admin) [2002] 3 WLR 24 at [62-63].

impulses. An inexhaustive list of examples of constitutional statutes was offered by Laws LJ in *Thoburn* and another was offered far more recently when a seven-panel bench of Supreme Court justices in the case of *HS2 Action Alliance*. In *HS2* the justices went further than *Thoburn* to suggest that not only does Britain have constitutional statutes but that some are more fundamental than others (Elliot 2014).[265]

This leads to the question of how political elites ought to deal with constitutional statutes and common-law constitutional principles when creating or amending them. The response is that political elites ought to be especially careful and particularly attuned to achieving cross-party consensus when constitutional instruments are to be repealed or abrogated by new legislation; that must particularly be the case where the rights of minorities or nations or others who may be dispossessed by majoritarian impulses.

In the absence of any parliamentary mechanism to entrench legislation through requirements of super-majorities or cross-party or cross-national consensus some form of formal consultation becomes critical. As current attacks on lawyers and judges have become widespread in Britain, it goes without saying that political elites of whatever persuasion ought to refrain from attacking the justice system and judiciary particularly where they are left with the difficult task of adjudicating on the protection of fundamental rights or on constitutional controversies which often stem—as they did in the Brexit cases of *Miller I* and *Miller II*—from the failure of political elites to follow convention, constitutional principles or, as a minimum, consult and seek cross-party or cross-national agreement.

In relation to conventions, political practice ought to revert to becoming aligned with constitutional rules, norms and practices. There are some statutes, such as those governing devolution, as discussed in Chapter 4, that allow Westminster to retain supreme legislative capability even when they concern devolved matters. This legislation contains two promises: that Westminster will not

---

[265] *R (HS2 Action Alliance Ltd) v Secretary of State for Transport* [2014] UKSC 3.

interfere with devolved competencies, and that the devolved administrations will be consulted where they are impacted by Westminster legislation. But the promises are not legally binding. The Act of Union 1707, the Statute of Westminster 1931, and the Scotland Act 2016 have in common the fact of being "both declaratory and promissory but not law-bearing" (McClean 2019, 331; Feldman 2016). Section 2 of the Scotland Act, for instance, recognizes that "the Parliament of the United Kingdom will not normally legislate with regard to devolved matters without the consent of the Scottish Parliament."

In recent times, from Brexit related matters, as in *Miller I*, to coronavirus legislation, Westminster has legislated on devolved matters without any synchronised negotiation or consent. That is notwithstanding that the Scottish, Welsh and Northern Ireland administrations have expressly rejected the matters legislated upon (Ascherson 2020). The Supreme Court in *Miller I* confirmed that section 2 of Scotland Act 2016 was merely a political convention[266] rather than a justiciable or legal one. That Westminster is *entitled* to do something, however, does not mean that it should. The harm to the integrity of the Union, the integrity of fundamental constitution instruments, and the centrifugal forces it generates in support of national secession, which the Scottish government duly threatened in response to *Miller I*, is obvious.

The significance would be plain to see if the constitutional importance of conventions and practices was better understood, primarily, by political elites. As noted in Chapter 1, conventions are unwritten rules of practice which are critical to the workings of the political system but are not directly committed into law usually in any written form at all (Blackburn 2015). The existence of the office of Prime Minister is purely conventional as is the rule upon which they are appointed, being whoever commands the confidence of the House of Commons. The monarch can refuse to appoint them, and she can also refuse to give assent to government Bills passed by both Houses of Parliament as both are conventions (Blackburn 2015). Whilst the monarch could do that, she does not because of

---

[266] *Miller v. Attorney-General*, [2017] UKSC 5 at [137, 149, 151]

the obvious constitutional crisis it would precipitate, not least, jeopardising her very existence. Commentators have considered whether the monarch should have ignored, for instance, Prime Minister Boris Johnson's advice to prorogue Parliament and she wisely did not for the aforementioned reason. The fact that commentators had to consider that to maintain the integrity of the parliamentary process, indeed for parliament's ability to convene itself, shows the seriousness that ought to be accorded to breaches of critical conventions.

Incidentally, the monarch in defence of democracy may also decide to exercise her constitutional discretion to refuse to pass legislation (for instance, legislation trying to turn the House Commons into a non-elected chamber), or the inappropriate dissolution of the House of Commons (Franklin and Baun 1995, 23). She could dismiss the Prime Minister, dissolve the Commons and be seen to be exercising her legal discretion appropriately. The royal veto has, however, not been used since 1702 (Ibid).

It is clear what political elites *should* do in Britain. What, however, are the incentives and disincentives for political elites to behave in this way when there is, seemingly, short-term advantage to be gained from breaking conventions, practices and rules?

Take not for granted good political culture

The second insight concerns the value of good political culture and that culture can progress as much as it can regress. An almost enigmatic problem in constitutional affairs as much as human affairs is how to make institutions, rules and practices democratic, legitimate and durable. Related to that enigma is understanding why people's values and beliefs about democracy and justice endure when the very institutions, rules and practices, that are supposedly democratic, fail them. Chapters 2 and 3 considered the question of political culture around which there was great, and misplaced, doubt when it came to Bosnia. The same is true of Britain, as Chapter 2 demonstrates, notwithstanding the problems emanating from the referendum to leave the EU.

Political culture is the bridge between written or unwritten rules. Good culture ensures an actual adherence to such rules which in turn leads to stability or order. Eskridge and Ferejohn (2001, 1215-1217) have argued that constitutional statutes or "super-statutes" can emerge out of consensus as much as they can come out of conflict. This suggests that co-operative people's movements may effect change on a written constitution including how it is understood, which over time may broadly reflect accepted political and even social norms. McClean (2019, 333), accepting that principle, has applied it to unwritten constitutions. She has, however, argued that it is quite hard to identify whether, for instance, constitutional statutes identified by Laws LJ's in the case of *Thoburn* were forged out of widespread societal consensus or they had actually come about through societal conflict. She says that "[…] is too early to say whether the norms they have created are likely to "stick" (Ibid). There are two responses. It is not too early but arguably too late that in 2020 the British are, apparently, still unclear (or choose not to be clear) on what they consider constitutional fundamentals and what norms they understand to be reflective of their political culture. There are certainly some.

McClean presupposes, as this book has demonstrated in the case of Bosnia, that "these norms have been created" by judges as opposed to the widespread consensus that can be gauged by modelling the preferences, across time, of political elites and importantly the vast majority of the people. In fact, in Britain, the data demonstrates people's clear preferences for tolerance, democracy, and a just and fair society albeit with a healthy distrust of government.[267] Where this book's author can agree with McClean (2019, 336) is that "regardless of whether one has a written or unwritten constitution, all constitutions ultimately require political commitment and political self-enforcement." She suggests that in a time of "polarized politics, constitutional actors need to think more seriously about the pre-commitments on which our democratic and political life depend" (2019, 340). Clear thinking is necessary but more so is action. There is much that can be found to be common

---

[267] See further, the analysis in Chapters 2 and 3.

between the people and political elites as a class; even amongst elites who oppose one-another in the day-to-day of politics.

There is a critical lesson for Britain from the game theory analysis in relation to Bosnia. That is that there are certain institutional features which allow political elites to operate in ways that accord with their own sectional interests rather than society's at large. Those features are set out in Chapter 5 and include: elites operating in ideological silos that isolate them from the people or from scrutiny by other political elites who may be opposed to them; elites fashioning or manipulating institutions to reward intransigence or non-cooperation in winner-takes-all scenarios; and elites ensuring that there are no political costs associated with poor decision making.

In Britain, we have seen attempts to create some of those features. For instance, there has been an increasing use of the courts and judiciary for high stakes constitutional issues. This use has acted as an ultimate check on government power when it has conducted itself in a way that is: manifestly contrary to international rules and norms; against centuries-old legal conventions that act as a check on arbitrary government; and to the detriment of fundamental rights or devolved powers. The check in the form of a robust judicial system has responded admirably. But the government's response has been to attack the judiciary further, including lawyers defending constitutional principles or representing individuals whose rights are violated by the State. In October 2020, this contestation has seen the Prime Minister, Boris Johnson, and the Home Secretary, Priti Patel, branding lawyers as "activist" and "lefty." Sustained criticism from the Home Secretary has seen some lawyers being targeted for physical attack (Bowcott 2020). These attacks, as noted in Chapter 4, follow on the back of policies to curtail parliamentary scrutiny, dilute human rights protections, weaken the power of judicial review of government decision-making, and circumventing adherence to international law.[268] In the UK context, without some of those institutional checks, a party with a majority in Parliament can wield untrammelled power.

These successively extreme criticisms of the judiciary by the executive may be interpreted as a tactic to achieve a longer-term strategy. That is to make extreme unconstitutional policies slightly more acceptable and create ideological silos within which government may operate unopposed. In US policy circles that strategy has become known as the 'Overton window' which entails positing an extreme solution to a problem in the hope that it will make an equally radical but slightly less extreme policy appear more reasonable. This technique not only makes unconstitutional policies more acceptable over time, but it also removes boundaries altogether. The campaign is concerted and consistent.

The influential Judicial Power Project (JPP), referred to in Chapter 4, and part of the thinktank Policy Exchange, for instance, recently questioned whether the Supreme Court should be abolished altogether on the grounds that it intervenes in matters that supposedly should be left to politicians (Bowcott 2020). This originally started with a criticism of the ECtHR and the ECJ because supposedly "foreign unelected judges" were ruling on British cases. The suggestion was that British judges ought to rule on "British matters", but now even "unelected" British judges are seen to be justifiable targets as they inhibit executive power. The JPP policy proposals, whilst presented as objective, have become successively more extreme.

A number of former Supreme Court justices came out in defence of the judicial system recently and disavowed baseless attacks. The late Lord Kerr "fully agreed" with comments made by the former President of the Supreme Court, Lord Neuberger, who said that the Internal Market Bill 2020, which would have enabled the government to breach international law and exempt some of its

---

[268] This has gone hand-in-hand with increasing the use of delegated legislation to bypass parliamentary scrutiny, (Sinclair 2020) increasing the proportion of government appointees to the House of Lords, (Fowler 2021) and controlling the order, and timing, of parliamentary bills being presented to skew decisions in favour of the Government (Russell 2021).

powers from legal challenge (through an ouster clause), was in danger of driving Britain down a "very slippery slope" towards dictatorship or tyranny (Bowcott 2020). Neuberger warned that any hearing putting the issue to the courts, including the fact that Scotland's express wishes against the Bill were rejected, would "put the judges in a position where they are on a collision course with the government or are seen to be craven … [But] you have to sort out problems in court, if you don't you have a civil war" (Bowcott 2020).[269] These troubling trends in Britain point towards short-term sectional interests having sway over long-term constitutional fundamentals.

Decisions on fundamentals, outside the constitutional framework, leave people who are side-lined or bypassed having little incentive in adhering to such decisions and fewer disincentives in breaking them. In the long run, the outcome is revolutionary. Elites of one factional group take over at the expense of the elites of the other faction and then mobilise people in their cause. O'Leary (2019, 186), has detailed how one of Britain's constitutional statute, the Government of Ireland Act 1920, partitioned Ireland and created a new Westminster style government in Belfast. Under those arrangements, the majoritarian arithmetic permitted the Ulster Unionist Party to exercise hegemonic control of executive, legislative, and judicial power for 50 years at the expense of Northern Ireland's Irish Catholic, nationalist minority. This statute went hand-in-hand with the 1921 and 1925 treaties obliging Ireland to remain in the British Empire, accept a British King and permit secession of Northern Ireland. The terms of those treaties precipitated civil war among the nationalists; a war that shaped the Irish party system and its policies including Ireland's claim to the whole island in its 1937 Constitution as an Irish Free State (Ibid). It was not until the Good Friday Agreement 1998 that simple majority rule in the Northern Ireland Assembly was blocked, that Ireland's territorial claim was modified in its

---

[269] At the time of writing, the Bill just passed through Parliament. The controversial provisions relating to international law were removed (although the symbolic harm was done). The Act was still heavily criticised for apparently ousting devolved competencies contrary to the wishes of the devolved administrations.

constitution to an aspiration (requiring concurrent majority affirmation by referendum in both nations) and that power-sharing institutions across Northern Ireland were established to incentivise cross-party and cross-national decision making (O'Leary 2019, 186). The 1920 Act shows that constitutional arrangements can create new problems and/or reinvigorate existing ones just as new arrangements (as under the 1998 Agreement) might resolve them.

Political practice in Britain — internalised, constantly iterated, and adapted to change — has led to the development of constitutional customs, practices and conventions. Some of those customs are new and some are old. McClean (2019) frames this development, with respect to constitutional statutes, as a question of trying to understand how and why constitutional norms are instituted. But the real challenge is to understand why constitutional norms, and in particular long-standing practices, are broken. Game theory and prospect theory help us to understand the mechanics of the behaviour of political elites. But the socio-cultural-political *milieu* that permits and makes permissive the breaking of fundamental rules is just as important.

Resist shibboleths and politically partisan practices

The third insight concerns piecemeal and partisan changes and the temptation to respond to them with simple solutions. Not everything that is wrong with politics in Britain is suggestive that the entirety of the constitutional framework is broken; far from it. The justice system, for instance, has reacted exactly as it should have when faced with a threat to its independence and the breaking of constitutional norms. Largely, across the left and right, there is a consensus in the legal community on adherence to the rule of law, a justice system free from government intimidation, and the right of courts to uphold the rule of law.[270]

The Labour Party, under Sir Keir Starmer QC, has professed regret at having started 'reforms' to legal aid and the dismantling

---

[270] Over a thousand leading lawyers, who act both on behalf of and against the government in proceedings, have signed letters asking the government to refrain from attacks on lawyers and uphold the role of law (Bowcott 2020).

of the court system that successive Conservative governments took to their logical conclusions. Lord Falconer, the former Labour Chancellor and Secretary of State for Constitutional Affairs, who presided over the first massive cuts to the system, has profoundly regretted the consequences to free legal representation to those who need it and, ultimately, access to justice for all (Falconer 2018).

There is also a strong consensus in Wales, Northern Ireland and Scotland on the need to uphold the rule of law, adhere to international law, norms and customs and augment promises, by Westminster, of not interfering in the competencies of the devolved administrations. They have used every constitutional means (including the courts to good effect, in the case of Northern Ireland and Scotland, in *Miller I* and *Miller II*) to challenge being bypassed on devolved matters. It should be noted that in *Miller II* there was also a large parliamentary majority against the actions of the government (which was in a minority).

Civil society, a free press, and practitioners have coalesced to defend possible repeal of the Human Right Act 1998 or dilution of rights currently guaranteed by the European Convention on Human Rights ("ECHR") under a replacement "British" instrument of rights. This is not withstanding that one of the strongest mechanisms for protecting human rights that ever-had effect in Britain, and that was more extensive than the ECHR, the EU's Charter of Fundamental Rights, was effectively repealed without any replacement as Britain left the EU. The fact that the Human Rights Act 1998 still stands on the statute books despite a Conservative Party Manifesto commitment since 2010 to repeal it, shows the strong defence emanating from civil society with hundreds of organisations and individuals committed to its defence[271] as well as opposition parties including Labour, Liberal Democrats, SNP, Plaid Cymru, and the Greens. That has partly precluded unilateral repeal.

In summary, the constitutional crises you would expect to see as a result of partisan challenges to the rule of law, adherence to

---

[271] See further, Position Statement. 2020. "Protect Human Rights and Judicial Review: Defend the Human Rights Act and Access to Justice." October 19, 2020.

international norms, rules and customs and adherence to British constitutional 'principles' have become manifest precisely as you would expect—around and in defence of the parliamentary system—by using and allowing the institutions of State to achieve legitimate goals. In some ways this is British political culture manifest. A social deference to each other as citizens, an absolute absence of political deference, but a clear disdain for *anti-systemic* action. People's responses on these issues are not only action against legislative proposals seen to be "really unjust and harmful" but is "of a rather orderly kind, directed *at* rather than *against* Parliament, and working *within* rather than *outside* the existing political system" (Heath and Topf 1987, 56-58).

The piecemeal and partisan constitutional changes to date, are, however, far reaching and fundamental. Depending on where you stand on the political spectrum, they are either right or wrong. Some, of late, clearly challenge foundational structures of the rule of law and democracy. There is, nevertheless, a sense of polarisation in Britain between a number of communities and constituencies. Between the well-off and the less well-off, the regions or nations and Westminster, the younger and older generations, and the liberal and the conservative. Whilst constitutional statutes may be repealed with just a simple majority, a majority is not as simple to achieve given the polar opposite views, of citizens, to the aforementioned crises.

Admittedly, stronger hurdles to amending the constitutional statutes—such as entrenchment, super majorities for amendment, or stronger bicameral approval, and calibrated cross-nation or cross-region referendums—may act as a greater check on the government, particularly for the protection of minorities and rights, but that is by no means certain. O'Leary (2019), for instance, believes, considering that the Good Friday Agreement can be repealed by ordinary legislation at Westminster, that Britain

> "cannot make fully credible constitutional bargains with its internal ethnic communities, or its neighbors, unless it resolves to create a genuine constitution, i.e., one in which constitutional laws, rights, and treaties, protected by courts, require extraordinary or "organic" majorities or distinct consensual procedures for their amendment" (O'Leary 2019, 189).

This book agrees that *something* to demonstrate credibility is needed but his prescription is hardly a cure. We need only look at Bosnia or, in fact, to the case study he himself cites, Northern Ireland. Create too strong a set of consensual and power-sharing arrangements and you have: deadlock and debilitation; the need for majorities which cannot be achieved where change is pressing; minorities who are locked out of politics precisely because of the consensual framework; constant challenges to the legitimacy of the constitution where simple non-partisan decision-making is not possible; and ultimately further entrenched polarisation. O'Leary seems to accept that constitutionalism *per se* is not enough by noting that: "constitutions may be the vehicles through which majority (or minority) tyrannies are organized" (2019, 189-192).

This does not mean that change in Britain is not necessary. Shibboleths as solutions—as we have seen in Bosnia and elsewhere in the world—call for a cautious approach. Two that are frequently advocated in Britain, in particular, require careful thought. The first is a written constitution and the second is a formalised federation.

The case for a written constitution, as noted in Chapters 2 and 4, has been made by many. Whether Britain, or indeed Bosnia, should or should not have a written constitution and what its terms should be, if it does, is not the focus of this book. This book maintains rather that the *process* by which any such outcome is reached is determinative. For the dangers of merely a written constitution—and a republican one at that—the British need not look to Bosnia. Britain did once have its own experiment with a written constitution. In 1653, the Instrument of Government (Britain's first and last written constitution) installed a Lord Protector, both the head of the executive and head of State, in the form of Oliver Cromwell. He had a role and powers not dissimilar to a modern-day president: "Cromwell was not just a figurehead but a chief executive whose emergency powers of taxation were to be subject to Parliament's endorsement or override, and who was forbidden to suspend or dispense with its legislation" (Sedley 2013). The Instrument was later to have its provisions on parliamentary approval of the monarch's tax and spending plans replicated in the

Bill of Rights 1689. By then Cromwell was dead, the monarchy was restored (by Parliament) and Britain's first written constitution, The Instrument, was torn-up. Monarchs though continued to purport to suspend legislation, in contravention of the idea of parliamentary supremacy, which both the 1689 Bill and The Instrument had enshrined, right up until the early 18th century (Loughlin 2013). Writing these constitutional provisions down, of course, had no special effect *per se*.

That experiment with written instruments has the same resonance today as it did then, as was noted in Chapter 4. Writing down constitutional rules can create or reinforce societal or political cleavages within society if the process is insufficiently inclusive, participatory and deliberative. Writing down a constitution, again without a very strong consensus, can also arrest political and social development; with the "risk [of] consolidating State power wherever it happens at that moment to reside" (Nolan 1997, 88).

The constitution must carefully calibrate institutional workability and operability with checks and balances between the branches of the government. It must also be careful not to accord too much power to one branch over another. (One need only think about the debates Britain already has about the judicialization of politics or a politicisation of the judiciary, as discussed in Chapter 4). Political elites must also be incentivised to work within a new constitutional arrangement and provisions must be made for political elites stretching any such system to its extreme limits. Finally, there needs to be a genuine will and desire on the part of the people—either implied or express—to be involved when they are consulted on, or asked to take part in, fundamental system change. In the last half of the last century, seminal works on political culture in Britain (Franklin and Baun 1995; Almond and Verba 1980) have found there was no empirical evidence supporting British preference for another system of governance although they certainly wished to see improvements to their existing one; major policy change, making government more accountable or democratic does not necessarily translate into complete system change (Franklin and Baun 1995, 27). In fact, there was a pretence between 1970 and 1990 of desire for gradual reforms over radical revolutionary change (Ibid, 27). A failure to respond, however, may well generate such centrifugal responses and the community that is constituted today may be differently constituted tomorrow with different aims, goals and aspirations.

Devolution, federalism, and confederalism are also not panacea and they are not in and of themselves more democratically progressive than less formalised federal arrangements. There are good grounds to suggest, for instance, that the SNP administration in Scotland has centralised power and authority itself whilst simultaneously calling for greater powers and authority from Westminster. In Spring 2013, for instance, the Labour Party in Scotland launched its own Devolution Commission, whose interim report argued persuasively for the cause of local government. It has, however, been roundly rejected by the incumbent SNP administration (Kidd 2014). Similarly, in its demands for independence, the SNP is in other ways subject to the charge of hypocrisy in failing to protect the interests of its own minorities. For instance, they have failed, despite being asked, to discuss the endowment of special resource rights to specific regions of Scotland. This seems particularly problematic given that Scotland is seeking to secede with the bulk share of Britain's natural resources. In 2013, the councils of Orkney, Shetland and the Western Isles formed an alliance to consider the implications of constitutional change for the remotest parts of Scotland (Kidd 2014). The islands had not ruled out some form of autonomy for themselves, including possible exclusivity to natural resources directly beneath their feet. As Kidd identifies: "The diktat of an uncomprehending Edinburgh three hundred miles away can seem just as distant and threatening as rule from London" (Kidd 2014). In response, the SNP outright rejected any suggestion of any devolution or autonomy to these Isles. In July 2020, Prime Minister Johnson suddenly made a one-day visit to Scotland where he suddenly announced additional funding for the Northern and Western Isles with an obvious goal to cement relationships to Westminster rather than Edinburgh (Ascherson 2020).

The secession and federalisation issue also comes with the perceived unfairness to the English people who comprise some 85 per cent of Britain's population. The, largely unarticulated, grievance is that England contains the bulk of Britain's infrastructure and wealth (Ascherson 2020) and yet it is suddenly expected to subsidise and imbue with wealth and resources a newly independent nation. A nation, as it happens, that shared an active and equal role (arguably disproportionately so) in empire and the conflicts that went together with the horrors of colonialism and slavery. It is again a classic 'beggar thy neighbour' problem of the kind witnessed in Bosnia. A literal race to the bottom and a manifestation of the lowest common denominator politics. The risk here is the kind that manifested in 1986 where talk was of 'power to the people and the regions', but actions were quite the opposite with further concentrations of power away from local government to centralised and competing Westminster fiefdoms or local fiefdoms. Prime Minister Margaret Thatcher, then, quite simply abolished democratically elected self-government of English 'metropolitan authorities' some of whom pursued policies opposing her own (Ascherson 2020).

The experience of federalism in Bosnia cautions against it being a ready solution to increasing nationalism (as that is what best characterises party politics in Britain currently). In the Bosnian case, the theory that ethno-national territorial solutions rarely provide peace and stability in divided states was proven true (Roeder and Rothschild 1999; Koneska 2016, 40). Territorial solutions, which try to neatly carve out new ethno-national majorities, the theory goes, encourage and empower local "ethnic entrepreneurs" who use their increased powers to mobilise their ethnic majorities to extract concessions or 'more independence' from the centre. Exclusive ethno-territorial separation is compounded when power-sharing consolidates local ethno-territorial monopolies and prevents trans-ethnic constituencies to form across the boundaries (Bassuener 2020, 221). There is some evidence to suggest that was precisely why Macedonia, another successor State from the SFRY that descended into ethnic conflict in

2001,[272] decided upon a non-federal arrangement with less prescriptive power-sharing arrangements than Bosnia (Koneska 2016, 39, 44; Keil 2015).[273] Bosnia was the only successor state of the former Yugoslavia that implemented a federal system (Keil, 2013a). In Macedonia, more functional forms of autonomy and policy devolution, including those relating to culture, were preferred over strict territorial devolution of political powers and competencies; this allows cross-ethnic and cross-territorial decision making (Koneska 2016, 41).[274] Macedonia, for instance, does not utilise any formal veto rights but rather uses special majorities[275] for decisions concerning important elements of minority protection or constitutional change (Keil 2015). This is not to say federal arrangements in any form cannot work but, in and of itself, simple federal solutions can entrench as well as foster division.

Federalisation, therefore, is not necessarily *the* answer and neither is secession; they are merely prescriptions, among many, that could be a product of a fair, negotiated and inclusive constitutional settlement process. The two major considerations when considering federalism, as noted in Chapter 4, is that the arrangements need to be: carefully adapted to the country and territory in question considering its history and political culture, and the arrangements must be arrived at through an inclusive process with attention given to key actors and spoilers (Keil and Alber 2020).

---

[272] Violent unrest broke out between Albanian rebels and Macedonian security services in 2000 up to the Ohrid Framework Agreement in 2001 which brought comprehensive peace.

[273] Keil (2015) states: "Article 1.2 of the Ohrid Agreement enforces this apathy against territorial autonomy, as it argues that 'Macedonia's sovereignty and territorial integrity, and the unitary character of the State are inviolable and must be preserved. There are no territorial solutions to ethnic issues.'"

[274] Koneska implies this was because of formal lessons learned from the Bosnian example but she herself concedes there is no evidence for that and that rather the lessons learned are likely to be inferred (Koneska 2016, 39-40). Keil (2015) notes that in addition to maintaining its territorial integrity, Macedonia provide extensive forms of cultural autonomy for members of minority nations, including in the areas of language, religion and education.

[275] Concurrent two thirds majority in the Assembly and two thirds of non-majority representatives.

Wading through the Great British muddle

There is a clear need for *something* other than the status quo to address constitutional issues in Britain outside of the day-to-day of parliamentary politics. The classic British fudge, muddling through and partisan ad hoc changes are neither workable nor sustainable.

The underlying unresolved constitutional issues have resulted in the following: attacks on judges by the media and the executive; bypassing of parliamentary scrutiny of the executive; centrifugal and centripetal forces that wrestle with secession from, or centralisation of, the Union respectively; and calls for reassertion of nativist or orthodox interpretations (depending on your view) of fundamental rights against accepted international norms and customs. Nothing seriously meaningful has, however, been proposed to date by way of solution by the party-political elites who are the ideological inspiration, proponents and sometimes causes of these *anti-systemic* practices. The book's author could not identify any major party leader who sought to make a sincere and serious commitment address the underlying issues that supposedly were the basis for partisan constitutional changes: that is, the creation of truly participatory, inclusive and deliberative mechanisms over and above shallow prescriptions.

Sumption (2019), for example, has lamented about the "empire of law" left by the "decline of politics" which is a threat to democracy. Yet, he proposes no alternatives to the status quo other than suggest we need to return to a "shared political culture" (2020). No suggestions for the revitalisation of democratic accountability mechanisms, no proposals for greater popular deliberation or participation in politics, no recommendation as to how to choose between rights he sees as fundamental from those he does not, and no method of determining why one interpretation about rights is orthodox and one impermissibly modern and, therefore, wrong.[276] The Liberal Democrats have proposed a 'citizens' convention' on the constitution consistently in their manifestos since 2010 although with a view for producing a full

---

[276] See further, O'Connor (2019).

written constitution (2010, 88). The First Minister of Wales, Carwyn Jones, argued in 2012 that "a constitutional convention will [sic] allow us to begin to redefine a modern UK".[277] The Scottish Government pledged to establish a constitutional convention *if* it won the "independence" referendum of September 2014.[278]

Most party manifestos for the 2015 general election other than the Conservative's, also proposed the establishment of some form public constitutional convention. Amongst those, Labour came the closest to 'set[ting] up a people-led constitutional convention" (Flinders 2016, 8). In November 2016, Gordon Brown called for the creation of "a UK-wide people's constitutional convention", to consider a "federal constitution." As Prime Minister, Gordon Brown had suggested reform proposals in a Green Paper, *The Governance of Britain 2007*, that suggested they would be as sweeping as those of the seventeenth century and were the most coherent and comprehensive political visions to date. They failed, however, in execution through a combination of poor planning, pitiable consultation, and palpable indecision; although it is to be added that Brown was dealing with multiple global crises and had little time and attention to give the serious thinking such fundamental reforms necessitate. The House of Lords Constitution Committee concluded: "this is no way to undertake the task of constitutional reform" (Tomkins and Turpin 2012, 30, 39). Labour and the Liberal Democrats have included proposals in their 2017 election manifestos to hold constitutional conventions. The Greens, UKIP, and others have also shown similar interest (Renwick and Hazell 2017).

The biggest problem is that many of these proposals came with pre-conceived desires or designs on constitutional outcomes. One party's or political leader's position does not accord with another's. The transactional nature of politics, it is presumed, will help them secure one reform over another. Brown had desired a fully written constitution and many sweeping constitutional

---

[277] Speech to an "Unlock Democracy" public meeting in the Westminster Parliament on 12 July 2012.
[278] Scottish Government, Scotland's Future: From the Referendum to Independence and a Written Constitution, February 2013.

reforms. Cameron had sought a Bill of Rights in tow with his "Big Society" and a particular view of what that entailed. Corbyn wished to abolish the House of Lords and undertake substantial land reform (Pickard and Shrimsley 2019). Johnson had wished to curtail judicial review, move the House of Lords out of London together with the civil service and revoke key human rights protections. But a serious and irrevocable manifesto commitment for a cross-party, cross-national and State-wide process for learning about, discussing and deliberating on constitutional changes without any pre-conceptions as to the outcome of intended reforms? It would be very welcome.

This is not to say there have not been proposals by academics, think-tanks, and parliamentary committees.[279] There have been a plethora, as highlighted in Chapter 4, but often, though not always, those affiliated with Parliament or political parties have been single-issue commissions and relatively narrow in focus and remit. They have dealt with the symptoms rather than the cause. A commission may be defined as "a group of people appointed by the Government to investigate a matter of public concern and to make recommendations on any actions to be taken" (HoC 2013). Over the years there have been many (HoC 2013; Renwick and Hazell 2017).[280]

Despite the recommendations from these commissions there has been no commission, and certainly no Royal Commission, since 1973 which has analysed the combined effect that these changes have had on the constitution as a whole. The last major Royal Commission on broad constitutional issues was the Kilbrandon Commission, established by a Labour Government, to consider the

---

[279] Some very instructive papers have been produced by The Constitutional Unit at University College London since 1996. They are cited in the reference list.

[280] For instance, the Calman Commission looking at further powers for Scotland; the Holtham, Richard, and Silk Commissions, looking at devolved powers for Wales; the McKay Commission, looking into solutions to the West Lothian Question; the Jenkins Commission on the electoral system; the Wakeham Commission on reform of the House of Lords; and the Commission on a British Bill of Rights, which looked at whether Britain should have its own Bill of Rights; and the Power Commission which examined the problem of democratic disengagement.

allocation of executive and legislative power within Britain, which reported in 1973 and produced the first substantial proposals for the devolution of power from Westminster (HoC 2013). The closest recent broad consideration of constitutional issues was an insightful report from the Commons', as it was then, Political and Constitutional Reform Committee, which asked whether a constitutional convention was needed for Britain.

What is then the route out of the seemingly mounting crises in Britain? This book is not one to offer prescriptive solutions; they are resisted for Britain as they are for Bosnia. There is, however, a starting point for inclusive, participatory and meaningful constitutional development in Britain, learning from the lessons of Bosnia, and cautious suggestions for *processes* for both countries to consider.

6.4 Pathways out of constitutional quagmires

This book makes the case for inclusive, participatory and deliberative mechanisms in constitutional creation and amendment processes. In comparing Bosnia and Britain, some insights are identified above that show the current deficiencies in how these two constitutions, sitting at the very opposite ends of a spectrum, are working and whether they are sufficiently in tune with the political culture of the people. These insights allow the author to recommend a revolving constitution for Bosnia and a new constitutional statute for Britain. The specific stages for implementing these two recommendations for the respective countries are consolidated below. There are, however, some common lessons that can be gleaned as a result of this book's research and analysis. They are the starting point for reform of both the British and Bosnian constitutions. Other constitutional design processes may find these instructive.

In any endeavour to reform a constitution or design a new one *process* is all critical. O'Leary (2019, 200), among others, have cautioned against "an obsessive focus on process in making constitutions" because "it is after all the end-product, a workable constitution for a deeply divided place that is the goal." If this book shows anything then it is that process is everything. The process determines why change should occur, when change is imperative, who to include, what should be the focus, and where and how change should happen. The analysis in Chapter 5, set outs the consequences of short-sightedness and miscalculation as well as the problems of framing and status quo biases in constitution making in a given context. The context matters as decisions may be made: in a period of crisis, where there are gaps in the information available to political elites and the people, and when the preferences of political elites and the people are not adequately understood. And, lastly, process is reflective of, and helps cultivate, good political culture (as elucidated upon in Chapters 2 and 3).

A fundamental problem in constitution-making processes, which remains characteristic, is that they are: insufficiently gender sensitive, poorly inclusive of women, and superficial when women's participation is provided for, either in the drafting process or in the content (Tamaru and O'Reilly 2018). Whilst women's participation has been increasing and women's inclusion is a standard *consideration* in constitution making, they are still under-represented across cases and regions (Houlihan 2019). For instance, from 1990 to 2015, in 75 countries in which there was either constitutional reform or a negotiated transition from authoritarianism to democracy following conflict or unrest, only 19 per cent of members of constitution-making bodies were women (Tamaru and O'Reilly 2018); today participation is around 26 per cent (Houlihan 2019, 10, 12). Early mobilisation around women's participation in constitution-making is critical in order to have inclusive processes and outcomes. That is particularly so in respect of women being in leadership roles and involved in the technical decisions to set up and compose any constitution-making body as well the design of the constitution itself. The general pattern is that women members of constitution-making bodies are often perceived by the public and men counterparts as representing so-called 'women's issues' (Houlihan 2019, 14). Quotas can be progressive depending on the context but may inadvertently create risks relating to delegitimising women members of constituent assemblies. Careful design, however, can mitigate such risks.

Broader equality in society, government and the judiciary help cement progressive constitutional outcomes and safeguard against reversal of inclusive provisions and rights (Houlihan 2019, 24-26). Women's representation is linked to more equitable legal frameworks, more inclusive socio-economic reforms and, in conflict-affected States, to more sustainable peace (O'Reilly *et al.* 2015; Krause *et al.* 2018; Lee-Koo and True 2018). An instructive example about inclusion, transparency and civic alliances can be gleaned from Hungary. Its 2012, its constitution was apparently drafted by three men in a single sitting (Houlihan 2019, 18). Women and other opposition groups were marginalized from the processes entirely and, therefore, the constitution reflected the ideological framework of Victor Orban's ruling Fidesz party. Women's interests (however defined) or their say on broader issues were completely supplanted by a "complementarity approach" to the role of women in the family and society as perceived, of course, by these men from Fidesz (Ibid).

There is a growing literature that shows active participation of the public in constitutional design processes can have positive empowering effects, increase civic understanding of State structures and create a culture of defence, and mobilisation, around the constitution which impacts effectiveness of State institutions (Wallis 2019, 278; Bernal 2019, 236-237; Landemore 2014). That is so even where there is a failure to amend or draft a new constitution. Applying the game theory analysis from Bosnia, one explanation is that public participation introduces new incentives and disincentives on the behaviour of political elites. Participation can, in particular, generate a legitimate expectation on the part of the public that they can have a say and, that when they do, outcomes will be respected. Elkins *et al* (2009) have found in a study of all constitutions made between 1789 and 2005 that public participation positively correlated with the endurance of the resulting constitution. Participation also has a connecting and legitimising effect—horizontal and vertical—between groups of people and between the national and the local which can foster a sense of community and even a sense of the constitution as a coalescing centre for activity (Ibid, Elster 1995). These studies are important particularly as power-sharing constitutional arrangements, which exclude active popular participation, remain the "off the shelf" template for "would-be international peace brokers, leaders of belligerent groups, as well as high-profile international affairs commentators" (Bassuener 2020). That is notwithstanding the failures in Bosnia of the consociational constitutional model, the increasing pressure on that model in Northern Ireland, as seen from 2017 to 2020, and the near collapse of that model in Lebanon and Iraq (Ibid, 12).

Britain has had a salutary lesson in exercising great caution over blunt tools of participation that bypass existing constitutional norms. Ghai and Galli (2006, 16) find that consultation or mere ratification are not adequate participatory processes, and that rather people should be given agency as decision-makers. This means receiving public views in narrative form, inviting citizen delegates to be part of deliberations and ensuring an independent mechanism (such as a convention) to seriously assess, analyse and translate public views on any proposed constitutional amendments (Ibid). Brexit was a failure not because people decided to leave the EU. It was a failure for a whole host of reasons related to the process and procedure of the referendum. The referendum was crude as it posed a binary question on a complicated issue. As a result, both the debate and outcome helped to create division rather than unity, rejection rather than legitimacy and uncertainty rather than clarity. Emerson (2020, 101) asks, quite sensibly, why the referendum question was not multi-option. This would have allowed people to provide a preference as to the outcomes they preferred. For instance, people could have ranked their most-desired outcome in terms of a future relationship with the EU: remain, leave on WTO rules, leave but stay in the EEA and so forth. That would have helped identify the locus of the "will of the people" slightly better. It would have led to a more constructive and nuanced national debate and provided a clear mandate for elites to act upon. Rather they contested whether the will of the people was for a hard or soft Brexit (Ibid). The referendum was problematic because it did not require a high threshold for a fundamental change or a mandatory turn-out requirement. Only 37 per cent of the electorate voted to leave once non-voters were accounted for. The referendum ignored the wishes of whole nations because a concurrent referendum in each nation was not held and the people's will in each could not be gauged and respected. Finally, as devolved matters were not subject to coordinated and concurrent negotiation and consultation at the outset, after the referendum there has been centrifugal tension between Westminster and the devolved administrations as to what Brexit will mean for devolved competencies. The lesson is that where participatory mechanisms are introduced, they must be introduced with caution, with careful analysis and calibration so that they are fair, inclusive and truly deliberative.

A number of scholars have identified that participation of the public needs to be meaningful and not perceived to be a sham or shallow (Ghai and Galli 2006; Wallis 2019). An example from Britain is the nature of Scotland's constitutional convention of 1989 that eventually led to devolution under the Scotland Act 1998.[281] No aspect of that constituent assembly was properly participatory, deliberative or inclusive. John McAllison, who cautioned in 2013 against the proposals by the SNP to create a constitutional convention if the 2014 referendum for independence was won, argued that it was likely to be encumbered by all the same biases of the convention that led to devolution (McAllison 2013).

McAllison is right that neither the first nor the intended second Scottish constitutional convention was directly elected, citizens had no active participation at all, and there was no broad-based stakeholder inclusion. For instance, the SNP withdrew from participation in the 1989 convention as independence was not on the agenda and the Conservative Party did not take part because

---

[281] The Convention's report in 1995 "formed the basis of further proposals which were brought forward in a white paper, Scotland's Parliament, by the Government in 1997. These proposals received considerable support in a referendum on 11 September 1997, with 74 per cent of those voting favouring the Government's proposals for a Scottish Parliament" (HoC 2013, 11).

they were against a devolved Scottish Parliament (HoC 2013, 10-11). Of those that did take part it was still a highly partisan body. Among its 159 members, only 16 were neither politicians nor party representatives (Renwick and Hazell 2017, 21). The issue with a lack of a broad-based platform or inadequate inclusion is that rather than the settle the issue of internal self-determination and autonomy, within the United Kingdom, devolution has opened up a constant re-opening and re-negotiation of who and what is the true heir of Scottish autonomy and self-determination. The people are merely co-opted into political elites pre-conceived designs rather than having a real and meaningful say.

The fact that constitutional reform is not on the public opinion pages of the national press says little about either the appetite or the desire for constitutional change; that is true of Scottish independence but also generally. There is a strand of literature suggesting only crises provide opportune moments for constitutional change where three things are present: public pressure for change, a galvanising constitutional entrepreneur and an ideational shift whereby political elites accept that change is inevitable (Flinders 2010). As Chapter 5 showed, however, this is not necessarily true, and neither is it necessary particularly because crises and conflict can result in bad choices—choices that may resolve the immediate conflict but may freeze of create the conditions for far worse conflict in the future. We need only think of Bosnia. Another example, as Chapter 4 noted, is that Brexit was not in the public's imagination or priority at all prior to the referendum in 2016 yet fundamental constitutional change has occurred in Britain because of a fringe party-political issue. Flinders (2010) does concede, however, that: "significant measures are generally led by one individual and usually in the absence of consensus. There was no consensus on the Great Reform Act, or universal suffrage, or Scottish devolution, or freedom of information, but that did not diminish their legitimacy." One must also account for dominant modes of thinking and structural impediments that previously hindered participation of groups in politics. In Kenya, the participatory nature of the constitutional reform process (of its 2010 constitution) gave visibility to, and empowered communities long marginalized by politics and the economy, such as the forest people, pastoralists, the disabled and ethnic minorities (Ghai and Galli 2006, 12).

Where an opportunity for meaningful participation has been created in a constitutional reform process, and where there have not been problems with communication or literacy, then take-up has often been enthusiastic. In South Africa, the political parties — who would have been distrustful and wary of each other given the history of apartheid — agreed, prior to the creation of a constituent assembly, on a number of constitutional principles which would govern the contents of the new constitution (Ghai and Galli 2006, 10). Remarkably in a pre-internet age, some two million public submissions were received from across the country, by the constituent assembly, as to what people would like to see in their future constitution (Bernal 2019, 235). These two processes went hand in hand with an interim constitution and an interim government of national unity, which helped to create an environment conducive to an inclusive and fair process (Ghai and Galli 2006, 10). As Chapter 2 set out, in Bosnia too there is a clear appetite for reform and, in particular, a feeling that better regulation of, and legal control over, political parties would be welcome (NDI 2019, 5). With better options, it is quite possible that a new constitutional process would result in unprecedented popular engagement.

In any constitutional reform endeavour, there needs to be wide stakeholder buy-in particularly from potential spoilers which means a clear understanding of the preferences of political elites and mechanisms for incentivisation. Pitfalls of participation have been noted, as in the process of drafting Kenya's 2010 constitution, where the short-term power interests of politicians or parties were sometimes pitted against the people. The people were largely concerned with ethical norms, social justice and human rights each of which had obvious implications for powerful elites who were perceived to be, and indeed some were, corrupt. Whilst there was clearly common ground among the people (whether left or right) on the issues — which elites were belatedly forced to consider — the politicians felt disempowered. A struggle then ensued which resulted in failure of the participatory process in producing a new constitution.

Iceland and Kenya serve as cases in point in which political elites blocked new constitutions that came about through highly participatory processes but over which they had little say (Landemore 2015). Of the three original citizens' assemblies — in British Columbia, the Netherlands, and Ontario — all excluded politicians and the outcome of those processes did not lead to any actual reform. In every case, that was partly because politicians did not back the assemblies' proposals (Renwick and Hazell 2017, 21). There is, therefore, as in Bosnia, some cause for caution against completely bypassing serving party or political elite interests; buy-in is critical (Ghai 2019, 237). Elster (1995) has suggested an hour-glass model so that there is high participation of the public at the beginning and end of the process so that there is significant early input and legitimacy. But he suggests that there would be less public participation and greater hard bargaining in between among elites and delegates (within a convention) to build consensus and push for tangible outcomes. Ghai and Galli (2006, 15) are right to caution that highly participatory processes can become unworkable due to complexity, diversity of actors, and challenges in maintaining interest, confidentiality and group cohesion. Whatever the model, there must be ever-present caution as elites can construct a veneer of public participation to provide cover for exclusive and partisan decision-making (Lerner 2019, 12). They can use intimidation, difficult procedural hurdles to participation or provide only passive participation opportunities to manufacture the consent that they seek.

Taking the road to reform

Inclusive, participatory and deliberative processes have to start somewhere and by some particular means and that process itself has to be inclusive and legitimate so as not to doom the whole constitutional reform endeavour to failure. The best way to achieve this, drawing from the scholarship and State practice that is available, would be the creation of a constitutional covenant. In both Bosnia and Britain, this would be the starting point for any constitutional reform agenda.

The terms of a constitutional covenant may generally relate to what form the process of debate, deliberation and then ultimately decision on a future constitutional settlement may look like. More specifically those terms may help clearly define the fundamentals of any constitutional design or amendment process which would create an assembly for discussion and deliberation: a constitutional convention. What purpose a constitutional convention will serve in Bosnia or Britain, or any other country, will differ greatly depending on what is the subject of reform. But in either case such a convention might serve as the beginning of a process: to inform the electorate and the elites about the constitution; to understand, after consultation with the people, the significance of reform and where it might really be needed; and ultimately to open a national debate between political elites and the people they represent. Some high-level considerations that would likely be relevant in a constitutional covenant are the following.

- What is the purpose and agenda of a future constitutional convention?
- Who decides the purpose and agenda?
- Who are 'the people' and where do they reside and how will they be reached?
- How might people's engagement be secured in the various stages of a constitutional design or amendment process?
    - How might the views of minorities, regions and nations be best gauged?
    - How might purely majoritarian outcomes be avoided?
    - How might gender sensitivity and equality be maintained in all aspect of the process?
- What form may public engagement in a convention take — referenda, civic initiatives, submissions, public meetings and deliberations and/or delegations to the convention?

- How frequent should public engagement be and at what stages would there be engagement?
- Would public participation be truly deliberative or merely symbolic allowing for ratification only?
- Would public engagement through delegates to a convention be secured by way of random selection or election?
    - How many delegates, if any, would there be?
    - How would fair and equal representation be maintained particularly where there are group cleavages?
    - If delegates were elected, what would be the procedural rules governing elections?
- Can the selected, or elected, delegates to a convention add, amend or remove items to the agenda in light of deliberation, consultation and agreement?
- Should politicians and political parties have delegates in the convention and, if so, in what numerical proportions and what weight, if any, should be accorded to their views?
- Should special committees for drafting be created within the convention and what form might appointment to such committees take?
    - Should the public have a passive role (i.e., ratifying decisions of the convention only) as well as an active role in drafting or making suggestions for drafting?
    - Might experts and civil society representatives be invited to give views as well as input into the drafting process and, if so, in what numerical proportions?
- What aspects of the convention process should be binding, or merely advisory, on the government and/or parliament?
- What form should ratification of a new constitution or constitutional amendment take, and should it be binding on the government and/or parliament or merely advisory?
- How long should the convention process last?
- How should a constitutional convention be financed, organised and resourced?

There will be a number of areas of contestation between political elites, the people and key constituencies in relation to the drafting of a constitutional covenant although not as many as the drafting of a constitution itself. This process is prior to elections or selections, referendums, deliberations and decisions on the fundamental constitutional rules. Therefore, some non-partisan, impartial and independent process for drafting it and allowing the compulsory consultation and consideration of a wide spectrum of views would help gauge what will objectively work in terms of process.

Relevant considerations will be who drafts the constitutional covenant, how preferences of participants are articulated and aggregated, and how the text will reflect political and social realities to ensure the process of discussion and deliberation on the constitutional amendments will be fair, inclusive and safe. Some form of independent vetting of the process would be necessary to ensure certain views are not side-stepped. As the discussion on Bosnia noted, there would be a need for very wide and pro-active consultation. There would be a need to inform the political elites and the people about the purpose of the constitutional covenant and the process it will initiate (Ghai and Galli 2006, 10). The process, thereby, may itself promote a sense of belonging, community and purpose that can be critical for the political community as a whole especially where a future convention is set to institutionalise participation and deliberation further.

Stages of a revolving constitution for Bosnia

Implementing the idea of a revolving constitution for Bosnia can be achieved via a complement of inter-twining and inter-locking mechanisms in a staged process. An evidence-based staged process is outlined below as a supplementation to the analysis in the preceding chapters. This is to merely encourage the opening of a creative process rather than determine an outcome. Such an endeavour would require, inevitably, further discussion, extensive peer review, and careful trial implementation or 'stress testing'. This book's author, though, does not disagree that, taken together, a revolving constitution whilst catalysing an evolutionary process could be revolutionary in outcome.

In terms of the actual mechanics of having a constitutional covenant leading to a constitutional convention—and then fixed and regular constitutional referendums, civic initiatives and deliberative assemblies—some insight is to be gained from the literature on initiatives and referendums applicable to constitution making in countries like Iceland, Cyprus, Switzerland, Nepal, South Africa, Ireland, Canada and Chile. Those were largely deliberative and participatory processes.

The process may begin, as noted as the start of this subchapter, with a widely debated and agreed constitutional covenant, drafted by a specialised and independent body, after a thoroughly inclusive, fair and transparent public process of consultation. Consultation that not merely receives submissions from the public at large but requires active, analysis and synthesis of recommendations by the independent body. The constitutional covenant will attempt to make operational the safeguards set out for any revolving constitution as set out in Chapter 5 and the three major insights noted at sub-chapter 6.2 above.

The process would then proceed by giving the electorate an opportunity to answer through a multi-option referendum (allowing the ranking of preferences) as to whether they would like to: (a) accept the constitutional covenant which would start the process of revolving the existing constitution at fixed and regular intervals, say, for instance, every 24 years or six electoral cycles; (b) keep the existing constitution in place unamended until the opportunity to have another say at the next electoral cycle; (c) revise the constitutional covenant through re-evaluation by the same independent body either by a convention of political elites and the people, or by a convention of just the people.

The referendum would precede, by a large margin, the usual State-wide elections so as to avoid conflation of ordinary political issues with constitutional issues. The referendum could either be State-wide with a very high voter turnout threshold (say 75 per cent) but preferably should take place simultaneously in both entities with a simple majority for reaching decisions with a relatively high-turnout threshold. It also ought to have a mandatory requirement for consent of a simple majority of the population in the 143 municipalities or each of the 10 Federation cantons and each of the 64 RS municipalities to avoid the suggestion that the less numerical Bosnian Croats or other minorities are being cut-out of the process.[282]

Buchanan and Tullock (1962) have talked about the necessity to have unanimity rule when making constitutional decisions despite the large costs involved in a decision with such a high threshold. They argue (1962, 93-96) that making decisions about the rules of the game implies potentially large external costs for most people i.e., costs that other people will decide on their behalf or coerce them. So great are the external costs, in fact, that the relative importance of decision costs is very small. They are right that unanimity rules would include everyone in the bargain and guarantees Pareto improvements from the status quo (i.e., that everyone is made better off without anyone being made worse off). Such rules are important to prevent a tyranny of the majority. But it should be noted that unanimity may preserve abhorrent or unjust situations in the status quo such as a tyranny of the minority:

> "For example, if some actors own slaves and emancipating slaves is a core part of a proposed constitution, then requiring all constitutional decisions to be Pareto improvements from the status quo may ultimately result in the preservation of slavery."

This was and remains an accepted and key failure of Dayton: allowing the gains of war crimes to be permanently enshrined as one would expect war criminals leading negotiations to insist upon. Unanimity rules in large referendums, therefore, would not be preferable in Bosnia (nor even perhaps super-majority) aside from the fact that unanimity rules would be completely unworkable. A higher threshold for the decision about the constitutional covenant would be the compromise noting that majority rules can also be

---

[282] See further, Dougherty and Edward (2011). There is precedent for super-majority voting with a super-imposed requirement for a concurrent super-majority in ethno-territorial sub-units.

Pareto optimal although not always improvements. Achieving Pareto optimal institutions is important. It that means that there is not another set of institutions that everyone prefers to the one just agreed. That again was not the case at Dayton. Everyone seemingly wanted something other than what they had just agreed.

Should the voters choose by a majority in each relevant canton and relevant municipality to institutionalise the constitutional covenant then the next step would be to convene the first constitutional convention. It would be specially convened in accordance with the rules of the constitutional covenant. Delegates would be either selected or elected so as to reflect the preferences of the voters. The elections for delegates could not be a State-wide alternative vote (AV) system even though this would encourage accommodation — given the exclusionary effect this will have on minorities and the risk that existing elites would canvass on de-legitimising the process for being exclusionary of 'their group' or 'their people'.[283] AV could be considered with high thresholds for selection in order to encourage accommodation among candidates but with great caution. Perhaps the most favourable form of vote would be one that would take place in each canton and each municipality with a threshold requirement for simple majorities or alternative votes for candidates — this would help cross-ethno-national candidates. Each canton or municipality could then send a fixed number of delegates to the convention. Delegates would be elected for the specific purpose of drafting the new constitution or amending the provisions of the existing one. Delegates, of course, would likely include representatives from the parties in the Parliamentary Assembly[284] and the entities but this need not be formal at all. Similarly, it would be important, particularly for drafting, that non-partisan experts be appointed (even possibly as delegates). All delegates would be empowered to vote and decide.

An alternative, and a preferable one, for appointing delegates would be to follow the citizen assemblies' model whereby a group

---

[283] The dangers of alternative voting or centripetlaist systems where divisions are deep are well-known if crudely adopted. See further, McCulloch, Allison (2013).
[284] Though they should not hold political office whilst the constitutional convention is convened.

of citizens are selected at random from the population (but filtered through "stratified random sampling" for representativeness, inclusion and removal of bias) to learn about, deliberate upon, and make recommendations in relation constitutional issues (Flinders 2015; Renwick and Hazell 2017). There is a lot to be said for random selection of ordinary people to avoid replicating the cleavages in the current system as well as pressures to conform whereby candidates might set-out pre-conceived ideas on reform in order to be elected. Whether that would be amenable to politicians is the difficult question.[285] It is helpful to remember that the Athenian system of democracy specifically disavowed elections for appointing citizens to the assembly because it was believed that elections would recreate the aristocratic biases and advantages at an electoral level. Preventing serving politicians from becoming delegates of the constitutional convention should seriously be considered to prevent reproducing cleavages and divisions in the parliamentary arena in the convention especially considering the different voting mechanisms used to elect delegates to the convention (Behnke 2008). But cutting out political elites altogether will almost doom any initiative to failure. They must play some part in the process; they need to agree to the covenant at the outset and they need to have something at stake in the deliberations and future outcomes.

The constitutional convention would then discuss, deliberate and decide on an agreed and amended constitution. The existing constitution would be the starting point and the one that was discussed. The public would be invited to participate through making submissions online and those would then be considered, synthesised (quantitatively and qualitatively in narrative form) and deliberated upon by delegates. Submissions from civil society and

---

[285] In the Icelandic Constitutional Council of 2011 twenty-five members, ordinary people, were chosen in November 2010 in an election. Politicians were excluded. In the three original citizens' assemblies — British Columbia (2004), the Netherlands (2006), and Ontario (2006-7) — its members, all ordinary citizens, were selected at random through stratified sampling to ensure representativeness on grounds of protected characteristics like gender, ethnicity, race and so forth (Renwick and Hazell 2017, 16).

individuals on provisions to reform or new provisions to be added can be invited for consideration by the convention; with a requirement that they should be considered 'of necessity' should certain procedural requirements be met—but the threshold should be low to encourage as much individual participation as possible.[286] Various mechanisms for allowing such submissions can be adopted as examples from Iceland, South Africa, Albania and Chile demonstrate (PILPG 2012; Arato 1989, 2009).

Offline meetings can also take place between the convention and the public, as they had during the Chilean reform process between April and August 2016, through local small group meetings (8,113 took place), and massive provincial meetings (71 were undertaken) and regional meetings (15 were carried out) (Bernal 2019, 236). Specialised experts would help faithfully translate any unrefined public views into workable provisions. Some independent oversight mechanism would be necessary on this 'translation' process. The deliberation process would need to be subject to high levels of confidentiality to allow for frank discussions although all agreed outcomes or formal dissents would require publication. In Chile, in its first constitutional assembly in 2015 there was a great concern that citizens' ideas and thoughts would not be faithfully interpreted by the President. This was a source of tension and formal discussions took place to ensure that the synthesising process had a binding and, therefore, verifiable aspect to it (Bernal 2019, 243). Ensuring that the people have another vote on the outcome can create a further check on the whole process.

An additional accommodating feature in terms of participation would be the introduction of joint-canton, joint-municipality and joint-entity civic initiatives.[287] This is when citizen

---

[286] It should be noted that aspects relating to human rights and fundamental freedoms would not be up for negotiation as under the current State Constitution, but additional stronger protections could be added.

[287] The idea emanates from the 'initiative for partial revision of the constitution' (precisely or generally formulated) in Switzerland which allows 100,000 electors to propose revisions to the current constitution. See further, Trechsel and Kriesi (1996).

groups accumulating a fixed number of signatories in each entity (say, 100,000 with specific support (say, 5,000-10,000)[288] in a majority if not all of the cantons and a majority in the RS municipalities) would be entitled to submit recommended provisions either precisely or generally formulated. The requirement for a majority plus a majority in the cantons and RS municipalities may be critical to ensure minority buy-in. The constitutional convention would then consider those submissions and a specialist elected sub-committee may re-formulate the submissions for consistency or workability and put the suggestions to a vote. Any provision would then be included as a separate line item for popular vote together with a vote, if any, on the revision of the existing constitution. Such a mechanism would increase cross-ethnic cooperation amongst citizens (Epple-Gass 1988; Trechsel 1996) and any abuse of process would still be checked by the requirement of support by the delegates of the constitutional convention.

Once provisions were drafted then versions of them could be subject to threshold agreement conditional on, say 50-75 per cent, support of the delegates—a check could be placed by ensuring that concurrent 50-75 per cent support emanated within all Federation canton and RS municipality delegates. It should be noted that a failure by the convention to draft an agreed constitution (or agree on no changes) would lead to consequences or a crisis. Consequences could result in a fall in the government and/or fresh elections in the Parliamentary Assembly (if parliamentary representatives are co-opted in the process) or fresh elections for the convention. This would ensure there are costs involved for politically partisan delegates who seek to hijack the process.

Agreement on a revised constitution would be put to a second civic referendum requiring wide-majority-support concurrent in both entities and even perhaps in a majority of smaller units in particular in a majority of the Federation cantons and the RS municipalities. Failure to receive the required equal support across

---

[288] With sufficient procedural safeguards such as a limitation period for signatures (e.g., 90 days), evidence of signature collections and so forth.

the entities (Federation cantons and RS municipalities) would end the process and the existing Bosnian constitution would remain in place unamended. A multi-option referendum would help make the process less binary and exclusionary and allow for instance amendment by groupings or no amendment at all. For instance, the options might be do you wish to: adopt the revised constitution with all amendments; adopt the revised constitutions with amendments grouped A or [B], or [C]; or retain the existing constitution unamended.

Numerous stakeholders, both domestic and international have insisted on greater civic involvement in Bosnia's democratic process but few have suggested how involvement could occur. The Venice Commission (2005, 12) came as close to being candid about the necessity for civic involvement as is possible for a diplomatic international institution noting all the while that the current arrangements are "largely based on the ethnic principle and maintaining it risks reproducing and reinforcing the ethnic divisions." The Commission went on to say:

> "It is desirable for the citizens at some stage to decide to have an entirely new constitution based on their own wishes and drafted during a period without ethnic strife [...] The ultimate goal should be to have democratically legitimate constitutions prepared with the participation of all political forces and civil society in a public and transparent process" (Venice Commission 2005, 16).

That ultimate goal will not be achieved if the road to reform is the most trodden. Desiring and achieving a State premised on individual rights and equality rather than collective equality of ethnic groups is to take the road least travelled or even the path unknown.

Routes along a clear constitutional path for Britain

Britain should convene a State-wide, non-partisan, public consultation to set the terms of reference for a non-binding constitutional covenant that would establish a constitutional convention outside of, but mandated by, the Westminster Parliament following consultation with the devolved legislatures.

A constitutional convention should not necessarily be convened to draft an entirely new written constitution or even to fundamentally alter Britain's constitutional make-up.

This book has envisaged only a specific role for any such process in Britain. The process would be to ascertain what aspects of Britain's uncodified constitution are clearly fundamental and around which cross-party and cross-national consensus may form leading to the drafting of a new constitutional statute as a one-off endeavour. This statute would, ideally, serve to address key constitutional issues that remain unresolved or are points of political contention in Britain. As outlined in Chapter 4, these issues may include among others: reform of, and representation in, the House of Lords; reform of, and election to, the House of Commons including issues of parliamentary scrutiny and procedure and MPs having control of their own business; an attempt to form a consensus on human rights including additions to rights such as economic, social and cultural rights; reform of party funding and electoral rules; devolution, particularly for the regions, and the nations; and future relationships with large regional organisations such as the European Union. But these are all questions for the people and the delegates (including elites) to any constitutional convention; canvassing their views in an informed, fair and inclusive process is precisely the point of such an endeavour.

It is an irony, as remarked by Blackburn (2015), that although Britain does not have a written constitution it has generated a rich heritage of "pioneering constitutional charters and documentation" (Ibid). There is no reason why it should not generate another. It would not be entirely without precedent. As noted in Chapter 1, Britain has previously convened a Convention Parliament in 1660. Long before that in 1295, there was also parliament that came to be popularly known as the 'Model Parliament' given how representative it was of the people for the very first time in Britain's history. A few principles, set-out below, might allow Britain to come to a new political understanding — towards a Magna Carta of the People[289] perhaps — around which political elites and the people

---

[289] Another title may be the *Millennium Magna Carta* or the *Charter of the People*.

across regions and nations may coalesce.[290] A constitutional statute, such as that, could strengthen national unity and territorial integrity, held define or enhance the idea of a modern and inclusive Britain, and develop a shared agenda for social and political change. A new Magna Carta would be a negotiated settlement rather than imposed at the behest of the ruling parties.

What might a Magna Carta of the People look like and what would be its status in the British constitution? The game theory analysis in this book demonstrates the benefits of the evolutionary mechanisms that have allowed Britain a remarkable flexibility in constitutional development especially allied with a political culture that has generally acted as a bulwark against despotism.

A new Magna Carta should, therefore, not be accorded some special treatment such as entrenchment *vis-à-vis* other constitutional statutes. If the process to getting to a new charter is sufficiently inclusive, participatory and consensus-oriented then it would tend to create a new status quo around which the contestations of day-to-day politics would revolve: with the legitimising effect that would entail. The lack of a definitive final outcome (forevermore), because the new Magna Carta would not have any special features of entrenchment, would create the game dynamics of an intertemporal bargain and avoid a single constitutional moment. It will provide an opportunity for elites to build mutual trust among themselves as well as trust with the people. Political elites would know the costs and consequences of unilateral change given the extensive involvement of the people. It also provides for the possibility—if a really bad bargain is seemingly struck—of amendment and revocation by the same

---

[290] There have been proposals in the UK for more limited constitutional charters that deal with specific constitutional problems often in response to immediate crises. They include: a 'Charter of the Union' to address devolution as a stop gap to the written constitution (BIICL 2005); a 'new Magna Carta' which would be a new written constitution as proposed by the Political and Constitutional Reform Select Committee (HoC 2014). The difference with the approach in this book is that the author: expressly cautions against a new written constitution as opposed to a constitutional statute; is hesitant about pre-determining what the content of a new constitution should be; and focuses on the process and procedure for determining a new constitutional statute.

parliamentary processes that would apply to the revocation of any other statute—simple majority—borne out of that classic British pragmatism.

Political science and comparative studies on constitutions find that fundamental constitutional change is often borne out of severe crises for two reasons. First, incumbent governments, in ordinary times, do not wish to be fettered by difficult constitutional issues which may not provide immediate results for their electorate (Flinders 2010). Second, only at a critical juncture might really radical change be possible to alter conventional assumptions and entrenched power relationships (Flinders 2010). Can Britain, like Bosnia, afford to wait for unilateral secession of its nations, the breakdown of the rule of law, the further undermining of Parliament, or radical populist sentiment altering the constitutional structure, piecemeal, to breaking point? The crisis is, in some ways, present right now providing for an opportune moment for reform before a more severe crisis renders the British constitution beyond rescue. And we know from the literature on status quo bias (in Chapter 5) that the choices people make in a crisis situation are very different from the choices made when there is relative peace and calm.

This book is not prescriptive on the content of any new constitutional statute and, therefore, expresses no view as to what a new Magna Carta should contain. There should not be any premature closure of issues that may require redress in such a Magna Carta. It must genuinely reflect the core of what society feels requires redress with some incentives to the entrenched and divisive elites to play 'the game'.

There are, however, some specific steps (in addition to the ones outlined at the start of this sub-chapter) that ought to be built into the constitutional covenant to mitigate against possible 'winner-takes-all' effects of convening a constitutional convention leading to the drafting a new constitutional statute. Safeguards are particularly important in relation to human rights and self-determination of groups.

The first consideration is that any constitutional reform process should be fair, transparent and inclusive. A very broad public exercise should precede any constitutional covenant being produced to instruct, inform and ascertain the preferences of political elites and the people. This would include receiving suggestions from the public prior to any formal consultation. There, therefore, needs to be leadership and direction in the setting of the purpose and agenda of a constitutional convention within the covenant (Renwick and Hazell 2017). Too broad an agenda risks the process becoming unworkable. Yet, too narrow an agenda risks ignoring what people want to be considered and, more fundamentally, risks the process becoming subject to all the biases of elite decision-making discussed in Chapter 5. Some room, therefore, still has to made for possible amendment, by convention delegates, if key public interests are ignored for whatever reason in the constitutional covenant itself.

A provision for civic initiatives to add or amend the issues on the agenda can be a good check on the terms of the constitutional covenant (as noted for Bosnia above) as can some deliberative mechanism within the convention's deliberative body to allow for additions or amendments to issues should a decision, with high-threshold support, suggest that is necessary. There should also be a body, perhaps the Supreme Court, that might act as an arbiter over disputes over the application, interpretation and fulfilment of any terms of reference in the constitutional covenant. That was the case in South Africa where the Constitutional Court verified whether the new permanent constitution complied with principles set out in a temporary one that initiated the constitution-making process. The Constitutional Court's involvement leant significant credibility to the process and removed contestation over disputes from partisan political actors (Landau and Lerner 2019, 6-7).[291]

The second consideration relates to human rights. There should be measures to ensure that there is no dilution of human rights below internationally accepted standards and norms which Britain is obligated to respect by virtue of being a ratifying State of

---

[291] See further, Arato (2016, 2017).

international treaties or because of the application of customary international law or common law. There is clearly elite contestation over rights and their adjudication, but one way to frame this discussion is to invite three specialist bodies to provide advisory opinions on what the accepted norms and standards are and then open up a discussion around what convention delegates as a whole would like to do within those boundaries. They may add to rights — such as economic, social and cultural rights — bolster existing ones — such as common law rights that have been rolled back by statute — and come up with forms of adjudication that allow for domestic internalisation of international rights given the objections, rightly or wrongly, in conservative circles to the Human Rights Act 1998. The three institutions could include: the highly respected Venice Commission; a Royal Commission formed for the purpose of considering the matter impartially; and the Supreme Court justices, who would finally determine the issue through an advisory opinion. The terms of reference of the constitutional covenant would then take that as its starting point on the issue of human rights. This way individuals, minorities, the disadvantaged and the dispossessed would not fear being cut out of a future Magna Carta. The issue of internal self-determination and autonomy can also be considered so that there is a minimum threshold for minority groups within devolved regions who might fear being bypassed by the majority in a debate on rights.

The third consideration relates to the regions, minority communities and the nations. There is an evident need to look at Scottish independence, possible re-unification of Ireland, further Welsh devolution as well how and in what manner the devolved administrations interact with one another. It goes without saying that there ought to be consideration of what a devolution settlement for England might look like. Last but not least, consideration may be given as to what the British population as a whole would like a Union of devolved countries or regions to look like (HoC 2013, 3-4, 6). To consider those questions, arguably, pre-convention hearings and submissions are probably necessary in each of the constituent parts of Britain and most importantly some guarantee that existing arrangements will not be rolled back without express agreement of the devolved administrations. There may also need to be a guarantee that the new arrangements will not be in place unless they comply with equitable terms (allowing for cross-nation and cross-party deliberation and high-threshold agreement) set out in the constitutional covenant.

In Britain, regular constitutional conventions are not necessary because that process is inbuilt in its unwritten constitution when the constitution is working as intended. Bearing in mind that the average life of the constitution of a sovereign State has recently been estimated to be just over 19 years the British approach is worth serious re-consideration before departure (Elkins and Ginsberg 2010). Well before Elkins and Ginsberg's (2010) study, they had traced back to an idea of one the US 'founding fathers', Thomas Jefferson. Jefferson argued that all constitutions and laws should expire when a new generation came into being on the basis of his belief that the "dead should never the govern living" and that the living should choose their own institutions (BBC 2017). Jefferson, in fact, created life expectancy tables of European citizens at the time — which he found were on average to be 19 years — and on that basis believed that every 19 years constitutions should expire, and people could choose to adopt a new constitution but only if they make that an active choice (BBC 2017).

The idea of choice really goes to the heart and centre of this book. Britain's constitution has had longevity, accommodation and co-operation allowing fundamental constitutional reforms including to the make-up of the country's political elites. Those reforms were essential and accommodated necessary civil and political change as well as socio-economic development. Movements that led to universal suffrage, the end of slavery, and greater civil rights are cases in point as well as more recent de-colonisation and independence processes. Looking, however, at the British and Bosnian cases we know that constitutional norms lapse and good political culture waxes and wanes.[292] In Britain it is time to provide a truly participatory and deliberative mechanism to renew, reinvigorate and revitalise politics although a wholesale overturning of the system is not warranted. The game theory and behavioural economics analysis in Chapter 5 suggested that — where the conditions are right — the British model with adaptations is favourable to better constitution-making. It makes less confrontational constitutional decision-making, allows inter-temporal bargains to lessen winner-takes-all effects and encourages an active constitutional culture to develop across generations. ✣

---

[292] For centuries Britain's House of Commons was elected by a small fraction of the adult male population, and in that classic British meandering and potted fashion, full adult male suffrage did not come about until 1918 a full hundred years after it was introduced in the US (at least for white adult males), and 60 years after adult male suffrage in France and Prussia (Franklin and Baun 1995, 16). In that same year, women (if they were 30 years old or over) were enfranchised with full suffrage. After this cautious first approach was tested on 'older' women, women generally were granted suffrage in 1928 (Ibid). It should be noted that in many other countries these reforms came about through violent revolutionary change. There could be a way to achieve these progressive evolutionary outcomes in the short-run as suggested in this book.

> "I understand you:
> You're a person in just one space and time
> Alive just here and now
> You don't know about the boundless
> Space of time
> In which I exist
> Present
> From a distant yesterday
> To a distant tomorrow
> Thinking
> Of you
>
> But that's not all"
>
> - Mak Dizdar, *The Stone Sleeper* [293]

BEYOND LAW, PRESCRIPTIONS AND CONCLUSIONS

This book compares the Bosnian and British constitutions. The two constitutions sit at the very opposite ends of a spectrum. Bosnia's constitution is a written, rigid and imposed document. Britain's constitution, by contrast, is an unwritten, flexible and evolving set of rules, conventions and practices. Making this comparison grants us an insight into whether these very different methods of designing the "rules that create all rules" affect the way people are governed and may also provide guidance in addressing the constitutional challenges facing the two countries.

The temptation, when embarking on an endeavour such as this, is to follow strictly the invocation often given by a master to their pupil: that it is dangerous to take general lessons from specific cases. The reverse, however, is also true. It is unwise to take only specific lessons from cases that are of general relevance. The pupil learns this over time as much as they become cautious of binary distinctions and compartmentalised thinking. That is why this unconventional comparison between Bosnia and Britain is instructive.

---

[293] An extract of a poem called "Roads" by Mak Dizdar [1917-1971] (2009, 18).

Constitutional design and amendment *processes* have common challenges. Therefore, common consideration is crucial in avoiding a situation where some people, at the expense of others, behave contrary to the common good. Aristotle was correct to say that "anyone who cannot form a community with others, or who does not need to because he is self-sufficient, is no part of a city-state — he is either a beast or a god."

At the beginning of this book there is an open question: whether a constitution can be seen as having a purely functional, mundane and mechanical role — creating the environment within which people operate but nothing more. In addressing this question, we have looked at the common challenges facing the British and Bosnian political communities in the following way. How can political elites be incentivised to play by the rules of the game? What set of codified rules, institutions and structures can constrain, by way of reward and punishment, the majoritarian impulse and political expediency?

An alternative question was also posed at the beginning: whether a constitution is something more elusive; something metaphysical and ultimately more human — akin to the soul of a state imbuing abstract laws with notions of values, culture and spirit. In that context, we might consider the common challenges facing the British and Bosnian political communities slightly differently. How might people *feel* a sense of belonging to, and ownership of, a constitution? Can we move beyond notions of reward and punishment? Is there a way to persuade political elites to embrace, endorse and employ constitutional rules even against their own narrow self-interest?[294] Which contexts and models might provide the best answers to such questions?

The traditional social contract explanations for adherence, by political elites, to constitutional norms are inadequate (Ordeshook, Levinson 2010). They fail to respond to some key questions: who are the guardians of the constitution? In other words, who enforces the constitution such that adherence is incentivised and non-

---

[294] For a very helpful framing of this paradox in the US context Levinson's (2010) piece is excellent.

adherence dis-incentivised? And who guards the guardians? This classic philosophical conundrum is still with us some two and a half millennia since Plato grappled with it in *The Republic*.

It is also clear that a codified constitution that is made difficult to amend is not guaranteed to protect the people's best interests. Committed political elites, backed by a constituency of 'their people', can frequently dismantle such constitutions. Courts, similarly, in and of themselves, are not always a sufficient check on political elites. The authority of courts springs largely from the constitutional structure itself. We know as much from the systematic breakdown of the rule of law in Hungary, Turkey, Poland and Russia in the past decade, which has often gone hand-in-hand with processes of state capture (Keil 2018). A given threshold for amending a constitution may be a high or a low barrier depending on particular electoral rules and the diverse constellations of political parties within a constitutional structure. By amending the constitution, however, it is possible to formally bypass the vital checks and balances upon which democracy depends, if those checks have not already been fatally undermined informally before-hand.[295]

We often find, in modern times, rhetorical references to constitutional preambles or principles that 'we the people' are the ultimate guardians of the constitution, and that it is in the people's name that the constitution is promulgated. If that is true then there is a forever risk that the people, when dissatisfied, can and are in fact entitled to rebel: legally within the constitutional framework but sometimes outside of it. But how does the risk of a rebellion from a diffuse, undisciplined, and undefined mass of people ensure that elites in their day-to-day actions adhere to constitutional rules or norms? Surely, the risk is so slim that unscrupulous political

---

[295] In Hungary, for instance, the electoral system uses a formula favourable to its largest party, the governing Fidesz (Hungarian Civic Union). By obtaining 44.5 per cent of the votes, Fidesz can gain a two-thirds majority of the seats in parliament, allowing it to amend — as it indeed has — the constitution at will (IDEA 2014, 12). The Netherlands, by contrast, uses a highly proportional electoral system, so that reaching a two-thirds majority may require agreement between four or more political parties, making it difficult to amend the constitution without *de facto*, cross-party support (Ibid).

elites, would break them whenever it serves an expedient political purpose? Political expediency may be even more pronounced where such political elites have taken it upon themselves to limit the social and civic spaces available to the people to get together to protest or rebel.

An analysis based on game theory and behavioural economics might serve as a better explanation.[296] A constitution, as an intertemporal bargain or coordination device, can be self-enforcing where a particular equilibrium is reached. It is easier to achieve that equilibrium where there is the presence of certain constitutional features. Some of these, as this book has highlighted, include repeated interaction between political elites, the provision of complete information to the people and the elites, greater communication between political elites and the people, credible punishments and reputational consequences for misbehaviour by political elites, meaningful rewards for honourable conduct, and strict provisions on enforcement of constitutional bargains.[297]

A successful constitution sits between the metaphysical and the mundane; providing some rational and mechanical rules that govern long-term political behaviour as well as instilling in the people, *if* they accept its terms, a sense of belonging to a wider political community and culture. This book, in search of that elusive equilibrium, has concerned itself with the constitutions of two countries, Bosnia and Britain, at the far ends of a continuum on constitutional design. What might we have gleaned about Bosnia and Britain?

Bosnia was devastated by violent conflict in the last decade of the last millennium. In the new millennium, whilst the threat of violent conflict has abated somewhat, a conflict of another kind is flourishing: latent low-level conflict amongst political elites of the 'constituent peoples': Bosniaks, Bosnian Croats and Bosnian Serbs. Political elites blame this conflict and their own intransigence on political culture. They say that they behave as they do in the name

---

[296] See further, Levinson (2010) and Ordeshook and Klochko (n.d.).
[297] The models in Chapter 5 showed that is the case even if we assume that individuals are completely self-interested.

of 'their people'. It has been taken for granted that conflict between political elites in the institutions of Bosnia is a mirror reflection of the latent conflict amongst the people. The people in Bosnia are characterised as poor democratic participants: anti-democratic and ethno-nationalist. Political elites, the narrative goes, merely represent faithfully the political preferences of their respective, and segmented, electorates. Political apathy and deadlock within state institutions, therefore, is a result of a lack of poor citizen participation, initiative and will. Such a narrative, however, is not supported by Bosnia's rich variegated and multi-ethnic history; a history predicated on accommodation and tolerance. This book has shown that the political apathy of the people *emanates* in fact from the actions of the post-war political elites working within the Bosnian constitutional framework. The structures created by the Bosnian constitution at Dayton not only institutionalised the aims of the war's architects, but they also amount to the primary causal variable resulting in political apathy of the people as well as intransigent or nationalist elite behaviour. As heirs of those war-time architects, today's political elites are now conducting war by other means.

Britain, by contrast to Bosnia, is a long-established democratic state, comprising four nations, with an uncodified, non-federal constitutional arrangement. This arrangement has endured for almost three and a half centuries without violent conflict threatening its core constitutional structure. Of course, the periphery of the British State, and in particular the countries of the empire, was never quite endowed with the peace, democracy and stability that endured at its centre. However, Britain's flexible constitutional arrangements, which make constitutional changes almost as easy as changes to day-to-day legislation, allow an accommodation between political elites and the people that has allowed seismic constitutional change without bypassing or overturning its core structure. Such changes include universal suffrage, ending slavery, domestic incorporation of a vast array of international legal instruments including on human rights, the expansion and contraction of its territory, entry and exit from the

European Union, decolonisation, deindustrialisation and devolution. The British uncodified constitution, however, is not entirely exemplary. Its unwritten constitutional practices and conventions are being tested to their limits. Britain has been racked by recent crises including Brexit, national separatism jeopardising the union, and perpetual executive undermining of the rule of law and parliamentary oversight.

Whilst the political culture of the people has remained surprisingly resilient in support of the current constitutional arrangements as a State, Britons appear polarised on many major policy issues. This polarisation has serious constitutional consequences and has *emanated* from piecemeal and partisan executive decision-making relating to a whole host of constitutional matters including from Britain's: fractured international relationships; domestic relationships with its own people affected by rising inequality; remote decision-making in Westminster; and the curtailment of human rights. The British people maintain a strong distrust of politicians. Such distrust is perhaps healthy, but it runs the risk of morphing into something more sinister.

This book has sought to show that, in both Bosnia and Britain political culture and identity 'emanate' from *something* and, because they are constructed, it must be the case that both are rarely ever fixed or unchanging. There is always the possibility of change. This book demonstrates that the people in both States (as opposed to elites) are increasingly moderate, accommodating and far more inclined to political participation than many have given them credit for.

In Britain, the public, and particularly the young, appear more interested in politics than they have ever been and seize upon using non-conventional forms of political communication, engagement and activity even where it relates to complex governance issues (Flinders 2016, 2). In Bosnia, the people are much more accommodating and capable of responsibility than the rigid elites representing them on an exclusively ethno-national basis.[298] There is, therefore, a discrepancy between elite preferences and the people's preferences in the constitutional space, i.e., where the rules of the game are set.

In Bosnia, constitutional structures, when combined with the legacy of the war, have tended to favour the election of ethno-nationalist elites; in fact, elites are incentivised to be such. Since the Bosnian constitution (and by extension its institutions) is the most significant impediment to bridging societal divides, its reform must be the priority and such reform must have a civic mandate. But political elites within the institutions, isolated from the people,[299] are unwilling and, in reality, unable to undertake reform that is conciliatory, moderate and accommodating. They are seemingly locked in revolving doors without an exit. Given their predicament, a *revolving constitution* may provide a possible way out. A revolving constitution would subject parts of the existing constitution to greater civic involvement and input (referendums, civic initiatives, deliberative assemblies) on a fixed and regular basis so the people can determine what, if anything, should change. This book demonstrates that fixed and repeated deliberation on the constitution, in a way that is properly institutionalised, accompanied by procedural safeguards, and set out in a constitutional covenant, will make people no worse off than the status quo. If anything, the mere possibility of joint and concurrent constitutional participation and deliberation in the cantons, municipalities and entities of Bosnia would guarantee that the outcomes of reform would accord with the median voter. This median voter, the evidence suggests, is more accepting, more tolerant and more democratic than the elites are able, or willing, to be in the current constitutional framework. At worst, if the people

---

[298] See Chapters 2 and 3. A limitation of the study are some gaps in the quantitative times series data preventing a comprehensive analysis, but significant and sufficient data is available to make the claim. At the very least the data confirms that culture is not fixed or unchanging and that the direction of change is positive in respect of accommodation amongst citizens.

[299] On the issue of constitutional reform, at least, and arguably on almost all policy issues given the way the elections, electoral laws and electoral districts operate.

are less accommodating than evidenced in this book, they and their representatives will maintain intransigence. At best, however, the carefully calibrated constitutional referendums, initiatives and assemblies would help reconcile intransigent elite and the moderate preferences of the people. Elites in the constitutional reform space, currently interacting only with each other in the parliamentary arena would be incentivised to truly consider the preferences of the people in the electoral arena.

The example of Bosnia is clearly of significance to Britain. Bosnia's constitutional underpinning provides a warning to Britain that codification, federalisation and entrenchment of some rules above others, in and of itself, is not a panacea. Short-term policy making in respect of core constitutional statutes—without local ownership, inclusion and deliberation—has led as linearly a lightning bolt to the crises that face Britain today. These crises could threaten the State's constitutional foundations as well as its union of nations. In light of this, Britain's historical unwritten arrangement—where political culture requires cultivation—is found to be worth understanding, defending and reinforcing—both in the civic and political spaces.

This book demonstrates that whilst the unwritten constitution is apt for Britain, the politics of old cannot continue without a major cross-party, cross-national constitutional covenant together with a re-assessment of political culture. The constitutional covenant would set in motion a process whereby politics, on a cross-party basis, can rally around the creation of a new constitutional statute; if you like, a Magna Carta of the People. Such a statute, whilst unentrenched like all other primary statutes, would aim to address key constitutional issues that cause division and polarisation between the state and the people. Its provisions will be determined by the people through informed and reasoned participation and debate within a constitutional convention convened as a once in a generation endeavour. Constitutional issues causing current polarisation may be settled, by a truly inclusive process, in a new statute around which the politics of the day may coalesce. It would act as a way to revive Britain's flexible constitutional arrangements rather than replace them. The covenant and the constitutional convention it would precipitate must, however, be a product of genuine public participation, deliberation and decision to give it legitimacy, direction and an enduring legacy.

In both Britain and Bosnia, the possibility of amending the constitution with genuine civic involvement would set in motion a process rather than determine an outcome. A process, whereby actors are incentivised to pursue moderate, inclusive, and accommodating reform, could alter political action and behaviour of both the people and political elites. Assessing and understanding the preferences of political elites and the people has valuable explanatory power as well as predictive potential; they allow us to think about how both countries might become, and be nudged into becoming, closer approximations of fairer, more just and more democratic states and societies. Britain and Bosnia might even set a standard even for other plural, multi-ethnic polities to follow.

The standard suggested in this book for Bosnia and Britain, to help circumvent the cycle of constitutional crises they face, raises two considerations. First, whether these models have wider application and, second, whether we might have to reassess contemporary understandings of what a constitution is.

Havel (1978) contended that conclusions on fundamental questions such as this that do not provide a common solution (that is not applicable to others) cannot be meaningful either for the political community or the individual. It would be akin to an individual who, faced with a difficulty, attempts to escape to an Indian ashram or an alternative political community rather than address the common problem. The escape may be wonderful for the individual but what about the political community that they leave behind? The escape to the ashram or the alternative political community, however, is not completely without relevance (1978, 117). Both points of departure leave within an individual an inescapable sense of contrast with, and perhaps even responsibility for, what they leave behind.[300] The individual would arguably feel bound, in some way, by the responsibility to their political community. What then is a constitution, if not a reflection of the individual, *the human being*, becoming responsible for themselves and their community?

This book has focused on rules, conventions and practices and the structures and systems that they generate: balancing competing variables using challenging equations. This is not because these variables and equations are important in and of themselves; they are not. But rather because they are a consequence of, and ultimately incidental to, a more esoteric variable, the people. Let us not forget, as Williams and Ferguson beautifully put it, that the intelligence we are able to see all around us is in the energy generated by the interaction of the living and the non-living: "the fire in the equations" (2019, 182).

It is incorrect, therefore, when we introduce the people into the equation, to ask what a constitution is for. It is even incorrect to ask whom a constitution is for. Both questions presuppose the involvement of the very people in whose name the abstract, and mathematical, processes of constitutional design take place. A constitution rather *is* of the people to whom it is of concern. The people in all their manifestations as nations, regions, groups and individuals. Not the people as they are idealised, romanticised, and conceptualised. But the people as they are when they come together: messy, difficult, and disorganised.

A constitution cannot, therefore, be incidental to something or someone. Neither can it be completely instrumental to some goal or objective. The obvious question that would raise is whose goal or objective? When changing any system or structure the answer is not, as Havel (1978, 115) cautioned, even in post-totalitarian States, about replacing one set with another: "after all, parallel structures do not grow *a priori* out of a theoretical vision of systemic changes [...] but from the aims of life and the authentic needs of real people."

---

[300] Contentious ideas about nationality, citizenship, ethnicity, race and culture come to mind.

Paradoxically, this book is predicated on identifying, measuring, and cultivating precisely the authentic needs of real people manifested by their political culture. This political culture exists but is often taken for granted and dismissed as too nebulous to be useful. The loss occurs as a result of improper instrumentalization: this is the 'will of the people' we are told. But as West (2018) has correctly articulated, "every democratic experiment we know has been shot through with structures of domination." The dangers, therefore, with mere abstract system or structural change is that they recreate the very hierarchies and modes of domination and subjugation that any new system is purportedly designed to overcome. Where then does the will of the people really reside? It resides, as Havel (1978, 130), Mahmutćehajić (2009, 129) and others have alluded, not in methods and systems of traditional politics that call for a fantastical tomorrow but instead in the ordinary here and now: the space in which protest, and dissent foments, and which sees a need in the struggles of the people. Struggles which are present today from Bosnia to Britain and further afield.

A constitution may be better understood as both the means and the end. An everyday struggle for a constant in a political community that has a chaotic and continuing set of commitments. These commitments—such as maintaining relationships with other States, defining citizenship, preventing crime and so forth—are in constant flux by virtue of people's changing practices, beliefs, and norms.

The political community today is not the Platonic *Republic* of Socrates that envisaged selfless and benign guardians, as philosopher-kings or queens, controlling a stratified society. Kings or queens who, with apparent gold in their souls, were supposedly predisposed to rule others in the political community and guide them to a future purpose of 'justice'. All built incidentally, on the 'noble lie' of class hierarchy: that some people were born predisposed to rule others. That lie has endured in Britain for long enough and has been newly created in Bosnia. We must rather grapple with the Socrates of radical egalitarianism. The cultivator of the soul, the dissenter against majoritarian impulse, the feminist and the confessor of the noble lie of class hierarchy. In that political community, each person has the *capacity, responsibility and capability* of the guardian.

To come back to the question posed at the beginning of this book, the constitution is better envisaged as akin to the soul of a person—a collection of people's beliefs, norms and practices as a political culture—even an amalgamation of souls. Political culture, therefore, is the starting and end point when it comes to discussions on constitutions, written or unwritten. The lesson for us all in the political community is simple: cultivate, maintain and enrich political, civil and socio-economic virtues (necessarily manifested by practice) that are important to the people's day-to-day lives. The day-to-day lives of individuals will then be worth living in the here and now. Otherwise, the people must reach for the temporal seclusion of the ashram or even the escape to the alternative political community. Inevitably those seclusions or escapes leave behind a less enriching, less free, and less just society for all.

What the political community must do is move away from passivity to activity. A politics of genuine responsibility accorded to the people again in decision-making so that deeper virtues, values and relationships, as Havel (1978, 140-143) suggests, and political sociologists have demonstrated, can be rehabilitated. Rehabilitation is in the form of trust in one another, openness to the other, responsibility to and for the State, solidarity with the dispossessed, marginalised and disenfranchised and love for oneself manifest as love for the other, even the supposed enemy (Badiou 2012). Love in its truest conception is a threat to the status quo, is a risk to comfort and presents a challenge to accept, without reservation, difference.

A truly deliberative and participatory process of constitutional design—through a covenant and convention—is not a destination and is not even a hope. Both give false comfort in an uncertain future that is ultimately the gift of some unknown, and probably unknowable, saviour. But a constitution of the people, truly, is an action in ordinary human hope. Each and every participant, at a particular snapshot in time, imbued with a sense of community and solidarity as a result of organised action to address a common problem: self-constituting, self-organising, and self-perpetuating. The structure of a constitutional covenant and convention, such as the terms of reference, institutions, deliberations and so forth, disappear when the immediate common task—a constitution—is attained. Much like the assembly and disassembly of people who gather in the commons. But the radical act itself, of individuals constituting for this common yet continuing purpose, is the most meaningful. An enduring reminder and a permanent testament against autocracy. ✺

AFTERWORD

Freedoms in democracies include the freedom to do absolutely nothing about the government of your village, town, county, nation or any international organisation of which your country is part, except in countries where voting in elections is a compulsory, but minimal, legal requirement.

These freedoms extend upwards, from participating *or* idle voters, to those with power—especially politicians and owners of media—to write, say and do things in defiance of truth in order to preserve power and consolidate the *status quo*.

These freedoms include the freedom for voters to take no steps—through the ballot box or elsewhere—to free themselves from shackles of a society divided, by its rulers, between those who have and those who do not, even to the extent of accommodating themselves to their own poverty, without complaint.

But if such shackles are, partly or wholly, a result of major limitations, shortcomings or failures of the very constitution within which voters have their limited powers, do voters ever *actually* get a chance to take steps to put *fundamental* things right? Experience reveals reality.

In Britain, the natural party of government—the Conservative Party—was out of office recently for 13 years of Labour Party rule in which period little significant was done to make *radical* changes to the distribution of wealth and to ensure the public as a whole was represented, in proportion, at government's highest levels, although Johnson's present 2021 government has a broader ethnic base than many previous governments. Yet both these issues might be counted as constitutional matters, even the one concerned with distribution of wealth. Within the sealed borders of our sovereign state, how we all share the state's assets may well be a constitutional issue, unless there is an embedded freedom—there is not— allowing anyone to make and keep as much as they can at whatever cost to others.

Seven or eight years ago, I dare say, few UK citizens had any detailed knowledge of the British constitution. Those with the advantage of good education may have heard of the constitution being 'unwritten' — whatever that means. Little more. Would they have understood the importance of Magna Carta or even heard of the Bill of Rights? I do not think so. Unlike citizens of the US — who may well be familiar with their Constitution and maybe the First and Second Amendments — UK citizens generally know nothing of the British constitution and are not to be blamed for that.

The referendums on proportional voting, the independence of Scotland and withdrawal from the EU, and elections since, may have enlightened us all a bit. As a new non-EU-member State, Britain is facing up to the dire economic consequences of Brexit as well as a global pandemic. Brexit *may*, on one reckoning (mine certainly), have been an act of *constitutional* folly. Both crises *may* have raised further public awareness of our constitution along with a connected understanding of primitive concepts of sovereignty, slowly being freed of their very simplest Union Jack wrappings. How long will this enhanced awareness last? Probably not long if that well-used shroud descends again, covering the constitution in a blinding red, white and blue romanticised history that allows governments to do what they wish on constitutional issues without proper, well-informed voter oversight.

With these realities in mind, will Britain — no longer a major world power whose parliament is sometimes perceived as there for entertainment rather than scrutiny of government policy and making informed decisions, carry on allowing its citizens to focus on consumer goods and possibly a holiday in the sun but not on politics, let alone on the founding documents of State?

Does Britain need change? Many things would suggest so. Do parliamentary dark arts — fixing time for debate and order papers for decision making — together with bludgeoning whips, who threaten, promise and blackmail, all reflect the *real* modern British political culture? Does the weekly Prime Minister's Questions really test the government or is it some form of all-comers boxing bout, where knock out blows can never happen? Is an unelected chamber of Parliament, with some 92 hereditary peers, stuffed with appointees of the of the Prime Minister of the day, acceptable in a modern democracy?

Nothing really suggests the British State has the best method of making decisions. We know from this book that the British public thinks very little of politicians although the citizens may *seem* happy with the overall political structure.

The citizens may well be happy to carry on as an island race doing little or nothing about the current structure until, just possibly, we suffer on-land violence of the kind so many *un*happy states suffer. And, by the way, we are not in fact especially happy, perhaps because of the confining structures or policies from which we choose *not* to escape. Why are we below all these countries on one reckoning of national happiness—Finland, Denmark, *Switzerland, Iceland, Norway, Netherlands, Sweden, New Zealand, Austria, Luxembourg, Canada, Australia*—given our historic power and present wealth? Are not some factors found, for this reckoning, as the most important to happiness—*freedom to make life choices, trust towards social and political institutions, healthy life expectancy, level of available support from friends and relatives in times of need, generosity as a sense of positive community engagement and income*—things that a good constitution might properly respect and help to provide?

This book is premised—for Britain *and* for Bosnia—on an optimistic, if demonstrable, view of enhanced citizen engagement in how both States are ruled and the willingness of both States' political elites to limit their privileges of money, property, rank, and power—over time.

Can the ideas in this book, if taken to heart by altruistic politicians and active, or even activist, citizens do anything to change—for the good—how these two countries (and others) are governed? Does consideration of Bosnia's post-Dayton fate give us any clues?

Unlike the people of Bosnia, UK citizens have no personal experience of politician-led slaughter on our own modest land. Unlike for my consideration of the UK, I am no native of Bosnia or any part of the Former Yugoslavia and, therefore, have no instinctive sense for how the present Bosnian constitution is or seems.

This much we all know, who know Bosnia at all. It is yesterday's problem. The world is not that bothered anymore, even if it looks on with some sympathy at a country stuck, as seems, from the consequences of the end of an *internal* war, although Republika Srpska's side was supported by Serbia itself in that war.

The Dayton Peace Agreement was forged, in large part, by the very international parties who had more than a mercy-mission role in what happened in Srebrenica and the bombing that followed. We may not know, in our lifetimes, precisely how deeply Britain, the USA, France and Germany were involved in the Srebrenica tragedy because the same parties that told Bosnia how to organise its affairs have no intention of revealing, in full, the way they had organised theirs. The UK and other states obstinately refused to acknowledge that genocide was happening in an area they owed both general and particular—Genocide Convention—duties. Those forcing the Dayton Peace Agreement and the new constitution onto the land of Bosnia—to be composed of Republika Srpska and the Federation—were content to negotiate with those who were later to be indicted for international crimes. They may have also been serving some unrevealed plan; for example, to avoid there ever being a Muslim state in the heart of Europe (See 'Clinton Tapes' by Taylor Branch). Any secondary objective lying behind the enforced Agreement, fixed with war criminals, might have made it extremely unlikely that a workable constitution would ever be a possibility. And so it has turned out to be.

Aarif Abraham's general idea of institutionalised deliberation and fixed and regular consideration of constitutional change may, on the face of it, be difficult to envisage where the first problem for Bosnia is how to deal with separation of the people through cantonisation and entitisation. That is particularly so where Republika Srpska's elites dream of secession and ultimate union with a Greater Serbia: proving to the world that genocide works well, in this case for Christians of a formerly multi faith land? And the subsequent difficulties of the Federation would not be much easier for relaxed discussion and conversation.

Shortly after the end of the conflict, Sarajevo was many visitor's 'favourite city'. A romantic sense of the danger through which it had journeyed; with its happy multi-ethnic past just about able to look ahead. Now, Bosnia has more politicians *per capita* than any country in the world and an inability accurately to chronicle its past because truth telling is incomplete and likely to remain so. The capital seems sadder and with little to encourage the visitor to any optimism—let alone the optimism needed for any exercise in constitutional reform. But must it remain so?

This book's suggestions—optimistic, idealistic, pragmatic, innovative—dare to look at two constitutions in crisis, neither a model for the other to copy.

The UK's citizens have, for a century or so, been given no chance to affect the way their nation is constituted and run except to vote in constituencies—where very substantial minorities may live a lifetime never electing an MP to Parliament whom they support—and to take part in occasional binary referendums. Assuming Scotland splits and Ireland unites, neither change will be by real informed consent of the people concerned. Each will be by political force and each will show Britain's unwritten constitution to have been as much a problem in its unrestrained flexibility (not attuned to it citizens wishes) as well as its entrenched particular elite interests (with their own networks of patronage and power). The processes advocated here—had they happened a long time ago and had they allowed more citizens to bring individual judgement into political decision making—would probably have saved the country from crashing out of Europe and quite possible could keep the Kingdom together once sensible decentralisation possibilities are properly considered by citizens from its four parts. But the UK's systems are all or nothing, and certainly nothing at present for the citizen to contribute between elections and referendums. So maybe nothing.

People in Bosnia do not rule out further armed conflict. Unsurprising. Yet the research revealed in the book suggests the citizens themselves are perhaps more capable of optimism and cooperation than others might think.

If Aarif Abraham is right, the desperate circumstances facing Bosnia and the wretched realities of the UK's inescapable constitutional commitment to sclerotic systems of government can be eased by gentle processes. They could start with citizen engagement and aim by degrees at better constitutions. Why not give the citizens a chance? They deserve it.

Sir Geoffrey Nice QC
Professor Emeritus Gresham College

The Hague, February 2021

APPENDICES

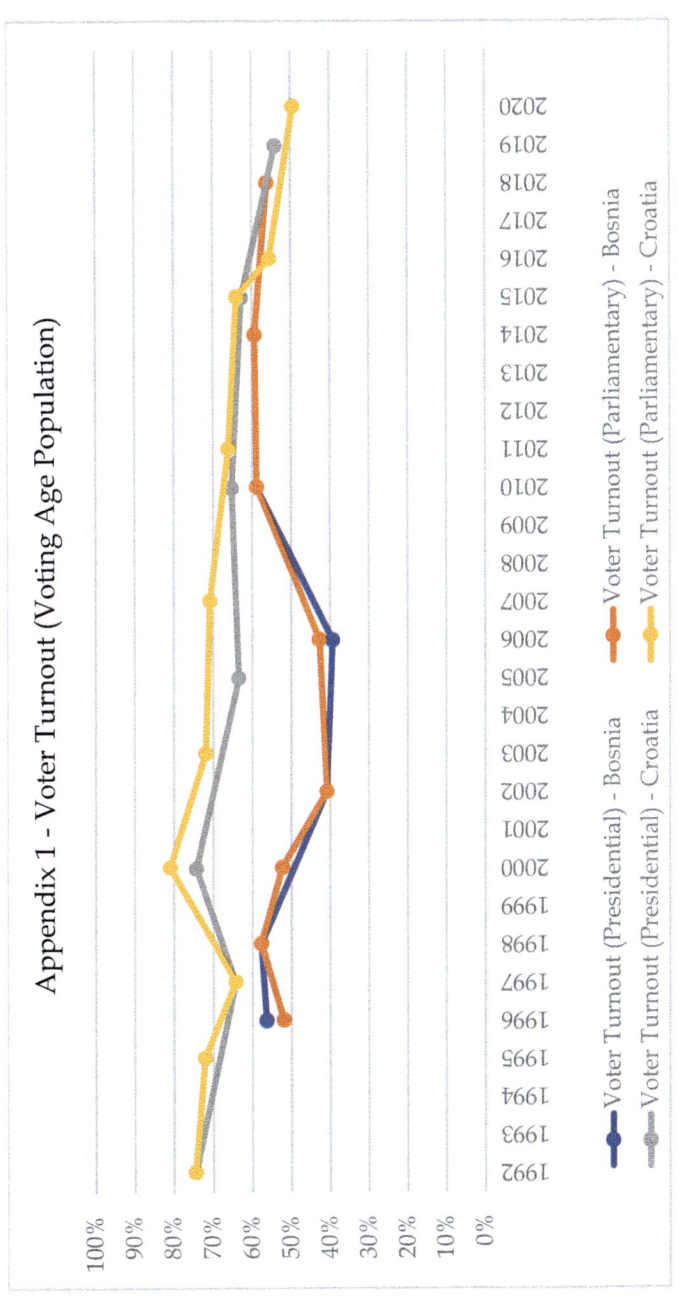

340 AARIF ABRAHAM

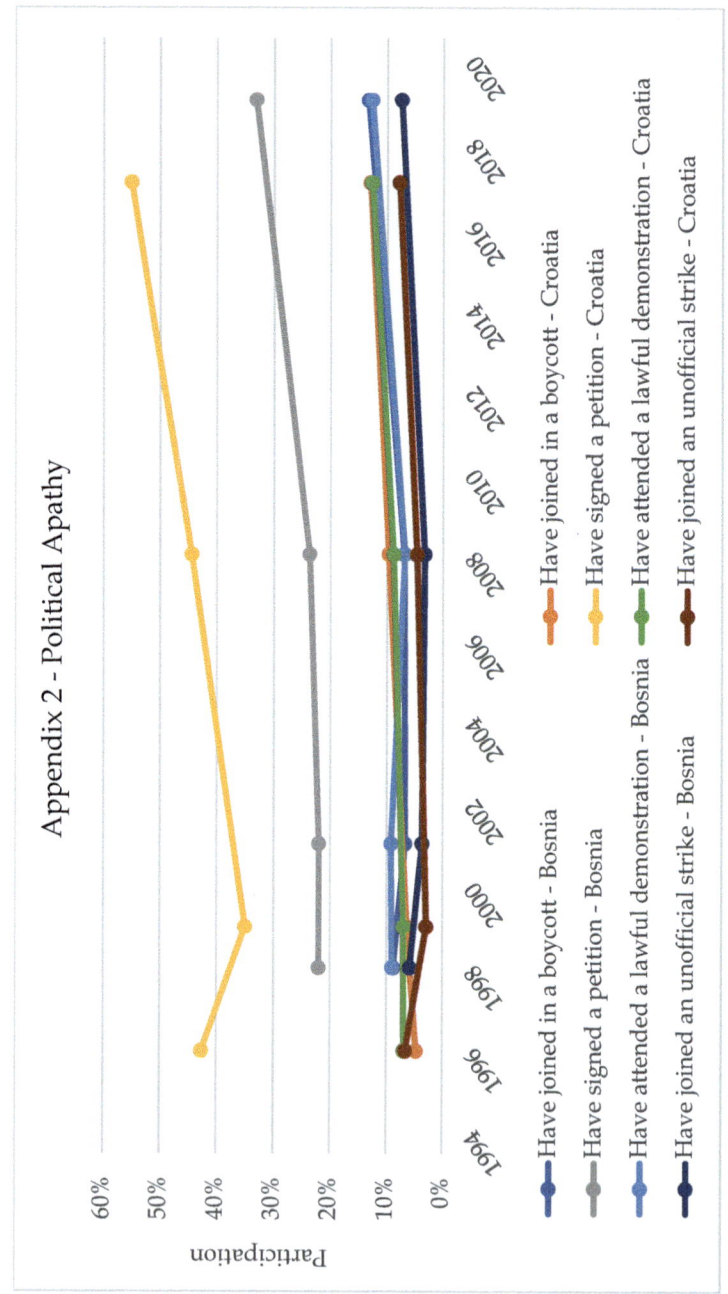

A CONSTITUTION OF THE PEOPLE AND HOW TO ACHIEVE IT 341

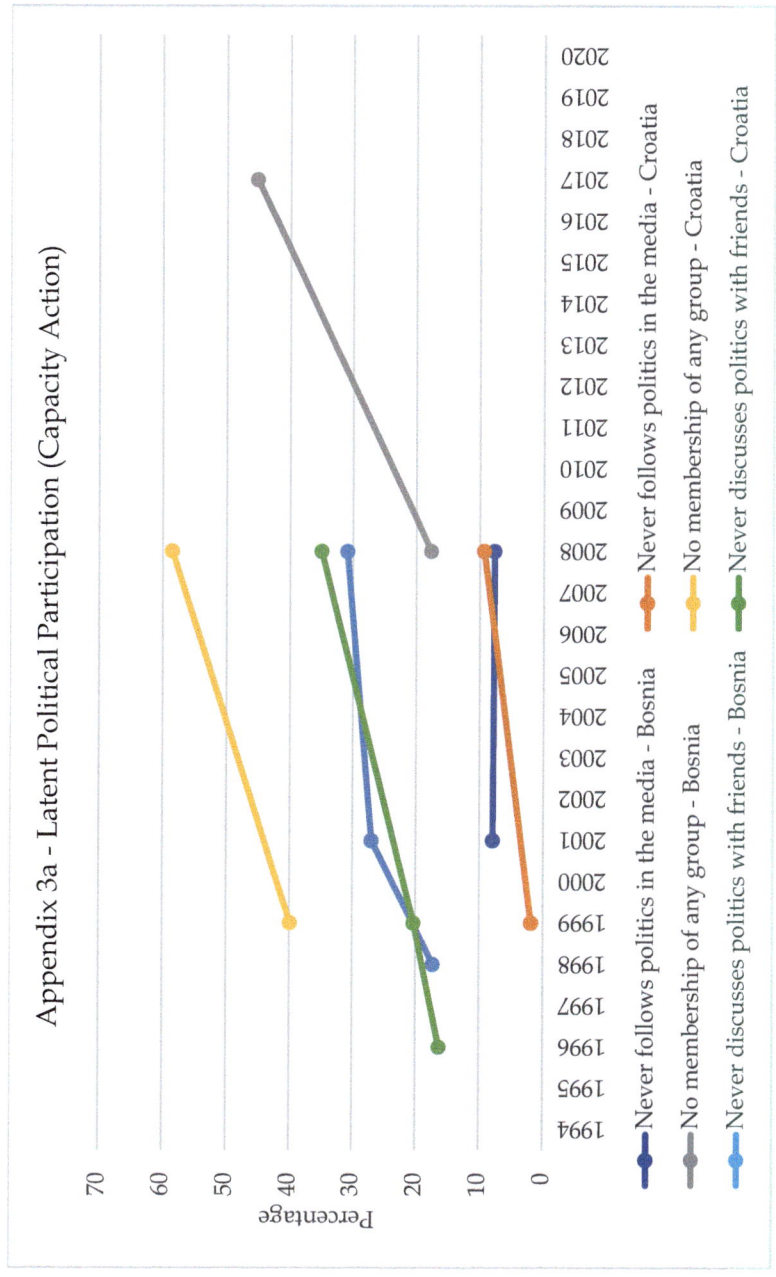

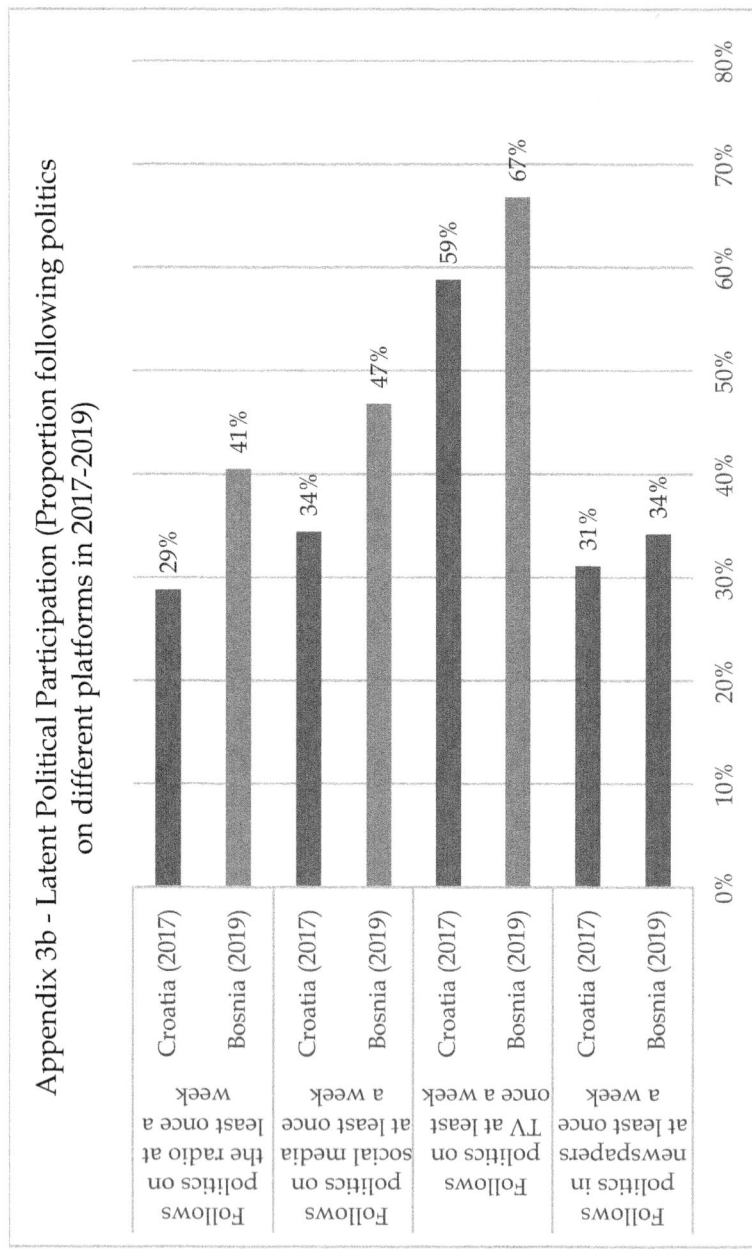

Appendix 3b - Latent Political Participation (Proportion following politics on different platforms in 2017-2019)

Appendix 4 - Political Culture: A-Systemic Measures (Confidence in Institutions)

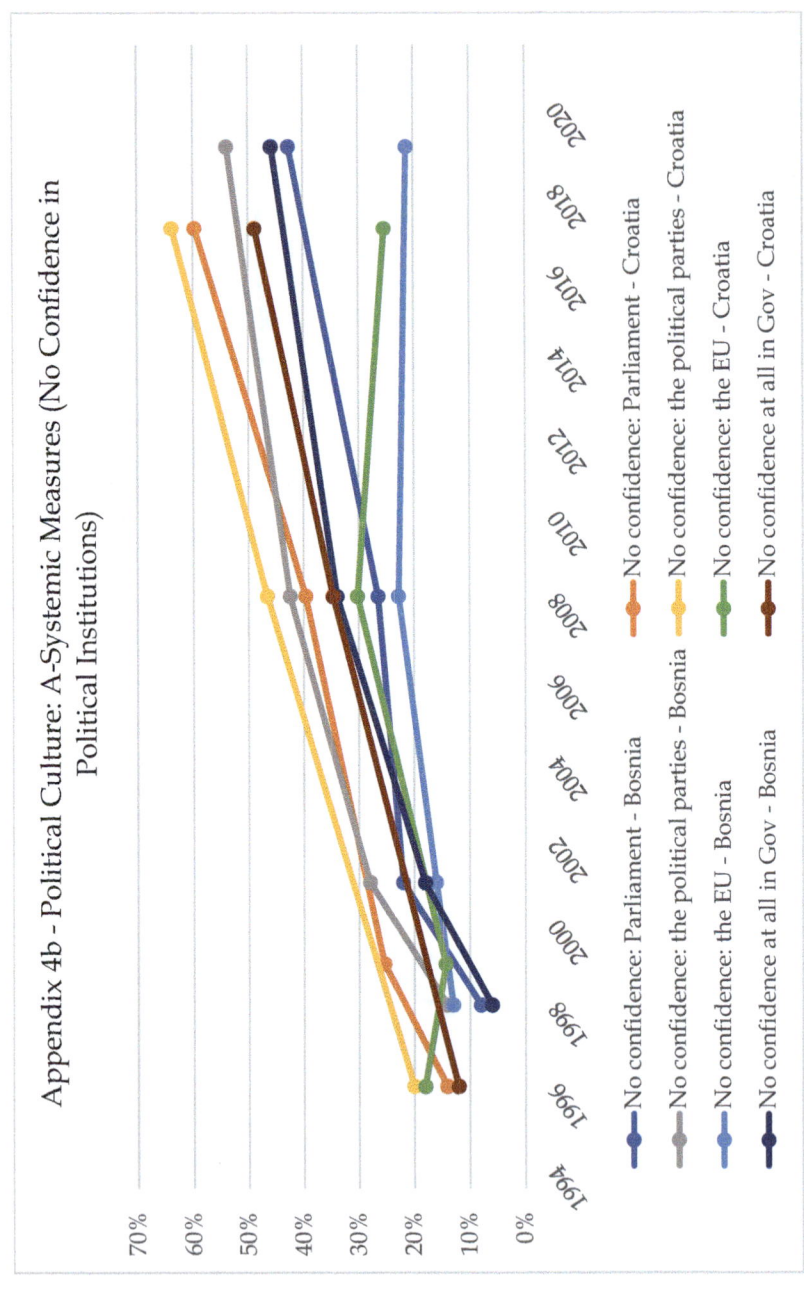

A CONSTITUTION OF THE PEOPLE AND HOW TO ACHIEVE IT   345

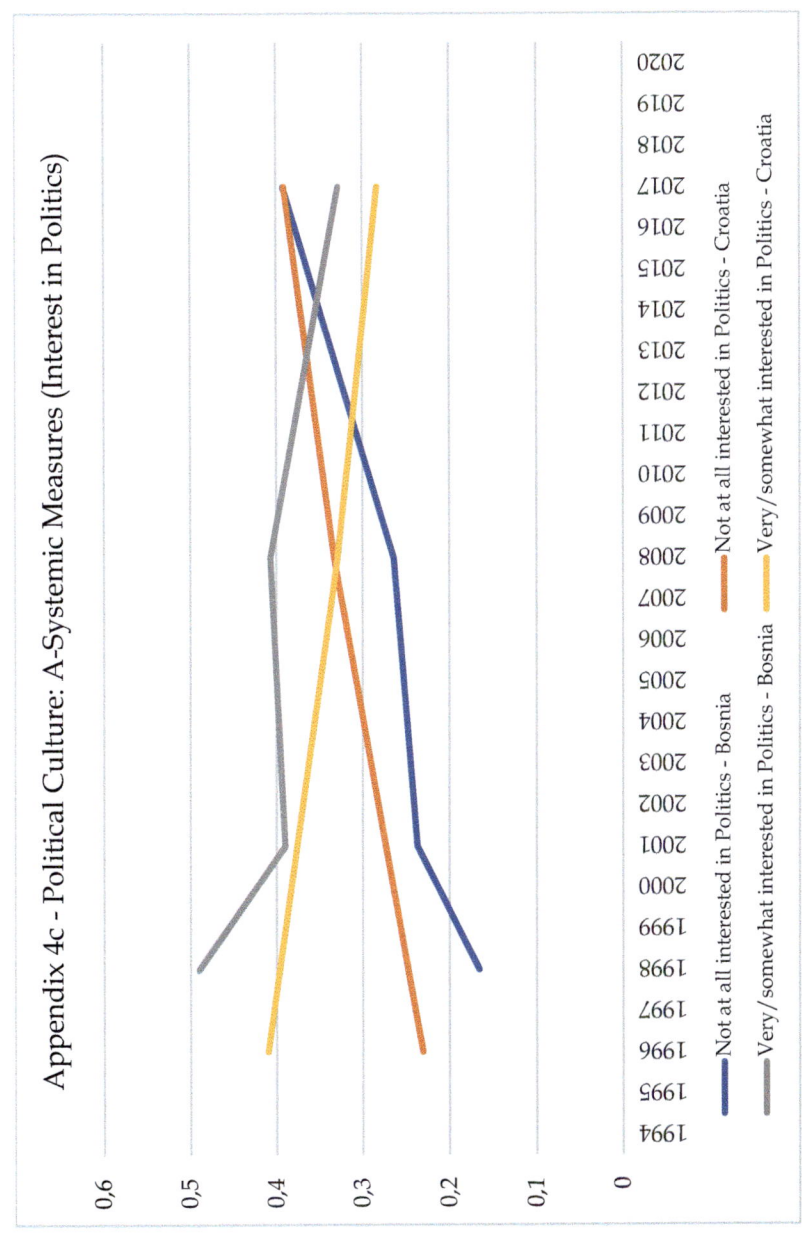

Appendix 4c - Political Culture: A-Systemic Measures (Interest in Politics)

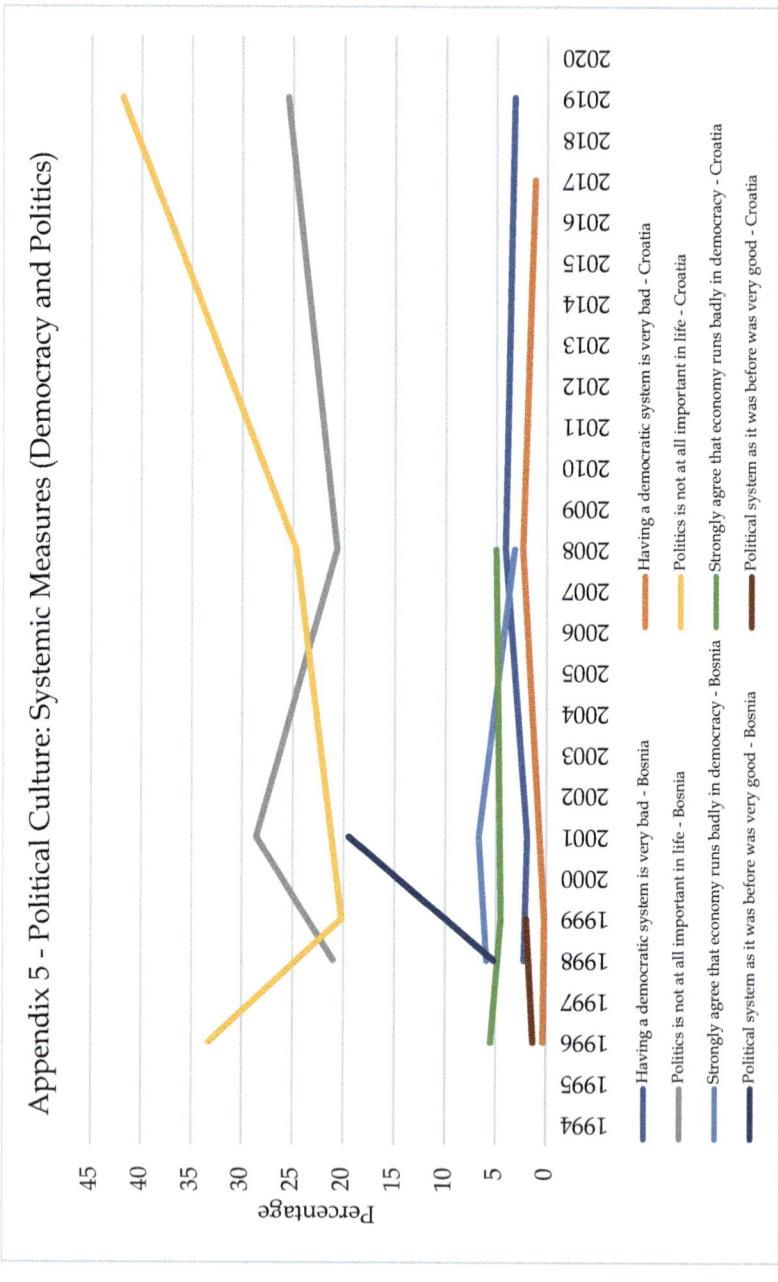

A Constitution of the People and How to Achieve It 347

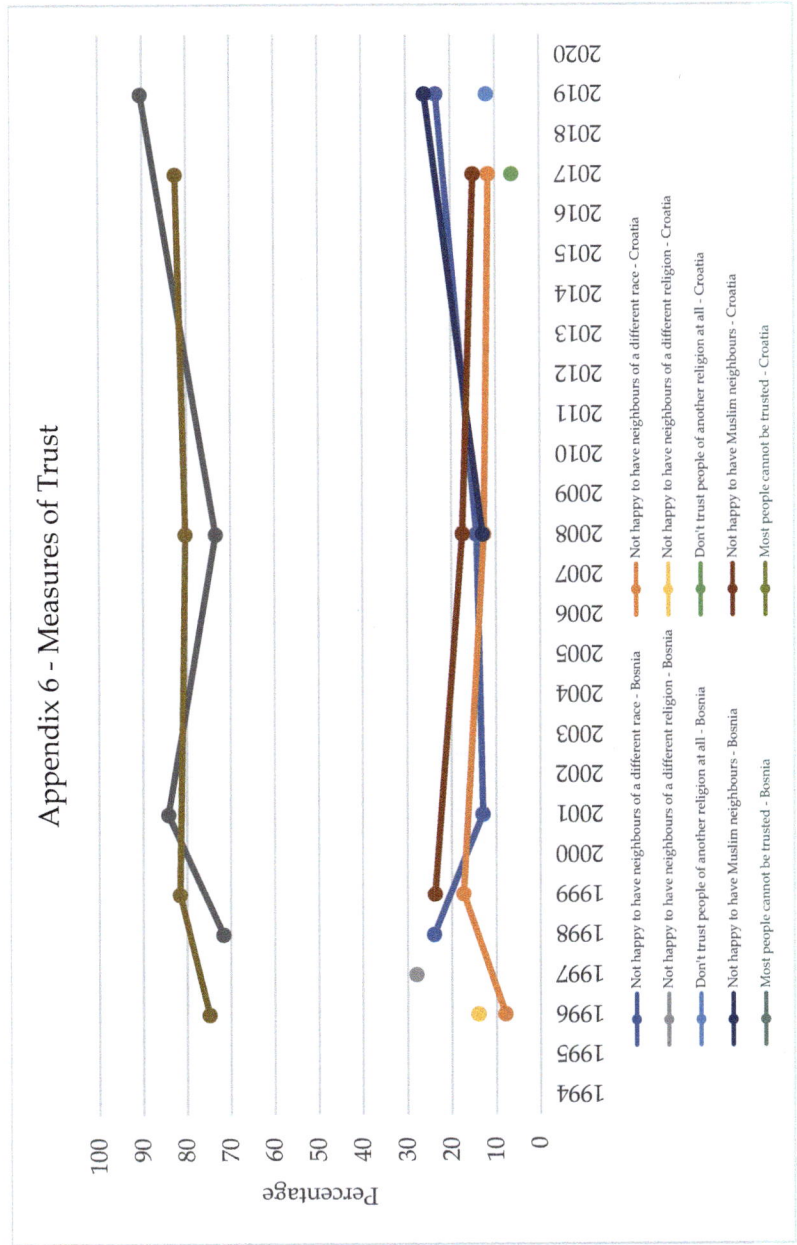

Appendix 6 - Measures of Trust

Appendix B

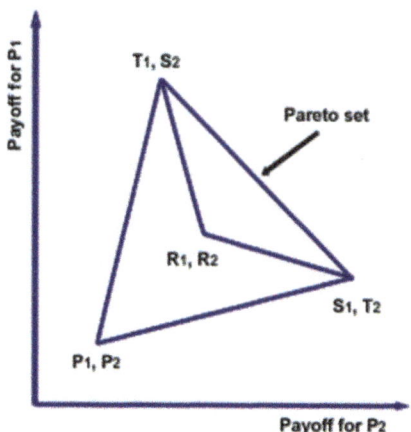

Figure 1A

DATE OF ELECTION	TABLE 2A: VETO PLAYERS FOR CONSTITUTIONAL CHANGE				
	HoR: COALITION VETO (SEATS) NOTE: TOTAL SEATS = 42	HoP: SIMPLE VETO	HoP: COALITION VETO (SEATS) NOTE: TOTAL SEATS = 15	HoP: SIMPLE VETO
2018	SDA (8-F)	EVV only if: ≥ 19 F SEAT COALITION	SDA (3-F)	VNIH
	SDP (5-F)		SDP (1-F)	
	HDZ-HSS-HSP-HKDU (5-F)		HDZ (4-F)	VNIH
	DF – Civic Alliance (3-F)		DF (1-F)	
	SBB (2-F)		SBB (1-F)	
	Our Party (2-F)			
	NB (1-F)			
	PDA (1-F)			
	A-SDA (1-F)			
	SDA (1-RS)	EVV		
	SNSD (6-RS)		SNSD (4-RS)	VNIH, EVV
	SDS-NDP-NS-SRS (3-RS)		SDS (1-RS)	
	PDP (2-RS)			
	DNS (1-RS)			
	SP (1-RS)			
2014	SDA (9-F)	EVV only if: ≥ 19 F SEAT COALITION	SDA (3-F)	VNIH
	DF (5-F)		DF (1-F)	
	SBB BiH (4-F)		SBB (1-F)	
	HDZ-HSS-HKDU (4-F)		HDZ (4-F) HSS (1-F)	VNIH
	SDP (4-F)			
	CDU 1990 (1-F)			

DATE OF ELECTION	HoR: COALITION VETO (SEATS) NOTE: TOTAL SEATS = 42	HoP: SIMPLE VETO	HoP: COALITION VETO (SEATS) NOTE: TOTAL SEATS = 15	HoP: SIMPLE VETO
	BPS (1–F)			
	A-SDA (1–F)			
	SDA (1–RS)	EVV		
	SNSD (6–RS)		SNSD (2–RS)	
	SDS (5–RS)		SDS (1–RS)	
	PDP–NDP (1–RS)		[Al for Change] (1–RS)	
2010	DNS (1–RS)		DNS (1–RS)	
	SDP (8–F)	EVV only if: ≥ 19 F SEAT COALITION	SDP (1–F)	
	SDA (7–F)		SDA (3–F)	VNIH
	SBB BIH (4–F)			
	SBIH (2–F)		SBIH (1–F)	
	HDZ BIH (3–F)		HDZ BiH (3–F)	VNIH
	HDZ 1990 (2–F)		HDZ 1990 (2–F)	
			PDP (1–RS)	
	SNSD (8–RS)	EVV	SNSD (3–RS)	VNIH, EVV
	SDS (4–RS)		SDS (1–RS)	
2006	SDA (8–F / 1–RS)	EVV only if: ≥ 19 F SEAT COALITION	SDA (3)	VNIH
	SBiH (7–F / 1–RS)		SBiH (1)	
	SDP (5–F)		SDP (1)	
	HDZ BiH (3–F)		HDZ BiH (3)	VNIH
	HDZ 1990 (2–F)		HDZ 1990 (2)	
	SNSD (7–RS)	EVV	SNSD (3–RS)	VNIH, EVV
	SDS (3–RS)		SDS (1–RS)	
2002	SDA (9–F / 1–RS)	EVV only if: ≥ 19 F SEAT COALITION	SDA (4)	VNIH
	SBiH (5–F / 1–RS)		SBiH (1)	
	SDP (4–F)		SDP (1)	
	DNZ–NP–BOSS (3–F)		HDZ–Christian Democrats (4)	VNIH
	NP–NHI–SPU (3–F)			
	HDZ–Christ. Dems. (5–F)		PDP (2–RS)	
	SDS (5–RS)		SDS (3–RS)	VNIH, EVV
	SNSD (3–RS)			
	CAV: 28 ≤ SEATS / EVV: 10 ≥ RS SEATS 19 ≥ F SEATS		CAV: 10 ≤ SEATS / EVV: 3 ≥ RS SEATS 7 ≥ F SEATS	
Preferred position of party elites to reform	Status-quo orientation			
	Unitary-civil State or greater centralisation			
	Greater autonomy or increased veto powers			

Source: Figures obtained from OSCE, CEC and the Parliamentary Assembly BiH

GLOSSARY

ARBiH	Army of Republic of Bosnia and Herzegovina
Bosnia	Bosnia and Herzegovina
Bosniak	Bosnian Muslim
Bosnian	Includes but is not limited to Bosniak, Bosnian Serb, Bosnian Croat, Bosnians, Citizens and Others
Bosnian Croat	Bosnian Catholic
Bosnian Serb	Bosnian Orthodox Christian
CoE	Council of Europe
CoM	Council of Ministers
Croat	Bosnian Croat unless otherwise stated
Dayton Peace Agreement	General Framework Agreement for Peace in Bosnia and Herzegovina and Annexes
DF	Demokratska Fronta
EC	European Community
ECHR	European Convention on Human Rights
ECtHR	European Court of Human Rights
EU	European Union
EUSR	European Union Special Representative
Federation	Federation of Bosnia and Herzegovina
HDZ	Hrvatska Demokratska Zajednica (Croatian Democratic Union), or HDZ BiH, largest predominantly Croat party in Bosnia
HoP	House of Peoples
HoR	House of Representatives
HRA	Human Rights Act 1998
HVO	Hrvatsko Vijeće Obrane (Croat Defence Council)
NS	Naša Stranka
OHR	Office of the High Representative.
PIC	Peace Implementation Council. It is a group of 55 countries and international organizations 'that sponsor and direct the peace implementation process'
PDP	Partija Demokratskog Progresa (Party of Democratic Progress), the third-strongest Serb party in RS currently in opposition
RS	Republika Srpska
RSNA	Republika Srpska National Assembly
SBB	Savez za Bolju Budućnost (Union for a Better Future).
SBiH	Stranka za Bosnia (Party for Bosnia), predominantly nationalist Bosniak party.
SDA	Stranka Demokratske Akcije (Party for Democratic Action), largest and oldest predominantly Bosniak party.

SDP	Socijaldemokratska partija (Social Democratic Party), large multi-ethnic party. Successor to League of Communists of Bosnia.
SDS	Srpska Demokratska Stranka (Serb Democratic Party), Serb nationalist party that governed RS during the 1992-1995 war and for many years thereafter.
SNP	Scottish National Party
Serb	Bosnian Serb unless otherwise stated
SFRY	Socialist Federal Republic of Yugoslavia
SNSD	Savez Nezavisnih Socijaldemokratska (League of Independent Social Democrats), largest predominantly Serb party.
UNGA	United Nations General Assembly
UNSC	United Nations Security Council
US	United States of America

REFERENCES

Acemoglu, Daron, Simon Johnson, and James A. Robinson. 2000. "The Colonial Origins of Comparative Development: an Empirical Investigation." *American Economic Review* 91: 1369-1401.

Ackerman, Bruce A. 1991. *We the People.* Cambridge, Mass: Belknap Press of Harvard University Press.

Addison, Tony and Murshed, S. Mansoob. 2002. "Credibility and Reputation in Peacemaking." *Journal of Peace Research* 39(4).

Agee, Chris. 2002. "Stone and Poppy: Mak Dizdar's Kameni Spavač / Stone Sleeper." *Forum Bosnae* 15.

Agency for Statistics of Bosnia and Herzegovina (AfS). 2013. *Bosnia and Herzegovina Population and Housing Census.* Sarajevo: AfS, October, 2013.

Almond, Gabriel A, Alan I. Abramowitz. 1980. *The Civic Culture Revisited.* Boston: Little, Brown, 1980.

Analitika. 2015. "Survey Results; The Trend of Citizens' Distrust in Political Parties and Institutions in Bosnia and Herzegovina Continues" *Analytika,* December, 2015.

Anderson, Benedict R. O'G. 1991. *Imagined Communities: Reflections on the Origin and Spread of Nationalism.* Verso.

Andrić, Ivo. 2013. The Damned Yard and Other Stories, Dufour: Forest Books.

Arangio-Ruiz, Gaetano. 1895. The Amendments to the Italian Constitution. *Annals of the American Academy of Political and Social Science* 6:31–57.

Arato, Andrew. 2009. "Redeeming the Still Redeemable: Post Sovereign Constitution Making". *International Journal of Politics, Culture, and Society* 22 (4): 427-443.

Arato, Andrew. 2016. *Post-Sovereign Constitution-Making: Learning and Legitimacy.* Oxford: Oxford University Press.

Arato, Andrew. 2017. *The Adventures of the Constituent Power: Beyond Revolutions?* Cambridge, UK: Cambridge University Press.

Arendt, Hannah. 1948. *Origins of Totalitarianism.* Orlando: Harcourt Brace & Company.

Aristotle, and William Ellis. 1952. *The Politics of Aristotle.* London: J M Dent & Sons Ltd.

Aristotle. 1998. *Politics.* Indianapolis: Hackett Publishing.

Ascherson, Neil. 2020. "Bye Bye Britain." *London Review of Books* 42(18), September 24, 2020.

Associated Press News (APN). 2018. "The Latest: Partial Tally Has Nationalist Bosnian Serb Ahead." *APN*, October 7, 2018.

Auer, Andreas. 2008. "On the Way to a Constitutional Convention for Cyprus." C2D — Centre for Research on Direct Democracy — *Working Paper Series* 29.

Badiou, Alain, Nicolas Truong, and Peter R. Bush. 2012. *In Praise of Love*. London: Serpent's Tail.

Bali, Asli U., and Hanna Lerner. 2016. "Constitutional Design Without Constitutional Moments: Lessons from Religiously Divided Societies." *SSRN Electronic Journal*.

Bahtić-Kunrath, Birgit. 2011. "Of Veto Players and Entity-Voting: Institutional Gridlock in the Bosnian Reform Process." *Nationalities Papers* 39 (6): 899-923.

Bar Council. 2020. *Judicial Review: Bar Council Reaction to Latest Comments on Reform*. London: Bar Council, Press Release, February 12, 2020.

Barzilai, Gad. 2003. *Communities and Law: Politics and Cultures of Legal Identities*. Michigan: University of Michigan.

Bassuener, Kurt. 2011. "Bosnia Cannot Disintegrate Without Violence." *Balkan Insight*, April 4, 2011.

Bassuener, Kurt and Weber, Bobo. 2014. *K-143's Municipalization Model for Bosnia and Herzegovina*. Sarajevo: Coalition 143 (K-143), July 2014.

Bassuener, Kurt. 2020. *Peace Cartels: Internationally Brokered Power-Sharing and Perpetual Oligarchy in Bosnia and Herzegovina and North Macedonia*. Unpublished Thesis: University of St Andrews, July 2020.

Bassuener, Kurt, Valery Perry, Toby Vogel, and Bodo Weber. 2021. *But Is There a Strategy? Defining a Transatlantic Consensus to Catalyze Progress in BiH*. Sarajevo: Democratization Policy Council, January 17, 2021.

Basta, Karlo. 2016. "Imagined Institutions: The Symbolic Power of Formal Rules in Bosnia and Herzegovina." *Slavic Review* 75 (4): 944-969.

Batt, Judy. 2007. "The Western Balkans." in White, Steven, Batt, Judy and Lewis Paul G. *Developments in Central and East European Politics*. New York: Palgrave.

BBC News. 2019. "David Cameron: EU referendum claim fact-checked, Reality Check Team." BBC News, September 19, 2019.

BBC Radio 4. 2017. "Analysis, Constitutions at Work." *BBC Radio 4*, July 3, 2017.

BBC Radio 4. 2020. "Today Programme, Interview with Jonathan Sumption." *BBC Radio 4*, September 14, 2020.

BBC. 1995. *The Death of Yugoslavia*. London: BBC, September 3, 1995.

Behnke, Nathalie and Benz, Arthur. 2009. "The Politics of Constitutional Change between Reform and Evolution." *Publius* 39 (2): 213-240.

Behnke, Nathalie. 2008. "Towards a New Organization of Federal States?" *Fern Universität ECPR Workshops 20*, April 11-16, 2008.

Bell, Christine and O'Rourke, Catherine. 2007. "The People's Peace? Peace Agreements, Civil Society, and Participatory Democracy." *International Political Science Review* 28 (3): 293-324.

Belloni, Roberto. 2007. *State Building and International Intervention in Bosnia.* Oxford: Routledge.

Belloni, Roberto. 2010. "Bosnia: Dayton Is Dead! Long Live Dayton!" In *Pathways from Ethnic Conflict: Institutional Redesign in Divided Societies*, edited by John Coakley, 95-115. London: Routledge.

Benedict, Robert. 1991. Review of Cronin (1989) *The American Political Science Review* 85 (1): 281-282.

Bernal, Carlos. 2019. "How Constitutional Crowdsourcing Can Enhance Legitimacy in Constitution Making." In *Comparative Constitution Making*, edited by Landau, David and Lerner, Hanna, 235-254. Cheltenham: Edward Elgar.

Bianco, William T., Ordeshook, Peter C., and Tsebelis, George. 1990. "Crime and Punishment: Are One-Shot, Two-Person Games Enough?" The American Political Science Review 84 (2): 569-586.

Bieber, Florian. 2006. *Post-war Bosnia: Ethnicity, Inequality and Public Sector Governance.* New York: Palgrave.

Bieber, Florian. 2010, "Constitutional Reform in Bosnia and Herzegovina: Preparing for EU Accession." *European Policy Centre. Policy Brief*, April 2010.

Bigio, Jamille, Rachel Vogelstein, Alexandra Bro, and Anne Connell. 2019. *Women's Participation in Peace Processes Interactive Guide.* New York: Council on Foreign Relations.

Bingham, Thomas H. 2011. *The Rule of Law, London.* England: Penguin Books.

Birnberg, Benedict. 2012. "Letters." *London Review of Books* 34(7).

Blackburn, Robert. 2015. *Britain's Unwritten Constitution.* London: The British Library, March 13, 2015.

Blaine, Harry R and Kettler, David. 1971. "Law as Political Weapon." *Politics & Society* 1: 479-526.

Blick, Andrew and Brian Salter. 2020. "Divided Culture and Constitutional Tensions: Brexit and the Collision of Direct and Representative Democracy," *Parliamentary Affairs.*

Bochsler, Daniel. 2011. "Let the people decide? Learning from Swiss Direct democracy in a Comparative Perspective." *Transitions* 51(1&2).

Bogdanor, Vernon. 1997. *The Monarchy and the Constitution.* Oxford: Oxford University Press.

Bogdanor, Vernon. 2009. "The New British Constitution Transcript of a Lecture." *Gresham College,* June 16, 2009.

Borger, Julian. 2015. "Bosnia's bitter, flawed peace deal, 20 years on." *Guardian,* November 10, 2015.

Borneman, John. 2007. "Reply to Hayden (2007)." *Current Anthropology* 48(1): 105-131.

Bose, Sumantra. 2002. *Bosnia After Dayton: Nationalist Partition and International Intervention.* New York: Oxford University Press.

Bougarel, Xavier, Elissa Helms and Ger Duijzings. 2007. *The New Bosnian Mosaic: Identities, Memories, and Moral Claims in a Post-war Society.* Aldershot: Ashgate Publishing.

Bowcott, Owen. 2020. "Brexit Strategy Risks UK 'dictatorship', says Ex-President of Supreme Court." *Guardian,* October 7, 2020.

Bowcott, Owen. 2020. "UK Needs Judges to Limit Government Power, Says Lord Kerr." *Guardian,* October 10, 2020.

Bowcott, Owen. 2020. "Government QCs Call for End to Ministers' Attacks on 'Lefty' Lawyers." *Guardian,* November 6, 2020.

Bowen, Paul. 2019. "Could Ministerial Advice to the Queen to Prorogue Parliament or to Refuse Assent to a Parliamentary Bill be Challenged in the Courts?" *Brick Court* (blog). April 8, 2019.

Bowring, Bill. 2008. *The Degradation of the International Legal Order: The Rehabilitation of Law and the Possibility of Politics.* Oxford: Routledge.

Bowring, Bill. 2013. "Protecting Minority Rights through an Individual Rights Mechanism." *European Yearbook on Minority Issues* 10: 437-460.

Brian, Barry. 1975. "The Consociational Model and Its Dangers." *European Journal of Political Research* 3, December 1975.

British Institute of International and Comparative Law (BIICL). 2015. *A Constitutional Crossroads: Ways Forward for the United Kingdom.* London: BIICL, May 2015.

Buchanan, J.M. and Tullock, G. 1962. *The Calculus of Consent.* Ann Arbor: University of Michigan Press.

Burgess, Michael and Tarr, G. Alan. 2012. *Constitutional Dynamics in Federal Systems: Sub-national Perspectives.* McGill-Queen's University Press.

Buturović, Amila, and Francis R. Jones. 2002. *Stone Speaker Medieval Tombs, Landscape, and Bosnian Identity in the Poetry of Mak Dizdar.* New York: Palgrave.

Cabada, Ladislav. 2009. "Political Culture and its Types in the Post-Yugoslav Area." *Politics in Central Europe* 5.

Cabinet Office. 2018. *State of the Estate in 2017–18*. London: Cabinet Office.

Capotorti, Francesco. 1991. *Study on the Rights of Persons Belonging to Ethnic, Religious and Linguistic Minorities*. New York: United Nations.

Carmichael, Cathie. 2015. *A Concise History of Bosnia*. Cambridge: Cambridge University Press, 2015.

Carpenter, David. 2015. *Magna Carta*. London: Penguin UK.

Carroll, John W. 1987. "Indefinite terminating points and the iterated Prisoner's Dilemma". *Theory and Decision* 22 (3): 247-256.

Caspersen, Nina. 2004. "Good Fences Make Good Neighbours? A Comparison of Conflict-Regulation Strategies in Postwar Bosnia." *Journal of Peace Research* 41 (5): 569-588.

Centri Civilnih Inicijativa (CCI). 2010. *Izvjestaj o Monitoringu Rada Skupstine Parlamentarne Skupstine BiH*. Sarajevo: CCI, October 30, 2010.

Chandler, David. 1999. Bosnia: *Faking Democracy After Dayton*. London: Pluto Press.

Clancy, Tim. 2013. *Bosnia and Herzegovina*. Chalfont St Peter: Bradt Travel Guides.

Coakley, John. 2010. *Pathways from Ethnic Conflict: Institutional Redesign in Divided Societies*. London: Routledge.

Cohen, Roger. 2013. "Enough of the Daytonians." *New York Times*, July 18, 2013.

Cohen, Roger. 2015. "The World; Bosnia, Where Facts Strangle Principles." *New York Times*, August 14, 1994.

Commission on a Bill of Rights. 2012. *A UK Bill of Rights? The Choice Before Us*. London: Commission.

Congleton, R.D and Swedenborg, B. 2006. *Democratic Constitutional Design and Public Policy: Analysis and Evidence*. Cambridge: MIT Press.

Congleton, R.D. 2011. *Perfecting Parliament: Constitutional Reform, Liberalism and the Rise of Western Democracy*. Cambridge: Cambridge University Press.

Congressional Research Service. 2019. *Bosnia and Herzegovina, Background and U.S. Policy*. Washington: CRS, R45691, April 15, 2019.

Conservative Party. 2010. *Manifesto: Invitation to Join the Government of Britain*. London: Conservative Party, April 2010.

Cooper, Christabel, and Christina Pagel. 2019. "Polling 'People vs Parliament': What a New Survey Says About Our Constitutional Mess." *Politics*, September 9, 2019.

Council of Europe (CoE). 2006. *Draft Resolution on Constitutional reform in Bosnia and Herzegovina*. Strasbourg: Council of Europe, Doc. 10982, June 27, 2006.

Cronin, Thomas E. 1989. *Direct Democracy: The Politics of Initiative, Referendum, and Recall*. Cambridge, MA: Harvard University Press.

Crosby, Alan. 2017. "Mixed Marriages Emerge as Another Casualty of Bosnia's War." *Radio Free Europe*, July 8, 2017.

Cubbon, John. 2020. "Written evidence from Mr John Cubbon (OOB0001) to the UK to Joint Human Rights Committee of the UK Parliament." *UK Parliament, Written Submission*, August 8, 2020.

Curtice, John, Elizabeth Clery, Jane Perry, Miranda Phillips, and Nilufer Rahim. 2019. "British Social Attitudes 36." *The National Centre for Social Research*.

Curtice, John. 2016. "How Leave Won Amongst the Politically Disengaged." *What UK Thinks*, December 20, 2016.

Dahl, Robert. 2007. *Polyarchy: Participation and Opposition*. New Haven: Yale University Press.

De Ridder, Martine, Robert L. Peterson, and Rex Wirth. 1978. "Images of Belgian Politics: The Effects of Cleavages on the Political System." *Legislative Studies Quarterly* 3 (1): 83-108.

De Tocqueville, Alexis. 1863. *Democracy in America*. Cambridge: Sever and Francis.

Dean, Alex. 2020. "Government Zealots Fix their Sights on Judicial Review." *Prospect Magazine*, August 28, 2020.

Denitch, Bogdan. 1993. "Learning from the Death of Yugoslavia: Nationalism and Democracy." *Social Text* 34: 3-16.

Derrida, Jacques. 2002. "Force of Law: The 'Mystical Foundation of Authority." In *Acts of Religion* edited by Gil Anidjar. New York: Routledge.

Dizdar, Mak. 2009. *Stone Sleeper*. Translated by Francis R. Jones. London: Anvil Press.

Dougherty, Keith L. and Edward, Julian. 2011. *The Calculus of Consent and Constitutional Design*. New York: Springer Science Business Media, LLC.

Douglas-Scott, Sionaidh. 2018. "Without Map or Compass on the constitutional implications of Brexit." *London Review of Books* 40 (10), May 24, 2018.

Druckman, James N. 2001. "Using Credible Advice to Overcome Framing Effects." *Journal of Law, Economics, & Organization* 17 (1): 62-82.

Duhaček, Gordana Daša. 1997. *Gender Perspectives on the Reconstruction of Political Identities in Yugoslavia.* New Brunswick, Rutgers University.

Duijzings, Ger. 2007. "Reply to Hayden (2007)." *Current Anthropology* 48 (1): 105-131.

Džankić, Jelena. 2016. *Citizenship in Bosnia and Herzegovina, Macedonia And Montenegro: Effects of Statehood and Identity Challenges.* London: Routledge.

Edwards, Maxim. 2019. "The President Who Wants to Break Up His Own Country." The Atlantic, January 2, 2019.

Ekman, Joakim and Irene, Erik. 2009. "Political Participation and Civic Engagement: Towards A New Typology." *Youth and Society (YeS)* Working Paper 2.

Ekman, Joakim. 2009. "Political Participation and Regime Stability: A Framework for Analyzing Hybrid Regimes." *International Political Science Review* 30 (1): 7-31.

Elkins, Zachary, Tom Ginsburg, and James Melton. 2010. *The Endurance of National Constitutions.* Cambridge: Cambridge University Press.

Elliot, Mark. 2014. "Reflections on the HS2 Case: A Hierarchy of Domestic Constitutional Norms and the Qualified Primacy of EU law." *Public Law for Everyone (blog).* January 23, 2014.

Elliot, Mark. 2020. "The (Constitutional) State We're In: A Week in British Politics." *Public Law for Everyone (blog).* September 2020.

Elster, Jon. 1995. "Forces and Mechanisms in the Constitution-Making Process". *Duke Law Journal* 45 (2): 364.

Elster, Jon. 2012. "Clearing and Strengthening the Channels of Constitution Making." In *Comparative Constitutional Design*, edited by Tom Ginsburg, 15-30. New York: Cambridge University Press.

Emerson, Peter. 2020. *Majority Voting as a Catalyst of Populism.* Cham: Springer International Publishing.

Engstrom, Richard L. 1992. Review of Cronin (1989). *Presidential Studies Quarterly* 22 (4): 786-788.

Eskridge, W. N., and J. Ferejohn. 2001. "Super-Statutes". *Duke Law Journal* 50: 1215-1276.

European Commission. 2020. "Report on Bosnia and Herzegovina." *European Commission*, October 6, 2020.

European Stability Initiative. 2004. *Governance and Democracy in Bosnia And Herzegovina: Post-Industrial Society and the Authoritarian Temptation.* Berlin, Sarajevo: European Stability Initiative.

European Western Balkans (EWS). 2019. "Hahn: The Case of David Dragičević Has to be Resolved Without Any Further Delay." *EWS*, March 11, 2019.

Evans, Paul. 2020. "Braking the law: is there, and should there be, an executive veto over laws made by parliament?" *The Constitution Unit*, October 16, 2020.

Ewing, Keith, and C. A. Gearty. 1993. *Freedom Under Thatcher: Civil Liberties in Modern Britain*. Oxford: Clarendon Press.

Falconer, Charles. 2018. "Labour Helped These Devastating Legal Aid Cuts Along. Now It's Time to Fix It." *Guardian*, December 31, 2018.

Farrell, Henry and Shalizi, Cosma. 2011. "'Nudge' policies are another name for coercion." *New Scientist Magazine* 2837, November 9, 2011.

Faulks, Edward. "This Opportunity to Repeal the Human Rights Act, Quit the ECHR and Bring Justice Home May Not Come Again." *Conservative Home*, April 26, 2017.

Faulks, Edward. 2020. "The Supreme Court's Prorogation Judgement Unbalanced Our Constitution. MPs Should Make a Correction." *Conservative Home*, February 7, 2020.

Fisher, Sharon. 2006. *Political Change in post-Communist Slovakia and Croatia: From Nationalist to Europeanist*. New York: Palgrave MacMillan.

Flinders, Matthew, et al. 2016. *Democracy Matters: Lessons from the 2015 Citizens' Assemblies on English Devolution*. London: The Constitution Unit, University College London, March 2016.

Flood, Merrill M. 1952. *Some Experimental Games*. Santa Monica, Calif: Rand Corp.

Fogel, Robert W. and North, Douglass C. 1993. "Economic Performance Through Time." *Nobel Prize Lecture to the Memory of Alfred Nobel*, December 9, 1993.

Franklin, Daniel P. and Baun, Michael J. 1995. *Political Culture and Constitutionalism: A Comparative Approach*. Oxford: Routledge.

Frease, Dean E. 1975. "A Politicization Paradigm: The Case of Yugoslavia." *The Sociological Quarterly* 16, (1): 33-47.

Fudenberg, Drew and Maskin, Eric. 1986. "The Folk Theorem in Repeated Games with Discounting or with Incomplete Information." *Econometrica* 54 (3): 533-554.

Gadzo, Mersiha. 2020. "Large increase in Anti-Bosnian, Anti-Muslim Bigotry: Report." *Al Jazeera News*, September 23, 2020.

Gaeta, Paul. 1996. "Symposium: The Dayton Peace Agreements: A Breakthrough for Peace and Justice?" *European Journal of International Law* 7: 147-163.

Gallagher, Michael and Uleri, Pier Vincenzo. 1996. *The Referendum Experience in Europe*. London: Macmillan Press Ltd.

Gallup Balkan Monitor (GBM). 2010. *Focus On Bosnia and Herzegovina*. GBM Focus On #04, November 2010.

Ganghof, Steffen. 2003. "Promises and Pitfalls of Veto Player Analysis." *Swiss Political Science Review* 9 (2): 1-25.

Ganghof, Steffen. 2009. "Veto Player." In *International Encyclopedia of Political Science*, edited by Bertrand Badie, Dirk Berg-Schlosser and Leonardo Morlino. Los Angeles, CA: Sage.

Gavrić, Saša. 2013. "Constitutional Reform in Bosnia and Herzegovina." *South East European Journal of Political Science* I (2), June 2013.

Gellner, Ernest. 1983. *Nations and Nationalism*. Oxford: Blackwell.

Georgievski, Jovana. 2020. "A Delicate Moment." Dodik Against the Constitutional Court of Bosnia and Herzegovina" *European Western Balkans*, March 11, 2020.

GfK. 2018. "Balkan Barometer 2018", *Regional Cooperation Council*, IV (4).

Ghai, Yash and Galli, Guido. 2006. "Constitution Building Processes and Democratization." In *Democracy, Conflict and Human Security* by IDEA. Stockholm: IDEA, September 2006.

Ghai, Yash. 2019. "Civil Society, Participation and the Making of Kenya's Constitution. In *Comparative Constitution Making*, edited by Landau, David and Lerner, Hanna, 212-234. Cheltenham: Edward Elgar.

Ginsburg, Tom. 2012. *Comparative Constitutional Design*. New York: Cambridge University Press.

Giorgi, Jacopo. n.d. "Minorities Protection: Between Legal Framework and Political Mechanisms." *Pubblicazioni Centro Studi per la Pace*.

Glaurdić, Josip. 2012. *The hour of Europe: Western powers and the breakup of Yugoslavia*. Hour of Europe. New Haven: Yale University Press.

Grebäck, K. and Zillén, E. 2003. *Peace Agreements as a Means for Promoting Gender Equality and Ensuring Participation of Women*. Ottowa: UN Division for the Advancement of Women Expert Group.

Greenberg, Jessica. 2010. "'There's Nothing Anyone Can Do about It': Participation, Apathy, and "Successful" Democratic Transition in Post-socialist Serbia." *Slavic Review* 69 (1): 41-64.

Guardian. 2013. "Secret Papers Show Extent of Senior Royals' Veto Over Bills." January 15, 2013.

Gutmann, Matthew. 2002. *Romance of Democracy*. Berkeley: University of California Press.

Håkansson, Peter and Hargreaves, Sarah. 2004. *Trust in Transition – Generalised trust in Bosnia and Herzegovina*. Sarajevo: Balkans Analysis Group.

Håkansson, Peter and Sarah Hargreaves. 2004. "Trust in Transition – Generalised Trust in Bosnia and Herzegovina." *Balkans Analysis Group*.

Håkansson, Peter and Sjöholm, Fredrik. 2007. "Who Do You Trust? Ethnicity and Trust in Bosnia and Herzegovina." *Europe-Asia Studies* 59 (6): 961-976.

Hallerberg, Mark. 2010. "Empirical Applications of Veto Player Analysis and Institutional Effectiveness." In *Reform Processes and Policy Change*, edited by Konig, Thomas, George Tsebelis, and Marc Debus, 21-42. New York: Springer Science Business Media, 2010.

Hamilton Daniel. 2020. *Fixing Dayton: A New Deal for Bosnia and Herzegovina*. Washington DC: NextEurope, Wilson Centre, No. 1, November 2020.

Hart, Vivien. 2010. "Constitution-Making and the Right to Take Part in a Public Affair." In *Framing the State in Times of Transition: Case Studies in Constitution Making*, edited by Miller, Laurel E. Washington: United States Institute of Peace.

Havel, Vaclav. 1978. *The Power of the Powerless*, London: Penguin Random House UK.

Hayden, Robert and Hitchner, R. Bruce. 2006. *Constitution Drafting in Bosnia and Herzegovina*. Somerville, MA: Tufts University: Meeting Report 323, May 10, 2006.

Hayden, Robert M. 2007. "Moral Vision and Impaired Insight: The Imagining of Other Peoples' Communities in Bosnia." *Current Anthropology* 48 (1): 105-131.

Hayden, Robert. 2021. "The Ethno-Territorial Separation of Bosnia Was the Key to Ending the War and Keeping Peace." *The National Interest*, January 10, 2021.

Hill, Christopher. 1991. *The World Turned Upside Down: Radical Ideas in the English Revolution*. Penguin Press.

Heath, Anthony and Topf, Richard. 1987. "Political Culture." In *British Social Attitudes: the 1987 Report*, edited by Roger Jowell, Sharon Witherspoon, and Lindsay Brook. London: Social and Community Planning Research.

Hennessy, Peter. 1995. *The Hidden Wiring: Power, Politics and the Constitution*. London: Fabian Society.

Hibbert, Christopher. 2010. *The Story of England*. London: Phaidon.

HM Treasury. 2019. *Public Expenditure: Statistical Analyses 2019*. London: HM Treasury, July 2019.

Hodson, Randy, Duško Sekulić, and Garth Massey. 1994. "National Tolerance in the Former Yugoslavia," *American Journal of Sociology* 99(6).

Hogarth, Raphael. 2020. *Judicial Review*. London: Institute for Government (IfG), March 9, 2020.

Holbrooke, Richard C. 1998. *To End a War*. New York: Random House.

Honig, Bonnie. 2001. "Dead Rights, Live Futures: A Reply to Habermas's 'Constitutional Democracy.'" *Political Theory* 29 (6): 792-805.

Horowitz, Donald L. 2000. *Ethnic Groups in Conflict*. Berkeley: University of California Press.

Horowitz, Donald L. 2003. "The Cracked Foundations of the Right to Secede". *Journal of Democracy* 14 (2): 5-17.

Horowitz, Donald L. 2013. *Constitutional Change and Democracy in Indonesia*. Cambridge: Cambridge University Press.

Horowitz, Donald, L. 1993. "The Challenge of Ethnic Conflict: Democracy in Divided Societies." *Journal of Democracy* 4: 18-37.

Horowitz, Donald, L. 2011. "Writing the New Rules of the Game." *The Wilson Quarterly* (1976-) 35 (3): 52-54.

Houlihan, Erin C. 2019. *Women Constitution-Makers: Comparative Experiences with Representation, Participation and Influence, First Annual Women Constitution-Makers' Dialogue*. Edinburgh: IDEA.

House of Commons (HoC) Library. 2018. *Research Briefing: Vellum – Printing Record Copies of Public Acts*. London: HoC. August 15, 2018.

House of Commons (HoC). 2014. *Political and Constitutional Reform – Second Report A New Magna Carta?* London: HoC, July 3, 2014.

House of Commons (HoC). Political and Constitutional Reform Committee. 2013. *Do We Need a Constitutional Convention for Britain?* London: HoC, March 25, 2013.

House of Commons (HoC) Political and Constitutional Reform Committee. 2011. *Parliament's Role in Conflict Decisions*. London: HoC, May 17, 2011.

Hug, Simon and Tsebelis, George. 2002. "Veto Players and Referendums Around the World." *Journal of Theoretical Politics* 14(4): 465-515.

Hulsey, John. 2015. "Electoral Accountability in Bosnia and Herzegovina under the Dayton Framework Agreement." *International Peacekeeping* 22 (5): 511-525.

Hulsey, John. 2018. "Institutions and the Reversal of State Capture: Bosnia and Herzegovina in Comparative Perspective." *Southeastern Europe and Black Sea Studies* 42 (1): 15-32.

Hulsey, John. and Keil, Soeren. 2019. "Ideology and Party System Change in Consociational Systems." *Nationalism and Ethnic Politics* 25 (4): 1353-7113.

Hulsey, John and Keil, Soeren. 2020. "Change Amidst Continuity? Assessing the 2018 regional elections in Bosnia and Herzegovina," *Regional & Federal Studies* 30 (3): 343-361.

Human Rights Watch. 2011. "Bosnia: A Move to End Discrimination." *New York: Human Rights Watch*, November 2, 2011.

Human Rights Watch. 2019. "Bosnia and Herzegovina: Ethnic Discrimination a Key Barrier." *New York: Human Rights Watch*, December 12, 2019.

Imamovic, Mustafa. 2006. *Bosnia and Herzegovina: Evolution of its Political and Legal Institutions*. Sarajevo: Magistrat.

Independent Balkan News Agency (IBNA). 2020. "BiH: Dragojlovic, Mladen, Milorad Dodik comes under fire for his visit to Zagreb." *Independent Balkan News Agency*, September 16, 2020.

Inglehart, Ronald. 1997. *Modernization and Postmodernization: Cultural, Economic, and Political Change in 43 Societies*. Princeton: Princeton University Press.

Institute for Government (IfG). 2014. *The Cost of Running Departments*. London: IfG, November 5, 2014.

Institute for Government (IfG). 2020. *Cost and Administration*. London: IfG, May 14, 2020

International Crisis Group (ICG). 1996. *Elections in Bosnia & Herzegovina*. Brussels: ICG, Europe Report 16, September 22, 1996.

International Crisis Group (ICG). 1999. *Why Will No One Invest In Bosnia and Herzegovina?* Brussels: ICG, Europe Report 64, April 21, 1999.

International Crisis Group (ICG). 2009. *Bosnia's Incomplete Transition: Between Dayton and Europe*. Brussels: ICG, Europe Report 198, March 9, 2009.

International Crisis Group (ICG). 2011. *Bosnia: What Does Republika Srpska Want?* Brussels: ICG, Europe Report 214, Oct 2011.

International Crisis Group (ICG). 2012. *Bosnia's Gordian Knot: Constitutional Reform*. Brussels: ICG, Europe Briefing 68, July 12, 2012.

International Institute for Democracy and Electoral Assistance (IDEA). 2014. *Constitutional Amendment Procedures*. Stockholm: IDEA, September 2014.

International Institute for Democracy and Electoral Assistance (IDEA). 2016. *Constitutional History of Bosnia and Herzegovina*. Stockholm: IDEA.
International Institute for Democracy and Electoral Assistance (IDEA). n.d. *Database on Voter Turnout in Bosnia and Herzegovina*. Stockholm: IDEA.
Išerić, Harun. 2016. "The European Court of the Human Rights Changes the Constitution of Bosnia and Herzegovina." *ELSA Malta Law Review*, 132.
Iveković, Rada. 1993. "Women, Nationalism and War: "Make Love Not War"." *Hypatia* 8 (4): 113-26.
Ivković, Aleksandar. 2018. "Elections in Bosnia and Herzegovina: Who Won and What it Means for the Future?" *European Western Balkans*, October 16, 2018.
Ivković, Aleksandar. 2018. "The Failure of the BiH Reform Agenda is the Failure of the EU." *European Western Balkans*, May 9, 2018.
J. T. 2011. "Bosnia's gridlock: Two visions for Bosnia." *The Economist, Eastern Approaches Blog*, April 13, 2011.
J. T. 2013. "Gorazde: A Microcosm of Bosnia." *The Economist, Eastern Approaches Blog*. March 18, 2013.
Jasiewicz, Krzystof. 2007. "Citizens and Politics." In *Developments in Central and East European Politics*, edited by Steven White, Judy Batt and Paul G. Lewis. New York: Palgrave and MacMillan.
Jeffrey, Alex. 2007. "The Politics of 'Democratization': Lessons from Bosnia and Iraq". *Review of International Political Economy* 14 (3): 444-466.
Jespersen, Andreas Maaløe and Hansen, Pelle Guldborg. 2013. "Nudge and the Manipulation of Choice." *EJRR* 1.
Jones, Carwyn. 2012. "A Constitutional Convention for Britain?" Westminster: Parliament, July 12, 2012.
Jones, Francis R. 2000. "The Poet and the Ambassador: Communicating Mak Dizdar's "Stone Sleeper." *Translation and Literature* 9 (1): 65-87.
Jones, Bill, and Philip Norton. 2019. *Politics UK*. Routledge.
Judah, Tim. 2014. "Bosnian protests: A Balkan Spring?" *BBC*, February 7, 2014.
Kapidžić, Damir. 2019. "A Mirror of the Ethnic Divide: Interest Group Pillarization and Elite Dominance in Bosnia and Herzegovina." *Journal of Public Affairs* 19(2).
Kasapović, Mirjana. 2005. "Bosnia and Herzegovina: Consociational or Liberal Democracy?" *Politička Misao* XLII (5): 3–30.

Kavish, Donovan. 2012. "Constitutional Reform in Bosnia and Herzegovina: State-Nation Theory and the Spirit of the Dayton Accords." *INTL* 494-01: Fall 2012.

Keech, William R. 1972. "Linguistic Diversity and Political Conflict: Some Observations Based on Four Swiss Cantons". *Comparative Politics.*

Keil, Soeren. 2015. "Power-Sharing Success and Failures in the Western Balkans". In *State-Building and Democratization in Bosnia and Herzegovina,* edited by Soeren Keil and Valery Perry, 193-212. Farnham: Ashgate.

Keil, Soeren. 2018. "The Business of State Capture and the Rise of Authoritarianism in Kosovo, Macedonia, Montenegro and Serbia." *Southeastern Europe* 42 (1). pp. 59- 82.

Keil, Soeren and Alber, Elisabeth. 2020. "Introduction: Federalism as a Tool of Conflict Resolution." *Ethnopolitics,* July 23, 2020.

Kennedy, Helena. 2020. "The Government is Bent on Constitutional Destruction." *Prospect Magazine,* August 30, 2020.

Kennedy, Helena. 2020. "The Government Should Keep Its Hands Off the Judiciary." Prospect Magazine, December 4, 2019.

Kentish, Benjamin. 2018. "Theresa May defends Syria air strikes amid criticism for refusal to grant parliamentary vote." *The Independent,* April 16, 2018.

Kidd, Colin. 2014. "A British Bundesrat?" *London Review of Books* 36 (8), April 17, 2014.

King, Anthony. 2007. *The British Constitution.* Oxford: Oxford University Press.

Koneska, Cvete. 2014. *After Ethnic Conflict – Policymaking in Post-conflict Bosnia and Herzegovina and Macedonia.* Farnham: Ashgate.

Koneska, Cvete. 2017. "On Peace Negotiations and Institutional Design in Macedonia." *Peacebuilding* 5 (1): 36-50.

Konig, Thomas, Tsebelis, George and Debus, Marc. 2010. *Reform Processes and Policy Change: Veto Players and Decision-Making in Modern Democracies.* New York: Springer Science Business Media.

Kovačević, Danijel. 2020. "Dodik Unveils Fresh Threat of Bosnian Serb Secession." *Balkan Insight,* February 13, 2020.

Kovačević, Danijel. 2020. "Serbian Party Banned from Bosnian Election Over 'Hateful' Video." *Balkan Insight,* October 8, 2020.

Krajnc, Marina Tavčar, Sergej Flere and Andrej Kirbiš. 2012. "Is Protest Participation in Post-Yugoslav Countries Motivated by Pro-democratic Political Culture? A Cross-National Study." *The Western Balkans Policy Review* 2 (2).

Krause, J., Krause, W. and Braňfors, P. 2018. "Women's Participation in Peace Negotiations and the Durability of Peace." *International Interactions* 44 (6): 985–1016.

Kuntz, Jessica. 2011. "(Re)Entering Europe: The Post-communist Transition of Croatian Political Culture." *Politička misao* 48 (5): 215-246.

Kuntz, Philipp and Thompson, Mark R. 2009. "More than Just the Final Straw: Stolen Elections as Revolutionary Triggers." *Comparative Politics* 41 (3): 253-272.

Kymlicka, Will. 1995. *The Rights of Minority Cultures*. Oxford: Oxford University Press.

Landau, David and Lerner, Hanna (ed.) 2019. *Comparative Constitution Making*. Cheltenham: Edward Elgar Publishing Limited.

Landemore, Hélène. 2015. "Inclusive Constitution-Making: The Icelandic Experiment". *Journal of Political Philosophy* 23 (2): 166-191.

Lee-Koo, K. and True, J. 2018. "Toward Inclusive Peace: Mapping Gender-Sensitive Peace Agreements 2000–2016." *Monash University*, April 2018.

Lee, Jihong and Sabourian, Hamid. 2011. "Efficient Repeated Implementation." *Econometrica* 79 (6): 1967–1994.

Leonard, Thomas. 2008. "Richard H. Thaler, Cass R. Sunstein, Nudge: Improving decisions about health, wealth, and happiness". *Constitutional Political Economy* 19 (4): 356-360.

Lerner, Hanna. 2011. *Making Constitutions in Deeply Divided Societies*. Cambridge: Cambridge University Press.

Less, Timothy. 2020. "Bosnia's 'Second Collapse' is Starting to Look Inevitable." *Balkan Insight*, February 28, 2020.

Levinson, Daryl J. 2010. "Parchment and Politics: The Positive Puzzle of Constitutional Commitment". *SSRN Electronic Journal*.

Levy, Jack S. 1992. "An Introduction to Prospect Theory". *Political Psychology* 13 (2): 171-186.

Leyton-Brown, Kevin and Shoham, Yoav. 2008. *Essentials of Game Theory: A Concise, Multidisciplinary Introduction*. Oregon: Morgan & Claypool.

Liberal Democrats. 2010. *Liberal Democrat manifesto 2010*. London: Chris Fox on behalf of the Liberal Democrats.

Lijphart, Arend. 1977. *Democracy in Plural Societies: A Comparative Exploration*. New Haven: Yale University Press.

Lijphart, Arend. 2004. "Constitutional Design For Divided Societies." *Journal of Democracy* 15 (2): 96-109.

Lijphart, Arendt. 2008. *Constitutional Design for Divided Societies in Lijphart, Thinking About Democracy: Power Sharing and Majority Rule in Theory and Practice.* London: Routledge.

Linz, Juan J. 1990. "The Perils of Presidentialism." *Journal of Democracy* 1 (1): 51-69.

Linz, Juan J. and Stepan, Alfred. 1996. *Problems of Democratic Transition and Consolidation.* Baltimore: The John Hopkins University Press.

Lipset, Seymour. 1959. *Some Social Requisites of Democracy: Economic Development and Political Legitimacy.* Indianapolis, Indiana: Bobbs-Merrill.

Loughlin, Martin. 2013. *British Politics: A Very Short Introduction.* Oxford: Oxford University Press.

Loughlin, Martin. 2016. "The End of Avoidance." *London Review of Books* 38 (15). July 28, 2016.

MacDowall, Andrew. 2017. "Bosnia's Serb Republic leader: No Breakaway Vote Next Year." *Politico*, June 29, 2017.

MacGregor, Neil. 2012. *TEDTalks: Neil MacGregor – 2,600 Years of History in One Object.* New York, N.Y.: Films Media Group.

Maddicott, J. R. 2010. *The Origins of the English Parliament 924-1327.* Oxford: Oxford University Press.

Mahoney, James and Thelen, Kathleen. 2009. "A Theory of Gradual Institutional Change." In *Explaining Institutional Change: Ambiguity, Agency, and Power* edited by James Mahoney and Kathleen Thelen, 16-18. Cambridge.

Mahmutćehajić, Rusmir. 2003. *Sarajevo Essays: Politics, Ideology, and Tradition.* New York: State University of New York Press.

Mahmutćehajić, Rusmir. 2005. *Learning from Bosnia: Approaching Tradition.* New York: Fordham University Press.

Mahmutćehajić, Rusmir. 2009. "The Text Beneath the Text: The Poetry of Mak Dizdar." In *Stone Sleeper,* by Mak Dizdar, translated by Francis R. Jones. London: Anvil Press, 2009.

Mahmutćehajić, Rusmir. 2011. "No Final Curtain: The Never-ending Drama of Bosnia and Herzegovina." *Forum Bosnae* 6 (1).

Mainwaring, Scott and Shugart, Matthew. Linz, Juan. 1993. "Presidentialism, And Democracy: A Critical Appraisal." *Working Paper #200.*

Majstorovic, Danijela. 2013. "Comments on Gerard Toal's 'Republika Srpska Will Have a Referendum': The Rhetorical Politics of Milorad Dodik." *Nationalities Papers* 41.

Malcolm, Noel. 1994. *Bosnia A Short History.* New York: New York University Press.

Mann, Michael. 1998. "The Dark Side of Democracy: The Modern Tradition of Ethnic and Political Cleansing." *Workshop "Democracy, the Use of Force and Global Social Change", University of Minnesota,* May 1-3, 1998.

Mansfield, Edward D. and Snyder, Jack. 2009. "Pathways to War in Democratic Transitions." *International Organization* 63 (2): 381-390.

Marjanovic, D., et al. 2005. "The Peopling of Modern Bosnia-Herzegovina: Y-chromosome Haplogroups in the Three Main Ethnic Groups". *Annals of Human Genetics* 69 (6): 757-763.

Marko, Joseph. 2000. "Bosnia and Herzegovina – Multi-ethnic or Multi-National?" In *Societies in Conflict: The Contribution of Law and Democracy in Conflict Resolution,* 92-118. Strasbourg: Council of Europe.

Marsh, David. 2018. "Brexit and the Politics of Truth." *British Politics* 13: 79-89.

Martin, Irene and Jan W. van Deth. 2007. *Citizenship and Involvement in European Democracies: A Comparative Analysis. Chapter on Political Involvement.* London and New York: Routledge.

Mašić, Adelisa. 2020. "The Nafaka" of the Sarajevo Haggadah." *Post-Conflict Research Center (PCRC), Balkan Diskurs,* November 20, 2020.

Merdzanovic, Adis. 2015. *Democracy by Decree: Prospects and Limits of Imposed Consociational Democracy in Bosnia and Herzegovina.* Stuttgart: Ibidem Verlag.

McAllison, John. "Ex-MP: Scotland 'In Trouble' If Lax on Constitution." *The Targe,* December 8, 2013.

McClean, Iain. 2012. *What's Wrong With the British Constitution?* Oxford, U.K.: Oxford University Press.

McClean, Janet. 2019. "Constitution Making: The Case of "Unwritten" Constitutions." In *Comparative Constitution Making,* edited by Landau, David and Lerner, Hanna, 324-340. Cheltenham: Edward Elgar Publishing Limited, 2019.

McCulloch, Allison. 2013. "The Track Record of Centripetalism in Deeply Divided Places." In *Power Sharing in Deeply Divided Places,* edited by Joanne McEvoy and Brendan O'Leary, 94–111. Philadelphia: University of Pennsylvania Press.

McDermott, Rose. 1998. *Risk-Taking in International Politics: Prospect Theory in American Foreign Policy.* Ann Arbor: University of Michigan Press.

McGann AJ. 2006. *The Logic of Democracy: Reconciling Equality, Deliberation, and Minority Protection.* Ann Arbor: University of Michigan Press.

McGarry, John, and Brendan O'Leary. 1993. *The Politics of Ethnic Conflict Regulation: Case Studies of Protracted Ethnic Conflicts*. London: Routledge.

McMahon, Patrice C. and Western, Jon. 2009. "The Death of Dayton: How to Stop Bosnia From Falling Apart." *Foreign Affairs* 88 (5): 69-83.

Mertus, Julie A. 2005. *Bait and Switch: Human Rights and U.S. Foreign Policy*. New York and London: Routledge.

Ministry of Justice (MoJ). 2013. *Grayling: No More Using Judicial Review as a Cheap Delaying Tactic*. London: MoJ, Press Release, April 23, 2013.

Ministry of Justice (MoJ). 2020. *Government Launches Independent Panel to Look at Judicial Review*. London: MoJ, Press Release, July 31, 2020.

Ministry of Justice (MoJ). 2020. *Independent Review of Administrative Law – Terms of Reference*. London: MoJ, September 2020.

Monitor. 2018. "Civic Space in Bosnia and Herzegovina in 2018", *Monitor*, October 2, 2018.

Montgomery, Tom and Baglioni, Simone. 2018. "The United Kingdom." In *Solidarity as a Public Virtue?* edited by Veronica Federico and Christian Lahusen, 179-192. Baden-Baden: Nomos Verlagsgesellschaft mbH.

Morrison, J. 2001. *Reforming Britain*. London, Reuters, 2001.

Morrison, Kenneth and Lowe, Paul. 2021. *Reporting the Siege of Sarajevo*. London: Bloomsbury Academic.

Mudde, Cas. 2007. "Civil Society" and "Citizens and Politics." In White, Steven, Batt, Judy and Lewis Paul G. *Developments in Central and East European Politics*. New York: Palgrave and MacMillan.

Mujanović, Jasmin. 2015. "Bosnia-Herzegovina after the German-British Initiative." *Balkanist*, June 12, 2015.

Murshed, Mansoob. 2010. Explaining *Civil War: A Rational Choice Approach*. Cheltenham: Edward Elgar Publishing.

N1 Sarajevo. 2020. "Dodik: Either We Agree on Constitutional Court, or Bosnia Will Be No More", *N1 Sarajevo*, February 12, 2020.

National Democratic Institute (NDI). 2019. *Public Opinion Poll: Bosnia and Herzegovina*. Washington: NDI, October 15, 2019.

Nezavisne Novine. 2015. "Anketa: Više od Polovine Ispitanika za Samostalnost RS, Vole Dodika, a Vjeruju Crkvi", August 11, 2015.

Nicole Smith and Katy Donnelly. 1996. *Delivering Constitutional Reform*. London: Constitution Unit.

Noel, Sid. 2005. *From Power Sharing to Democracy: Post-Conflict Institutions in Ethnically Divided Societies*. McGill-Queen's University Press: September.

Nolan, Michael, Patrick Nolan, Stephen Sedley, and Geoffrey Wilson. 1997. *The Making and Remaking of the British Constitution*. London: Blackstone.

Norton, Philip. 2007. "Tony Blair and The Constitution". *British Politics* 2 (2): 269-281.

Norris, Pippa. 2002. *Democratic Phoenix*. Cambridge: Cambridge University Press.

North, Douglass C. 1991. "Institutions". *The Journal of Economic Perspectives* 5 (1): 97-112.

O'Brien, James. 2010. "The Dayton Constitution of Bosnia and Herzegovina." In *Framing the State in Times of Transition: Case Studies in Constitution Making*, edited by Miller, Laurel E. Washington: United States Institute of Peace.

O'Connor, Patrick. 2019. "'Judicial Overreach': A Response to Sumption." *Counsel Magazine*, August 2019.

O'Leary, Brendan. 2019. "Making Constitutions in Deeply Divided Places." In *Comparative Constitution Making*, edited by David Landau and Hanna Lerner, 186-212. Cheltenham: Edward Elgar.

O'Reilly, M., Ó Súilleabháin, A. and Paffenholz, T. 2015. *Re-Imagining Peacemaking: Women's Roles in Peace Processes*. New York: International Peace Institute, June 2015.

Office for Budget Responsibility (OBR). 2020. *A Brief Guide to the Public Finances*. London: OBR, November 2020.

Office of the High Representative (OHR). 1995. *Agreed Basic Principles*. Geneva: OHR, September 8, 1995.

Office of the High Representative (OHR). 1995. *Further Agreed Basic Principles*. New York: OHR, September 26, 1995.

Office of the High Representative (OHR). 2020. *Fifty-eighth Report of the High Representative for Implementation of the Peace Agreement on Bosnia and Herzegovina*. Sarajevo: OHR, May 11, 2020.

Office of the UN Resident Coordinator. 2015. *Public Opinion Poll Results: Analytical Report*. Sarajevo: Office of the UN Resident Coordinator.

Office of National Statistics (ONS). 2020. *Long-term International Migration 2.01a, Citizenship, UK and England and Wales*. London: ONS, November 26, 2020.

Oireachtas. 2012. *Frequently Asked Questions about the Houses of the Oireachtas*. Belfast: Oireachtas. March 28, 2012

Ordeshook, Peter C. and Klochko, Marianna. n.d. "Toward a General Theory of Constitutional Design." Cornell University, California Institute of Technology.

Oxford Economics. 2018. "Country Economic Forecast: Bosnia and Herzegovina", *Oxford Economics*.

Parish, Matthew. 2011. "Comment: Croat Crisis Pushes Bosnia Towards Endgame." *Balkan Insight*, March 21, 2011.

Parish, Michael. 2010. *A Free City in the Balkans: Reconstructing a Divided Society in Bosnia*. London: IB Tauris & Co.

Peace Implementation Council Steering Board (PIC). 2005. *The Communiqué of the Steering Board of the PIC*. London: PIC, February 3, 2005.

Peck, Tom. 2018. "Theresa May says 'element of surprise' was crucial to Syria bombing, a week after Trump announced it on Twitter." *The Independent*, April 17, 2018.

Pellet, Allain. 1992. "The Opinions of the Badinter Arbitration Committee: A Second Breath for the Self-Determination of Peoples," *European Journal of International Law* 3 (1): 178–185.

Perry, Valery, and Keil, Soeren. 2018. "The Business of State Capture in the Western Balkans — An Introduction." *Southeastern Europe* 42 (1): 1–14.

Perry, Valery. 2019. "Frozen, Stalled, Stuck, or Just Muddling through." *Asia Europe Journal* 17 (1): 107-127.

Perry, Valery. 2020. "A Different Kind of Veil of Ignorance." *Democratization Policy Council*, June 22, 2020.

Perry, Valery. 2021. "The Myth of Incremental Education Reform in BiH." *Democratization Policy Council*, February 3, 2021.

Piacentini, A. 2019. "Trying to Fit In": Multiethnic Parties, Ethno-Clientelism, and Power-Sharing in Bosnia and Herzegovina and Macedonia." *Nationalism and Ethnic Politics* 25 (3): 273–291.

Pickard, Jim and Shrimsley, Robert. 2019. "Jeremy Corbyn's plan to rewrite the rules of the UK economy." *Financial Times*, September 1, 2019.

Plato, and C. J. Rowe. 2012. *Republic*. London: Penguin.

Poggioli, Sylvia. 2006. "Milosevic: The Life and Death of a Strongman." *NPR*, March 11, 2006.

Political and Constitutional Reform Committee. 2014. "A New Magna Carta?", *House of Commons*, July 3, 2014.

Pravda Za Davida. N.d. "Pravda Za Davida Facebook Group." *Facebook: Pravda Za Davida*.

PILPG. 2012. *Participatory Constitutional Reform. Legal Memorandum*. Sarajevo: PILPG, April, 2012.

Putnam, Robert D., Robert Leonardi and Rafaella Y. Nanetti. 1993. *Making Democracy Work: Civic Traditions in Modern Italy*. Princeton: Princeton University Press.

Raduta, Raluca. 2015. *Constitutional and Governance Reforms in Bosnia and Herzegovina: Does Public Opinion Matter?* Sarajevo: Democratization Policy Council, January 2015.

Renwick, Alan and Hazell, Robert. 2017. *Blueprint for a UK Constitutional Convention.* London: The Constitution Unit, University College London, June 2017.

Riga, Liliana and Kennedy, James. 2013. "To Build a Notion: US State Department Nation Building Expertise and Postwar Settlements in 20th Century East Central Europe." *Sociological Research Online* 18 (2): 21.

Roeder, Philip G., and Donald S. Rothchild. 2005. *Sustainable Peace: Power and Democracy after Civil Wars.* Ithaca, N.Y.: Cornell University Press.

Rohde, David. 2012. *Endgame: The Betrayal and Fall of Srebrenica, Europe's Worst Massacre Since World War II.* New York: Penguin Books.

Ron, James. 2000. "Boundaries and Violence: Repertoires of State Action along the Bosnia/Yugoslavia Divide." *Theory and Society* 29 (5): 609-649.

Roosevelt, Eleanor. 1948. *On the Adoption of the Universal Declaration of Human Rights.* Paris: United Nations General Assembly, December 9, 1948.

Rozenberg, Joshua. 2020. "Lockdown: navigating the moral maze." *Law Society Gazette,* August 3, 2020.

Rubin, James P. 2019. "The In-Your-Face Diplomat." Politico Magazine, May 12, 2019.

Russell, Meg and Daniel Gover. 2021. *Taking Back Control: Why the House of Commons Should Govern its Own Time.* The Constitution Unit, University College London, January 2021.

Saati, Abrak. 2017. "Participatory Constitution-Making as a Transnational Legal Norm." *U.C. Irvine Journal of Transnational and Comparative Law* 2: 113.

Sahadžić, Maja. 2009. "The Electoral System of Bosnia and Herzegovina: A Short Review of Political Matter and/or Technical Perplexion." *Contemporary Issues* 2(1).

Sands, Philippe. 2015. "This British Bill of Rights Could End the UK." *Guardian,* May 14, 2015.

Sands, Philippe. 2015. "Britain, Europe & Human Rights—What Next?" *Elson Ethics Lecture – Windsor Castle,* October 20, 2015

Sarajlić, Eldar and Davor, Marko. 2011. *State or Nation? The Challenges of Political Transition in Bosnia and Herzegovina.* Sarajevo: Centar za Interdisciplinarne Postdiplomske Studije.

Schneckener, Ulrich. 2002. "Making Power-Sharing Work: Lessons from Successes and Failures in Ethnic Conflict Regulation". *Journal of Peace Research* 39 (2): 203-228.

Schulte, F. 2020. *Peace Through Self-Determination – Success and Failure of Territorial Autonomy.* Palgrave Macmillan.

Sedley, Sir Stephen. 1998. "The Crown in its own Courts". In *The Golden Metwand and the Crooked Cord,* edited by William Wade, C. F. Forsyth, and Ivan Hare, 253-266. Oxford: Clarendon Press.

Sedley, Stephen. 2012. "Judicial Politics: Stephen Sedley on the separation of powers." *London Review of Books* 34 (4), February 23, 2012.

Sedley, Stephen. 2013. "Beware Kite-Flyers." *London Review of Books* 35 (17), September 12, 2013.

Sedley, Stephen. 2019. "A Boundary Where There Is None, London Review of Books." *London Review of Books* 41 (17), September 12, 2019.

Sells, Michael Anthony. 2007. *The Bridge Betrayed: Religion and Genocide in Bosnia.* Berkeley: University of California Press, 1998.

Serwer, Daniel. 2019. *From War to Peace in the Balkans, the Middle East and Ukraine.* Palgrave Critical Studies in Post-Conflict Recovery.

Serwer, Daniel. 2020. *A Clear-Eyed Assessment of Bosnia and Herzegovina A Quarter-Century After Dayton.* Washington DC: American Foreign Service Association, December 2020.

Sinclair, Alexandra and Tomlinson, Joe. 2020. *Tsunami' of EU Withdrawal Laws 'Rubber Stamped'.* London: Public Law Project (PLP), October 13, 2020.

Skocpol, Theda. 1996. "Unravelling From Above." *The American Prospect* 25: 20-25.

Stepan, Alfred, Juan J. Linz, and Yogendra Yadav. 2011. *Crafting State-Nations: India and Other Multinational Democracies.* Baltimore: Johns Hopkins.

Stojanović, Nenad. 2011. "Limits of Consociationalism and Possible Alternatives Centripetal Effects of Direct Democracy in a Multiethnic Society." *Transitions* 51(1&2).

Stoker, Gerry. 2012. "The Politics of Nudge." *University of Southampton,* August 2012.

Suljagic, Emir. 2020. "Analysis – Peacefully dismantling Dayton: Cynical and delusional." *Anadolu Agency,* November 10, 2020.

Sumption, Jonathan, and Anita Anand. 2019. The Reith Lectures. BBC Radio 4, May 25, 2019.

Sumption, Jonathan. 2019. *Trials of the State: Law and the Decline of Politics.* London : Profile Books Ltd.

Sumption, Jonathan. 2020. "Brexit and the British Constitution: Reflections on the Last Three years and the Next Fifty." *The Political Quarterly*, Vol. 91, No. 1, January–March 2020.

Surk, Barbara. 2015. "In Bosnia, a Father's Grief Swells into an Anti-government Movement," *New York Times*, January 8, 2015.

Tamaru, N. and O'Reilly, M. 2018. *How Women Influence Constitution Making After Conflict and Unrest, Inclusive Security*. Washington DC: Inclusive Security, 2018a.

Taniyici, Saban. 2008. "EU's Copenhagen Political Criteria and the Political Culture of the Western Balkan Countries: Are They Compatible?" *International Conference on Balkan Studies 2008*. 88-103.

Tanjug. 2012. "Bosnian Party Leaders Agree on Cooperation." *Tanjug*, November 1, 2012.

Tarrow, Sidney. 1996. "Making Social Science Work Across Space and Time." *American Political Science Review* 90(2).

Tate, C. Neal, and Torbjörn Vallinder. 1995. *The Global Expansion of Judicial Power*. New York: New York University Press.

Taylor, Charles and Gutmann, Amy, and. 2017. *Multiculturalism: Examining the Politics of Recognition*. Princeton: Princeton University Press, 1994.

Taylor, Charles. 2007. "Democratic Exclusion (and its Remedies?)." *Eurozine Magazine*, February 2002.

Taylor, Diane. 2020. "Lawyers Express Concern Over Ministerial Code Rewrite." *Guardian*, October 22, 2015.

Teorell, Jan, Mariano Torcal, and José Ramón Montero. 2007. "Political participation: mapping the terrain". In *Citizenship and Involvement in European Democracies*, edited by Anders Westholm, José Ramón Montero, and Jan W. van Deth A., 334-357. New York, NY: Routledge.

Thaler, Richard H., and Cass R. Sunstein. 2009. Nudge: *Improving Decisions About Health, Wealth, and Happiness*. New York: Penguin Books.

The Economist. 2013. "Bosnia and the European Union: A Balkan dysfunction." *The Economist*, March 16, 2013.

Toal, Gerard and Maksić, Adis. 2011. "Is Bosnia-Herzegovina unsustainable?" *Eurasian Geography and Economics* 52 (2).

Toal, Gerard, and Carl Dahlman. 2011. *Bosnia Remade: Ethnic Cleansing and Its Reversal*. New York: Oxford University Press.

Touquet, Heleen. 2015, "Non-Ethnic Mobilisation in Deeply Divided Societies: The Case of the Sarajevo Protests," *Europe-Asia Studies* 67 (3): 388-408.

Transparency International (TI). 2011. *An Overview of Budget Appropriations for Political Parties in BiH*. Sarajevo: TI, June 2011.

Traynor, Ian. 2011 "Bosnia in Worst Crisis Since War as Serb Leader Calls Referendum." *Guardian*, April 28, 2011.

Trechsel, Alexander and Kriesi, Hanspeter. 1996. "Switzerland: The Referendum and Initiative as a Centrepiece of the Political System." In *The Referendum Experience in Europe*, edited by Michael Gallagher, 187-190. London: Macmillan Press Ltd, 1996.

Trigilia, Carlo. 1995. *Italy At a Crossroads*. Cambridge: Minda de Gunzburg Center for European Studies, Harvard University.

Trnka, Kasim. 2009 *Proces Odlučivanja u Parlamentarnoj Skupštini Bosne i Hercegovine: Stanje, Komparativna Rješenja, Prijedloz*. Sarajevo: Fondacija Konrad Adenauer.

Tsebelis, George. 1990. *Nested Games: Rational Choice in Comparative Politics*. Berkeley: University of California Press.

Tsebelis, George. 1995. "Decision Making in Political Systems: Veto Players in Presidentialism, Parliamentarism, Multicameralism and Multipartyism." *British Journal of Political Science* 25 (3): 289-325.

Tsebelis, George. 1998. "Nested Games: The Cohesion of French Electoral Coalitions." *British Journal of Political Science*, 18 (2): 145-170.

Tsebelis, George. 2002. *Veto Players: How Political Institutions Work*. Princeton: Princeton University Press.

Tucker, H. W. 1950. *Contributions to the Theory of Games*. Princeton: Princeton University Press.

Turpin, Colin, and Adam Tomkins. 2012. *British Government and the Constitution: Text and Materials*. Cambridge: Cambridge University Press.

Tversky, A. and Kahneman, D. 1974. "Judgment Under Uncertainty: Heuristics and Biases." *Science* 185: 1124-1130.

UNDP. 2009. *The Ties that Bind: Social Capital in Bosnia and Herzegovina*. Sarajevo: UNDP BiH, Oct 3, 2013

UNDP. 2013. *Public Opinion Poll Results, Bosnia and Herzegovina Conflict Analysis*. Sarajevo: UNDP BiH, conducted by PRISM Research, 2013

United Nations Security Council (UNSC). 2011. *Comments made by High Representative, Valentin Inzko*. New York: UNSC, 6659th Meeting, November 11, 2011.

United States, Institute for Peace (USIP). 2006. *Special Report: From Dayton to Brussels – Constitutional Preparations for Bosnia's EU Accession*. Washington: USIP, October, 2006.

United States, State Department (USD). 1996. *Dayton History Project, Interview: Richard C. Holbrooke, Assistant Secretary for European and Canadian Affairs, Roberts Owen, Senior Legal Advisor, Bosnia Negotiating Team*. Washington: USD, June 18, 1996. Unclassified and released in full, October 16, 2012.

United States, State Department (USD). 1996. *Dayton History Project, Interview: Jim O-Brien, Legal Advisor State Department; Miriam Shapiro, Legal Adviser State Department*. Washington: USD, August 14, 1996. Unclassified and released in full, October 16, 2012.

Várady, Tibor. 1997. "Minorities, Majorities, Law, and Ethnicity: Reflections of the Yugoslav Case." *Human Rights Quarterly* 19 (1): 9-54.

Verba, Sidney and Gabriel Almond. [1963] 1989. *The Civic Culture*. London: Sage.

Verba, Sidney, Nie, Norman H. and Kim, Jae-on. 1978. *Participation and Political Equality: A Seven-Nation Comparison*. New York and London: Cambridge University Press.

Vile, M. J. C. 1967. *Constitutionalism and the Separation of Powers*. Oxford: Clarendon Press.

Volcansek, Mary L. 1992. *Judicial Politics and Policy-Making in Western Europe*. London, England: F. Cass.

Vozab, Dina. 2012. "Communication Models of Civil Society Organizations in Croatia." *Observatorio (OBS*) Journal*, 079-099.

Wallis, Joanne. 2019. "Constitution Making and State Building." In *Comparative Constitution Making*, edited by David Landau and Hanna Lerner, 278-301. Cheltenham: Edward Elgar.

Walzer, Michael. 1980 "Civility and Civic Virtue in Contemporary America." In *Radical Principles*, by Walzer, Michael. New York: Basic Books.

Walzer, Michael. 1997. *On Toleration*. Yale University Press, New Haven.

Washington Post. 1998. "Albright Pledges $5 Million in Aid to Bosnian Serbs." *Washington Post*, February 21, 1998.

Welzel, Christian and Ronald Inglehart. 2008. "The Role of Ordinary People in Democratization." *Journal of Democracy* 19 (1): 126-140.

Welzel, Christian and Ronald Inglehart. 2005. *Modernization, Cultural Change, and Democracy*, New York: Cambridge University Press.

Wenzel, Nikolai G. 2012. "Towards a Research Agenda on the Emergence of (Informal) Constitutional Culture into (Formal) Constitutional Order." *Studies on Emergent Order* 5.

Werlin, H. and Eckstein, Harry. 1990. "Political Culture and Political Change." *American Political Science Review* 84(1).

White, Hannah. 2020. *The Extension of Coronavirus Powers and the "Brady Amendment*. London: Institute for Government (IoG), September 29, 2020.

Widner, Jennifer. 2005. "Constitution Writing and Conflict Resolution." *The Round Table* 94 (381): 503-518.

Williams, Rowan. 2019. "Afterword." In *This is Not a Drill: An Extinction Rebellion Handbook* edited by Farrell, Clare, Alison Green, Sam Knights, and William Skeaping. 2019. London: Penguin Books.

Wood, Michael. 2010. "The Story of England." *BBC TV Production*.

Woolrych, Austin. 2002. *Britain in Revolution, 1625–1660*. Oxford: Oxford University Press.

World Bank. 2020. *National Accounts Data, and OECD National Accounts Data Files: GDP (current US$) – United Kingdom*. Washington: World Bank.

Wucherpfennig, Julian and Deutsch, Franziska. 2009. "Modernization and Democracy." *Living Reviews in Democracy* 1.

Yeung, Karen. 2012. "Nudge as Fudge. Review Article on Sunstein." *Modern Law Review* 75 (1): 122-148.

Yuval-Davis, Nira. 1997. *Gender & Nation*. London: Sage Publishing.

Zimmerman, Joseph F. 1990. "Review of Cronin (1989)." *Annals of the American Academy of Political and Social Science* 507: 159-160.

ibidem.eu